I AM STAN

A GRAPHIC BIOGRAPHY OF THE LEGENDARY STAN LEE

TOM SCIOLI

TEN SPEED GRAPHIC
An imprint of TEN SPEED PRESS
California | New York

AUTHOR'S NOTE

This graphic biography is adapted from a number of sources including interviews given throughout Stan's life. There are differences of opinion and other points of view about the events depicted in this work.

This graphic biography is not approved or endorsed by Stan Lee, his estate, his family, Marvel Comics, or any other person/corporate entity depicted within its pages.

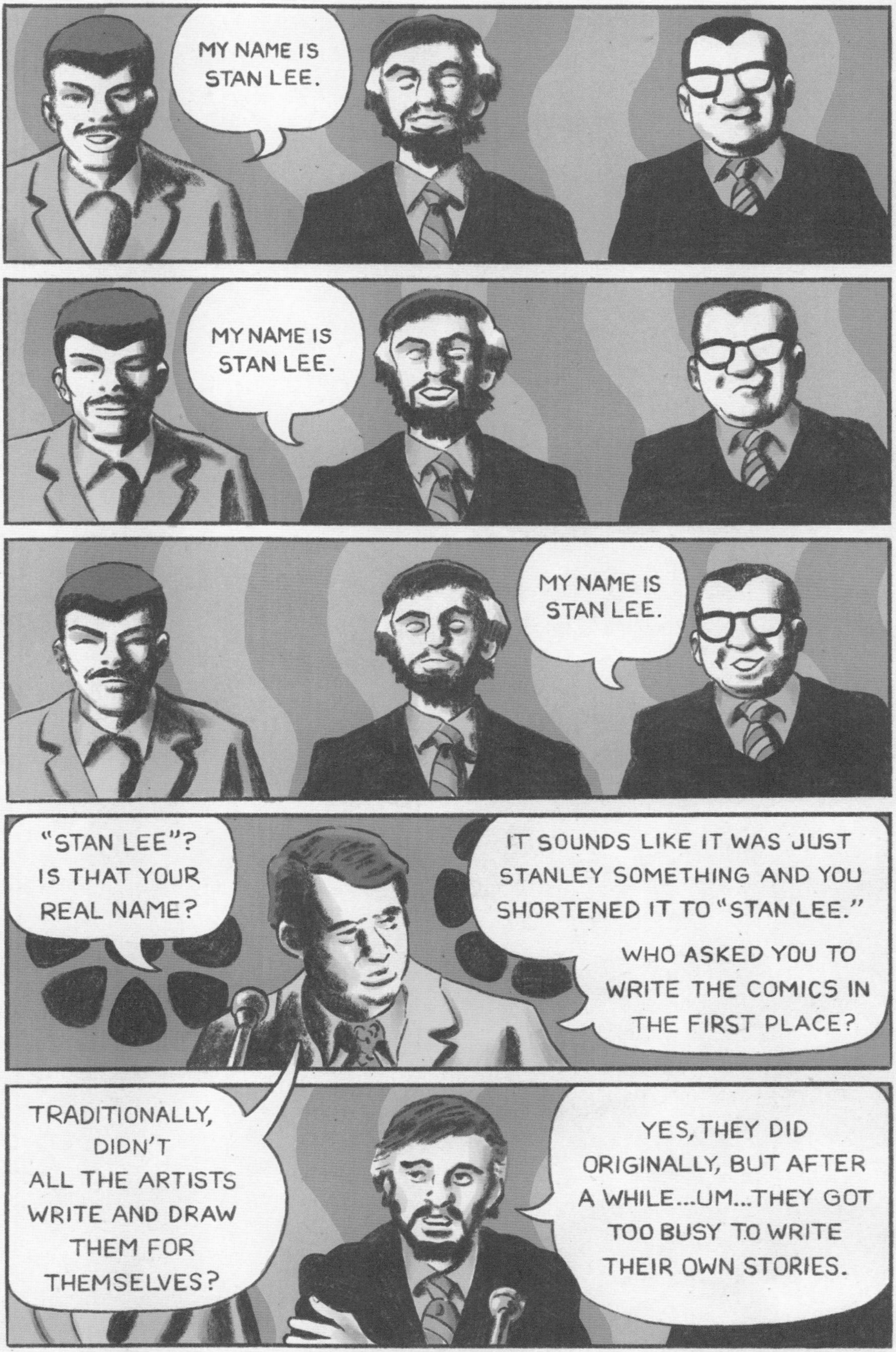

MY NAME IS STAN LEE.
MY NAME IS STAN LEE.
MY NAME IS STAN LEE.
"STAN LEE"? IS THAT YOUR REAL NAME?
IT SOUNDS LIKE IT WAS JUST STANLEY SOMETHING AND YOU SHORTENED IT TO "STAN LEE."
WHO ASKED YOU TO WRITE THE COMICS IN THE FIRST PLACE?
TRADITIONALLY, DIDN'T ALL THE ARTISTS WRITE AND DRAW THEM FOR THEMSELVES?
YES, THEY DID ORIGINALLY, BUT AFTER A WHILE...UM...THEY GOT TOO BUSY TO WRITE THEIR OWN STORIES.

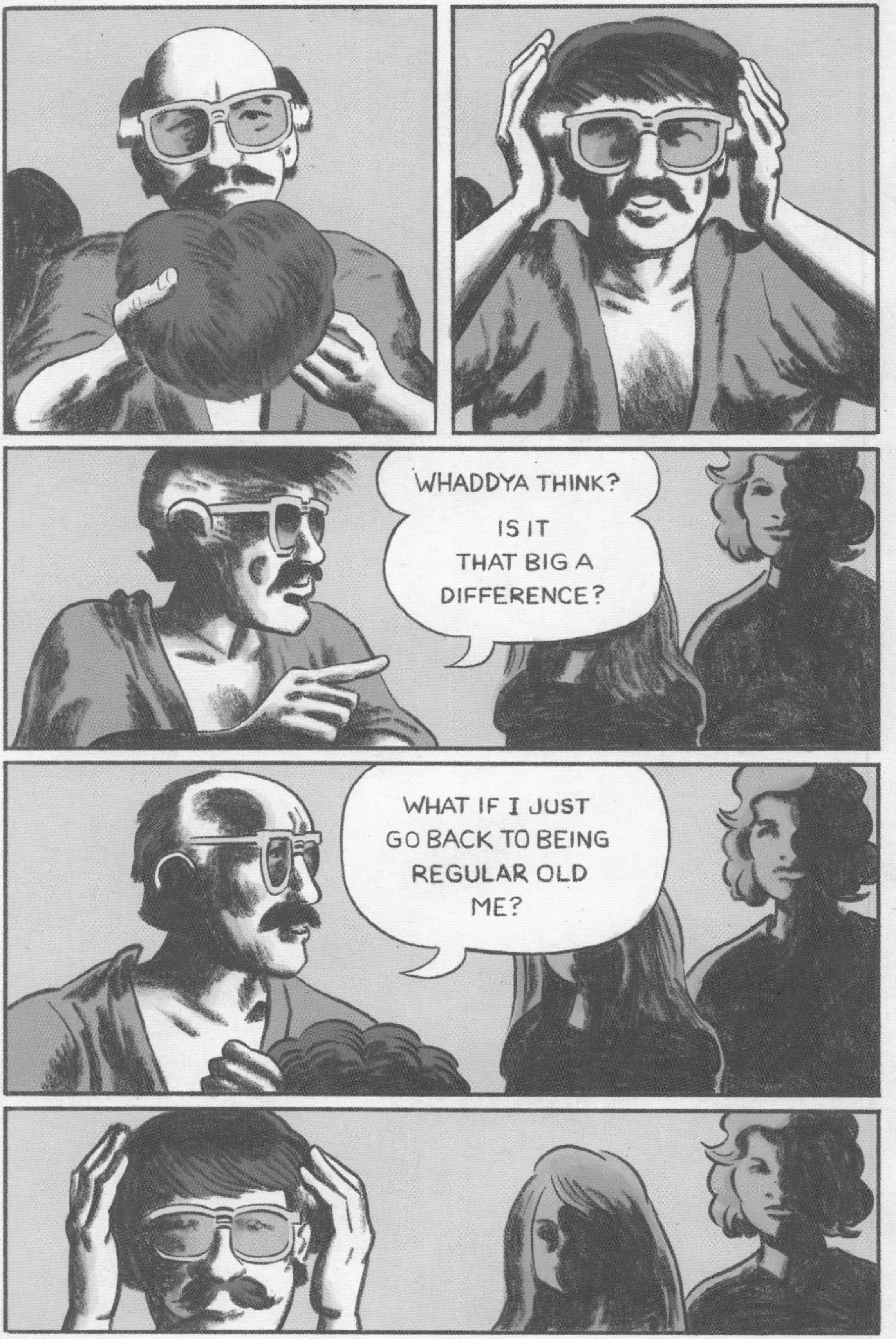
WHADDYA THINK? IS IT THAT BIG A DIFFERENCE?
WHAT IF I JUST GO BACK TO BEING REGULAR OLD ME?

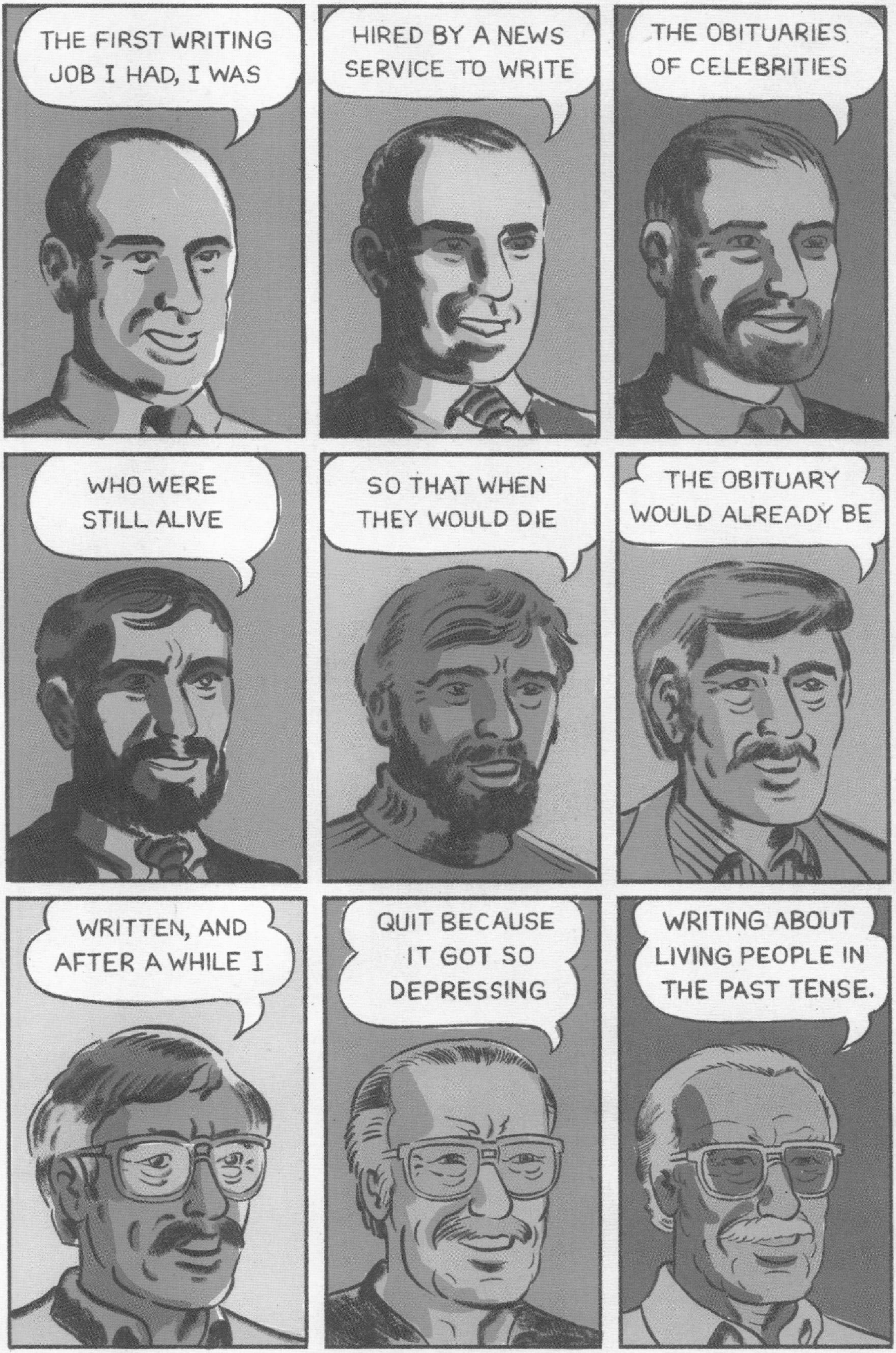
THE FIRST WRITING JOB I HAD, I WAS
HIRED BY A NEWS SERVICE TO WRITE
THE OBITUARIES OF CELEBRITIES
WHO WERE STILL ALIVE
SO THAT WHEN THEY WOULD DIE
THE OBITUARY WOULD ALREADY BE
WRITTEN, AND AFTER A WHILE I
QUIT BECAUSE IT GOT SO DEPRESSING
WRITING ABOUT LIVING PEOPLE IN THE PAST TENSE.

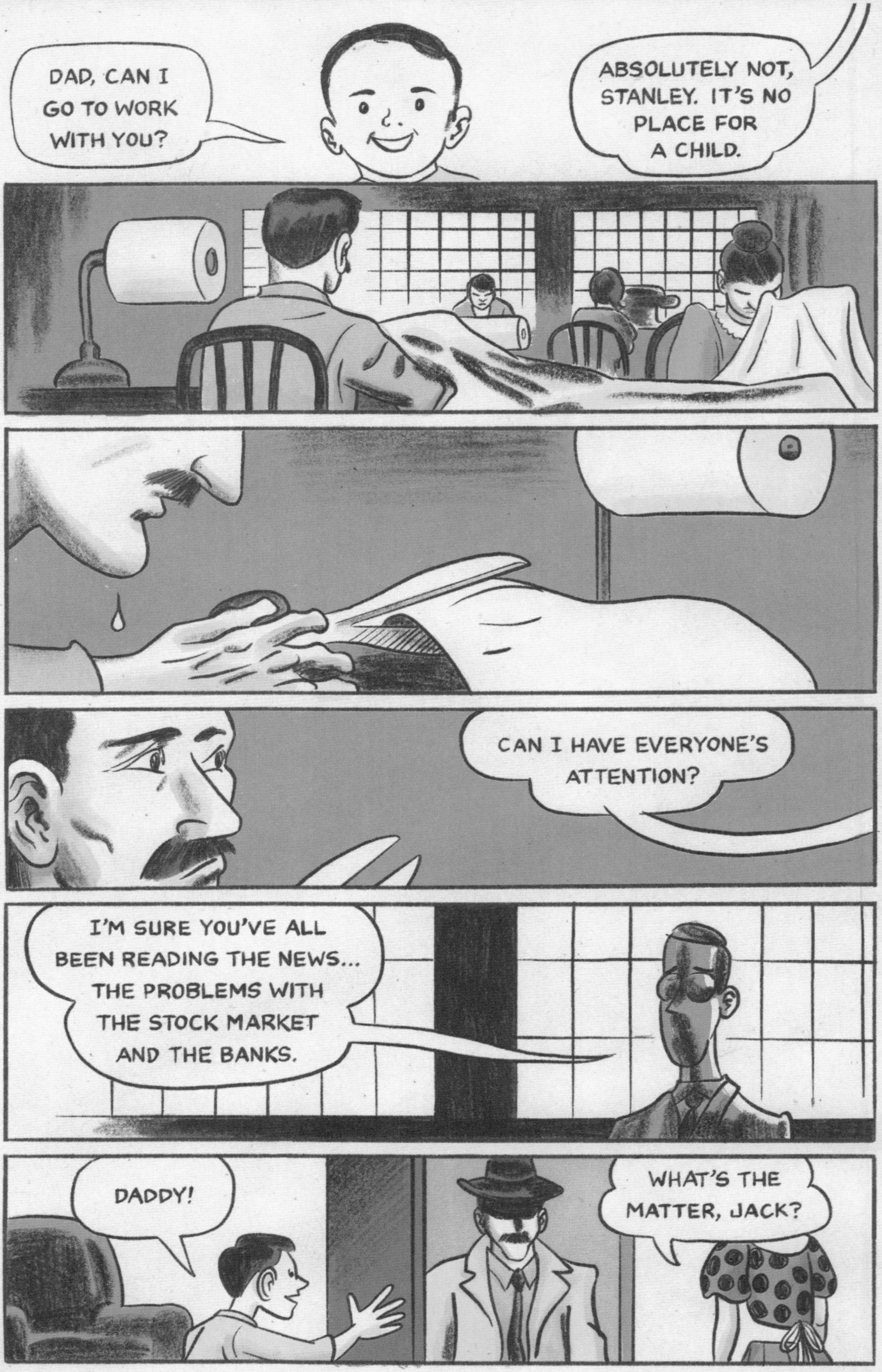
DAD, CAN I GO TO WORK WITH YOU?
ABSOLUTELY NOT, STANLEY. IT'S NO PLACE FOR A CHILD.
CAN I HAVE EVERYONE'S ATTENTION?
I'M SURE YOU'VE ALL BEEN READING THE NEWS... THE PROBLEMS WITH THE STOCK MARKET AND THE BANKS.
DADDY!
WHAT'S THE MATTER, JACK?

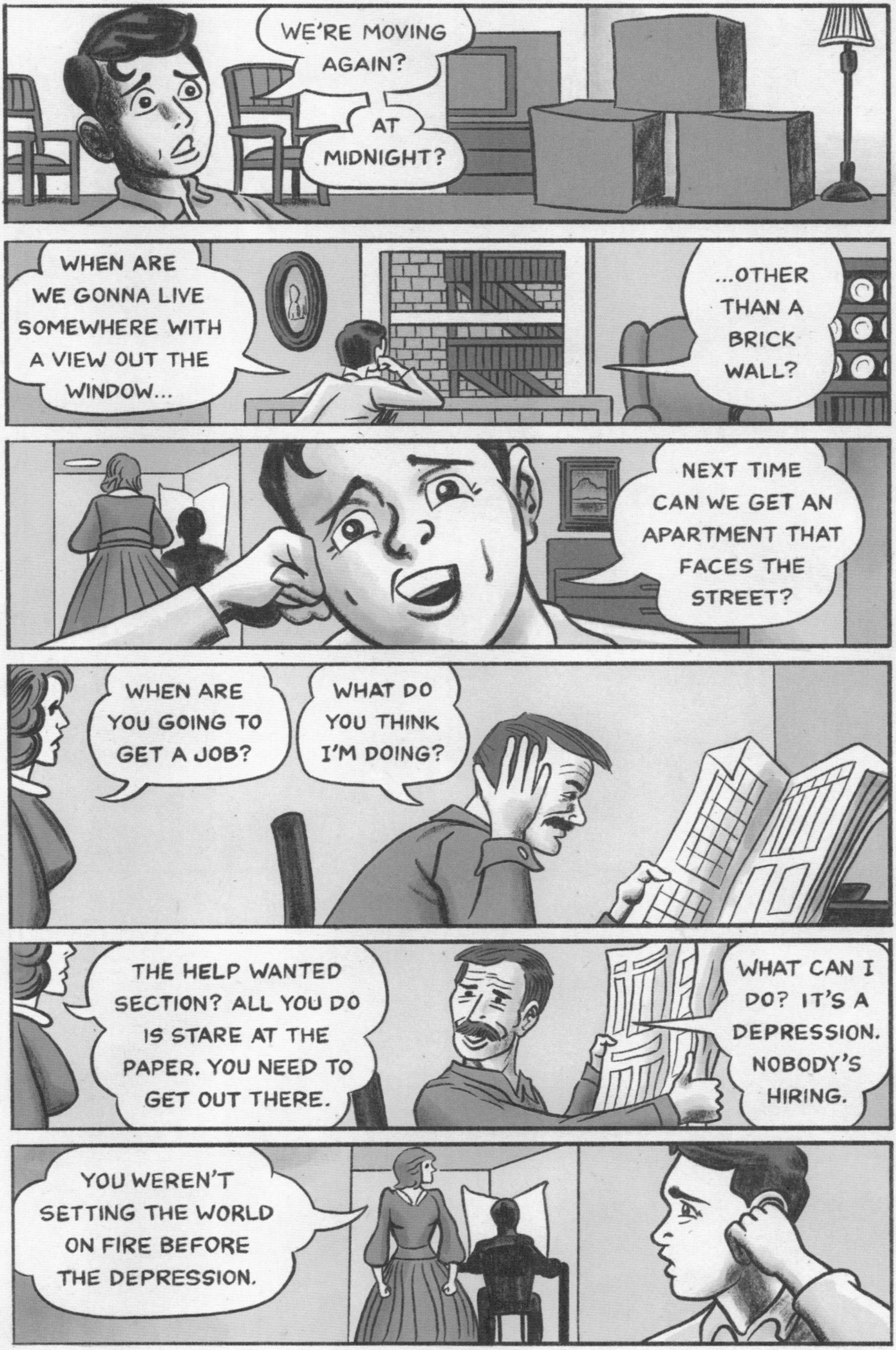
WE'RE MOVING AGAIN?
AT MIDNIGHT?
WHEN ARE WE GONNA LIVE SOMEWHERE WITH A VIEW OUT THE WINDOW...
...OTHER THAN A BRICK WALL?
NEXT TIME CAN WE GET AN APARTMENT THAT FACES THE STREET?
WHEN ARE YOU GOING TO GET A JOB?
WHAT DO YOU THINK I'M DOING?
THE HELP WANTED SECTION? ALL YOU DO IS STARE AT THE PAPER. YOU NEED TO GET OUT THERE.
WHAT CAN I DO? IT'S A DEPRESSION. NOBODY'S HIRING.
YOU WEREN'T SETTING THE WORLD ON FIRE BEFORE THE DEPRESSION.

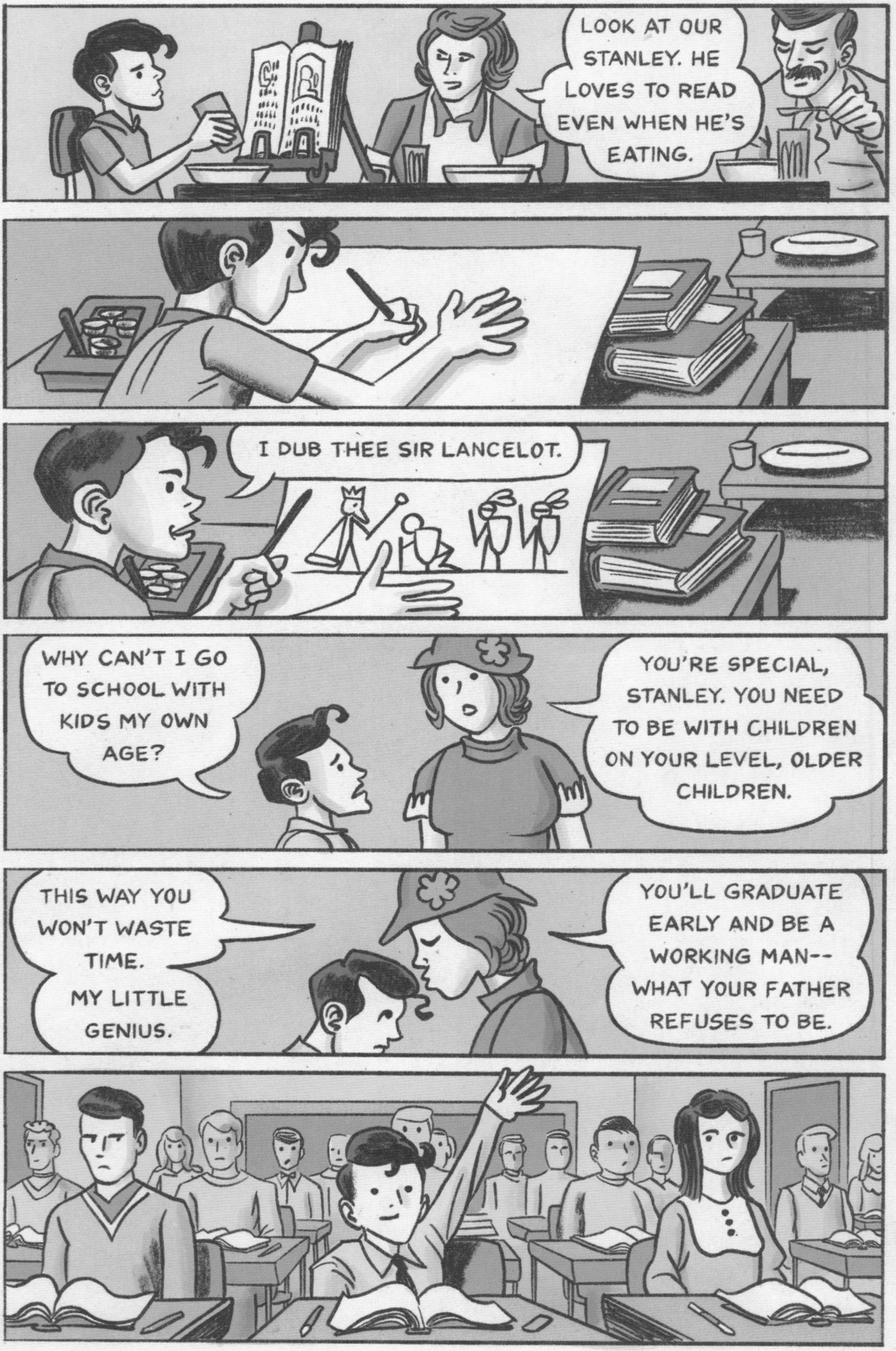
LOOK AT OUR STANLEY. HE LOVES TO READ EVEN WHEN HE'S EATING.
I DUB THEE SIR LANCELOT.
WHY CAN'T I GO TO SCHOOL WITH KIDS MY OWN AGE?
YOU'RE SPECIAL, STANLEY. YOU NEED TO BE WITH CHILDREN ON YOUR LEVEL, OLDER CHILDREN.
THIS WAY YOU WON'T WASTE TIME.
MY LITTLE GENIUS.
YOU'LL GRADUATE EARLY AND BE A WORKING MAN--WHAT YOUR FATHER REFUSES TO BE.

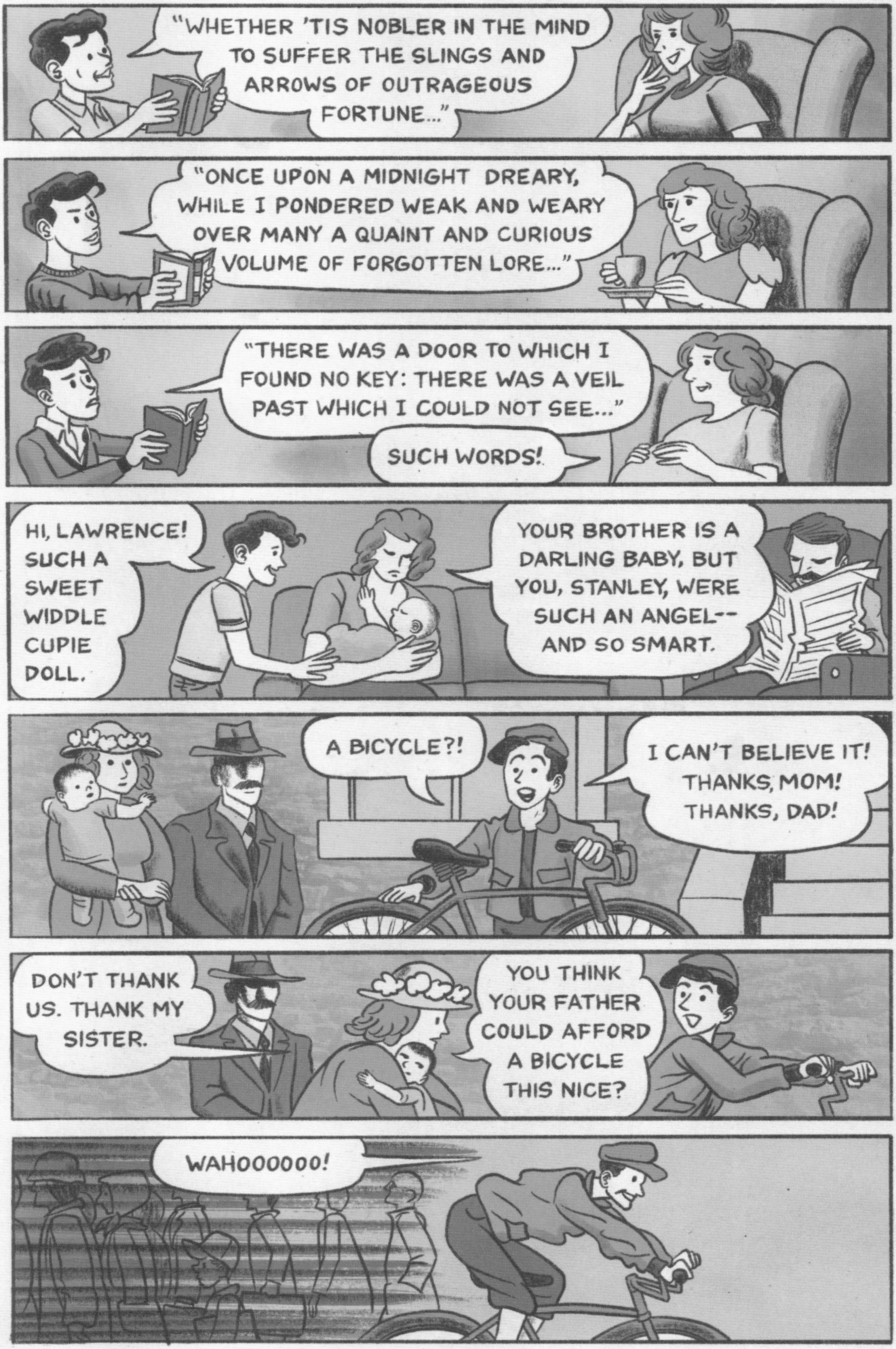
"WHETHER 'TIS NOBLER IN THE MIND TO SUFFER THE SLINGS AND ARROWS OF OUTRAGEOUS FORTUNE..."
"ONCE UPON A MIDNIGHT DREARY, WHILE I PONDERED WEAK AND WEARY OVER MANY A QUAINT AND CURIOUS VOLUME OF FORGOTTEN LORE..."
"THERE WAS A DOOR TO WHICH I FOUND NO KEY: THERE WAS A VEIL PAST WHICH I COULD NOT SEE..."
SUCH WORDS!
HI, LAWRENCE! SUCH A SWEET WIDDLE CUPIE DOLL.
YOUR BROTHER IS A DARLING BABY, BUT YOU, STANLEY, WERE SUCH AN ANGEL-- AND SO SMART.
A BICYCLE?!
I CAN'T BELIEVE IT! THANKS, MOM! THANKS, DAD!
DON'T THANK US. THANK MY SISTER.
YOU THINK YOUR FATHER COULD AFFORD A BICYCLE THIS NICE?
WAHOOOOOO!

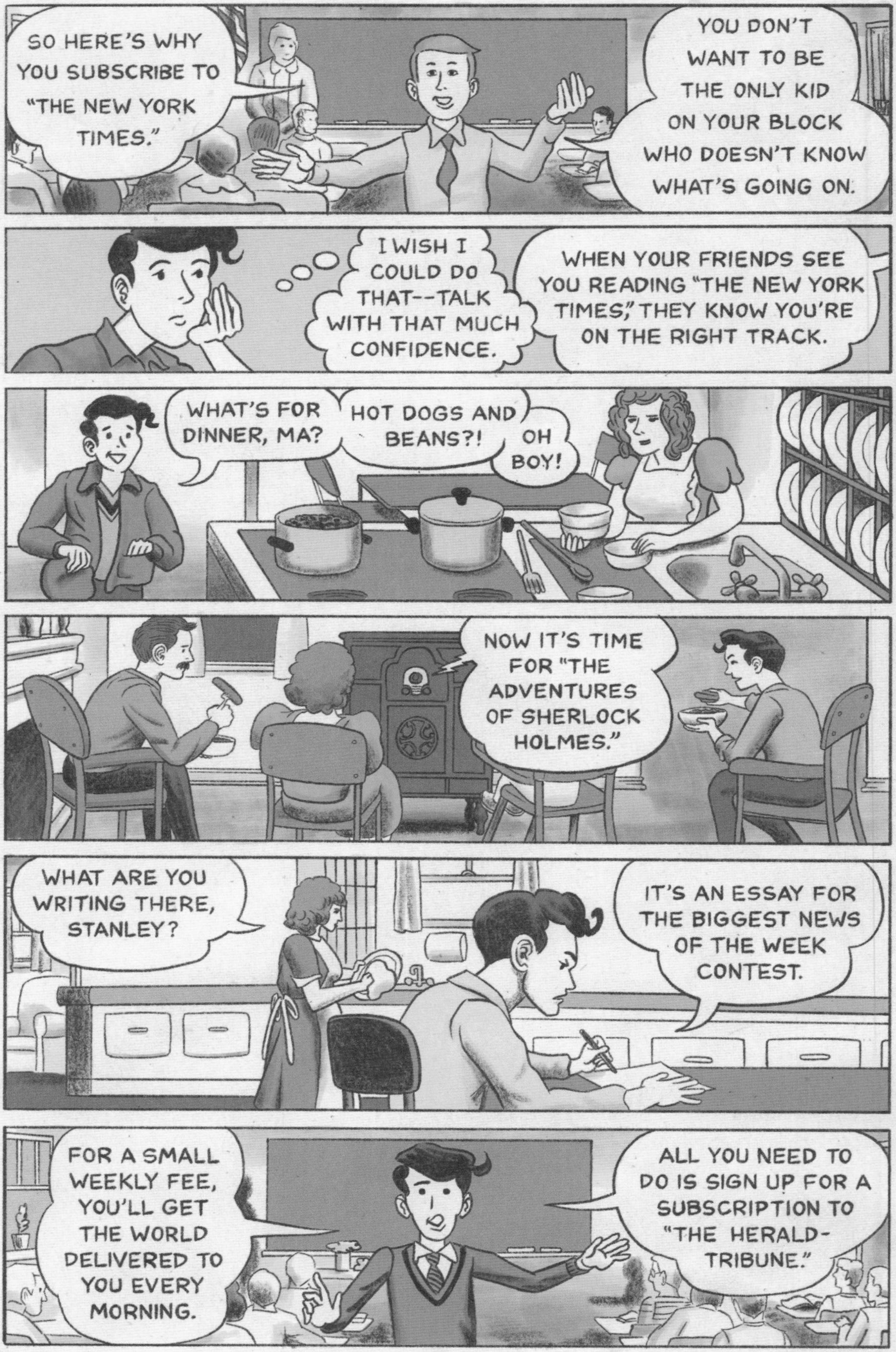
SO HERE'S WHY YOU SUBSCRIBE TO "THE NEW YORK TIMES."
YOU DON'T WANT TO BE THE ONLY KID ON YOUR BLOCK WHO DOESN'T KNOW WHAT'S GOING ON.
I WISH I COULD DO THAT--TALK WITH THAT MUCH CONFIDENCE.
WHEN YOUR FRIENDS SEE YOU READING "THE NEW YORK TIMES," THEY KNOW YOU'RE ON THE RIGHT TRACK.
WHAT'S FOR DINNER, MA?
HOT DOGS AND BEANS?!
OH BOY!
NOW IT'S TIME FOR "THE ADVENTURES OF SHERLOCK HOLMES."
WHAT ARE YOU WRITING THERE, STANLEY?
IT'S AN ESSAY FOR THE BIGGEST NEWS OF THE WEEK CONTEST.
FOR A SMALL WEEKLY FEE, YOU'LL GET THE WORLD DELIVERED TO YOU EVERY MORNING.
ALL YOU NEED TO DO IS SIGN UP FOR A SUBSCRIPTION TO "THE HERALD-TRIBUNE."

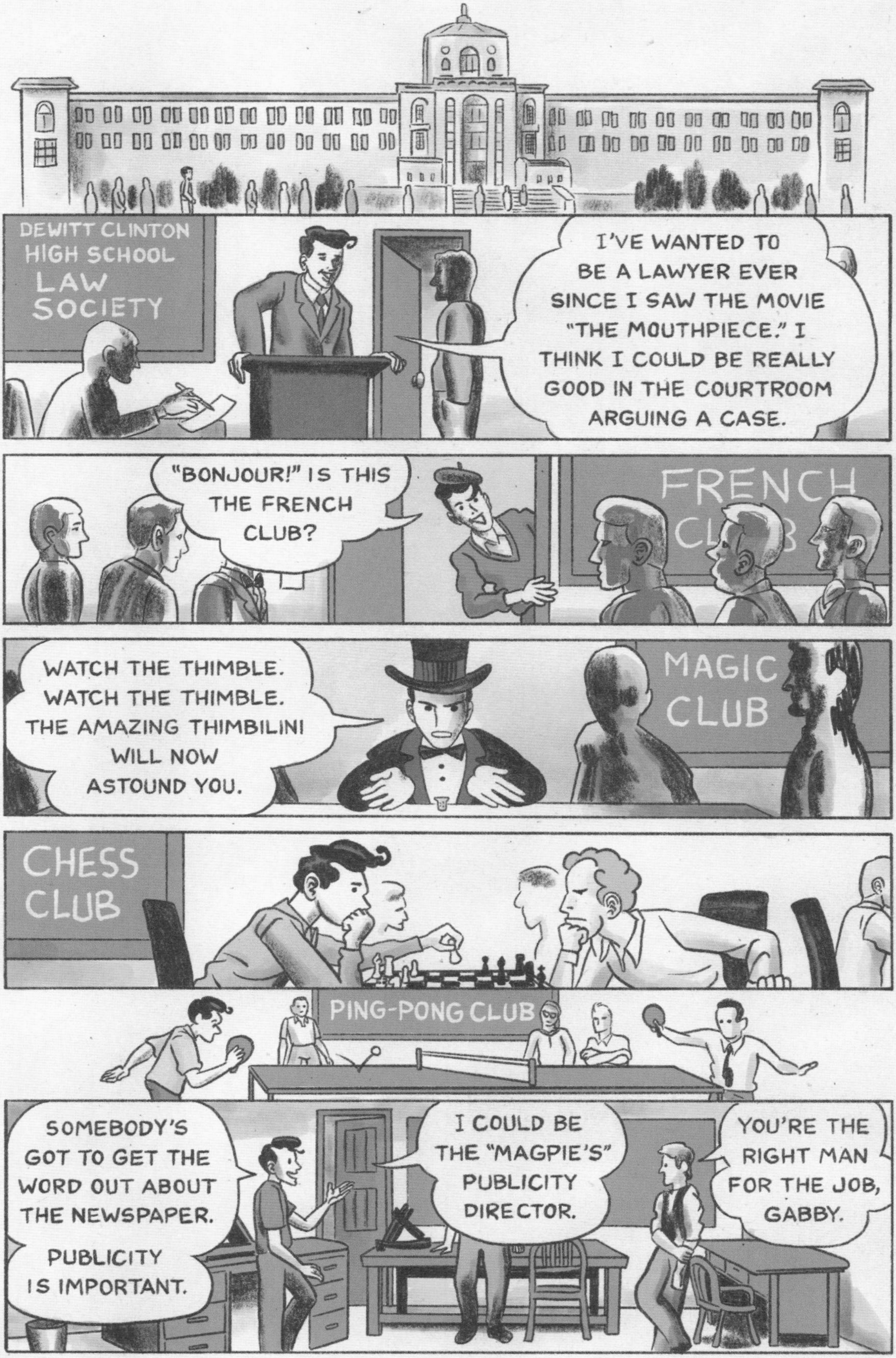
DEWITT CLINTON HIGH SCHOOL LAW SOCIETY
I'VE WANTED TO BE A LAWYER EVER SINCE I SAW THE MOVIE "THE MOUTHPIECE." I THINK I COULD BE REALLY GOOD IN THE COURTROOM ARGUING A CASE.
"BONJOUR!" IS THIS THE FRENCH CLUB?
FRENCH CLUB
WATCH THE THIMBLE. WATCH THE THIMBLE. THE AMAZING THIMBILINI WILL NOW ASTOUND YOU.
MAGIC CLUB
CHESS CLUB
PING-PONG CLUB
SOMEBODY'S GOT TO GET THE WORD OUT ABOUT THE NEWSPAPER.
PUBLICITY IS IMPORTANT.
I COULD BE THE "MAGPIE'S" PUBLICITY DIRECTOR.
YOU'RE THE RIGHT MAN FOR THE JOB, GABBY.

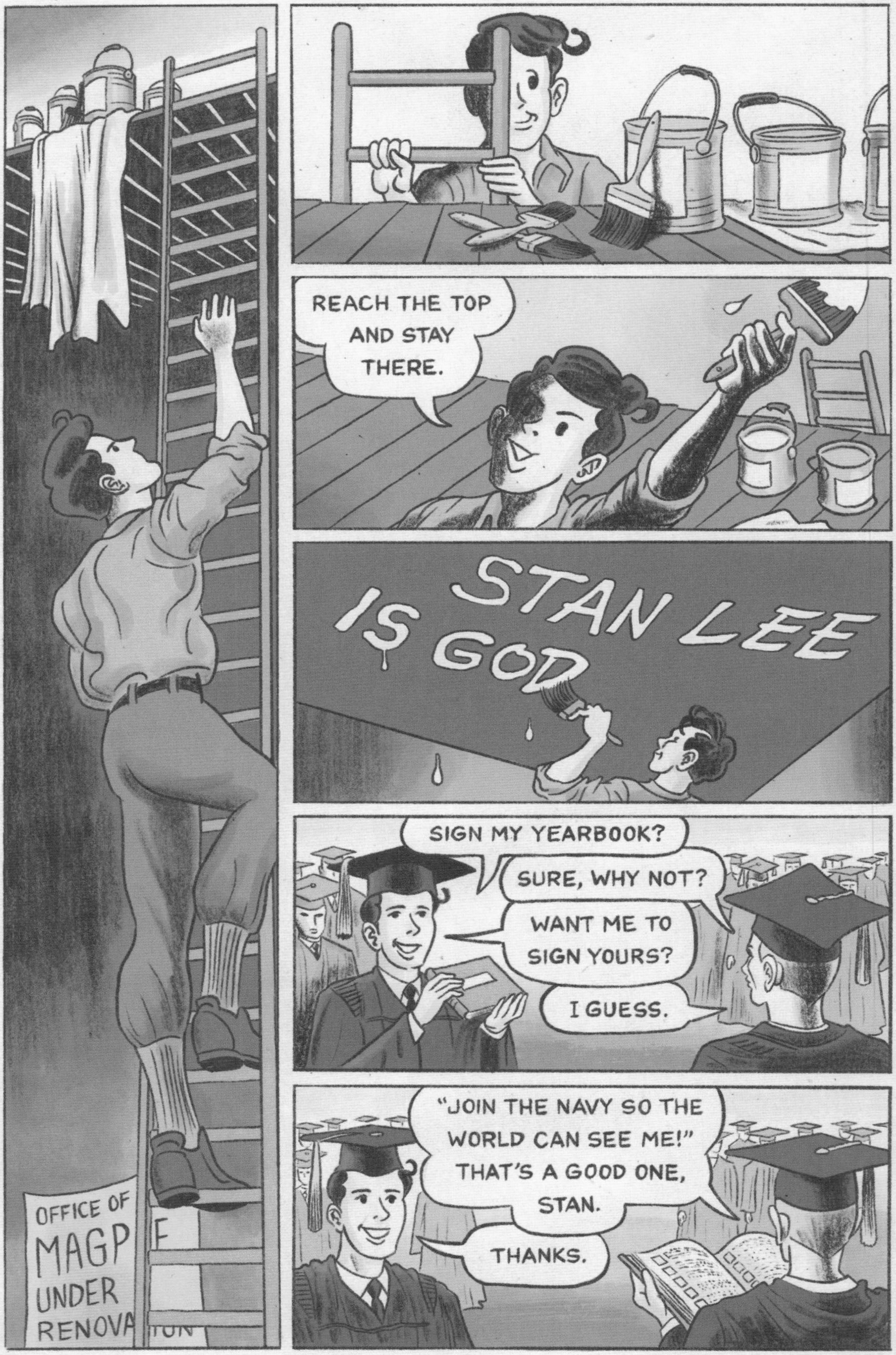
OFFICE OF
MAGP
UNDER
RENOVA
REACH THE TOP AND STAY THERE.
STAN LEE IS GOD
SIGN MY YEARBOOK?
SURE, WHY NOT?
WANT ME TO SIGN YOURS?
I GUESS.
"JOIN THE NAVY SO THE WORLD CAN SEE ME!" THAT'S A GOOD ONE, STAN.
THANKS.

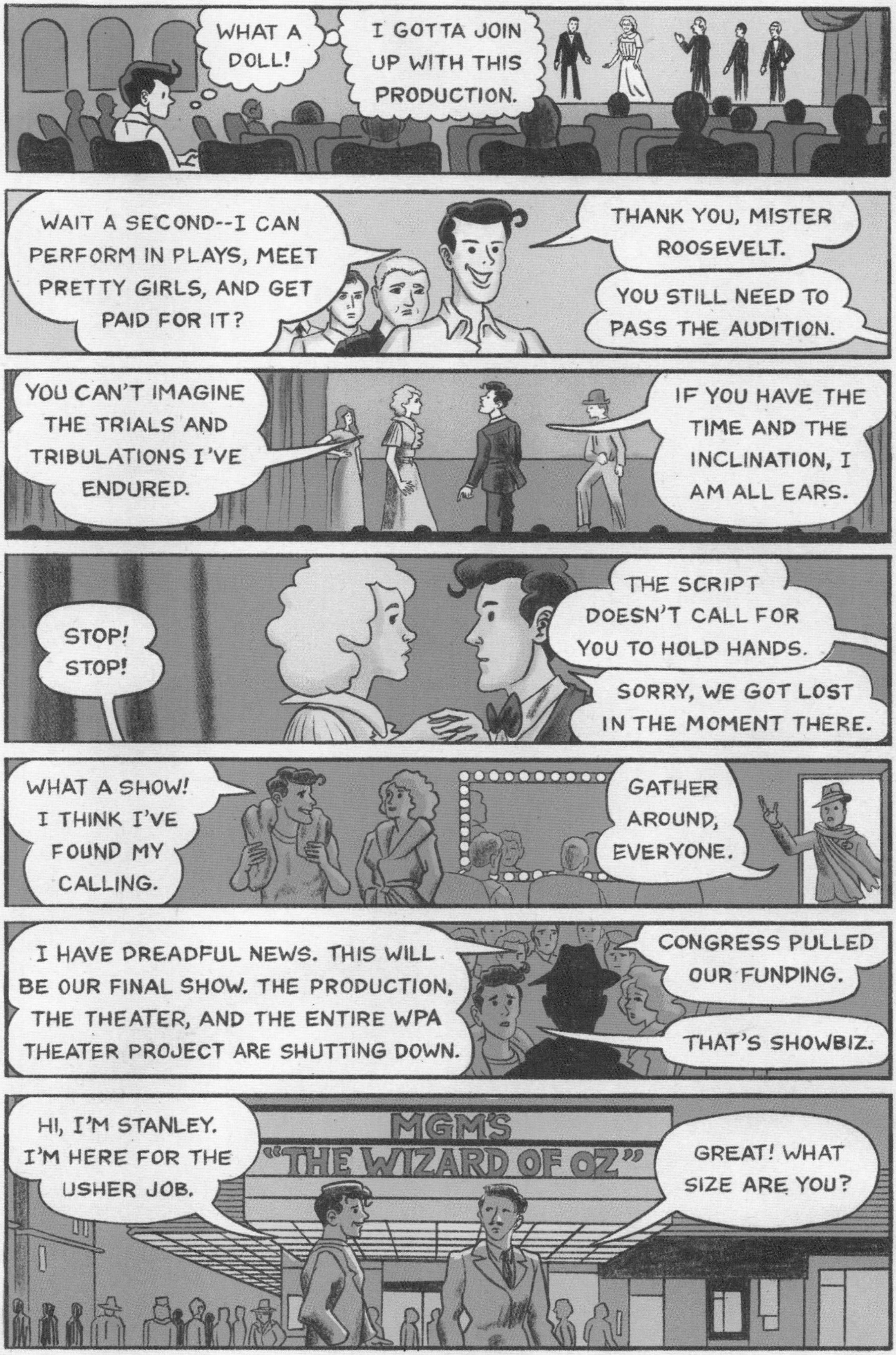
WHAT A DOLL!
I GOTTA JOIN UP WITH THIS PRODUCTION.
WAIT A SECOND--I CAN PERFORM IN PLAYS, MEET PRETTY GIRLS, AND GET PAID FOR IT?
THANK YOU, MISTER ROOSEVELT.
YOU STILL NEED TO PASS THE AUDITION.
YOU CAN'T IMAGINE THE TRIALS AND TRIBULATIONS I'VE ENDURED.
IF YOU HAVE THE TIME AND THE INCLINATION, I AM ALL EARS.
STOP! STOP!
THE SCRIPT DOESN'T CALL FOR YOU TO HOLD HANDS.
SORRY, WE GOT LOST IN THE MOMENT THERE.
WHAT A SHOW! I THINK I'VE FOUND MY CALLING.
GATHER AROUND, EVERYONE.
I HAVE DREADFUL NEWS. THIS WILL BE OUR FINAL SHOW. THE PRODUCTION, THE THEATER, AND THE ENTIRE WPA THEATER PROJECT ARE SHUTTING DOWN.
CONGRESS PULLED OUR FUNDING.
THAT'S SHOWBIZ.
HI, I'M STANLEY. I'M HERE FOR THE USHER JOB.
MGM'S "THE WIZARD OF OZ"
GREAT! WHAT SIZE ARE YOU?

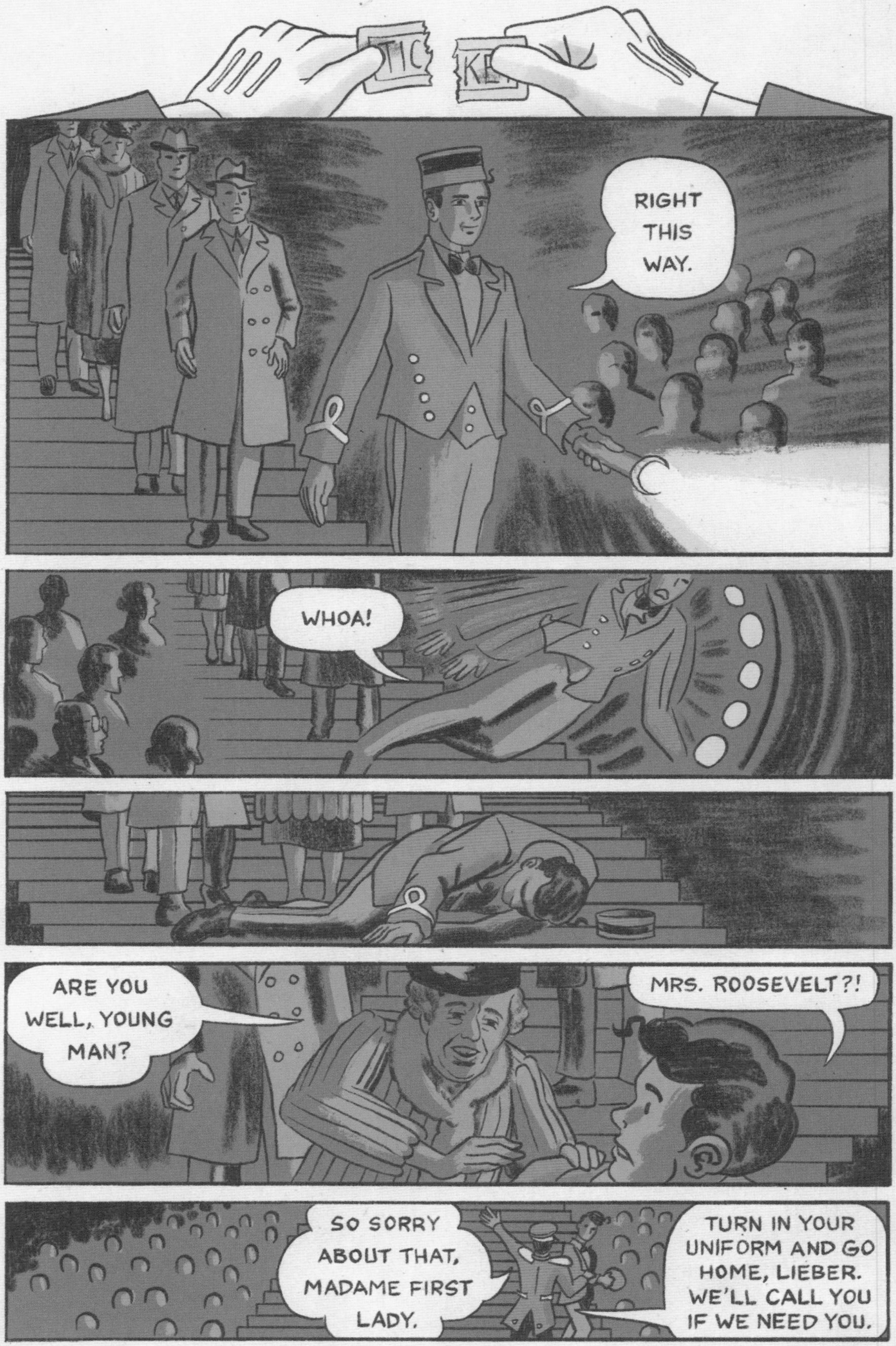
TIC
KE
RIGHT THIS WAY.
WHOA!
ARE YOU WELL, YOUNG MAN?
MRS. ROOSEVELT?!
SO SORRY ABOUT THAT, MADAME FIRST LADY.
TURN IN YOUR UNIFORM AND GO HOME, LIEBER. WE'LL CALL YOU IF WE NEED YOU.

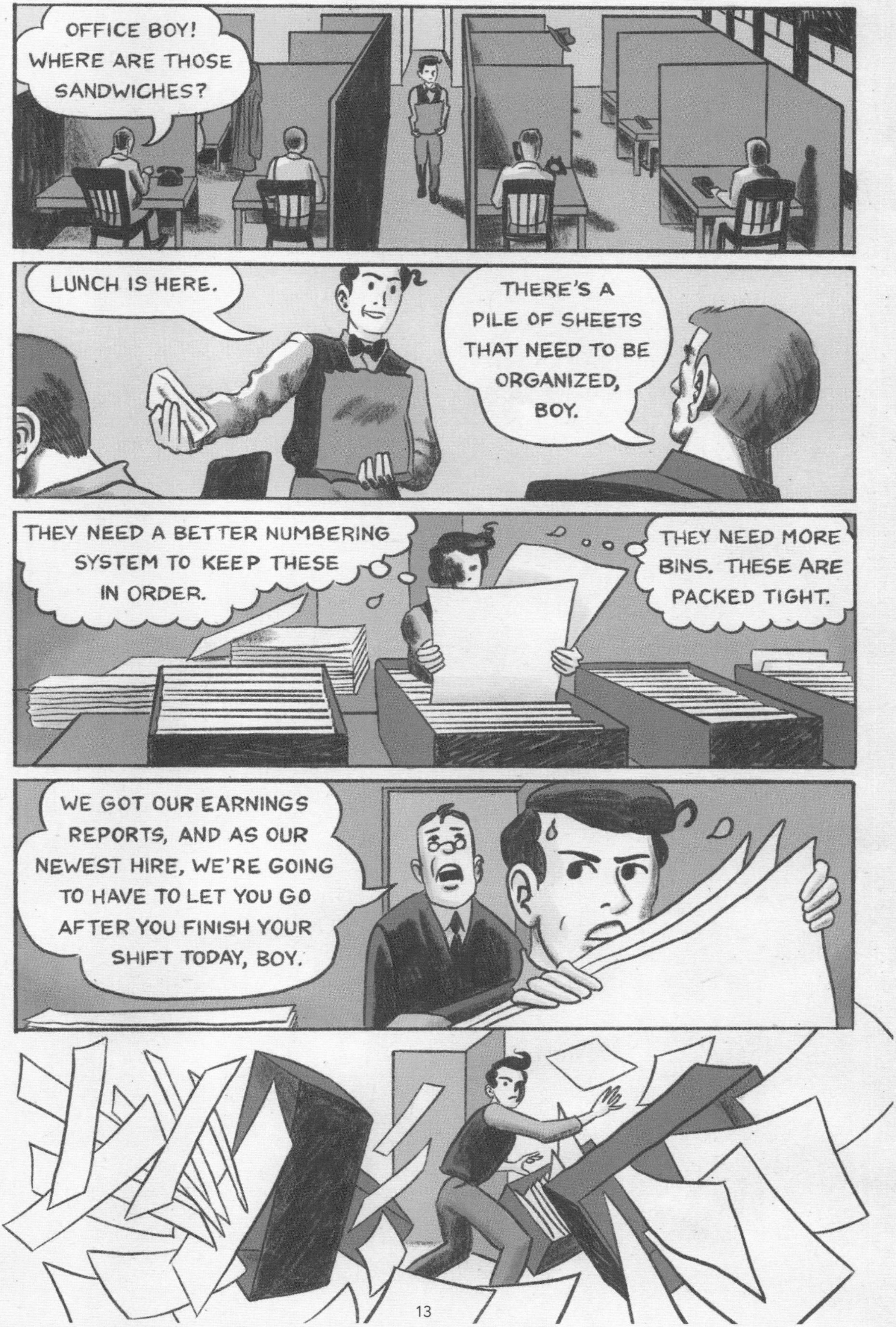
OFFICE BOY! WHERE ARE THOSE SANDWICHES?
LUNCH IS HERE.
THERE'S A PILE OF SHEETS THAT NEED TO BE ORGANIZED, BOY.
THEY NEED A BETTER NUMBERING SYSTEM TO KEEP THESE IN ORDER.
THEY NEED MORE BINS. THESE ARE PACKED TIGHT.
WE GOT OUR EARNINGS REPORTS, AND AS OUR NEWEST HIRE, WE'RE GOING TO HAVE TO LET YOU GO AFTER YOU FINISH YOUR SHIFT TODAY, BOY.

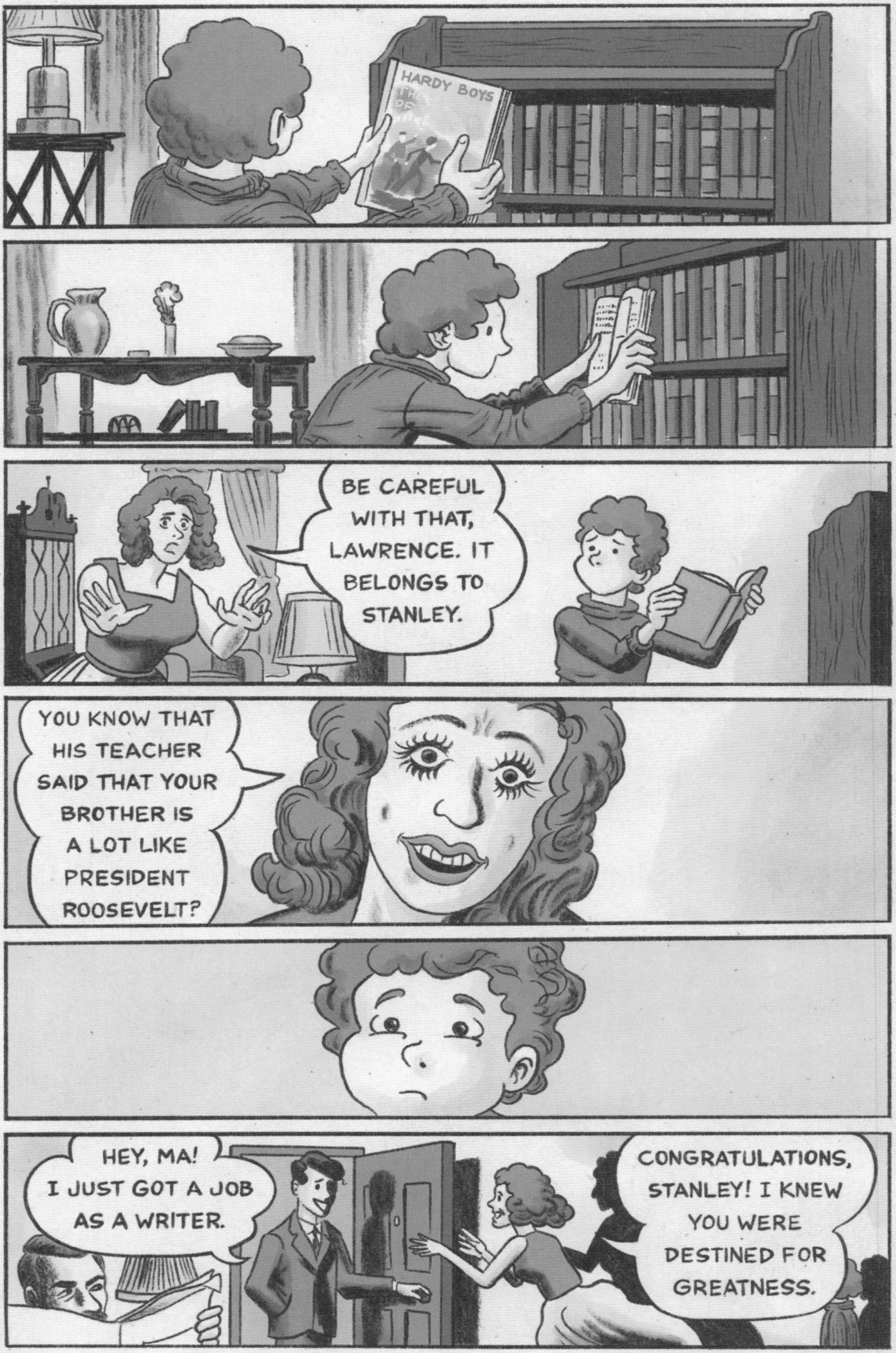
HARDY BOYS
BE CAREFUL WITH THAT, LAWRENCE. IT BELONGS TO STANLEY.
YOU KNOW THAT HIS TEACHER SAID THAT YOUR BROTHER IS A LOT LIKE PRESIDENT ROOSEVELT?
HEY, MA! I JUST GOT A JOB AS A WRITER.
CONGRATULATIONS, STANLEY! I KNEW YOU WERE DESTINED FOR GREATNESS.

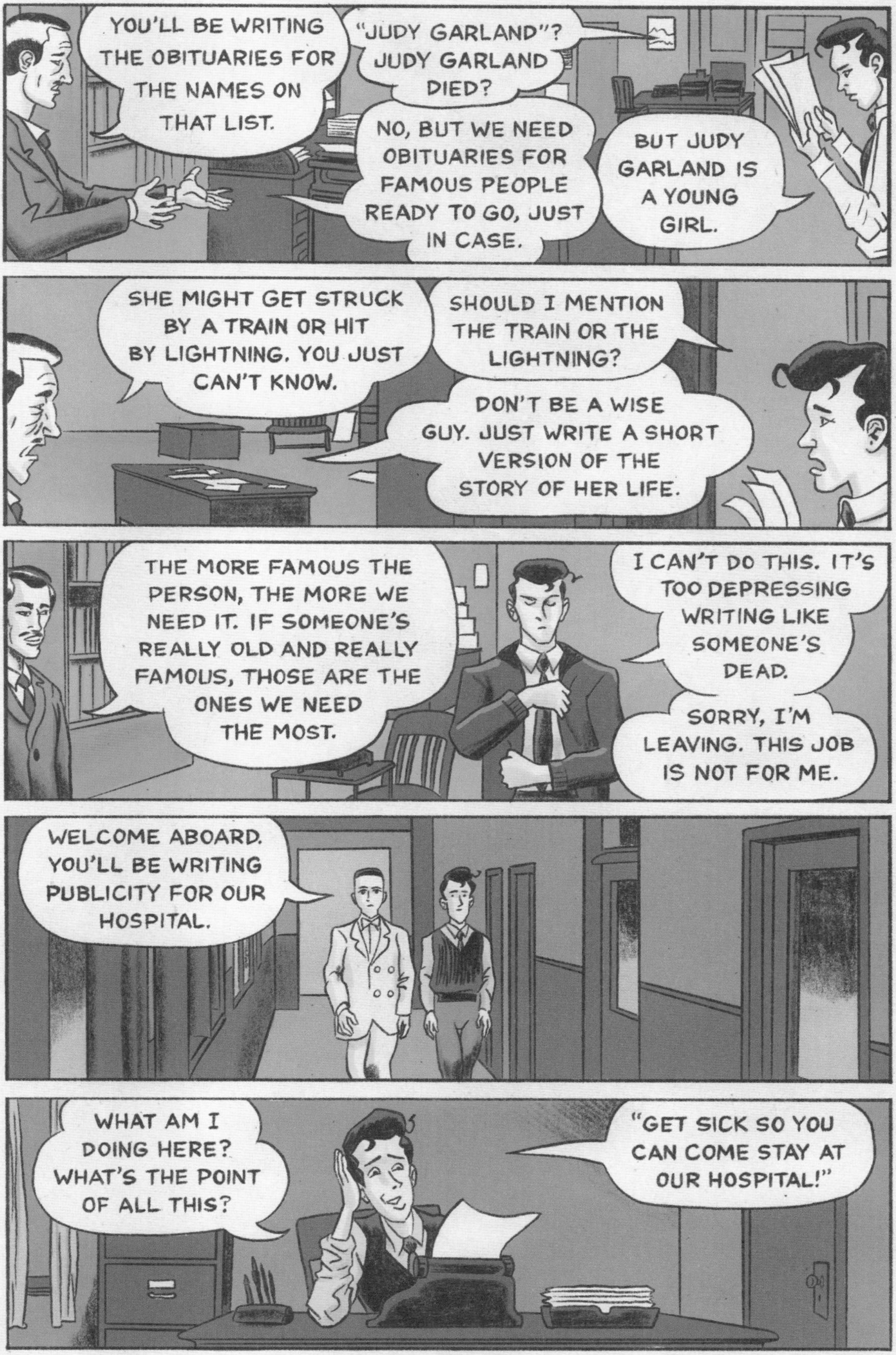
YOU'LL BE WRITING THE OBITUARIES FOR THE NAMES ON THAT LIST.
"JUDY GARLAND"? JUDY GARLAND DIED?
NO, BUT WE NEED OBITUARIES FOR FAMOUS PEOPLE READY TO GO, JUST IN CASE.
BUT JUDY GARLAND IS A YOUNG GIRL.
SHE MIGHT GET STRUCK BY A TRAIN OR HIT BY LIGHTNING. YOU JUST CAN'T KNOW.
SHOULD I MENTION THE TRAIN OR THE LIGHTNING?
DON'T BE A WISE GUY. JUST WRITE A SHORT VERSION OF THE STORY OF HER LIFE.
THE MORE FAMOUS THE PERSON, THE MORE WE NEED IT. IF SOMEONE'S REALLY OLD AND REALLY FAMOUS, THOSE ARE THE ONES WE NEED THE MOST.
I CAN'T DO THIS. IT'S TOO DEPRESSING WRITING LIKE SOMEONE'S DEAD.
SORRY, I'M LEAVING. THIS JOB IS NOT FOR ME.
WELCOME ABOARD. YOU'LL BE WRITING PUBLICITY FOR OUR HOSPITAL.
WHAT AM I DOING HERE? WHAT'S THE POINT OF ALL THIS?
"GET SICK SO YOU CAN COME STAY AT OUR HOSPITAL!"

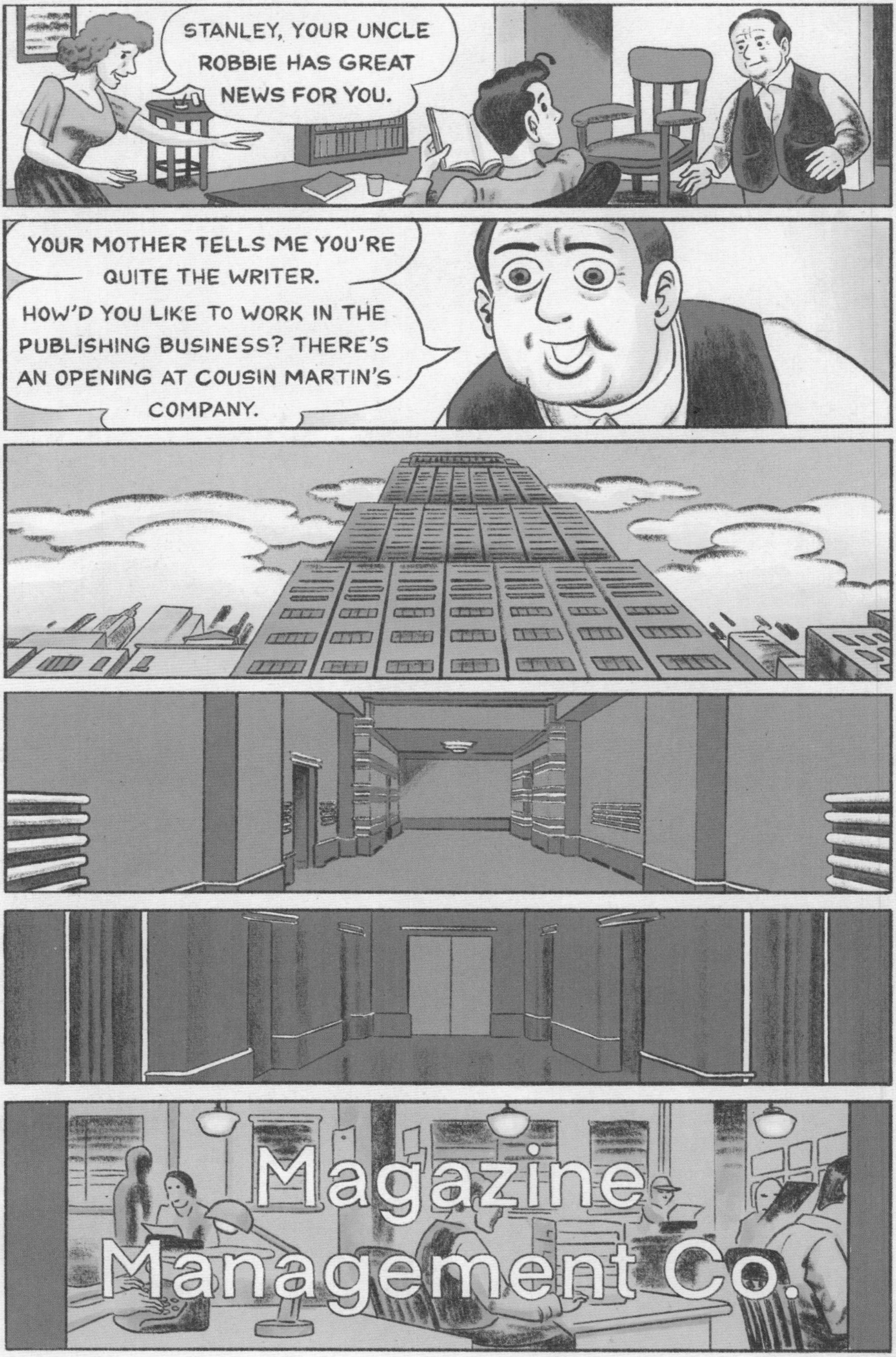
STANLEY, YOUR UNCLE ROBBIE HAS GREAT NEWS FOR YOU.
YOUR MOTHER TELLS ME YOU'RE QUITE THE WRITER. HOW'D YOU LIKE TO WORK IN THE PUBLISHING BUSINESS? THERE'S AN OPENING AT COUSIN MARTIN'S COMPANY.
Magazine Management Co.

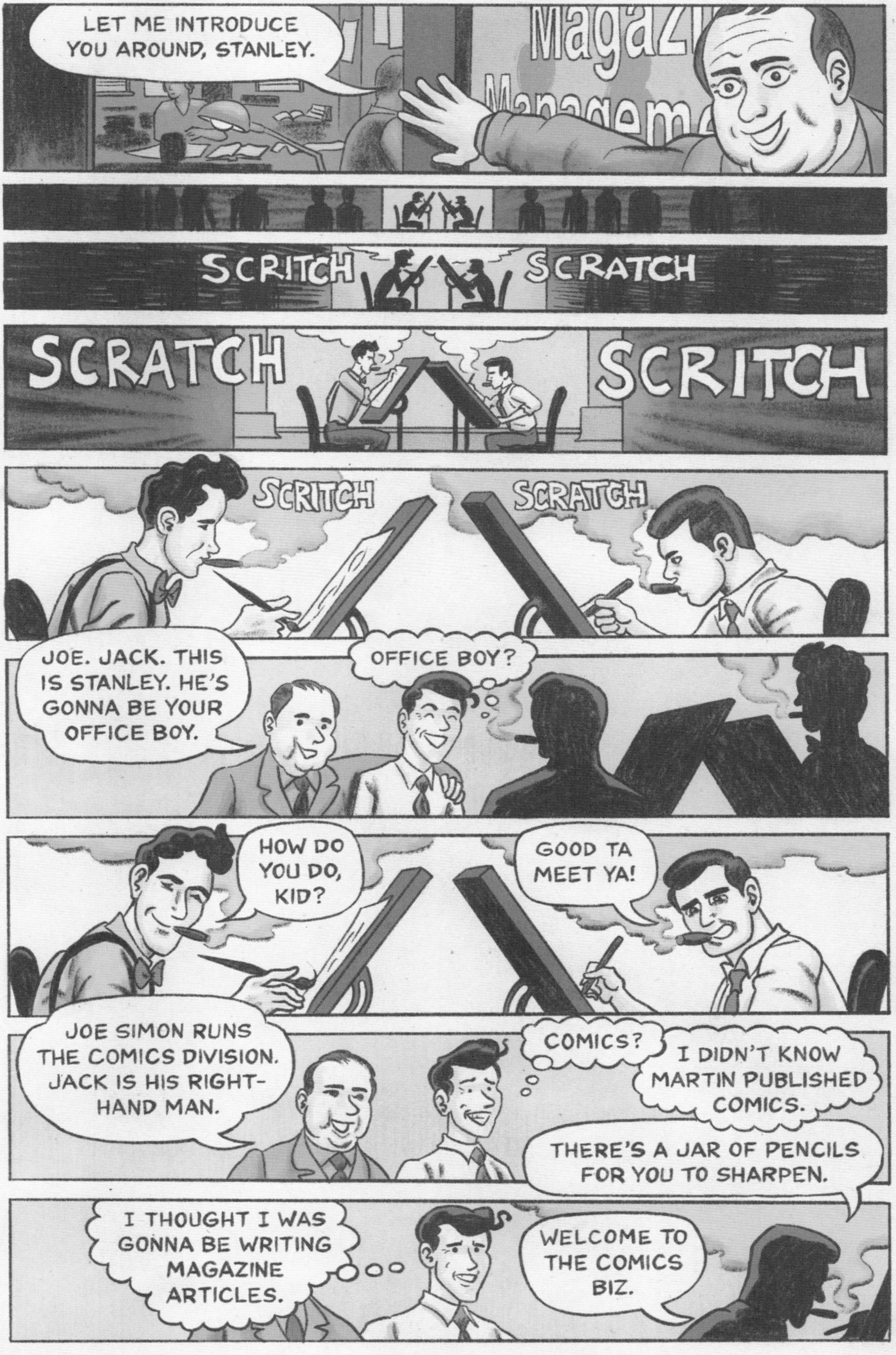
LET ME INTRODUCE YOU AROUND, STANLEY.
SCRITCH
SCRATCH
SCRATCH
SCRITCH
SCRITCH
SCRATCH
JOE. JACK. THIS IS STANLEY. HE'S GONNA BE YOUR OFFICE BOY.
OFFICE BOY?
HOW DO YOU DO, KID?
GOOD TA MEET YA!
JOE SIMON RUNS THE COMICS DIVISION. JACK IS HIS RIGHT-HAND MAN.
COMICS?
I DIDN'T KNOW MARTIN PUBLISHED COMICS.
THERE'S A JAR OF PENCILS FOR YOU TO SHARPEN.
I THOUGHT I WAS GONNA BE WRITING MAGAZINE ARTICLES.
WELCOME TO THE COMICS BIZ.

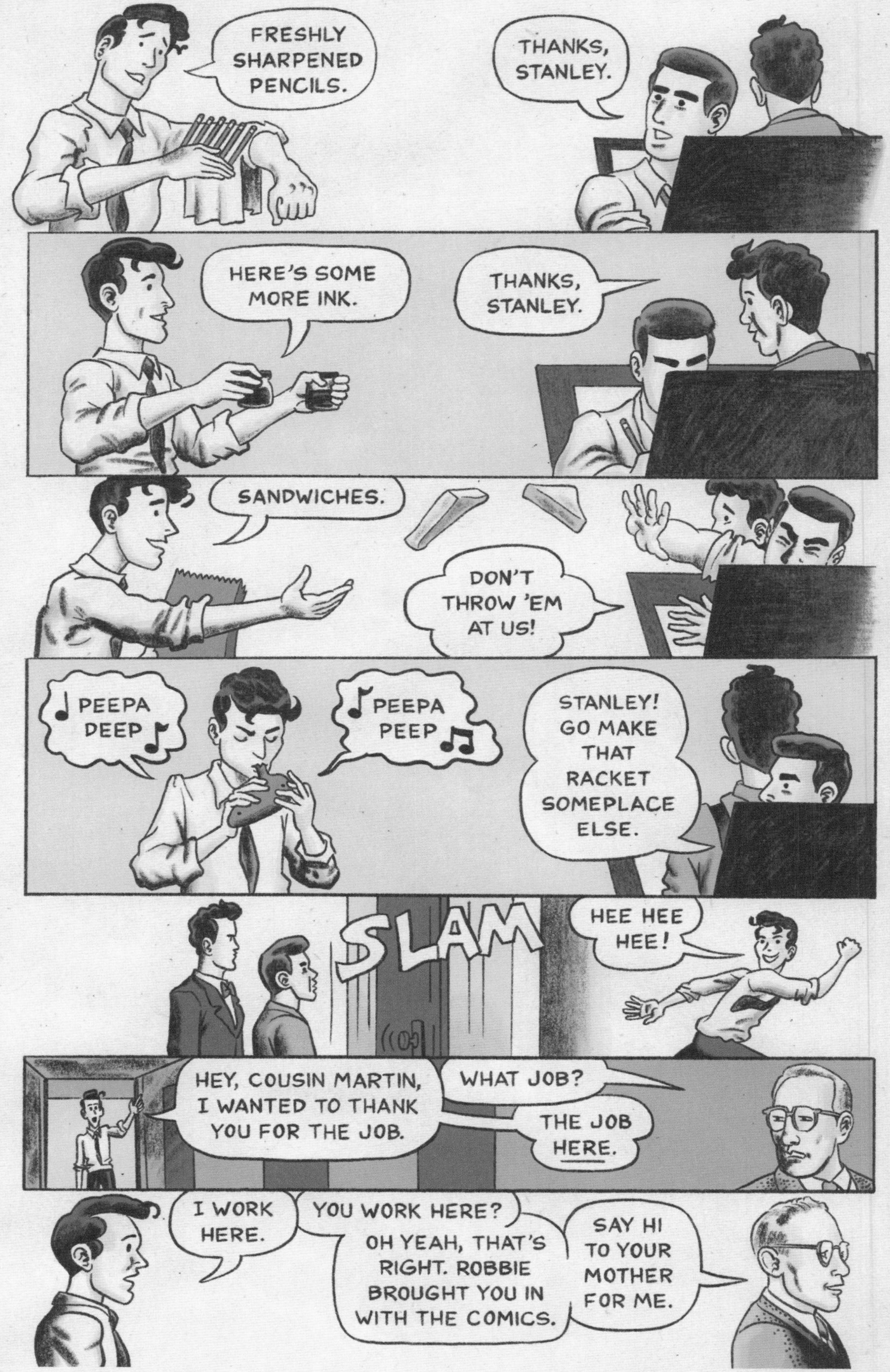
FRESHLY SHARPENED PENCILS.
THANKS, STANLEY.
HERE'S SOME MORE INK.
THANKS, STANLEY.
SANDWICHES.
DON'T THROW 'EM AT US!
PEEPA DEEP
PEEPA PEEP
STANLEY! GO MAKE THAT RACKET SOMEPLACE ELSE.
SLAM
HEE HEE HEE!
HEY, COUSIN MARTIN, I WANTED TO THANK YOU FOR THE JOB.
WHAT JOB?
THE JOB HERE.
I WORK HERE.
YOU WORK HERE?
OH YEAH, THAT'S RIGHT. ROBBIE BROUGHT YOU IN WITH THE COMICS.
SAY HI TO YOUR MOTHER FOR ME.

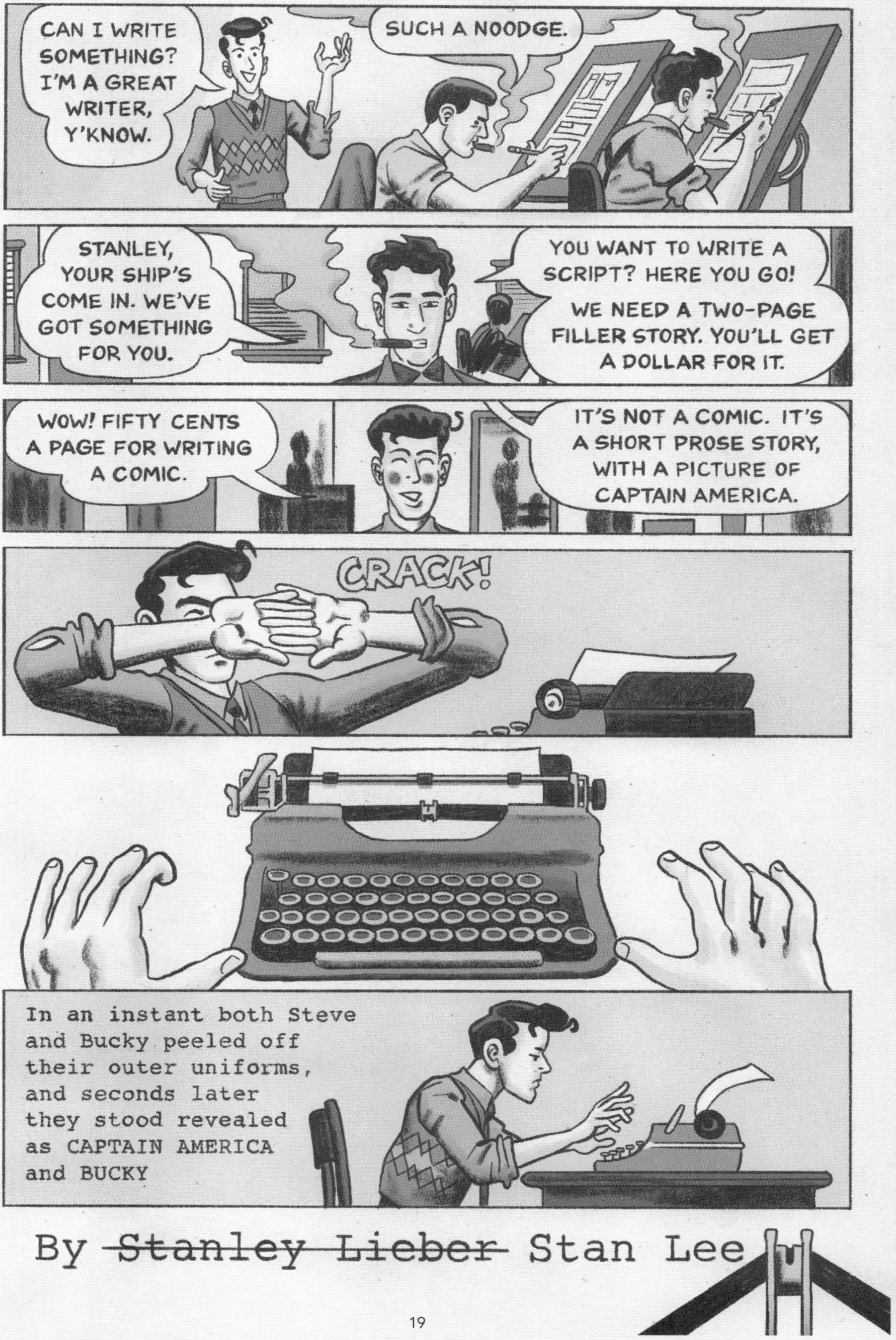
CAN I WRITE SOMETHING? I'M A GREAT WRITER, Y'KNOW.
SUCH A NOODGE.
STANLEY, YOUR SHIP'S COME IN. WE'VE GOT SOMETHING FOR YOU.
YOU WANT TO WRITE A SCRIPT? HERE YOU GO!
WE NEED A TWO-PAGE FILLER STORY. YOU'LL GET A DOLLAR FOR IT.
WOW! FIFTY CENTS A PAGE FOR WRITING A COMIC.
IT'S NOT A COMIC. IT'S A SHORT PROSE STORY, WITH A PICTURE OF CAPTAIN AMERICA.
CRACK!
In an instant both Steve and Bucky peeled off their outer uniforms, and seconds later they stood revealed as CAPTAIN AMERICA and BUCKY
By ~~Stanley Lieber~~ Stan Lee

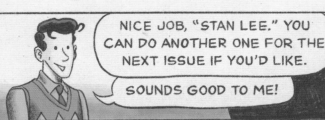

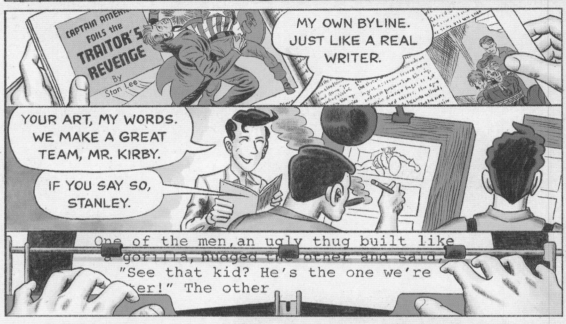

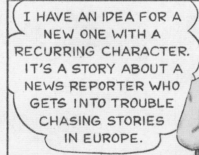

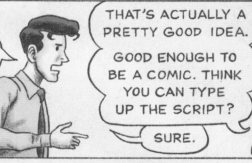

NICE JOB, "STAN LEE." YOU CAN DO ANOTHER ONE FOR THE NEXT ISSUE IF YOU'D LIKE.
SOUNDS GOOD TO ME!
CAPTAIN AMERI FOILS the TRAITOR'S REVENGE By Stan Lee
MY OWN BYLINE. JUST LIKE A REAL WRITER.
YOUR ART, MY WORDS. WE MAKE A GREAT TEAM, MR. KIRBY.
IF YOU SAY SO, STANLEY.
One of the men,an ugly thug built like a gorilla, nudged the other and said, "See that kid? He's the one we're ter!" The other
I HAVE AN IDEA FOR A NEW ONE WITH A RECURRING CHARACTER. IT'S A STORY ABOUT A NEWS REPORTER WHO GETS INTO TROUBLE CHASING STORIES IN EUROPE.
THAT'S ACTUALLY A PRETTY GOOD IDEA.
GOOD ENOUGH TO BE A COMIC. THINK YOU CAN TYPE UP THE SCRIPT?
SURE.
HEADLINE HUNTER
Foreign Correspondent
By Stan Lee
IN LONDON WE FIND JERRY HUNTER -- KNOWN TO HIS FRIENDS AS "HEADLINE" HUNTER -- SPEAKING TO HIS NEW YORK EDITOR
I CAN'T HELP IT, CHIEF--HOW CAN I GET A SCOOP IN LONDON? EVERY TIME SOMETHING HAPPENS, EVERY PAPER IN TOWN GETS WIND OF IT AS SOON AS I DO!
HECK, HOW CAN I FIND A SCOOP IF THERE JUST AIN'T NONE?
MR. HUNTER, THE MANAGING EDITOR WANTS YOU RIGHT AWAY!

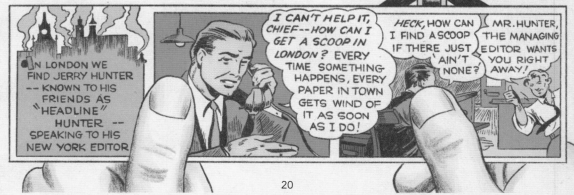

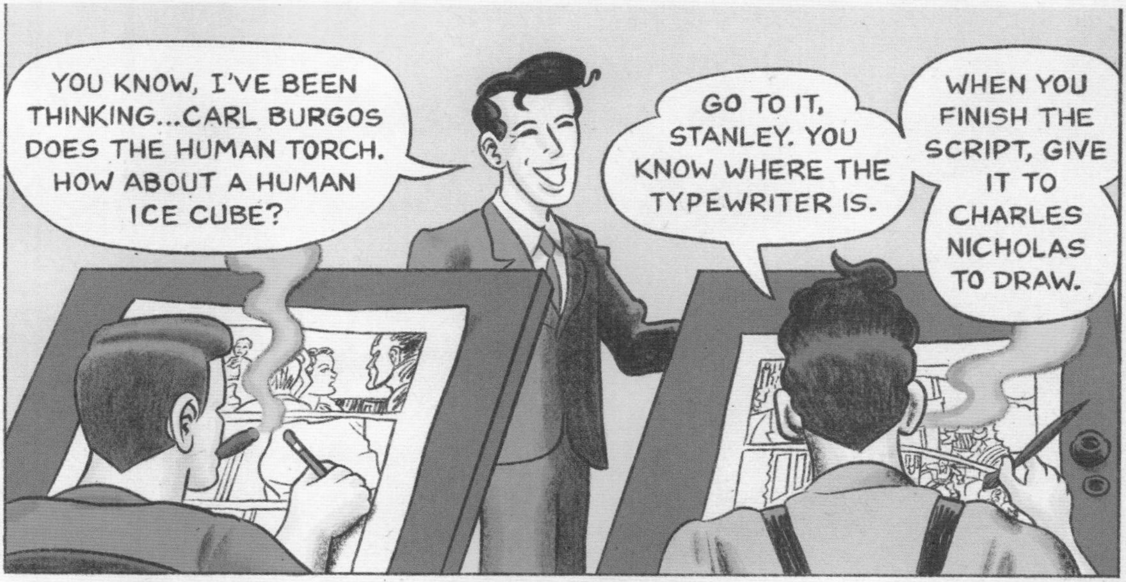
YOU KNOW, I'VE BEEN THINKING...CARL BURGOS DOES THE HUMAN TORCH. HOW ABOUT A HUMAN ICE CUBE?
GO TO IT, STANLEY. YOU KNOW WHERE THE TYPEWRITER IS.
WHEN YOU FINISH THE SCRIPT, GIVE IT TO CHARLES NICHOLAS TO DRAW.

JACK FROST
Story by Stan Lee

The Far North! Challenging! Mysterious! Foreboding! The land that no man really knows...in this gr

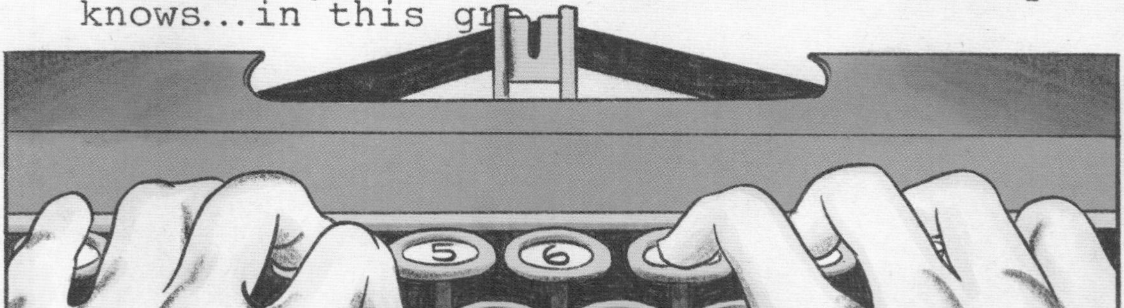
5
6
T
Y
U
G

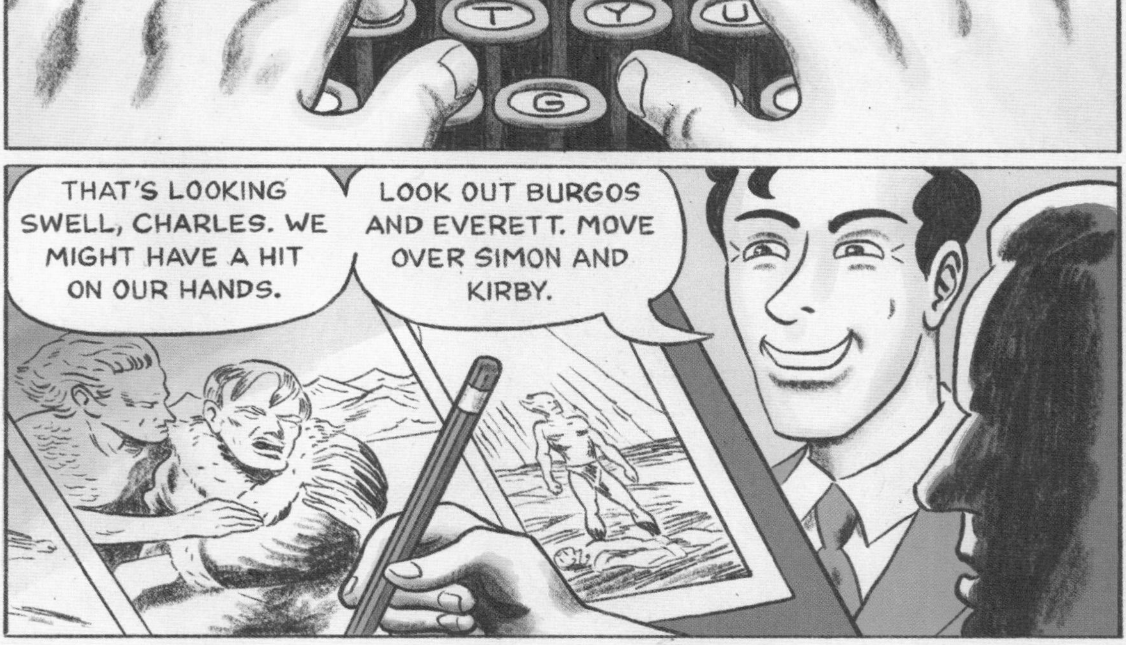
THAT'S LOOKING SWELL, CHARLES. WE MIGHT HAVE A HIT ON OUR HANDS.
LOOK OUT BURGOS AND EVERETT. MOVE OVER SIMON AND KIRBY.

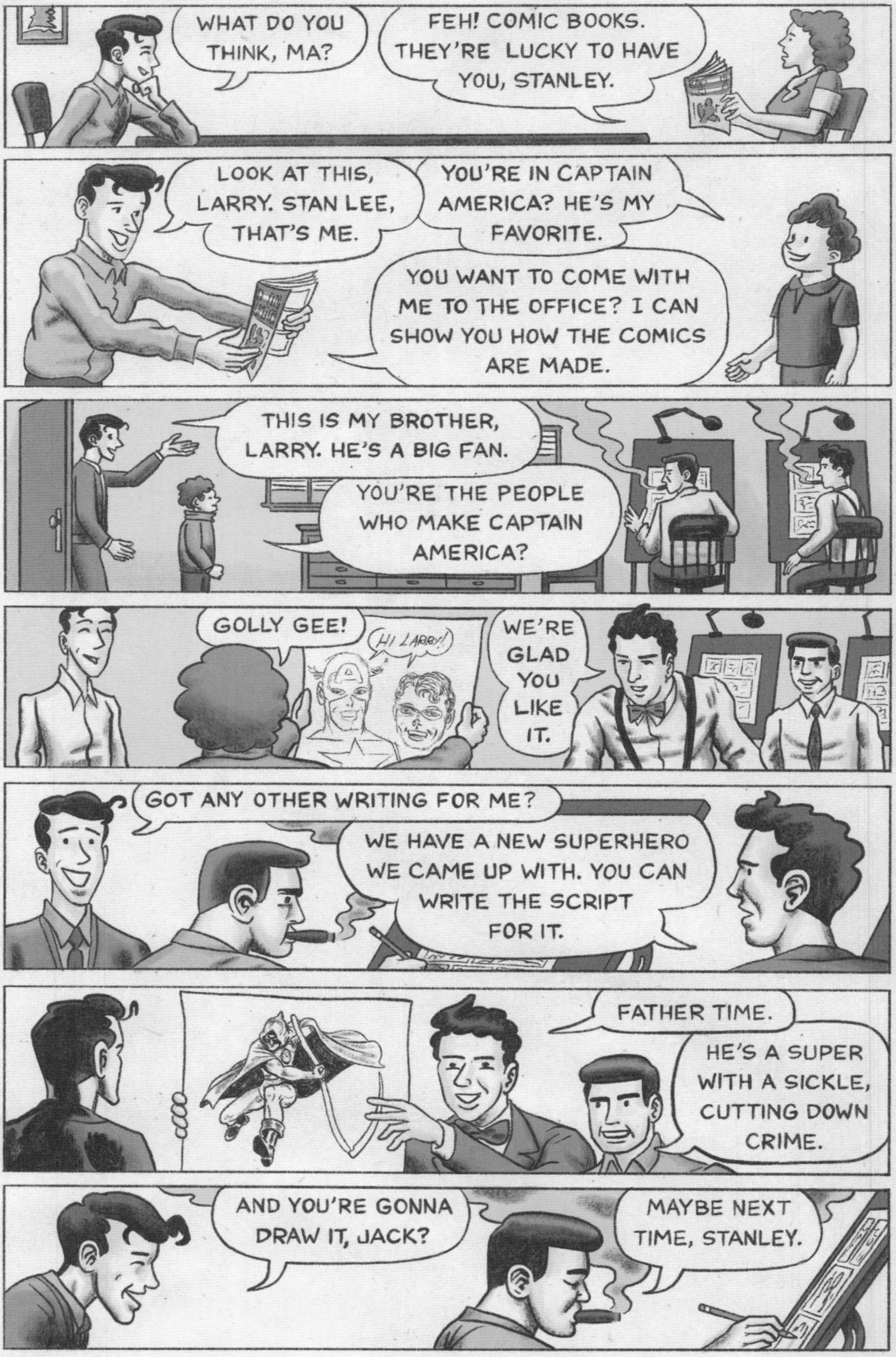
WHAT DO YOU THINK, MA?
FEH! COMIC BOOKS. THEY'RE LUCKY TO HAVE YOU, STANLEY.
LOOK AT THIS, LARRY. STAN LEE, THAT'S ME.
YOU'RE IN CAPTAIN AMERICA? HE'S MY FAVORITE.
YOU WANT TO COME WITH ME TO THE OFFICE? I CAN SHOW YOU HOW THE COMICS ARE MADE.
THIS IS MY BROTHER, LARRY. HE'S A BIG FAN.
YOU'RE THE PEOPLE WHO MAKE CAPTAIN AMERICA?
GOLLY GEE!
HI LARRY!
WE'RE GLAD YOU LIKE IT.
GOT ANY OTHER WRITING FOR ME?
WE HAVE A NEW SUPERHERO WE CAME UP WITH. YOU CAN WRITE THE SCRIPT FOR IT.
FATHER TIME.
HE'S A SUPER WITH A SICKLE, CUTTING DOWN CRIME.
AND YOU'RE GONNA DRAW IT, JACK?
MAYBE NEXT TIME, STANLEY.

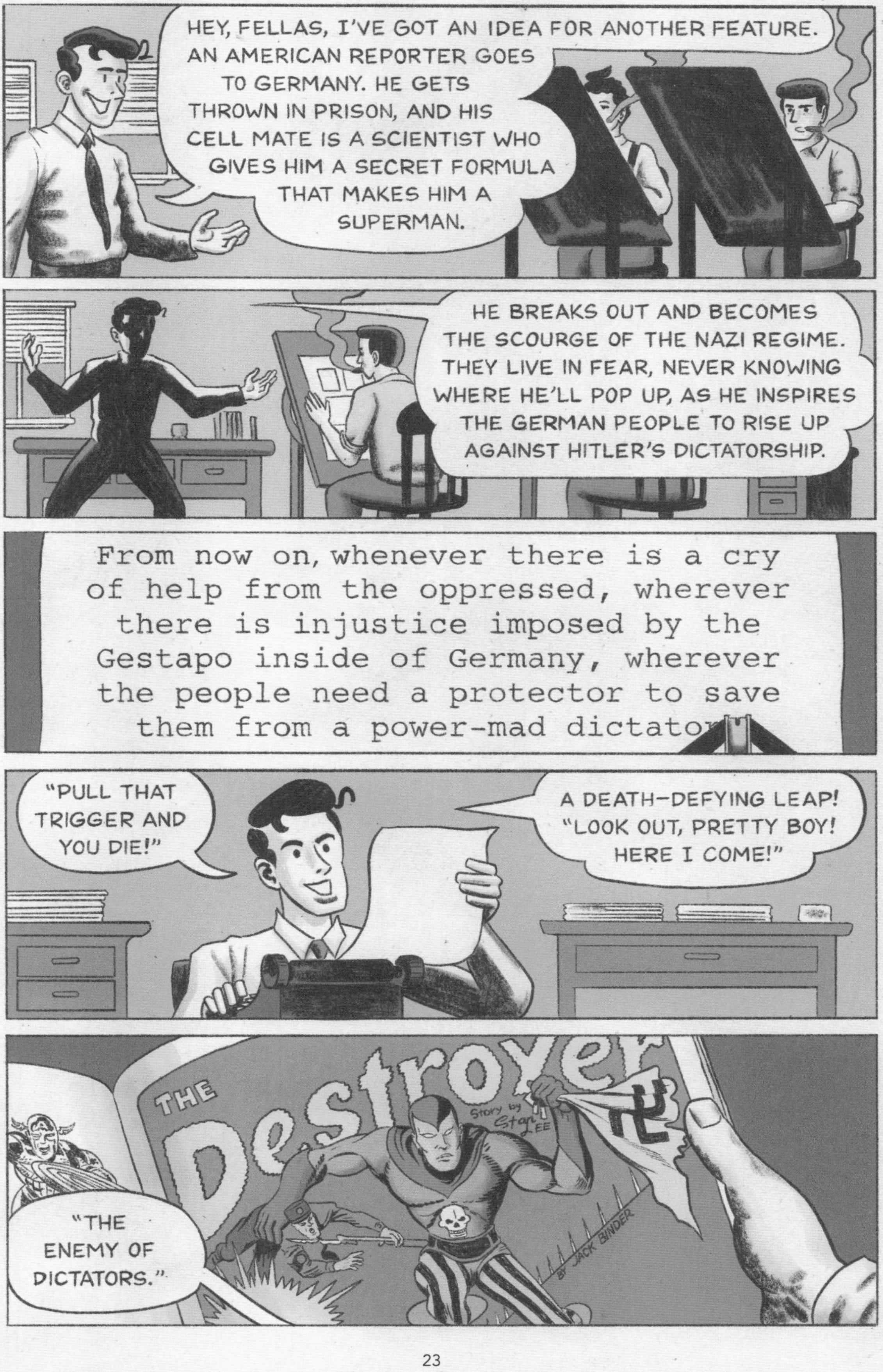

HEY, FELLAS, I'VE GOT AN IDEA FOR ANOTHER FEATURE. AN AMERICAN REPORTER GOES TO GERMANY. HE GETS THROWN IN PRISON, AND HIS CELL MATE IS A SCIENTIST WHO GIVES HIM A SECRET FORMULA THAT MAKES HIM A SUPERMAN.
HE BREAKS OUT AND BECOMES THE SCOURGE OF THE NAZI REGIME. THEY LIVE IN FEAR, NEVER KNOWING WHERE HE'LL POP UP, AS HE INSPIRES THE GERMAN PEOPLE TO RISE UP AGAINST HITLER'S DICTATORSHIP.
From now on, whenever there is a cry of help from the oppressed, wherever there is injustice imposed by the Gestapo inside of Germany, wherever the people need a protector to save them from a power-mad dictato
"PULL THAT TRIGGER AND YOU DIE!"
A DEATH-DEFYING LEAP! "LOOK OUT, PRETTY BOY! HERE I COME!"
THE Destroyer
Story by Stan Lee
BY JACK BINDER
"THE ENEMY OF DICTATORS."

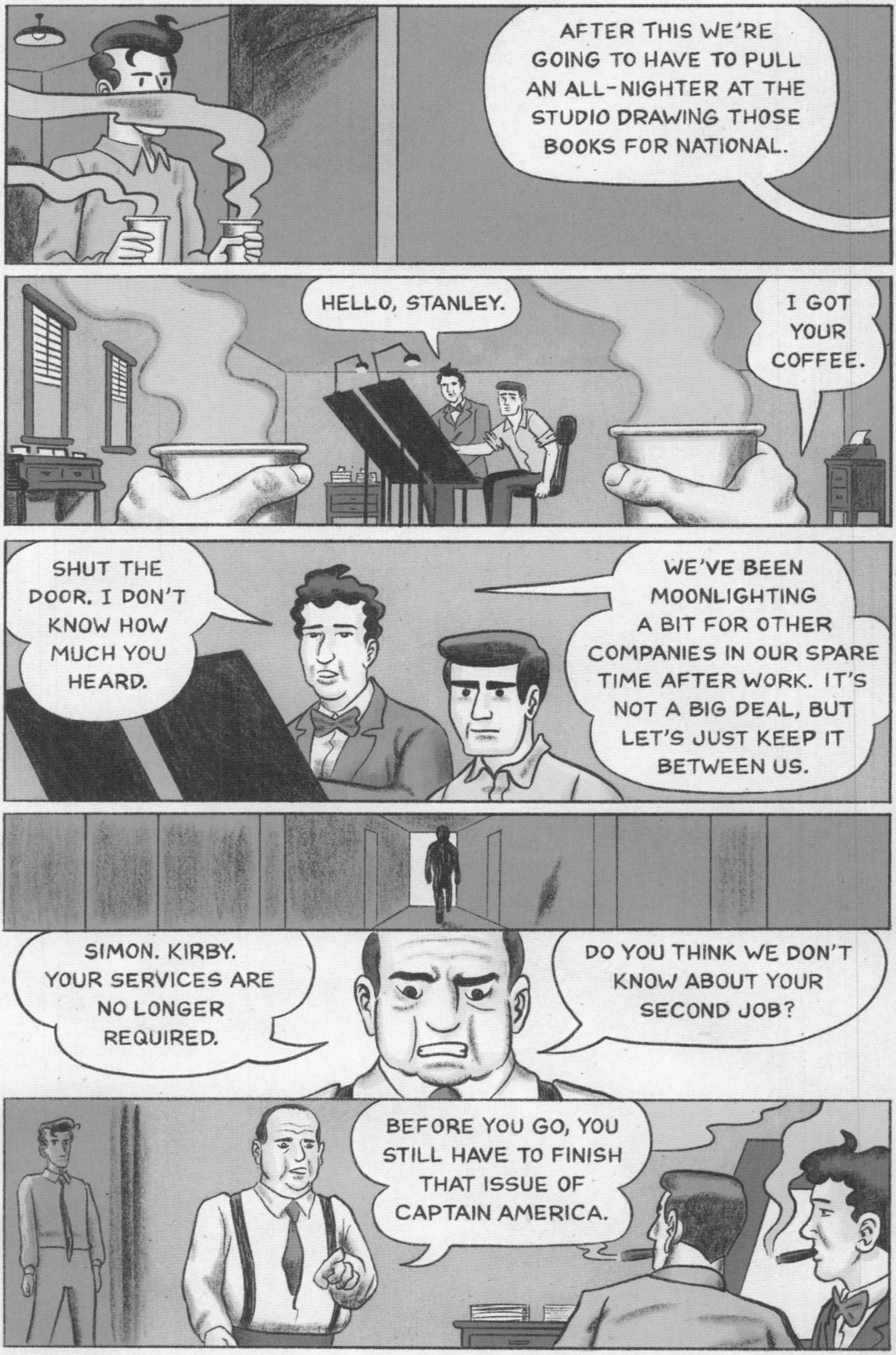
AFTER THIS WE'RE GOING TO HAVE TO PULL AN ALL-NIGHTER AT THE STUDIO DRAWING THOSE BOOKS FOR NATIONAL.
HELLO, STANLEY.
I GOT YOUR COFFEE.
SHUT THE DOOR. I DON'T KNOW HOW MUCH YOU HEARD.
WE'VE BEEN MOONLIGHTING A BIT FOR OTHER COMPANIES IN OUR SPARE TIME AFTER WORK. IT'S NOT A BIG DEAL, BUT LET'S JUST KEEP IT BETWEEN US.
SIMON. KIRBY. YOUR SERVICES ARE NO LONGER REQUIRED.
DO YOU THINK WE DON'T KNOW ABOUT YOUR SECOND JOB?
BEFORE YOU GO, YOU STILL HAVE TO FINISH THAT ISSUE OF CAPTAIN AMERICA.

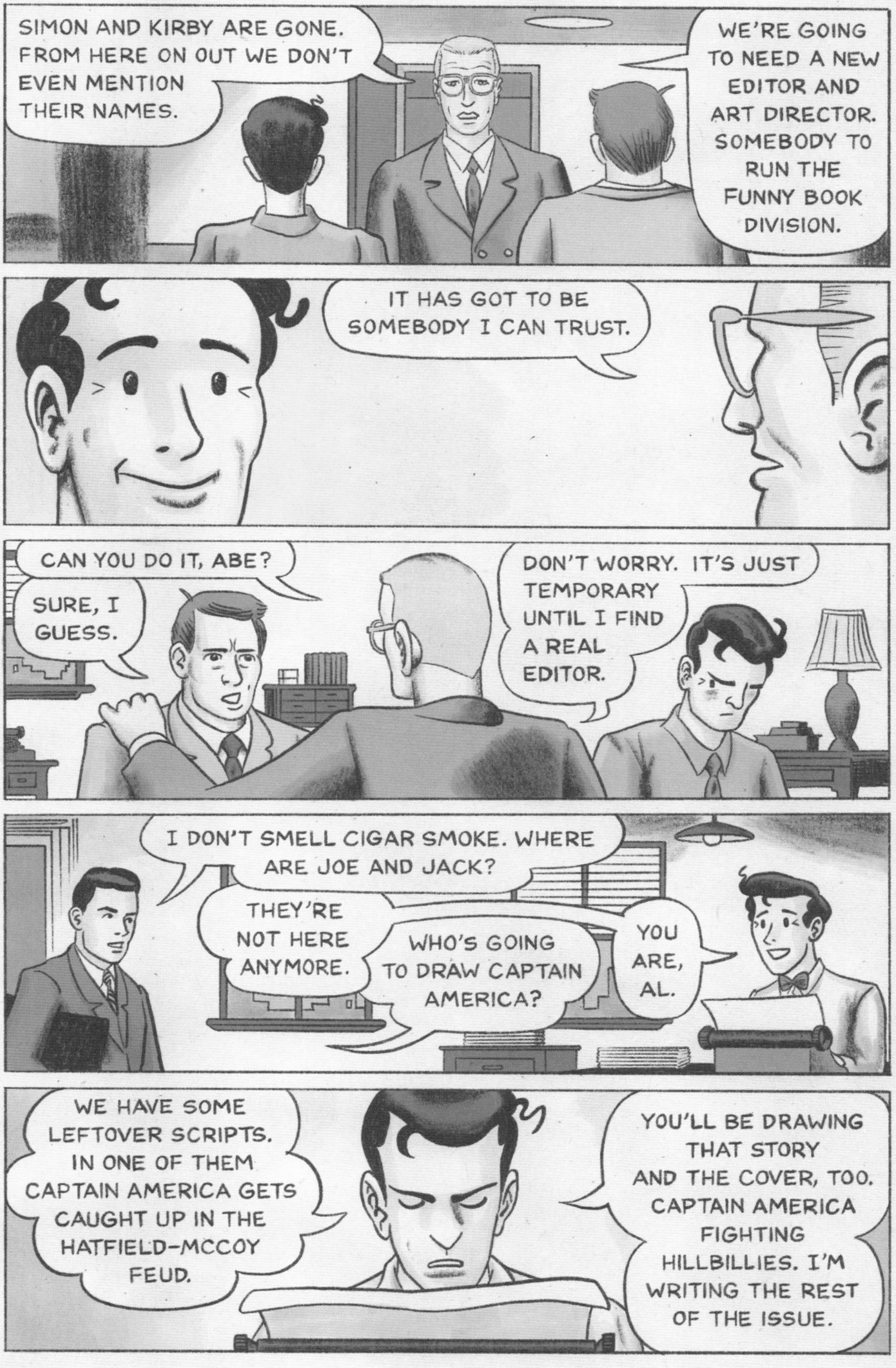
SIMON AND KIRBY ARE GONE. FROM HERE ON OUT WE DON'T EVEN MENTION THEIR NAMES.
WE'RE GOING TO NEED A NEW EDITOR AND ART DIRECTOR. SOMEBODY TO RUN THE FUNNY BOOK DIVISION.
IT HAS GOT TO BE SOMEBODY I CAN TRUST.
CAN YOU DO IT, ABE?
SURE, I GUESS.
DON'T WORRY. IT'S JUST TEMPORARY UNTIL I FIND A REAL EDITOR.
I DON'T SMELL CIGAR SMOKE. WHERE ARE JOE AND JACK?
THEY'RE NOT HERE ANYMORE.
WHO'S GOING TO DRAW CAPTAIN AMERICA?
YOU ARE, AL.
WE HAVE SOME LEFTOVER SCRIPTS. IN ONE OF THEM CAPTAIN AMERICA GETS CAUGHT UP IN THE HATFIELD-MCCOY FEUD.
YOU'LL BE DRAWING THAT STORY AND THE COVER, TOO. CAPTAIN AMERICA FIGHTING HILLBILLIES. I'M WRITING THE REST OF THE ISSUE.

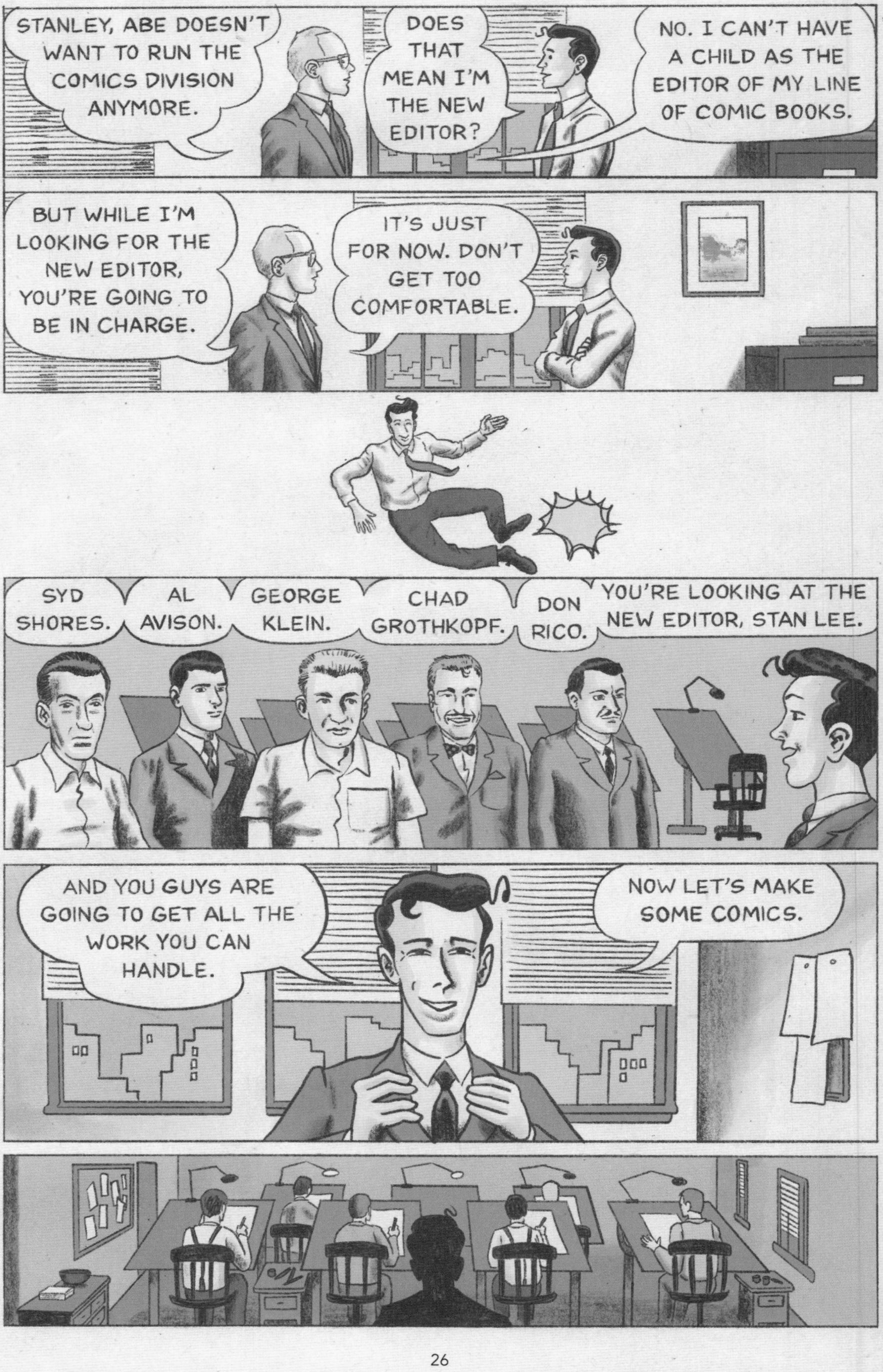
STANLEY, ABE DOESN'T WANT TO RUN THE COMICS DIVISION ANYMORE.
DOES THAT MEAN I'M THE NEW EDITOR?
NO. I CAN'T HAVE A CHILD AS THE EDITOR OF MY LINE OF COMIC BOOKS.
BUT WHILE I'M LOOKING FOR THE NEW EDITOR, YOU'RE GOING TO BE IN CHARGE.
IT'S JUST FOR NOW. DON'T GET TOO COMFORTABLE.
SYD SHORES.
AL AVISON.
GEORGE KLEIN.
CHAD GROTHKOPF.
DON RICO.
YOU'RE LOOKING AT THE NEW EDITOR, STAN LEE.
AND YOU GUYS ARE GOING TO GET ALL THE WORK YOU CAN HANDLE.
NOW LET'S MAKE SOME COMICS.

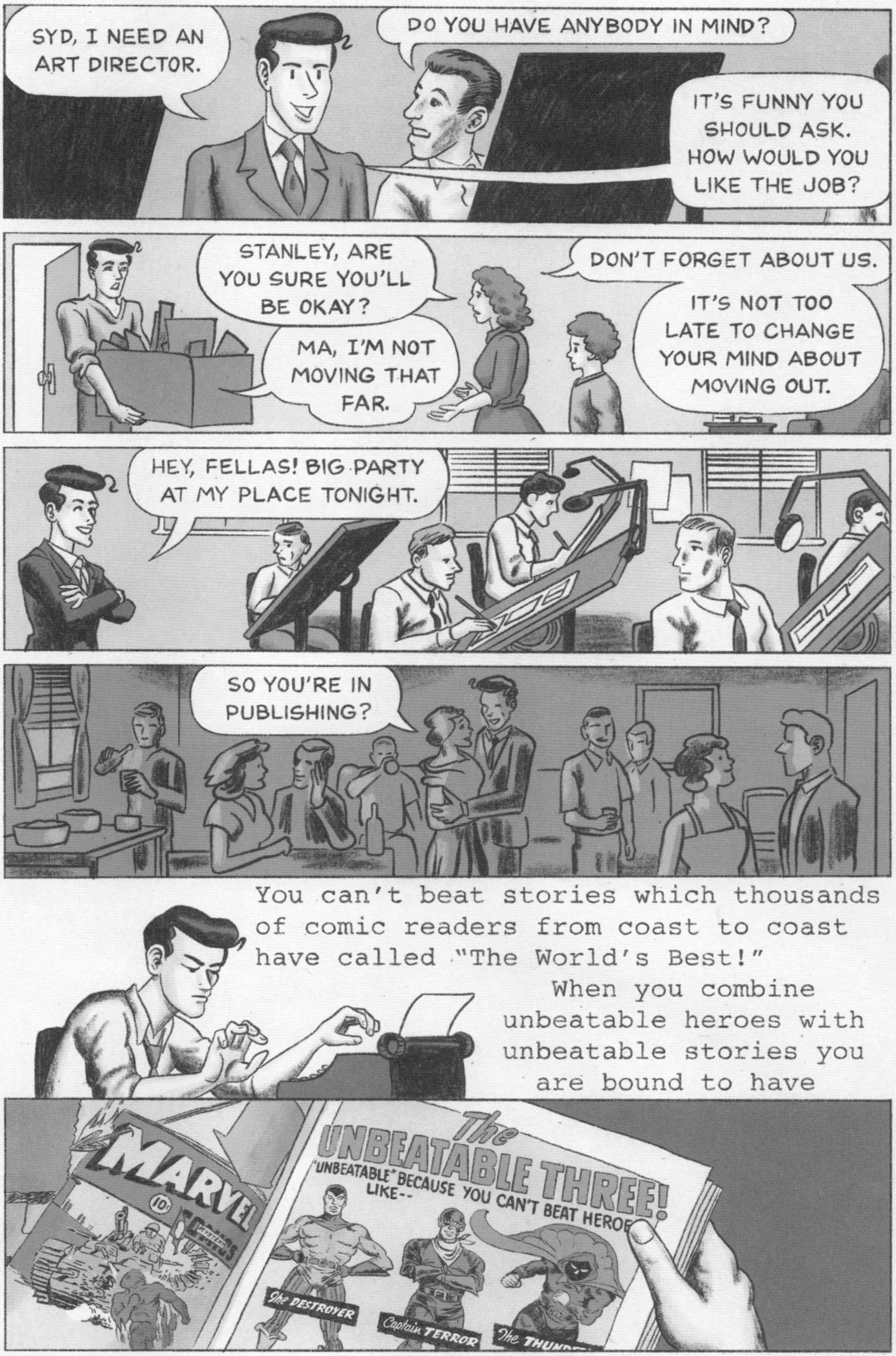
SYD, I NEED AN ART DIRECTOR.
DO YOU HAVE ANYBODY IN MIND?
IT'S FUNNY YOU SHOULD ASK. HOW WOULD YOU LIKE THE JOB?
STANLEY, ARE YOU SURE YOU'LL BE OKAY?
MA, I'M NOT MOVING THAT FAR.
DON'T FORGET ABOUT US.
IT'S NOT TOO LATE TO CHANGE YOUR MIND ABOUT MOVING OUT.
HEY, FELLAS! BIG PARTY AT MY PLACE TONIGHT.
SO YOU'RE IN PUBLISHING?
You can't beat stories which thousands of comic readers from coast to coast have called "The World's Best!"
When you combine unbeatable heroes with unbeatable stories you are bound to have
MARVEL
10¢
The UNBEATABLE THREE!
"UNBEATABLE" BECAUSE YOU CAN'T BEAT HERO
LIKE--
The DESTROYER
Captain TERROR

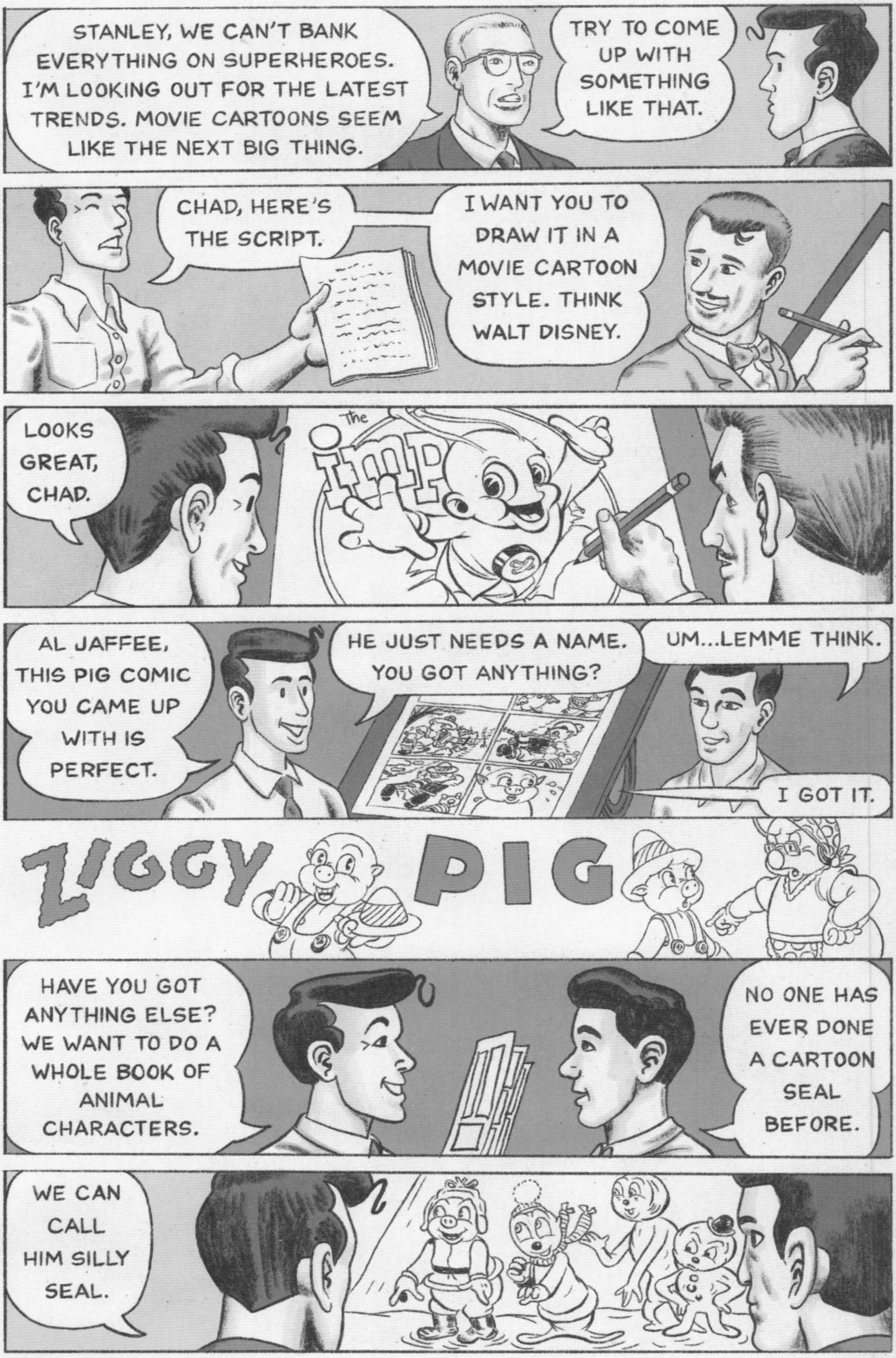
STANLEY, WE CAN'T BANK EVERYTHING ON SUPERHEROES. I'M LOOKING OUT FOR THE LATEST TRENDS. MOVIE CARTOONS SEEM LIKE THE NEXT BIG THING.
TRY TO COME UP WITH SOMETHING LIKE THAT.
CHAD, HERE'S THE SCRIPT.
I WANT YOU TO DRAW IT IN A MOVIE CARTOON STYLE. THINK WALT DISNEY.
LOOKS GREAT, CHAD.
The imp
AL JAFFEE, THIS PIG COMIC YOU CAME UP WITH IS PERFECT.
HE JUST NEEDS A NAME. YOU GOT ANYTHING?
UM...LEMME THINK.
I GOT IT.
ZIGGY PIG
HAVE YOU GOT ANYTHING ELSE? WE WANT TO DO A WHOLE BOOK OF ANIMAL CHARACTERS.
NO ONE HAS EVER DONE A CARTOON SEAL BEFORE.
WE CAN CALL HIM SILLY SEAL.

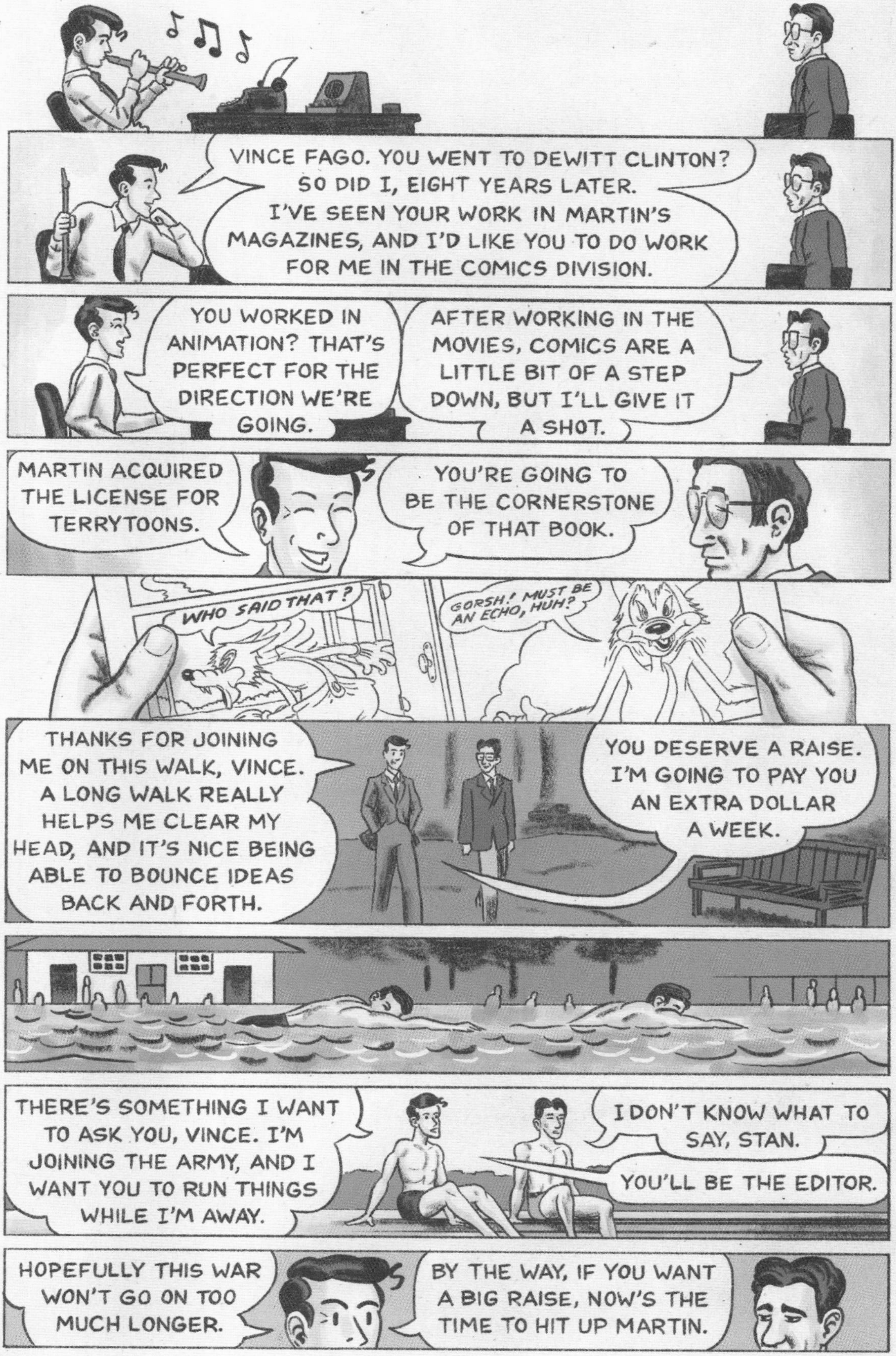
VINCE FAGO. YOU WENT TO DEWITT CLINTON? SO DID I, EIGHT YEARS LATER. I'VE SEEN YOUR WORK IN MARTIN'S MAGAZINES, AND I'D LIKE YOU TO DO WORK FOR ME IN THE COMICS DIVISION.
YOU WORKED IN ANIMATION? THAT'S PERFECT FOR THE DIRECTION WE'RE GOING.
AFTER WORKING IN THE MOVIES, COMICS ARE A LITTLE BIT OF A STEP DOWN, BUT I'LL GIVE IT A SHOT.
MARTIN ACQUIRED THE LICENSE FOR TERRYTOONS.
YOU'RE GOING TO BE THE CORNERSTONE OF THAT BOOK.
WHO SAID THAT?
GORSH! MUST BE AN ECHO, HUH?
THANKS FOR JOINING ME ON THIS WALK, VINCE. A LONG WALK REALLY HELPS ME CLEAR MY HEAD, AND IT'S NICE BEING ABLE TO BOUNCE IDEAS BACK AND FORTH.
YOU DESERVE A RAISE. I'M GOING TO PAY YOU AN EXTRA DOLLAR A WEEK.
THERE'S SOMETHING I WANT TO ASK YOU, VINCE. I'M JOINING THE ARMY, AND I WANT YOU TO RUN THINGS WHILE I'M AWAY.
I DON'T KNOW WHAT TO SAY, STAN.
YOU'LL BE THE EDITOR.
HOPEFULLY THIS WAR WON'T GO ON TOO MUCH LONGER.
BY THE WAY, IF YOU WANT A BIG RAISE, NOW'S THE TIME TO HIT UP MARTIN.

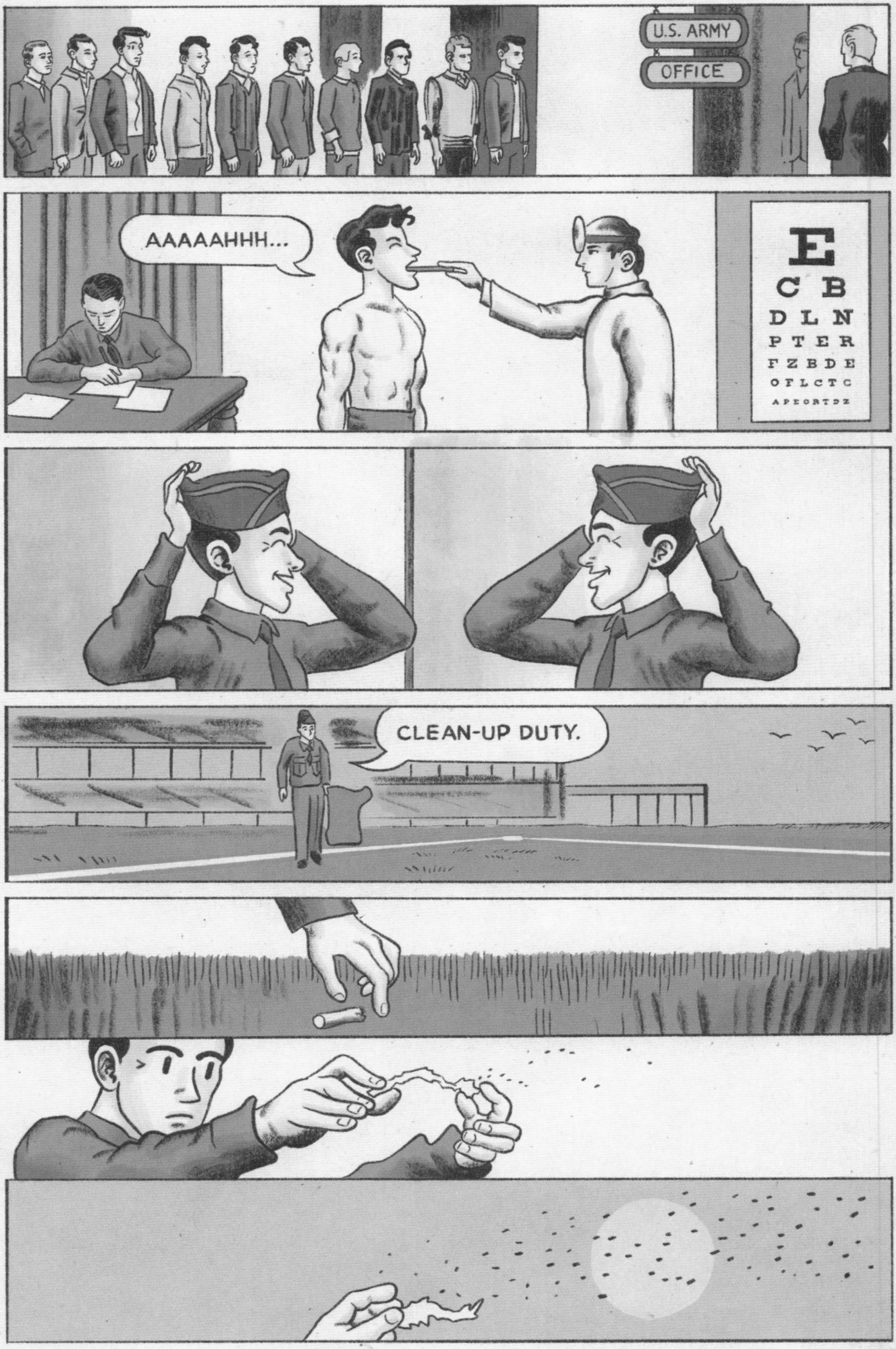
U.S. ARMY
OFFICE
AAAAAHHH...
E
C B
D L N
P T E R
F Z B D E
O F L C T C
CLEAN-UP DUTY.

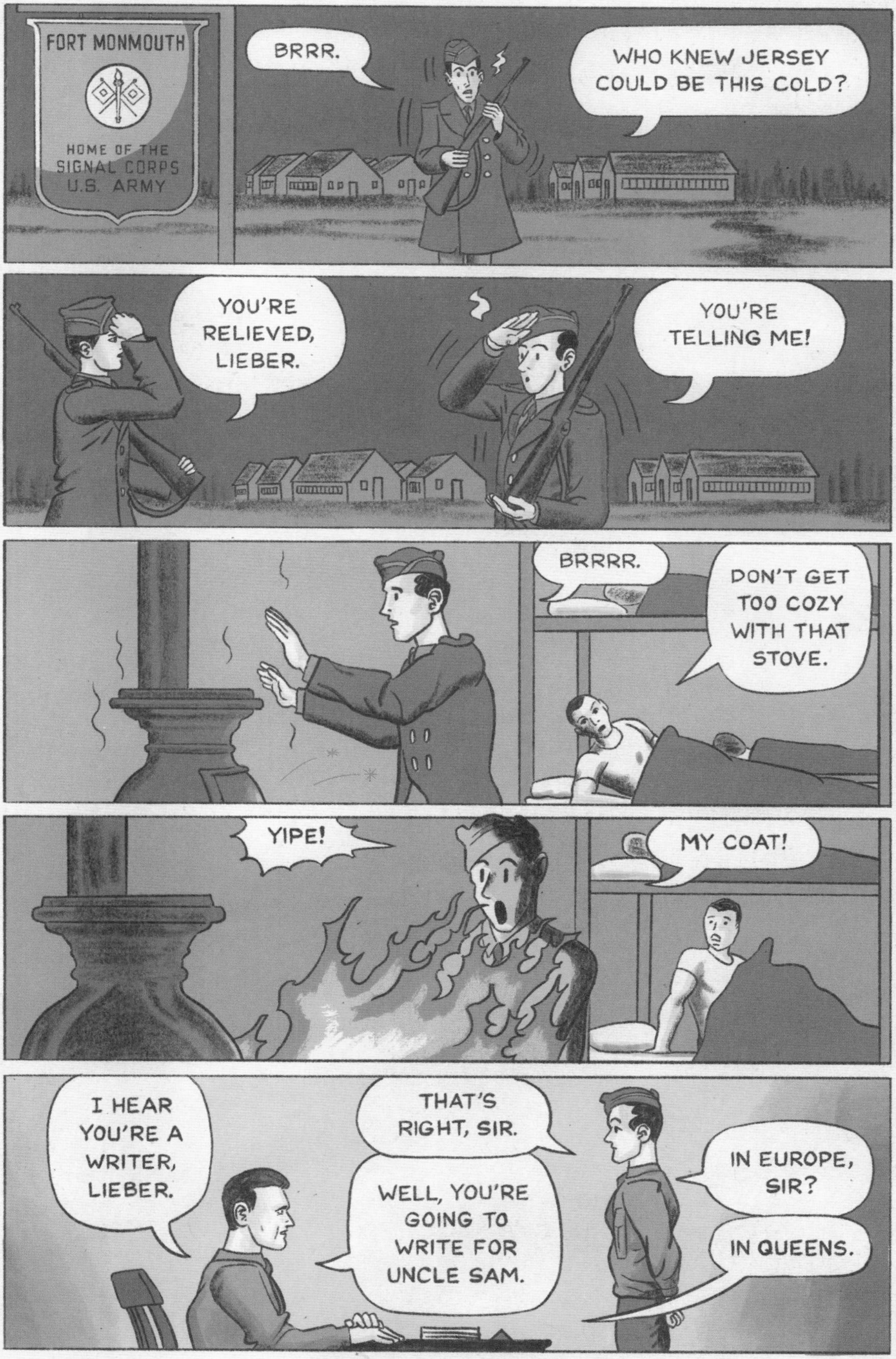
FORT MONMOUTH
HOME OF THE SIGNAL CORPS U.S. ARMY
BRRR.
WHO KNEW JERSEY COULD BE THIS COLD?
YOU'RE RELIEVED, LIEBER.
YOU'RE TELLING ME!
BRRRR.
DON'T GET TOO COZY WITH THAT STOVE.
YIPE!
MY COAT!
I HEAR YOU'RE A WRITER, LIEBER.
THAT'S RIGHT, SIR.
WELL, YOU'RE GOING TO WRITE FOR UNCLE SAM.
IN EUROPE, SIR?
IN QUEENS.

WELCOME TO THE ARMY PICTORIAL CENTER. WE PRODUCE TRAINING FILMS AND LITERATURE.
I GUESS I JOINED THE ARMY TO SEE QUEENS, NEW YORK.
THIS IS WHERE WE SHOOT THE INSTRUCTIONAL FILMS.
THIS IS LIKE A REAL HOLLYWOOD STUDIO.
THAT'S MORE OR LESS WHAT IT WAS BEFORE THE GOVERNMENT BOUGHT IT.
HERE'S THE TRAINING MANUAL. YOU NEED TO BREAK THIS INFORMATION DOWN INTO A SCRIPT.
STANLEY! WHAT ARE YOU DOING HERE?
I'M STATIONED IN QUEENS FOR NOW, SO I CAN COME VISIT.
YOU LOOK WONDERFUL.
SO DO YOU, MA.
STANLEY!
LOOKS LIKE YOU'RE HOLDING THINGS DOWN ON THE HOME FRONT, LARRY.
IT'S GOOD TO SEE YOU, STANLEY.
I'M PLANNING ON SWINGING BY THE NEW OFFICE LATER.
STAN! BACK ALREADY?
STANLEY, MY BOY!
TIMELY COMICS
VINCE! MARTIN! LOVE THE NEW DIGS. BUSINESS MUST BE BOOMING TO MOVE INTO THE EMPIRE STATE BUILDING.
HOW'S THE ARMY, STANLEY?
I'D SIGN UP, BUT THE ARMY DOESN'T WANT ME AND MY BAD EYE.
THE ARMY'S A LITTLE BORING. I HAVE A LOT OF TIME ON MY HANDS IF YOU WANT TO THROW SOME WORK MY WAY.
WE CAN GIVE YOU AS MUCH WORK AS YOU CAN HANDLE.

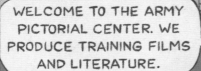

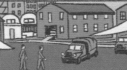

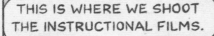

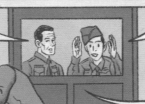

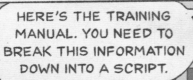

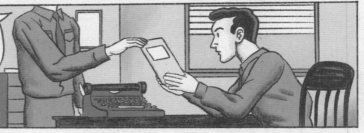

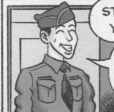

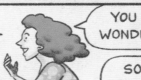

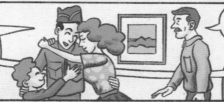

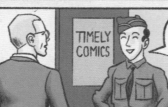

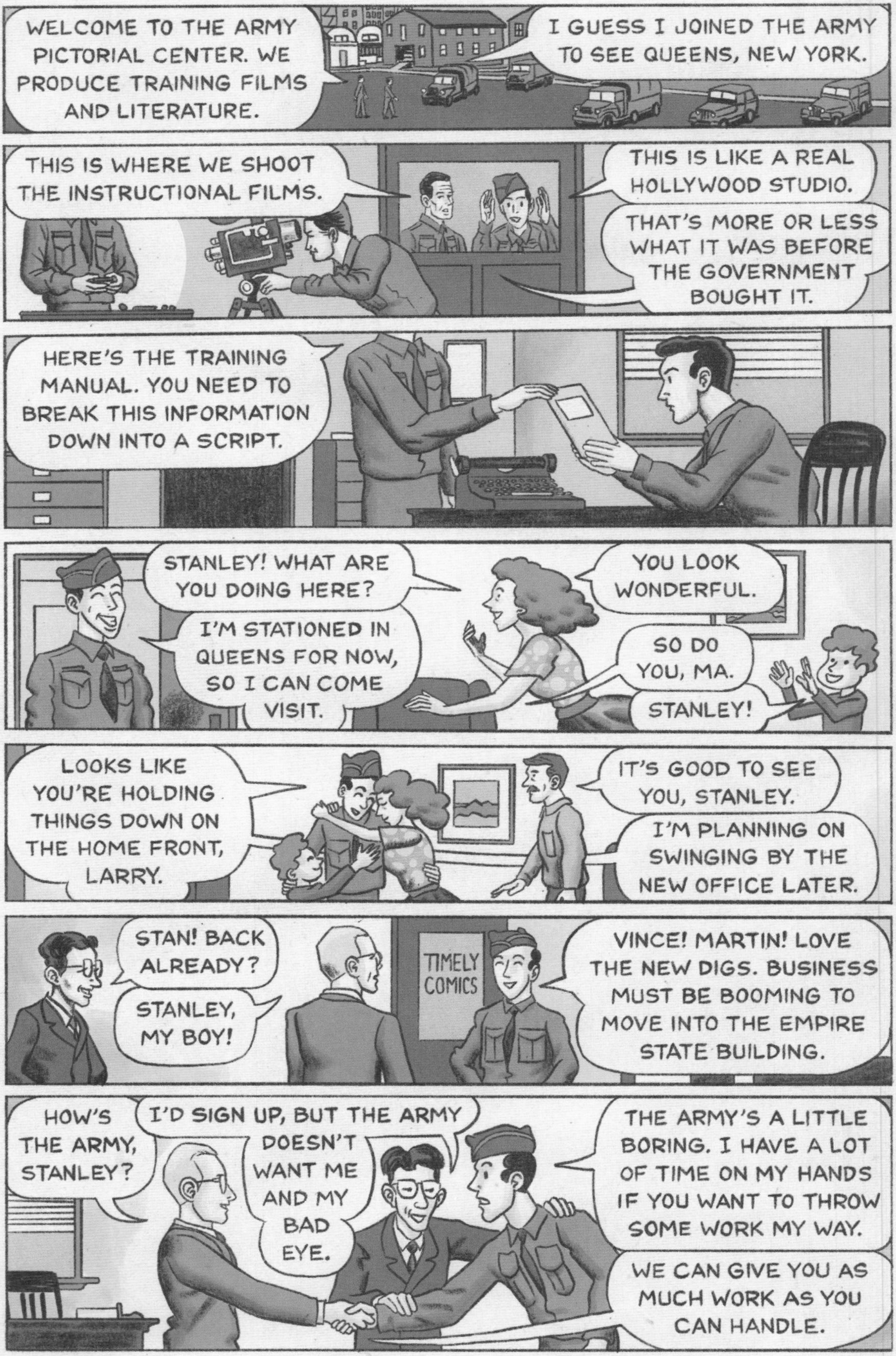

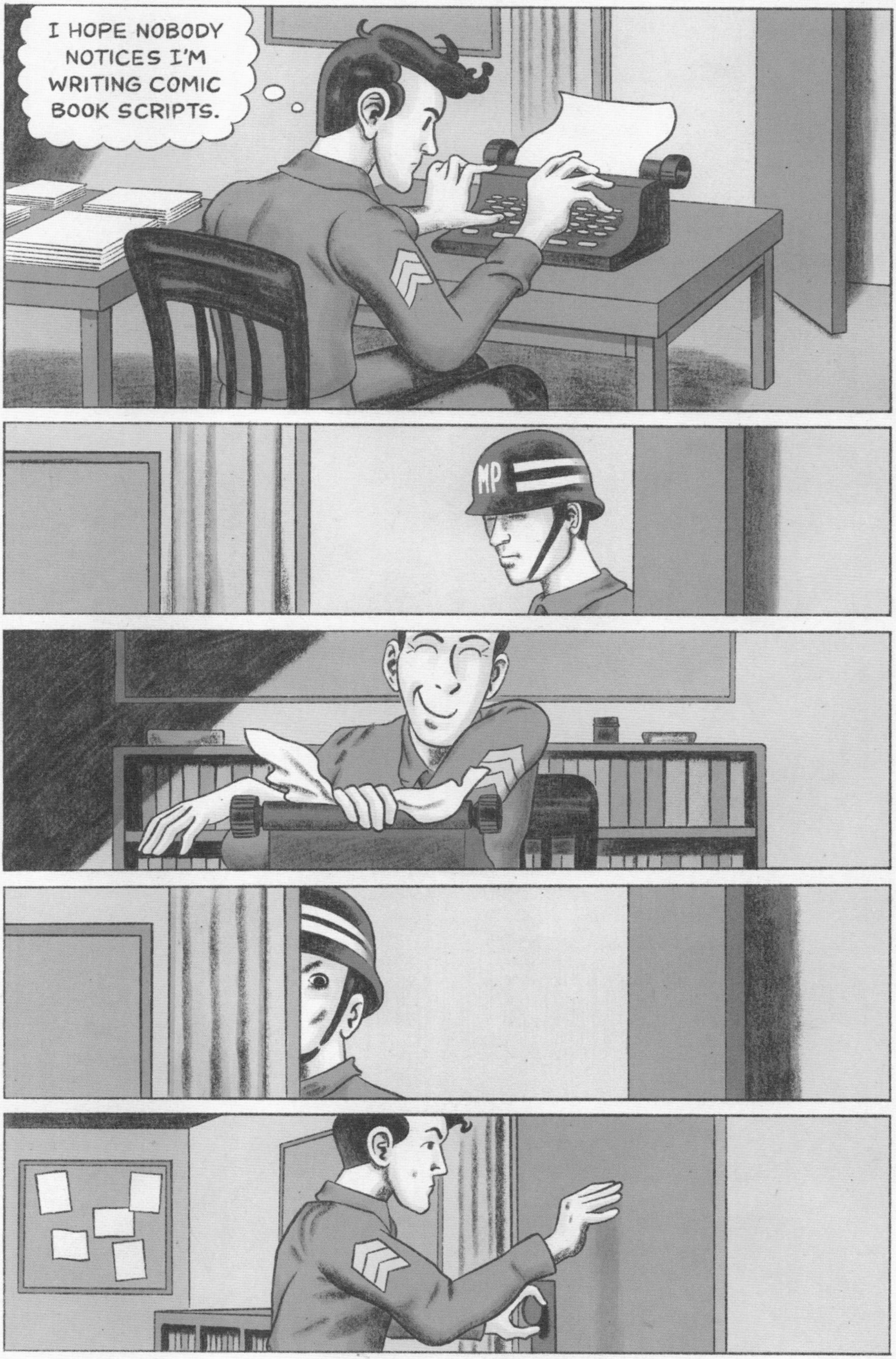
I HOPE NOBODY NOTICES I'M WRITING COMIC BOOK SCRIPTS.
MP

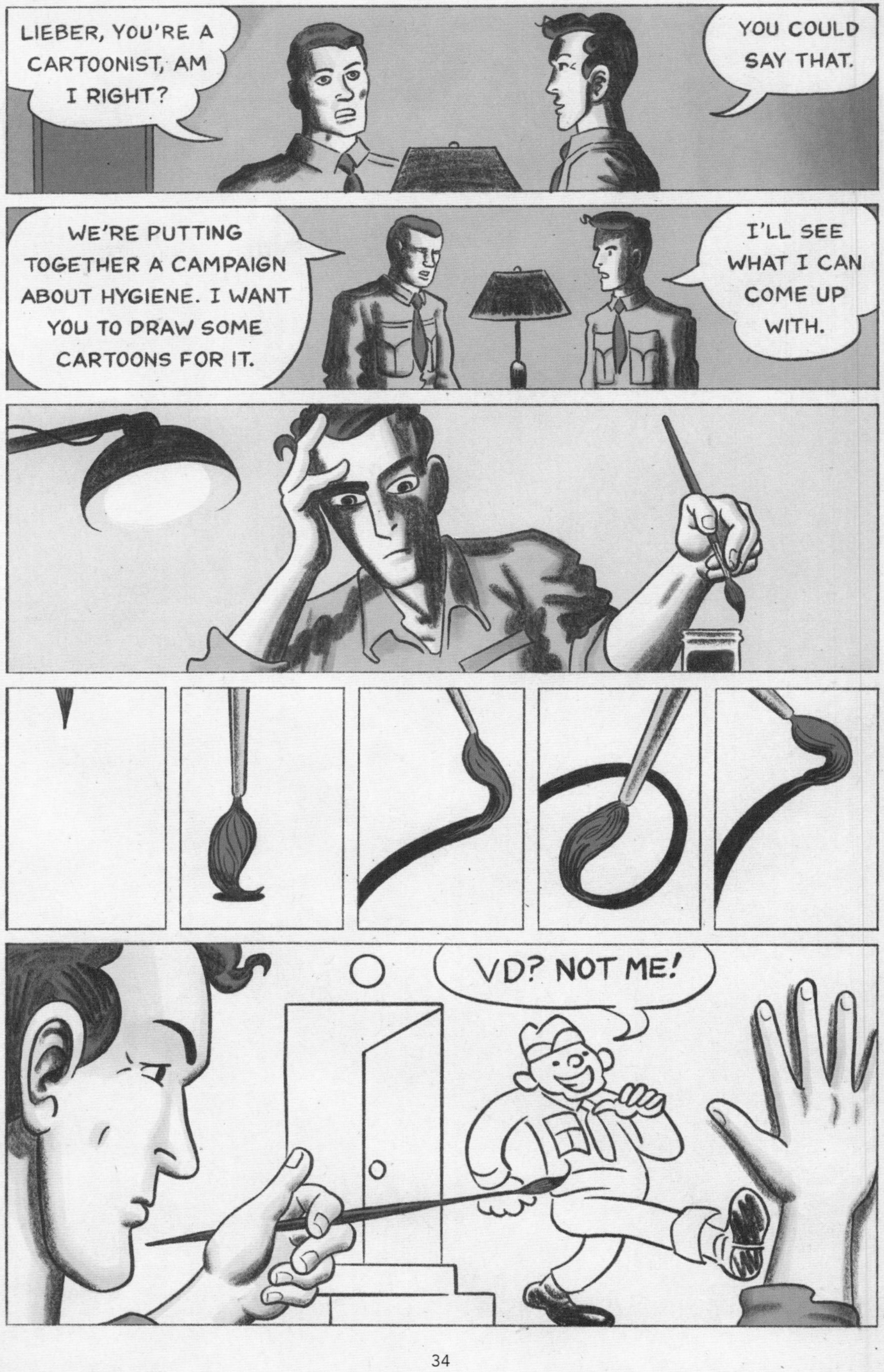
LIEBER, YOU'RE A CARTOONIST, AM I RIGHT?
YOU COULD SAY THAT.
WE'RE PUTTING TOGETHER A CAMPAIGN ABOUT HYGIENE. I WANT YOU TO DRAW SOME CARTOONS FOR IT.
I'LL SEE WHAT I CAN COME UP WITH.
VD? NOT ME!

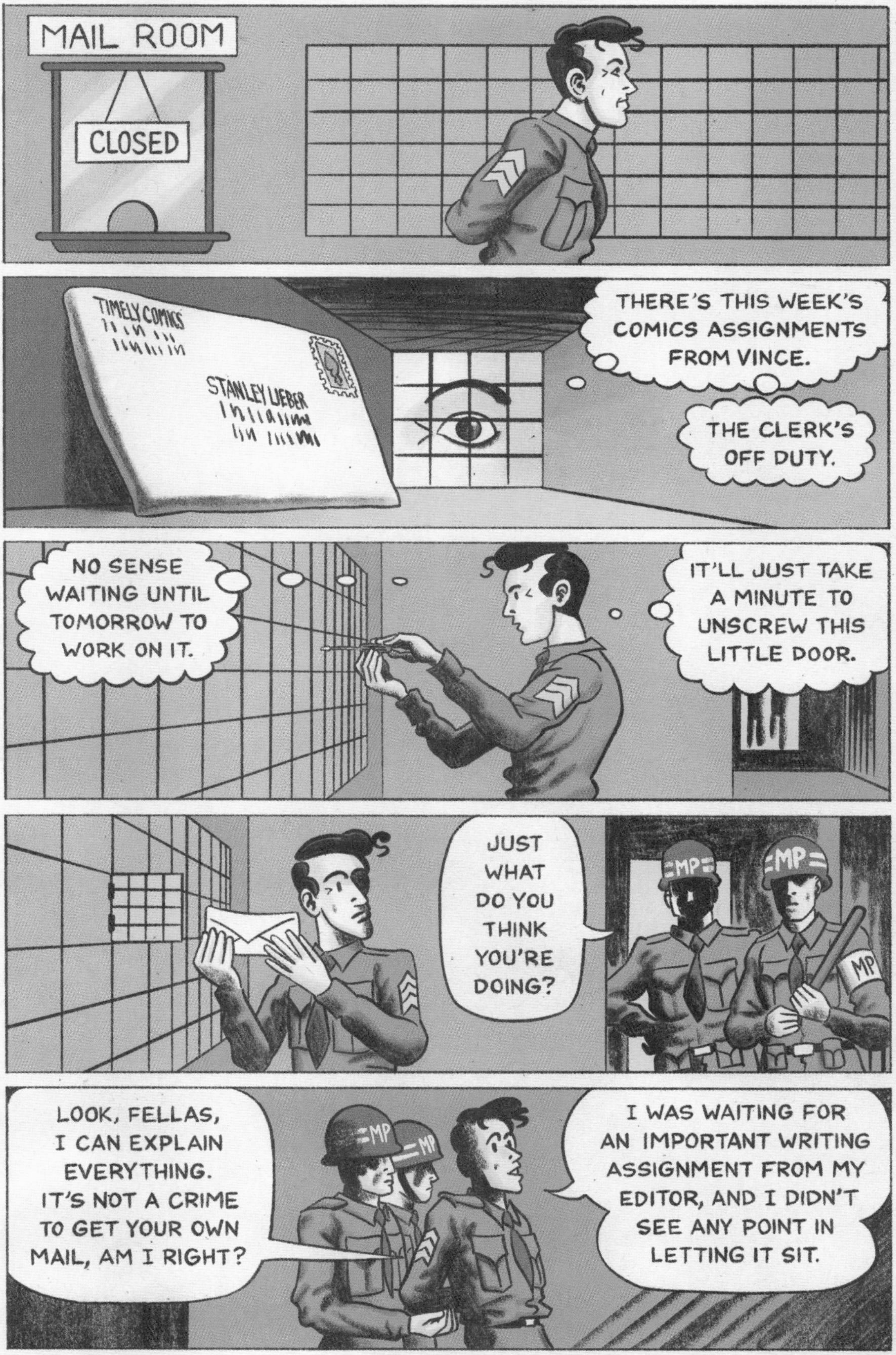
MAIL ROOM
CLOSED
TIMELY COMICS
STANLEY LIEBER
THERE'S THIS WEEK'S COMICS ASSIGNMENTS FROM VINCE.
THE CLERK'S OFF DUTY.
NO SENSE WAITING UNTIL TOMORROW TO WORK ON IT.
IT'LL JUST TAKE A MINUTE TO UNSCREW THIS LITTLE DOOR.
JUST WHAT DO YOU THINK YOU'RE DOING?
MP
MP
MP
LOOK, FELLAS, I CAN EXPLAIN EVERYTHING. IT'S NOT A CRIME TO GET YOUR OWN MAIL, AM I RIGHT?
I WAS WAITING FOR AN IMPORTANT WRITING ASSIGNMENT FROM MY EDITOR, AND I DIDN'T SEE ANY POINT IN LETTING IT SIT.
MP
MP

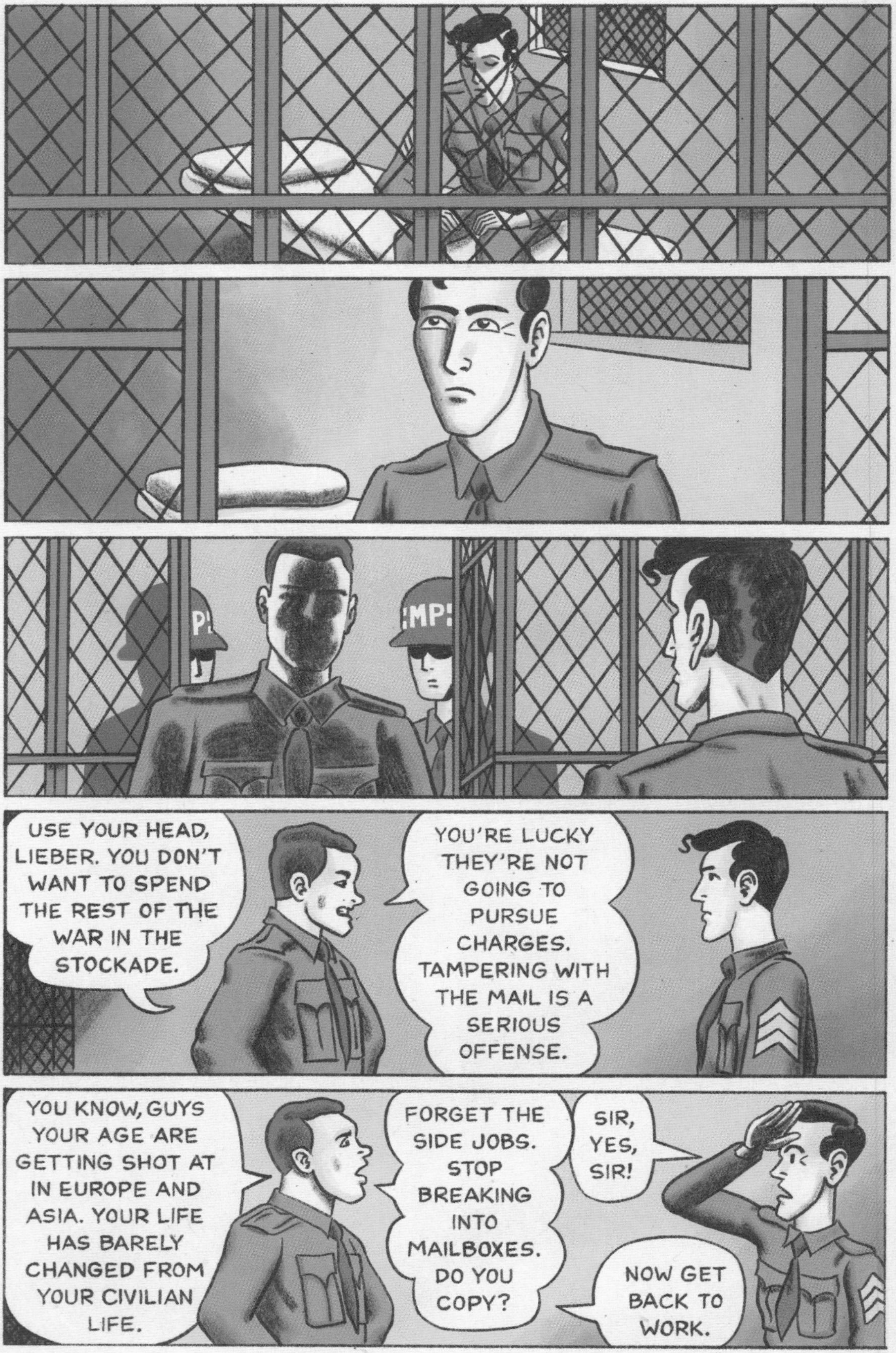

MP
MP
USE YOUR HEAD, LIEBER. YOU DON'T WANT TO SPEND THE REST OF THE WAR IN THE STOCKADE.
YOU'RE LUCKY THEY'RE NOT GOING TO PURSUE CHARGES. TAMPERING WITH THE MAIL IS A SERIOUS OFFENSE.
YOU KNOW, GUYS YOUR AGE ARE GETTING SHOT AT IN EUROPE AND ASIA. YOUR LIFE HAS BARELY CHANGED FROM YOUR CIVILIAN LIFE.
FORGET THE SIDE JOBS. STOP BREAKING INTO MAILBOXES. DO YOU COPY?
SIR, YES, SIR!
NOW GET BACK TO WORK.

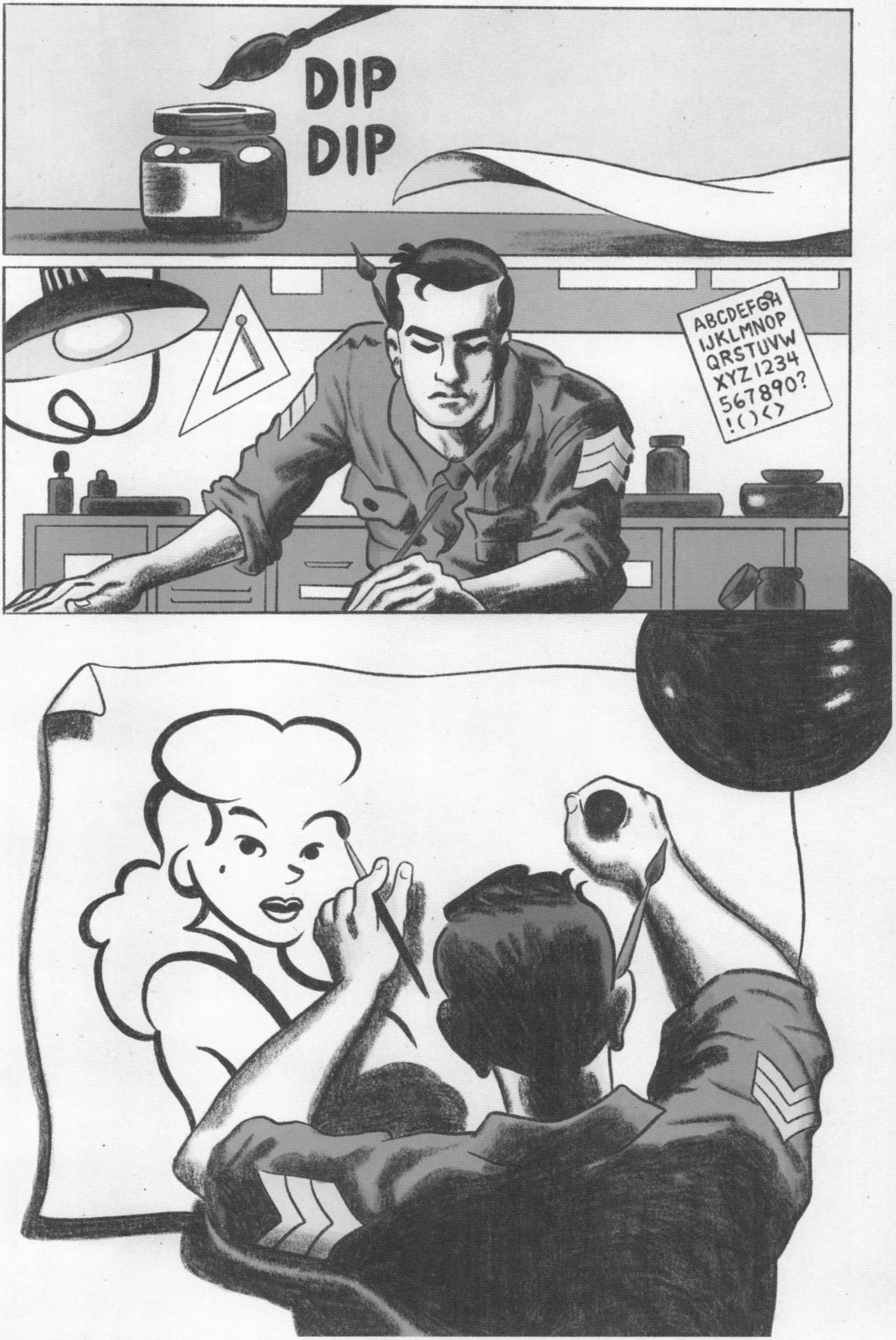
DIP
DIP
ABCDEFGH
IJKLMNOP
QRSTUVW
XYZ1234
567890?
!()<>

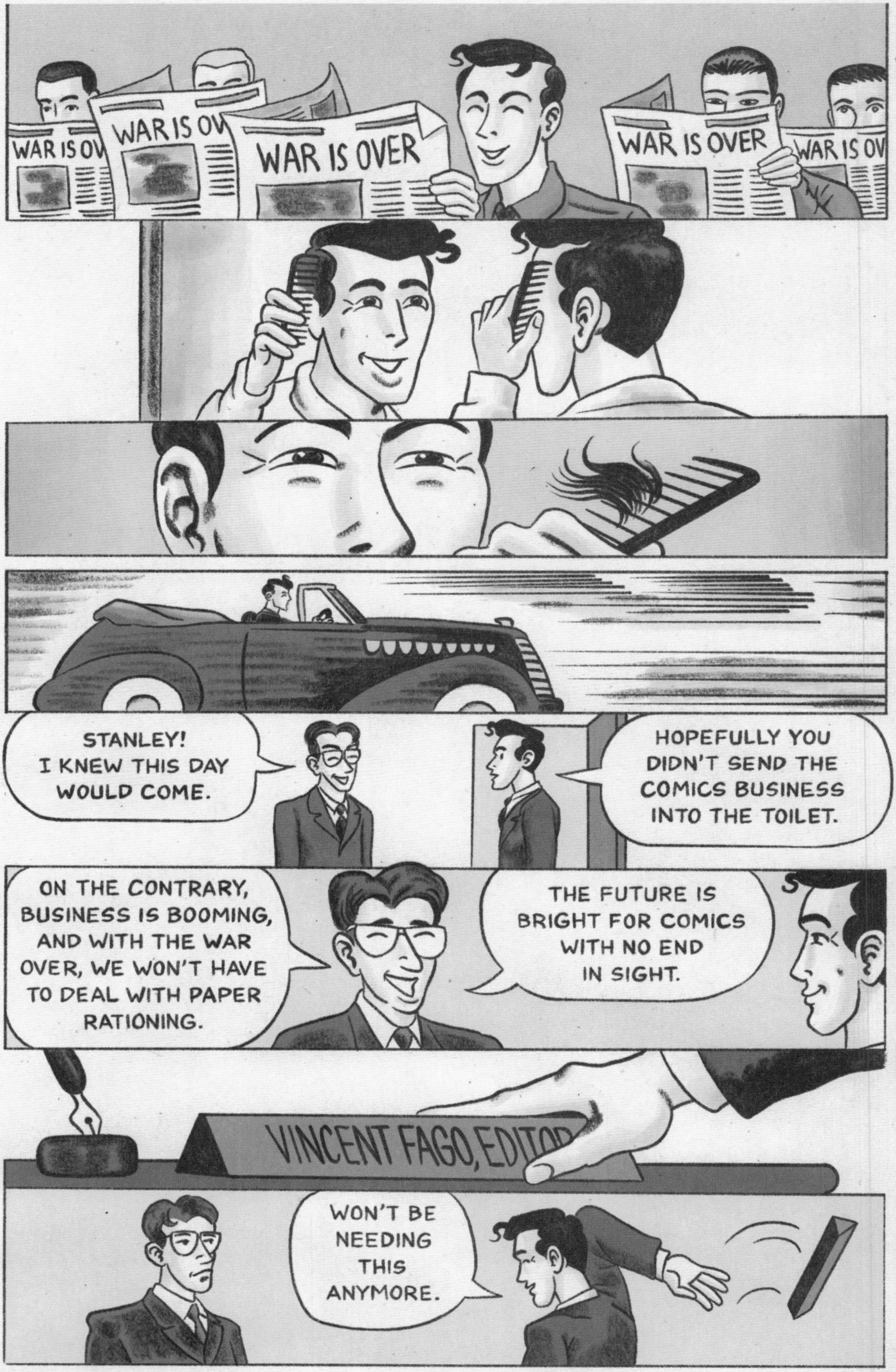
WAR IS OV
WAR IS OV
WAR IS OVER
WAR IS OVER
WAR IS OV
STANLEY! I KNEW THIS DAY WOULD COME.
HOPEFULLY YOU DIDN'T SEND THE COMICS BUSINESS INTO THE TOILET.
ON THE CONTRARY, BUSINESS IS BOOMING, AND WITH THE WAR OVER, WE WON'T HAVE TO DEAL WITH PAPER RATIONING.
THE FUTURE IS BRIGHT FOR COMICS WITH NO END IN SIGHT.
VINCENT FAGO, EDITO
WON'T BE NEEDING THIS ANYMORE.

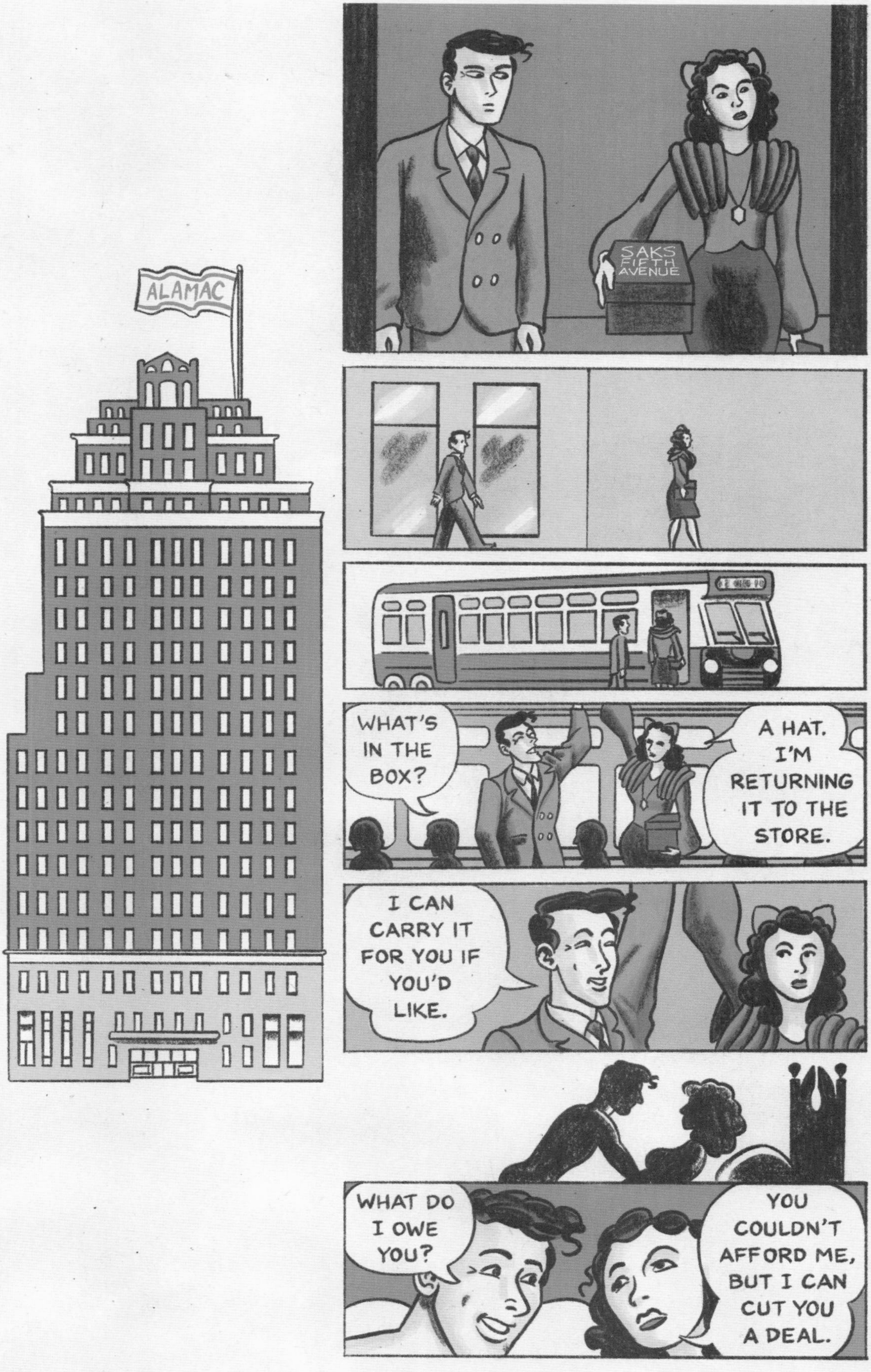
ALAMAC
SAKS FIFTH AVENUE
WHAT'S IN THE BOX?
A HAT. I'M RETURNING IT TO THE STORE.
I CAN CARRY IT FOR YOU IF YOU'D LIKE.
WHAT DO I OWE YOU?
YOU COULDN'T AFFORD ME, BUT I CAN CUT YOU A DEAL.

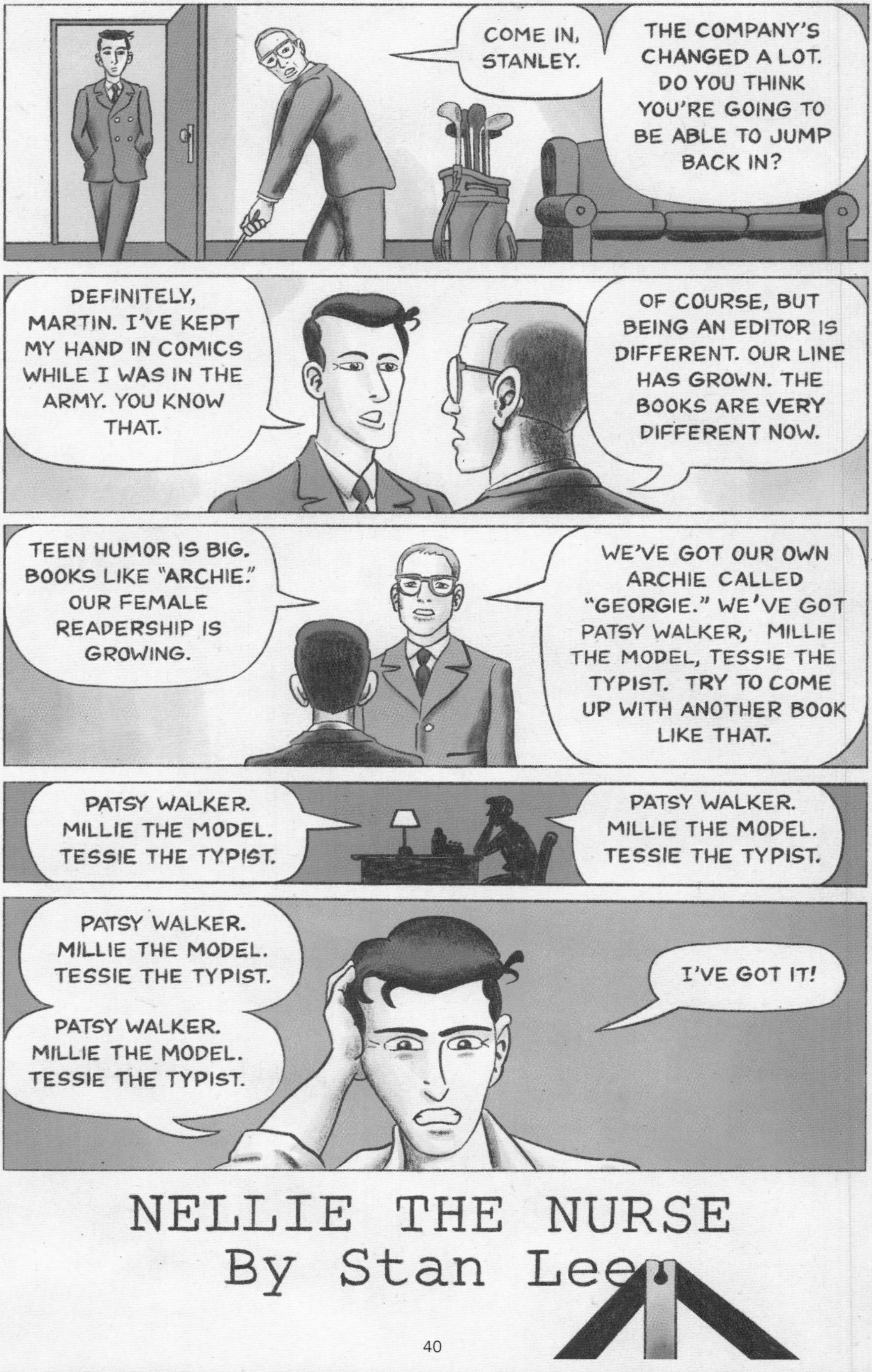
COME IN, STANLEY.
THE COMPANY'S CHANGED A LOT. DO YOU THINK YOU'RE GOING TO BE ABLE TO JUMP BACK IN?
DEFINITELY, MARTIN. I'VE KEPT MY HAND IN COMICS WHILE I WAS IN THE ARMY. YOU KNOW THAT.
OF COURSE, BUT BEING AN EDITOR IS DIFFERENT. OUR LINE HAS GROWN. THE BOOKS ARE VERY DIFFERENT NOW.
TEEN HUMOR IS BIG. BOOKS LIKE "ARCHIE." OUR FEMALE READERSHIP IS GROWING.
WE'VE GOT OUR OWN ARCHIE CALLED "GEORGIE." WE'VE GOT PATSY WALKER, MILLIE THE MODEL, TESSIE THE TYPIST. TRY TO COME UP WITH ANOTHER BOOK LIKE THAT.
PATSY WALKER. MILLIE THE MODEL. TESSIE THE TYPIST.
PATSY WALKER. MILLIE THE MODEL. TESSIE THE TYPIST.
PATSY WALKER. MILLIE THE MODEL. TESSIE THE TYPIST.
PATSY WALKER. MILLIE THE MODEL. TESSIE THE TYPIST.
I'VE GOT IT!
NELLIE THE NURSE
By Stan Lee

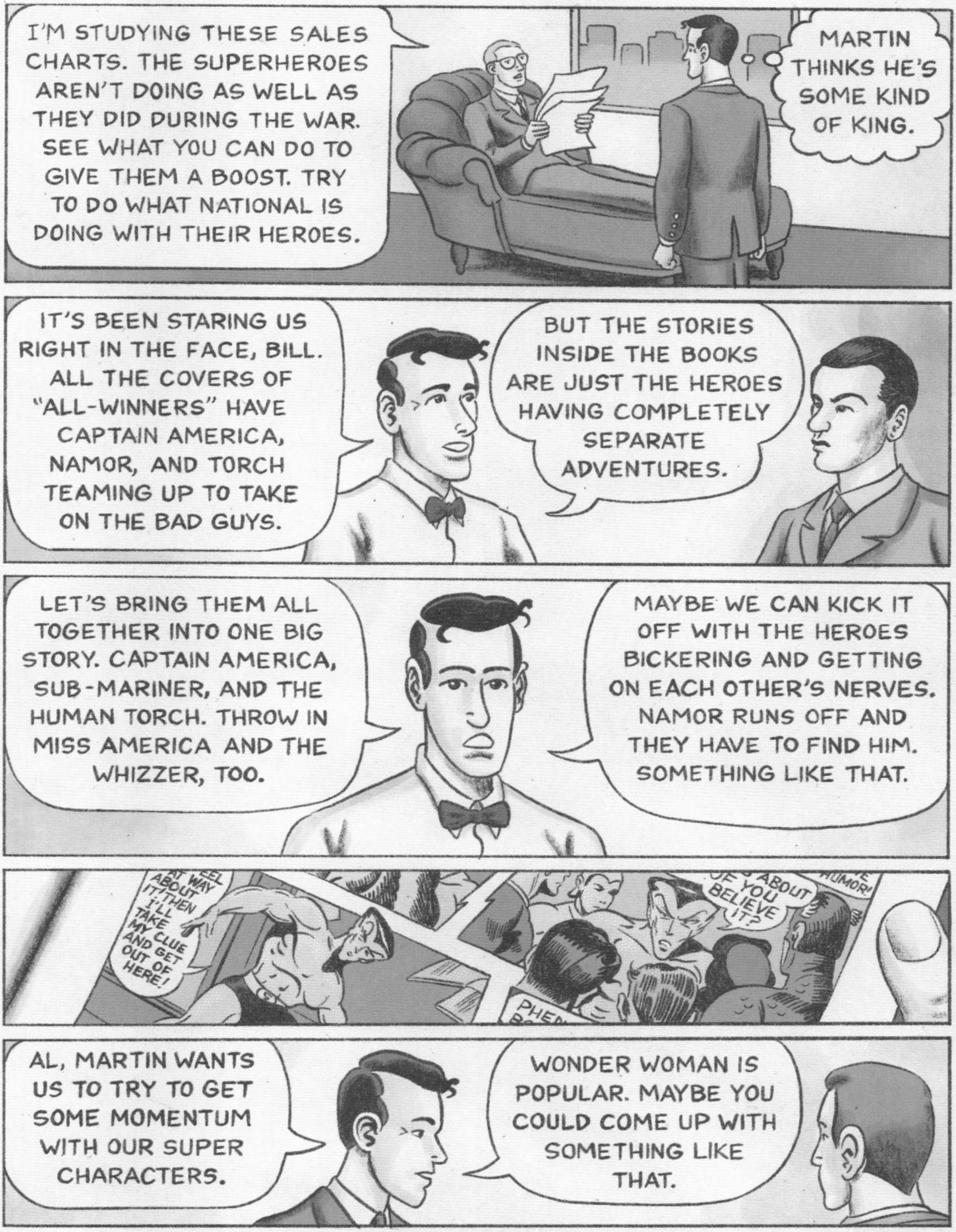
I'M STUDYING THESE SALES CHARTS. THE SUPERHEROES AREN'T DOING AS WELL AS THEY DID DURING THE WAR. SEE WHAT YOU CAN DO TO GIVE THEM A BOOST. TRY TO DO WHAT NATIONAL IS DOING WITH THEIR HEROES.
MARTIN THINKS HE'S SOME KIND OF KING.
IT'S BEEN STARING US RIGHT IN THE FACE, BILL. ALL THE COVERS OF "ALL-WINNERS" HAVE CAPTAIN AMERICA, NAMOR, AND TORCH TEAMING UP TO TAKE ON THE BAD GUYS.
BUT THE STORIES INSIDE THE BOOKS ARE JUST THE HEROES HAVING COMPLETELY SEPARATE ADVENTURES.
LET'S BRING THEM ALL TOGETHER INTO ONE BIG STORY. CAPTAIN AMERICA, SUB-MARINER, AND THE HUMAN TORCH. THROW IN MISS AMERICA AND THE WHIZZER, TOO.
MAYBE WE CAN KICK IT OFF WITH THE HEROES BICKERING AND GETTING ON EACH OTHER'S NERVES. NAMOR RUNS OFF AND THEY HAVE TO FIND HIM. SOMETHING LIKE THAT.
I'LL TAKE MY CLUE AND GET OUT OF HERE!
IF YOU BELIEVE IT?
AL, MARTIN WANTS US TO TRY TO GET SOME MOMENTUM WITH OUR SUPER CHARACTERS.
WONDER WOMAN IS POPULAR. MAYBE YOU COULD COME UP WITH SOMETHING LIKE THAT.
LOOKING FOR ME?
OOPS!

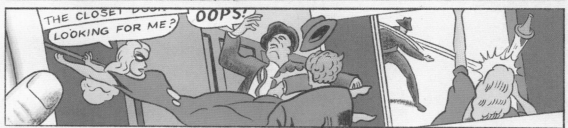

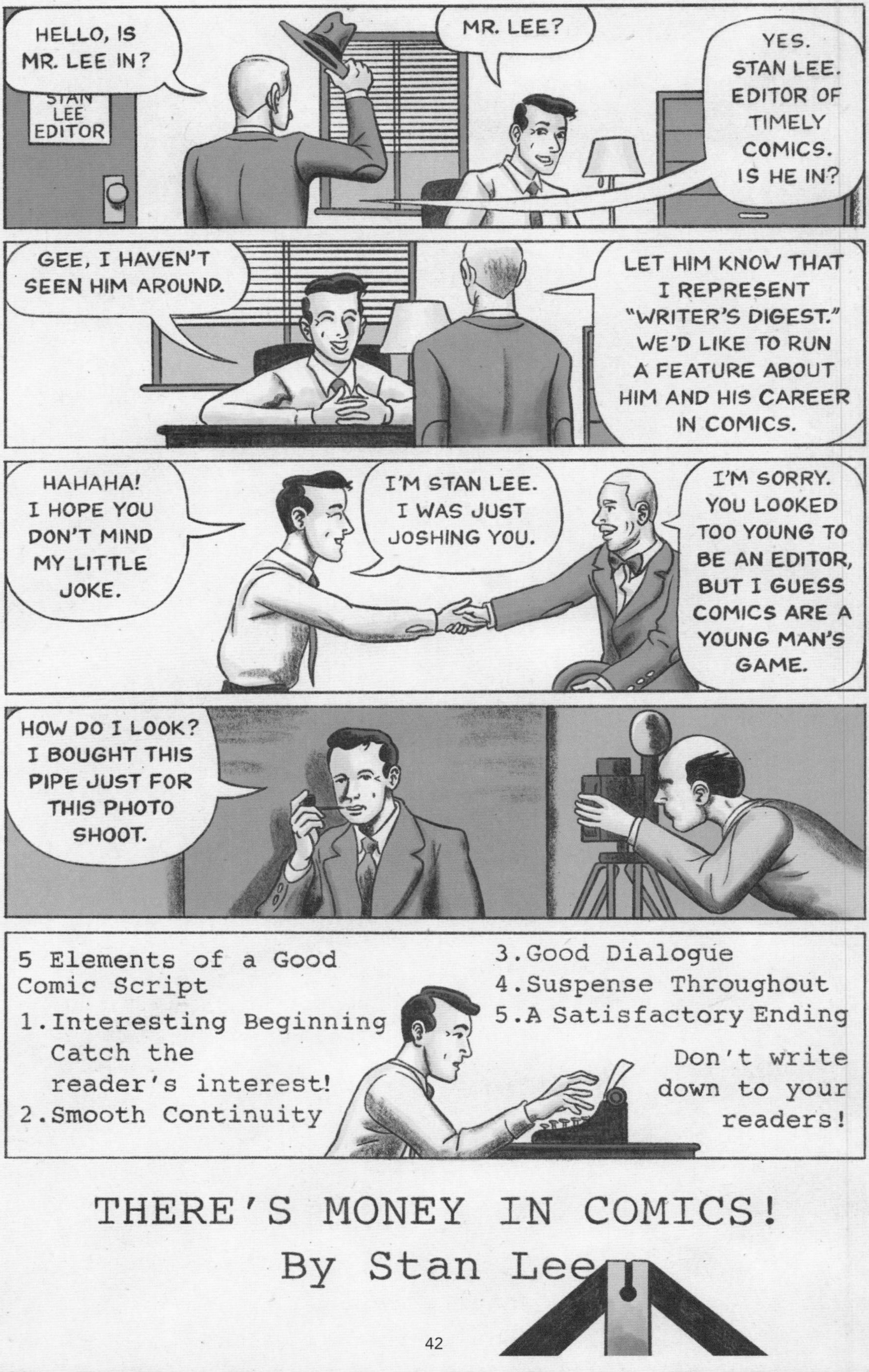
HELLO, IS MR. LEE IN?
STAN LEE EDITOR
MR. LEE?
YES. STAN LEE. EDITOR OF TIMELY COMICS. IS HE IN?
GEE, I HAVEN'T SEEN HIM AROUND.
LET HIM KNOW THAT I REPRESENT "WRITER'S DIGEST." WE'D LIKE TO RUN A FEATURE ABOUT HIM AND HIS CAREER IN COMICS.
HAHAHA! I HOPE YOU DON'T MIND MY LITTLE JOKE.
I'M STAN LEE. I WAS JUST JOSHING YOU.
I'M SORRY. YOU LOOKED TOO YOUNG TO BE AN EDITOR, BUT I GUESS COMICS ARE A YOUNG MAN'S GAME.
HOW DO I LOOK? I BOUGHT THIS PIPE JUST FOR THIS PHOTO SHOOT.
5 Elements of a Good Comic Script
1.Interesting Beginning Catch the reader's interest!
2.Smooth Continuity
3.Good Dialogue
4.Suspense Throughout
5.A Satisfactory Ending
Don't write down to your readers!
THERE'S MONEY IN COMICS!
By Stan Lee

HEY, STANLEY! I SAW YOUR ARTICLE IN "WRITER'S DIGEST," MR. BIG SHOT.

YOU'RE COMING UP IN THE WORLD.

THIS TURNED OUT GREAT. I NEED TO FOLLOW THIS UP WITH SOMETHING. STRIKE WHILE THE IRON IS HOT.

"SECRETS BEHIND THE COMICS!" By Stan Lee
Never before have you read a book like this! It will amuse you and astound you! Take good care of this book, for you will want to read it and re-read it and show it to your friends.

WHO WRITES AND DRAWS THE COMICS?
The answer to this question will surprise you! The answer is: the man whose name is signed to a comic is not always the man who really writes and draws the strip!

HI, MARTIN, HERE'S THAT BOOK I TOLD YOU ABOUT.

FAMOUS ENTERPRISES, INCORPORATED? WHO'S THAT?

IT'S MY OWN LITTLE IMPRINT. I SELF-PUBLISHED THE BOOK.

GOOD LUCK WITH YOUR ENDEAVOR.

THIS PUBLISHER WAS MARTIN GOODMAN, THE YOUNG BRILLIANT MAGAZINE KING WHO IS TODAY ONE OF THE GREATEST NAMES IN COMIC

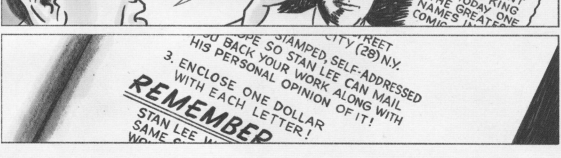

...TREET
...CITY (28) N.Y.
...OPE SO STAN LEE CAN MAIL
...BACK YOUR WORK ALONG WITH
...U HIS PERSONAL OPINION OF IT!
STAMPED, SELF-ADDRESSED
3. ENCLOSE ONE DOLLAR WITH EACH LETTER!

REMEMBER
STAN LEE W...
SAME S...
WO...

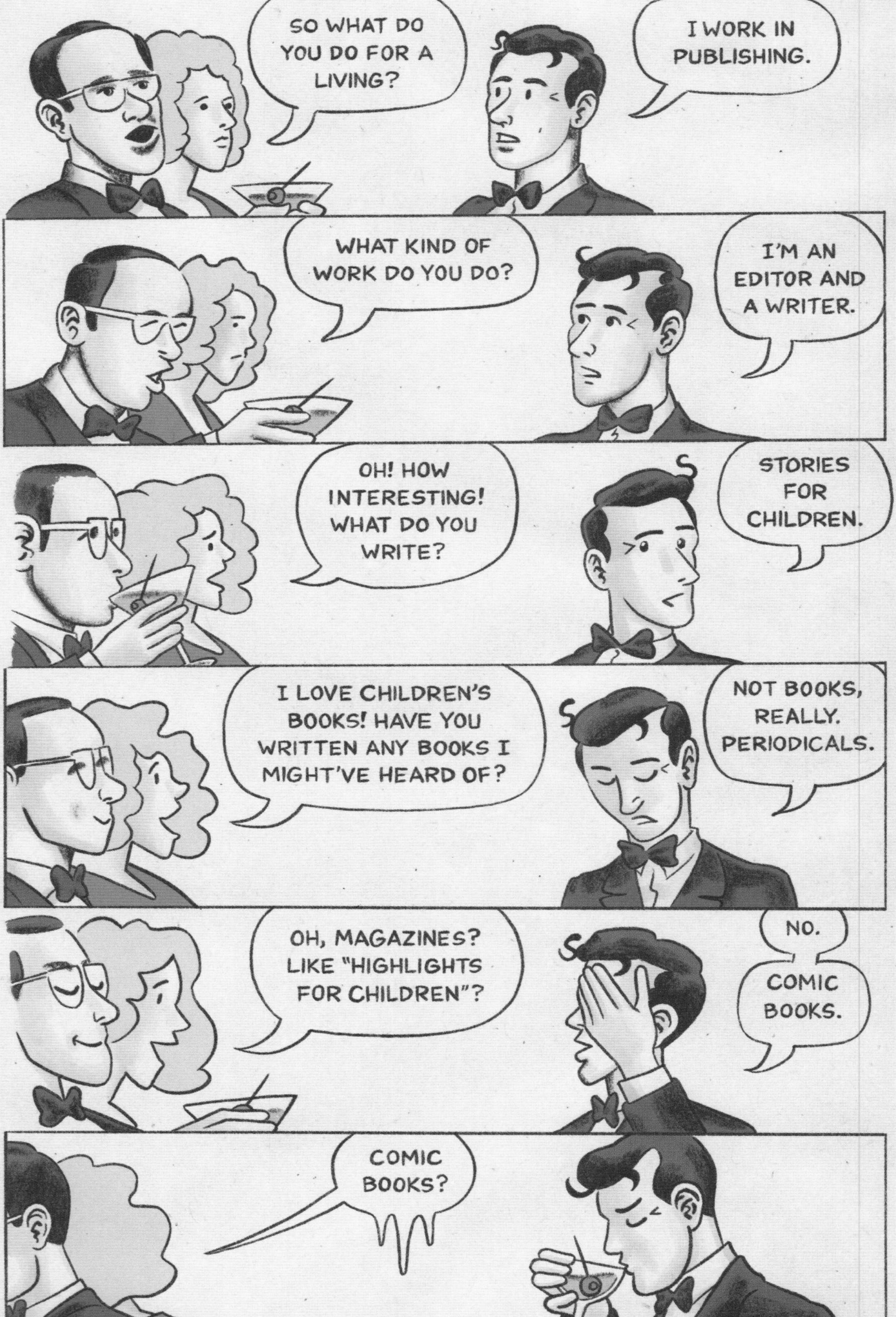
SO WHAT DO YOU DO FOR A LIVING?
I WORK IN PUBLISHING.
WHAT KIND OF WORK DO YOU DO?
I'M AN EDITOR AND A WRITER.
OH! HOW INTERESTING! WHAT DO YOU WRITE?
STORIES FOR CHILDREN.
I LOVE CHILDREN'S BOOKS! HAVE YOU WRITTEN ANY BOOKS I MIGHT'VE HEARD OF?
NOT BOOKS, REALLY. PERIODICALS.
OH, MAGAZINES? LIKE "HIGHLIGHTS FOR CHILDREN"?
NO.
COMIC BOOKS.
COMIC BOOKS?

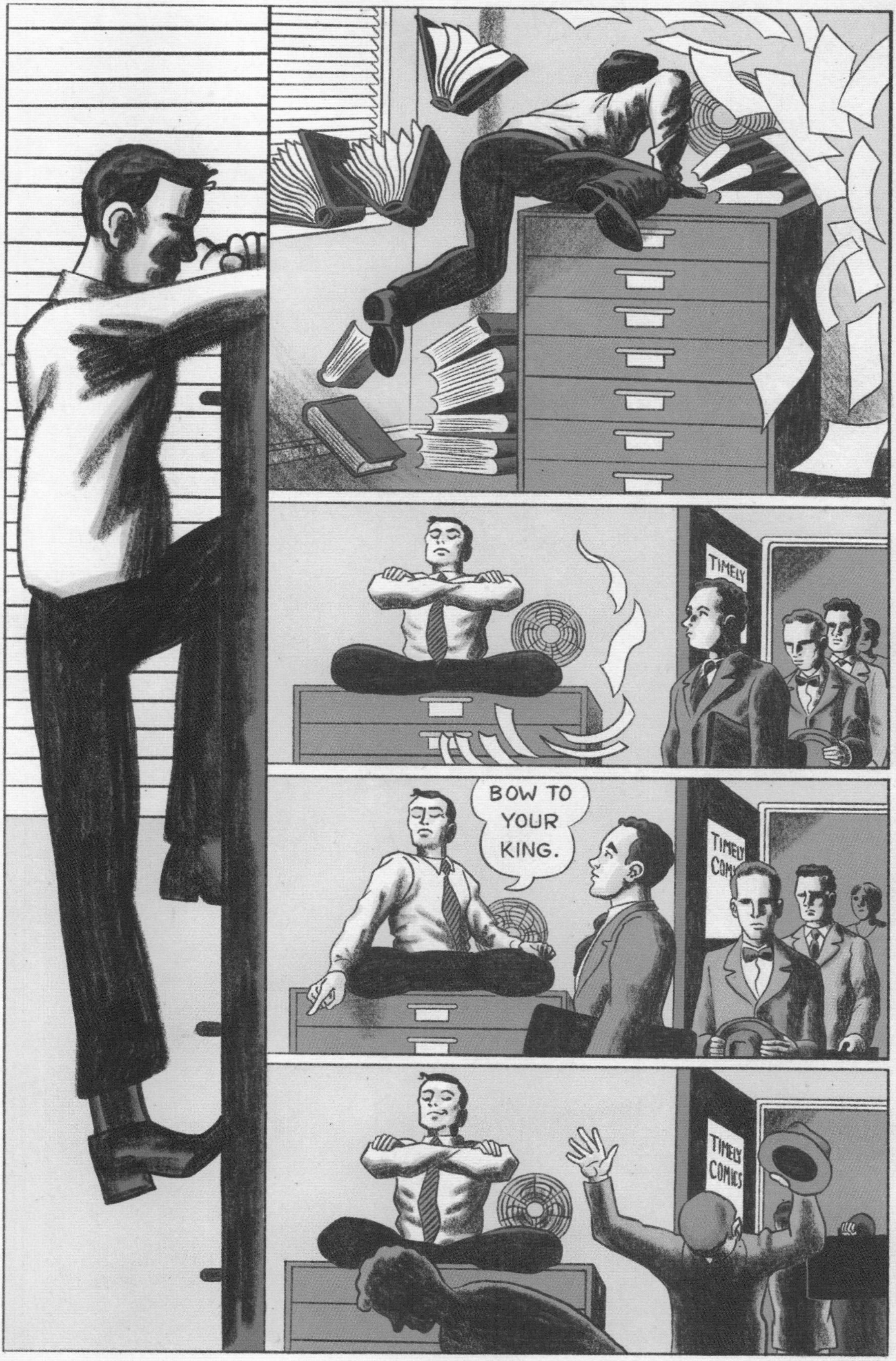
TIMELY
BOW TO YOUR KING.
TIMELY COMI
TIMELY COMICS

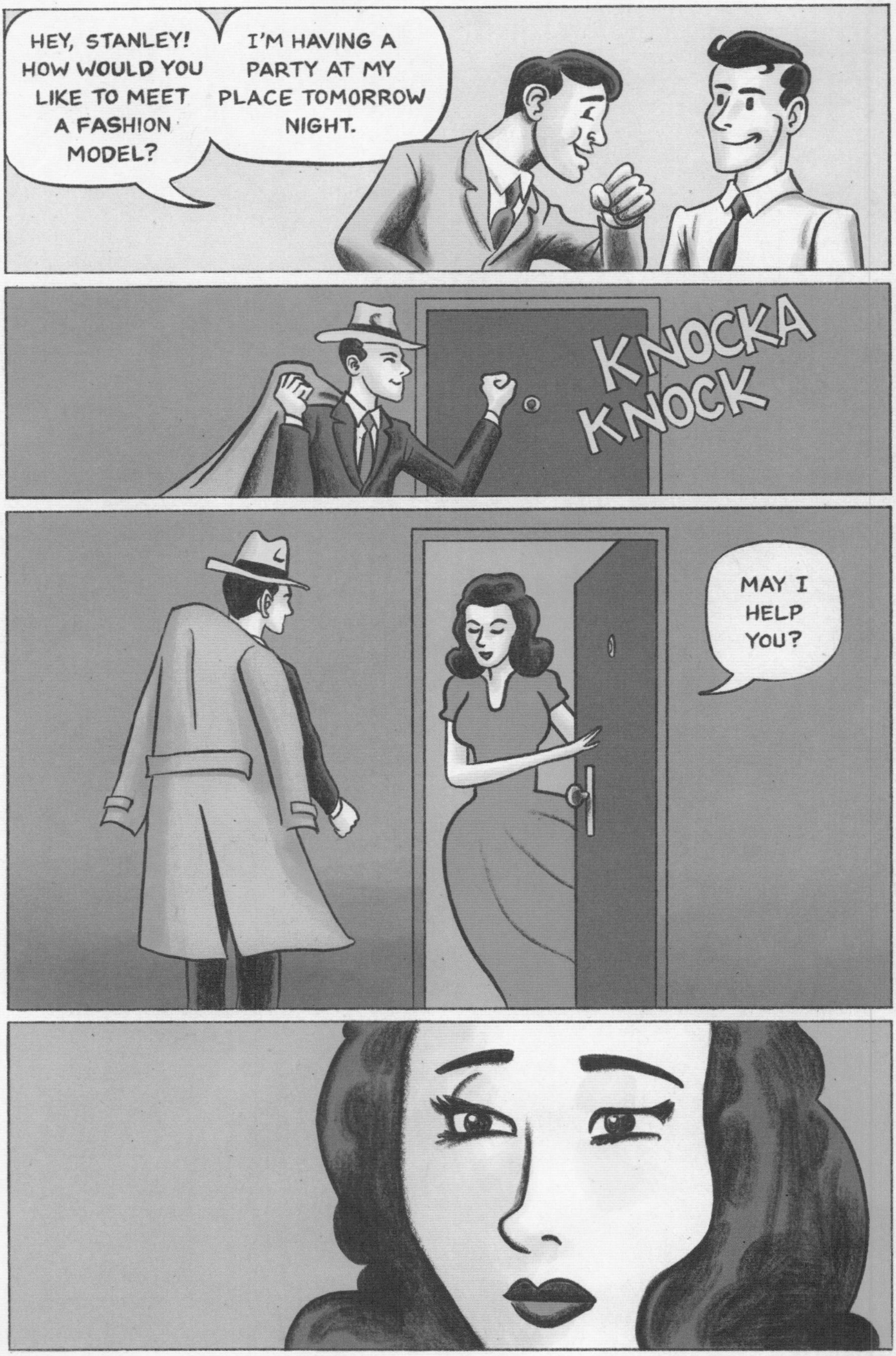
HEY, STANLEY! HOW WOULD YOU LIKE TO MEET A FASHION MODEL?
I'M HAVING A PARTY AT MY PLACE TOMORROW NIGHT.
KNOCKA KNOCK
MAY I HELP YOU?

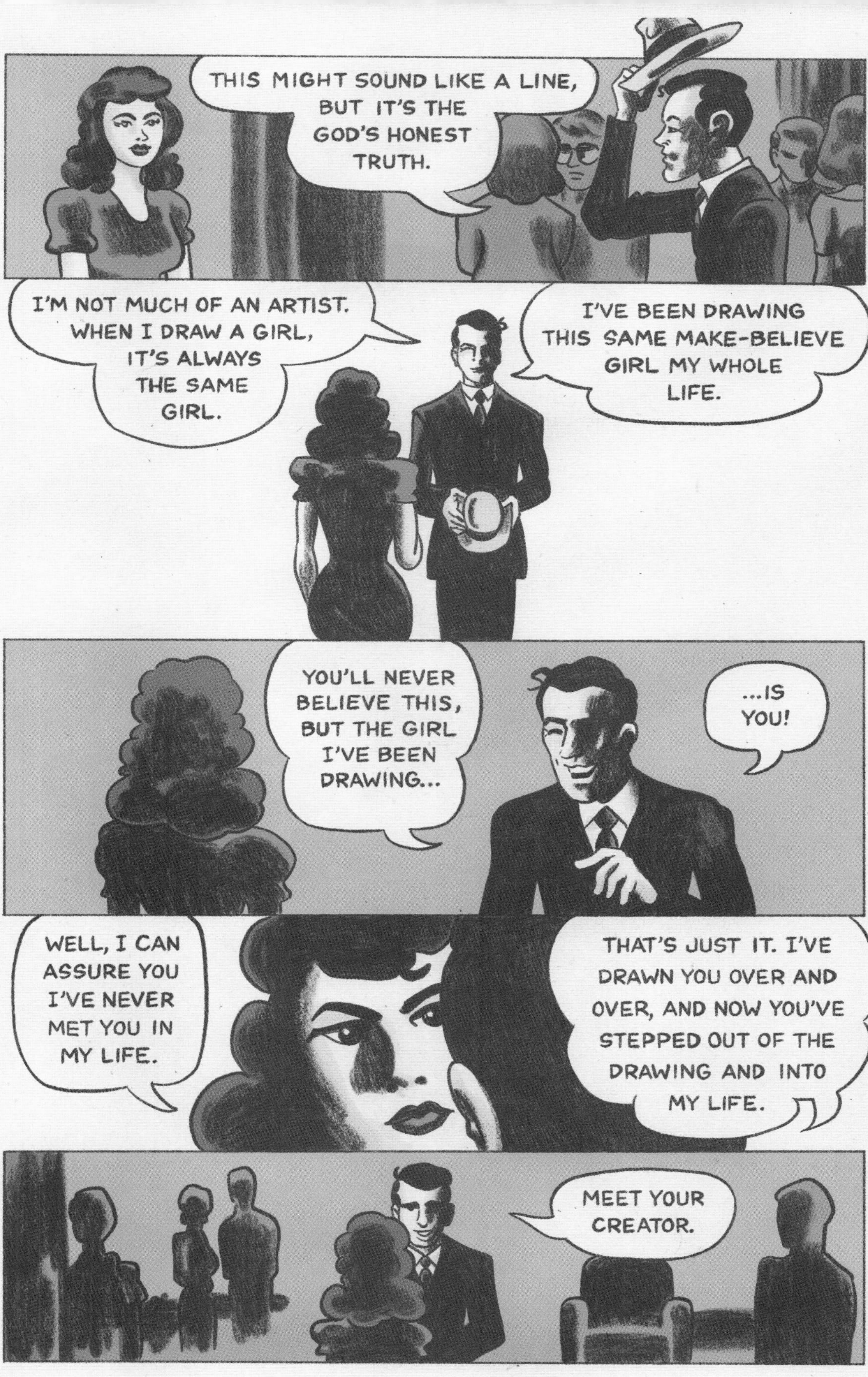

THIS MIGHT SOUND LIKE A LINE, BUT IT'S THE GOD'S HONEST TRUTH.
I'M NOT MUCH OF AN ARTIST. WHEN I DRAW A GIRL, IT'S ALWAYS THE SAME GIRL.
I'VE BEEN DRAWING THIS SAME MAKE-BELIEVE GIRL MY WHOLE LIFE.
YOU'LL NEVER BELIEVE THIS, BUT THE GIRL I'VE BEEN DRAWING...
...IS YOU!
WELL, I CAN ASSURE YOU I'VE NEVER MET YOU IN MY LIFE.
THAT'S JUST IT. I'VE DRAWN YOU OVER AND OVER, AND NOW YOU'VE STEPPED OUT OF THE DRAWING AND INTO MY LIFE.
MEET YOUR CREATOR.

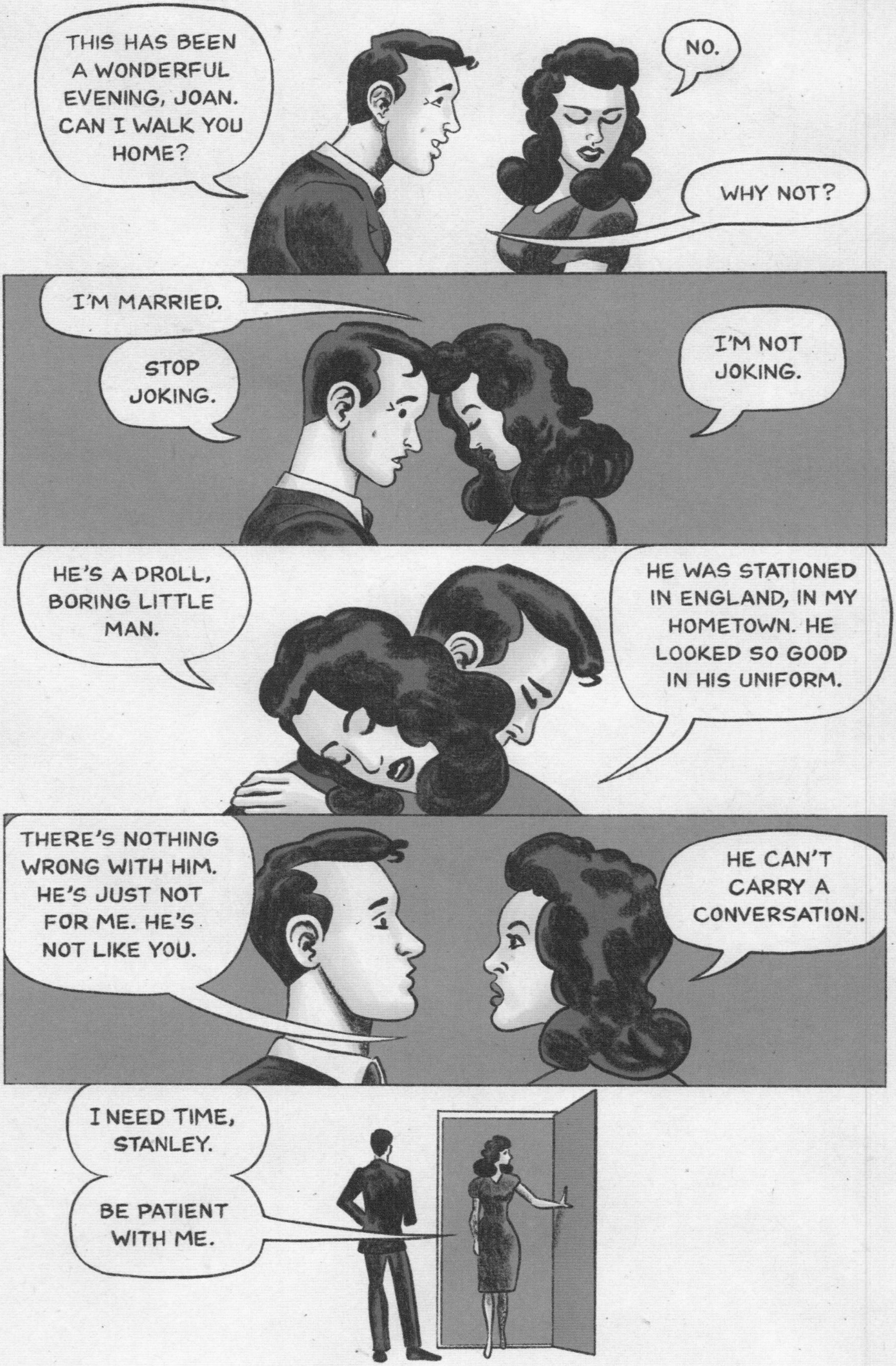
THIS HAS BEEN A WONDERFUL EVENING, JOAN. CAN I WALK YOU HOME?
NO.
WHY NOT?
I'M MARRIED.
STOP JOKING.
I'M NOT JOKING.
HE'S A DROLL, BORING LITTLE MAN.
HE WAS STATIONED IN ENGLAND, IN MY HOMETOWN. HE LOOKED SO GOOD IN HIS UNIFORM.
THERE'S NOTHING WRONG WITH HIM. HE'S JUST NOT FOR ME. HE'S NOT LIKE YOU.
HE CAN'T CARRY A CONVERSATION.
I NEED TIME, STANLEY.
BE PATIENT WITH ME.

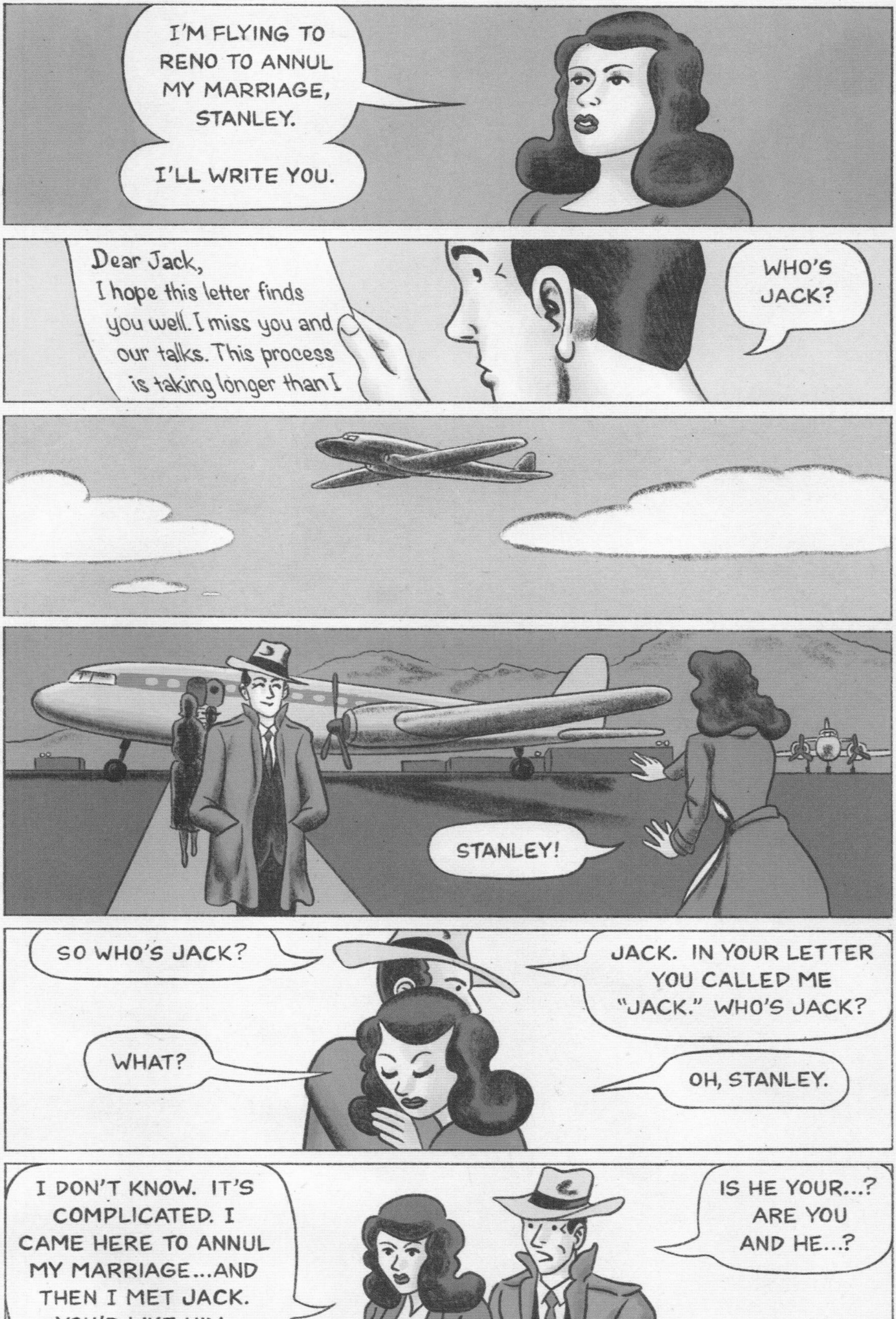
I'M FLYING TO RENO TO ANNUL MY MARRIAGE, STANLEY.
I'LL WRITE YOU.
Dear Jack,
I hope this letter finds you well. I miss you and our talks. This process is taking longer than I
WHO'S JACK?
STANLEY!
SO WHO'S JACK?
WHAT?
JACK. IN YOUR LETTER YOU CALLED ME "JACK." WHO'S JACK?
OH, STANLEY.
I DON'T KNOW. IT'S COMPLICATED. I CAME HERE TO ANNUL MY MARRIAGE...AND THEN I MET JACK. YOU'D LIKE HIM.
IS HE YOUR...? ARE YOU AND HE...?

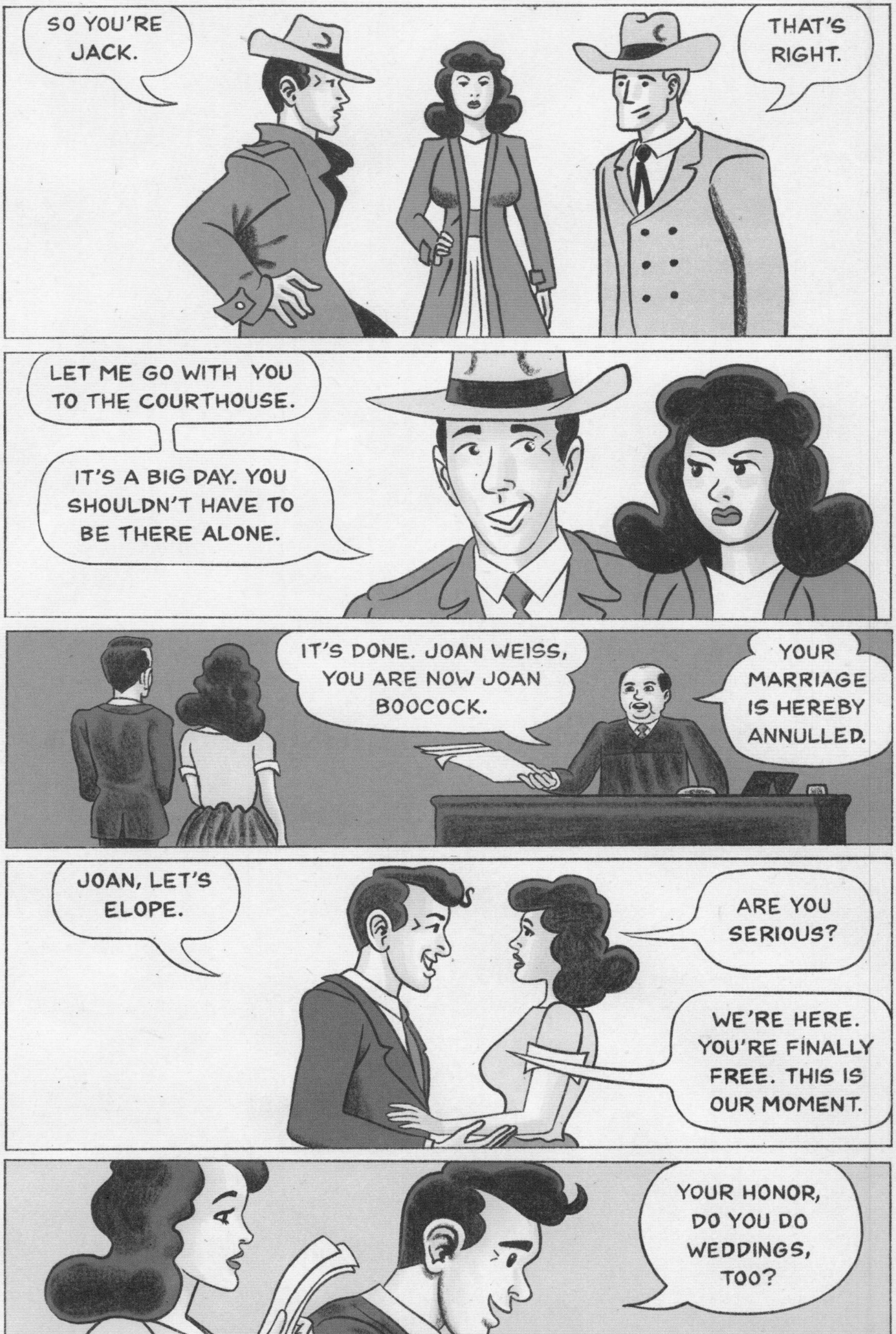
SO YOU'RE JACK.
THAT'S RIGHT.
LET ME GO WITH YOU TO THE COURTHOUSE.
IT'S A BIG DAY. YOU SHOULDN'T HAVE TO BE THERE ALONE.
IT'S DONE. JOAN WEISS, YOU ARE NOW JOAN BOOCOCK.
YOUR MARRIAGE IS HEREBY ANNULLED.
JOAN, LET'S ELOPE.
ARE YOU SERIOUS?
WE'RE HERE. YOU'RE FINALLY FREE. THIS IS OUR MOMENT.
YOUR HONOR, DO YOU DO WEDDINGS, TOO?

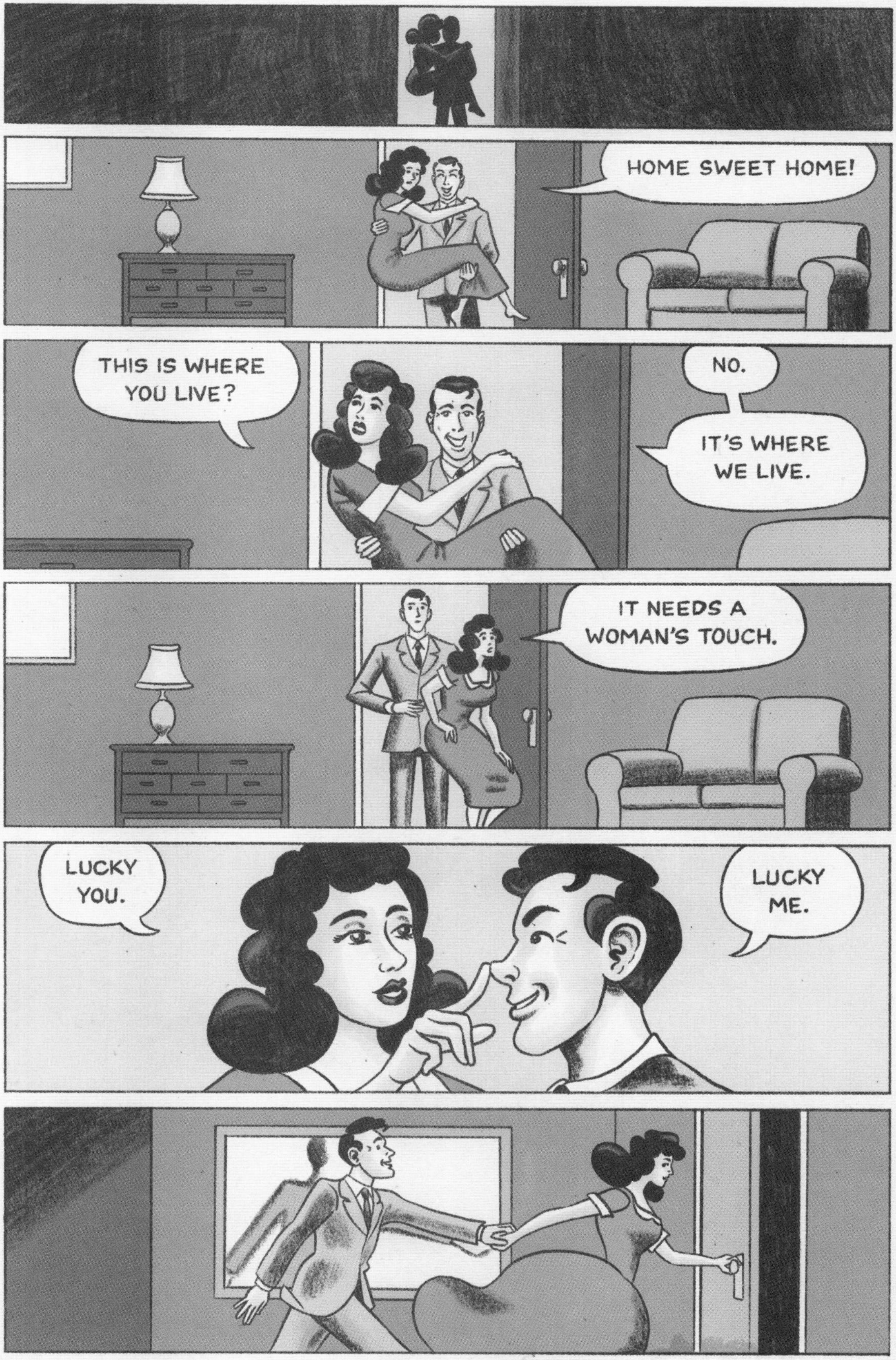
HOME SWEET HOME!
THIS IS WHERE YOU LIVE?
NO.
IT'S WHERE WE LIVE.
IT NEEDS A WOMAN'S TOUCH.
LUCKY YOU.
LUCKY ME.

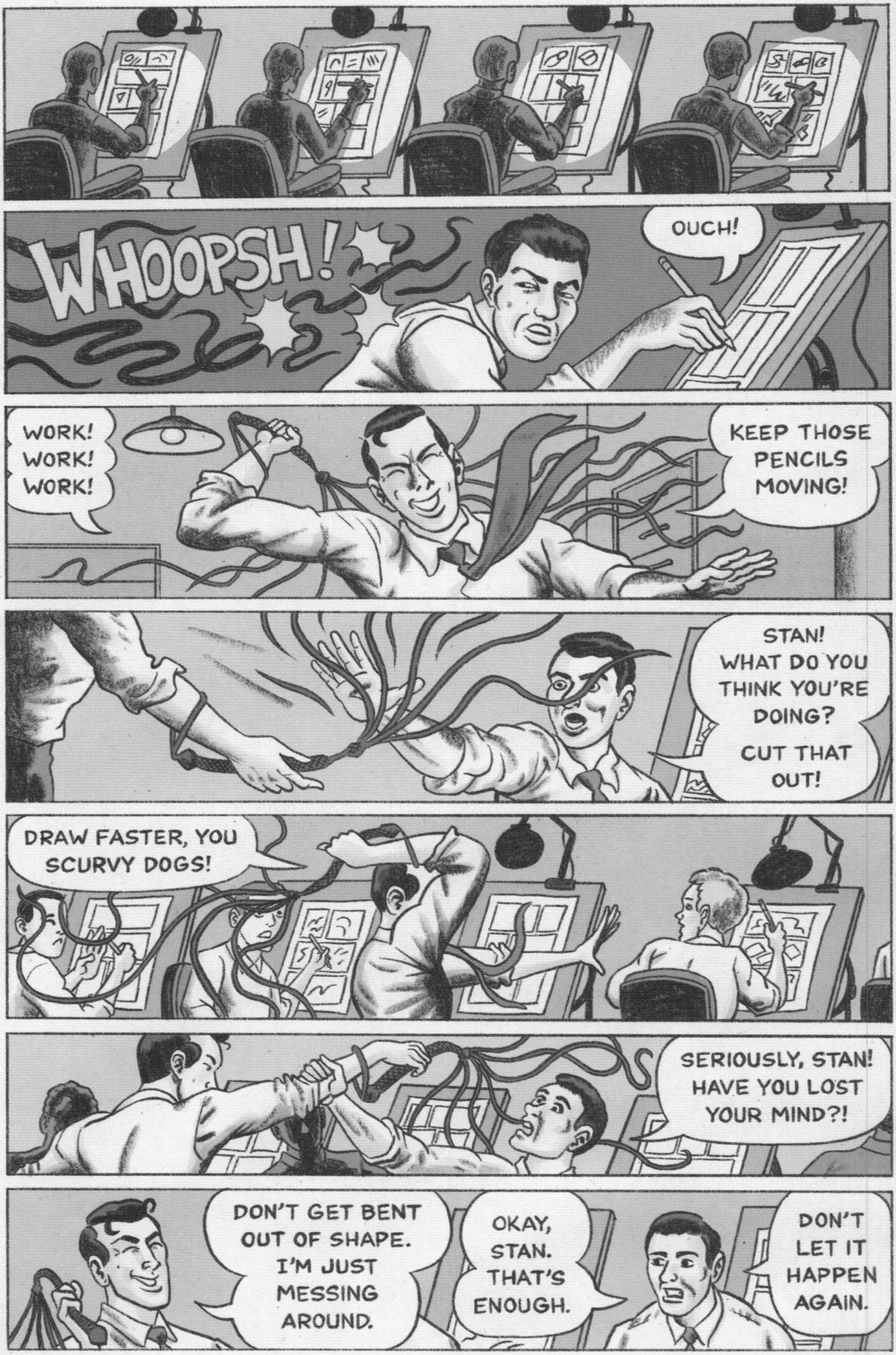
WHOOPSH!
OUCH!
WORK! WORK! WORK!
KEEP THOSE PENCILS MOVING!
STAN! WHAT DO YOU THINK YOU'RE DOING?
CUT THAT OUT!
DRAW FASTER, YOU SCURVY DOGS!
SERIOUSLY, STAN! HAVE YOU LOST YOUR MIND?!
DON'T GET BENT OUT OF SHAPE. I'M JUST MESSING AROUND.
OKAY, STAN. THAT'S ENOUGH.
DON'T LET IT HAPPEN AGAIN.

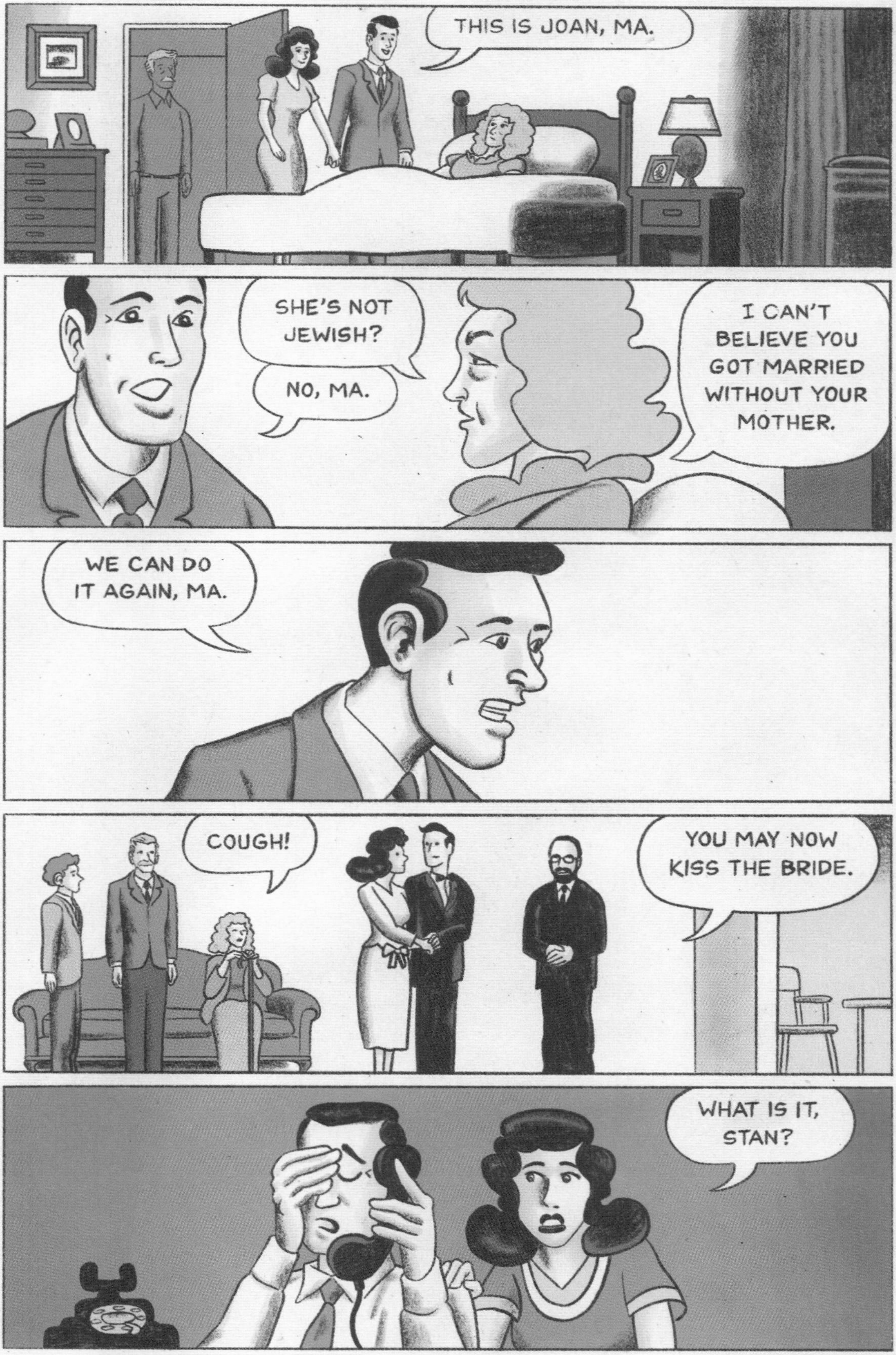
THIS IS JOAN, MA.
SHE'S NOT JEWISH?
NO, MA.
I CAN'T BELIEVE YOU GOT MARRIED WITHOUT YOUR MOTHER.
WE CAN DO IT AGAIN, MA.
COUGH!
YOU MAY NOW KISS THE BRIDE.
WHAT IS IT, STAN?

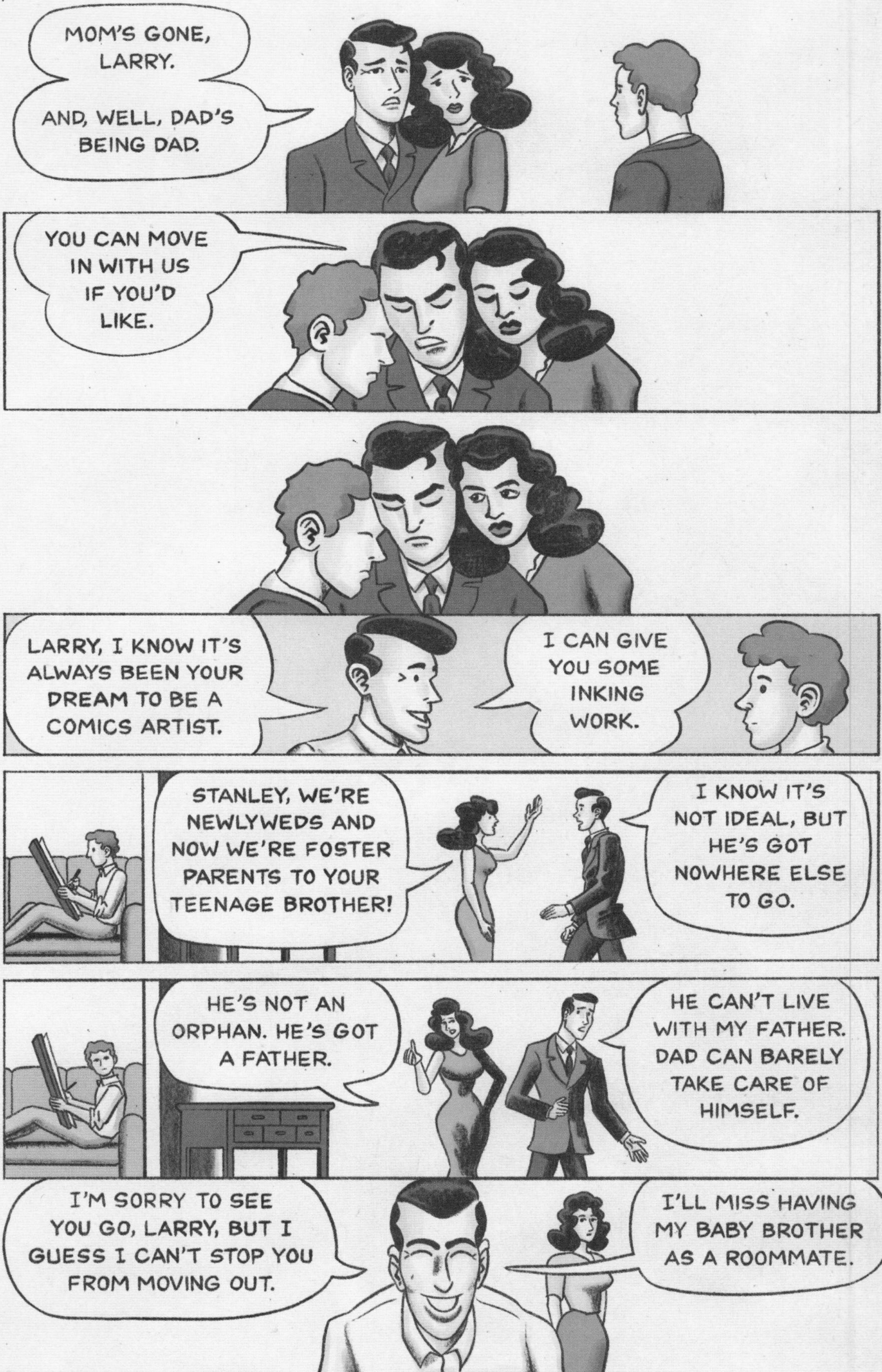
MOM'S GONE, LARRY.
AND, WELL, DAD'S BEING DAD.
YOU CAN MOVE IN WITH US IF YOU'D LIKE.
LARRY, I KNOW IT'S ALWAYS BEEN YOUR DREAM TO BE A COMICS ARTIST.
I CAN GIVE YOU SOME INKING WORK.
STANLEY, WE'RE NEWLYWEDS AND NOW WE'RE FOSTER PARENTS TO YOUR TEENAGE BROTHER!
I KNOW IT'S NOT IDEAL, BUT HE'S GOT NOWHERE ELSE TO GO.
HE'S NOT AN ORPHAN. HE'S GOT A FATHER.
HE CAN'T LIVE WITH MY FATHER. DAD CAN BARELY TAKE CARE OF HIMSELF.
I'M SORRY TO SEE YOU GO, LARRY, BUT I GUESS I CAN'T STOP YOU FROM MOVING OUT.
I'LL MISS HAVING MY BABY BROTHER AS A ROOMMATE.

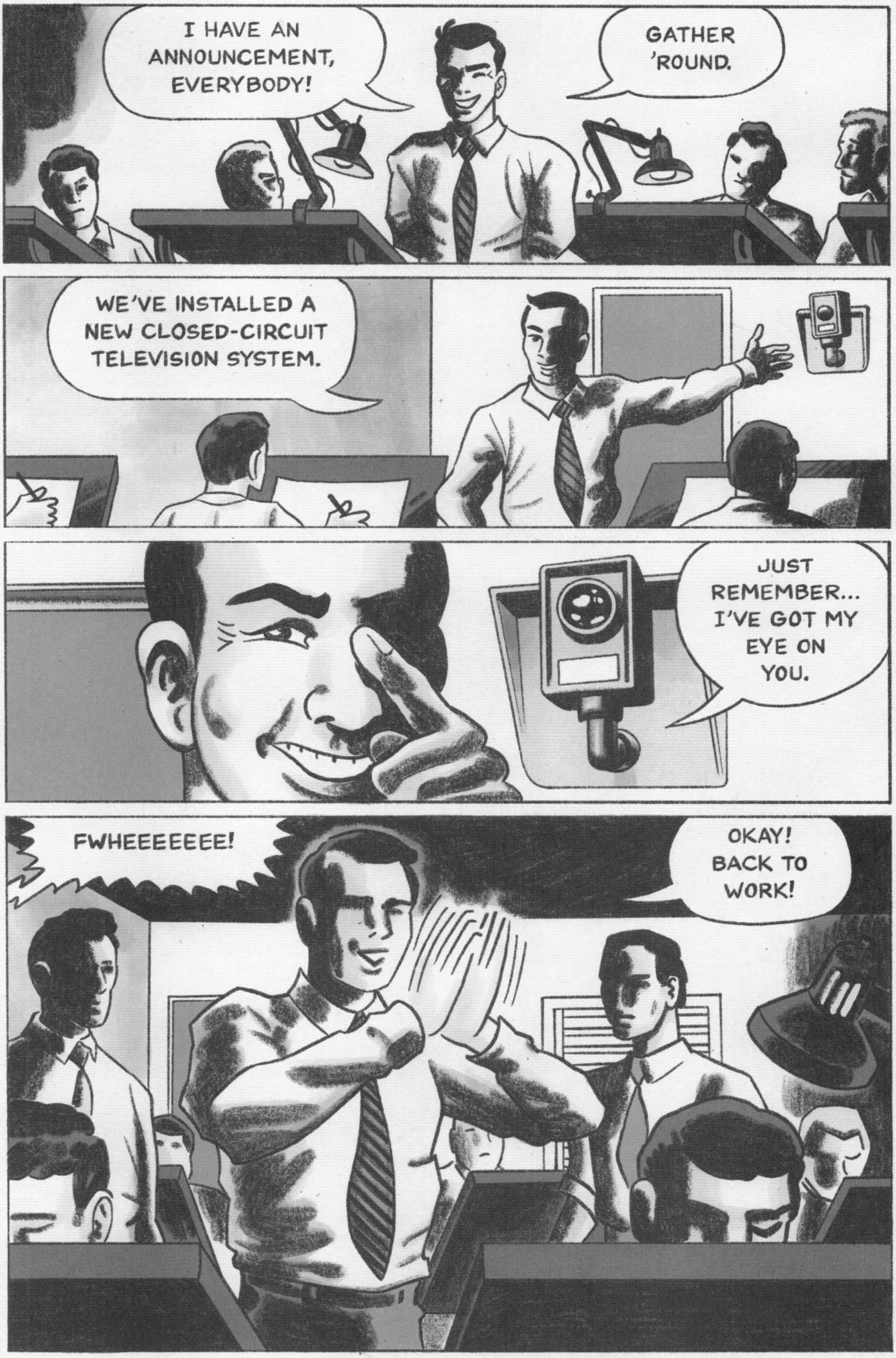
I HAVE AN ANNOUNCEMENT, EVERYBODY!
GATHER 'ROUND.
WE'VE INSTALLED A NEW CLOSED-CIRCUIT TELEVISION SYSTEM.
JUST REMEMBER... I'VE GOT MY EYE ON YOU.
FWHEEEEEEE!
OKAY! BACK TO WORK!

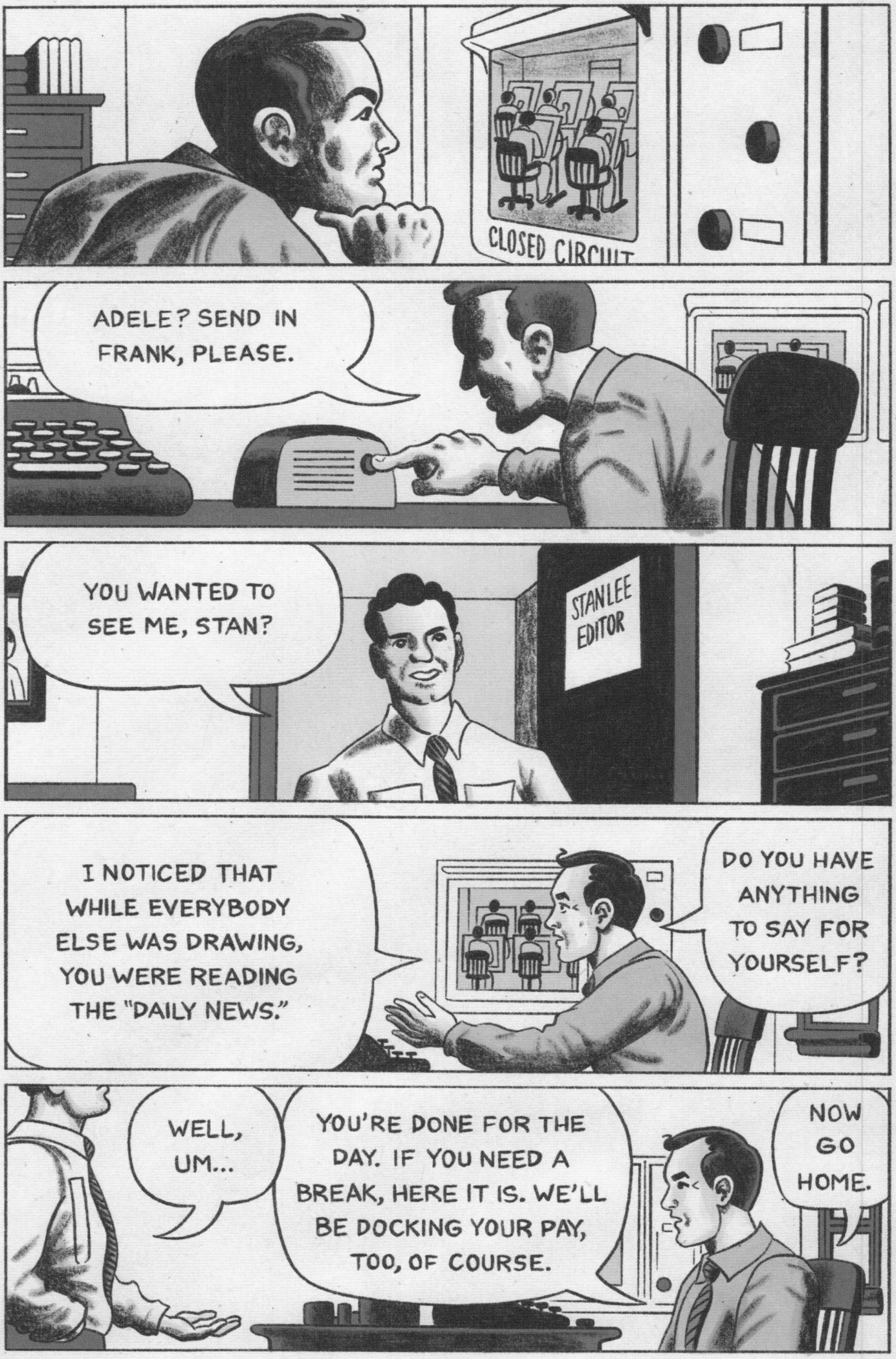
CLOSED CIRCUIT
ADELE? SEND IN FRANK, PLEASE.
STAN LEE EDITOR
YOU WANTED TO SEE ME, STAN?
I NOTICED THAT WHILE EVERYBODY ELSE WAS DRAWING, YOU WERE READING THE "DAILY NEWS."
DO YOU HAVE ANYTHING TO SAY FOR YOURSELF?
WELL, UM...
YOU'RE DONE FOR THE DAY. IF YOU NEED A BREAK, HERE IT IS. WE'LL BE DOCKING YOUR PAY, TOO, OF COURSE.
NOW GO HOME.

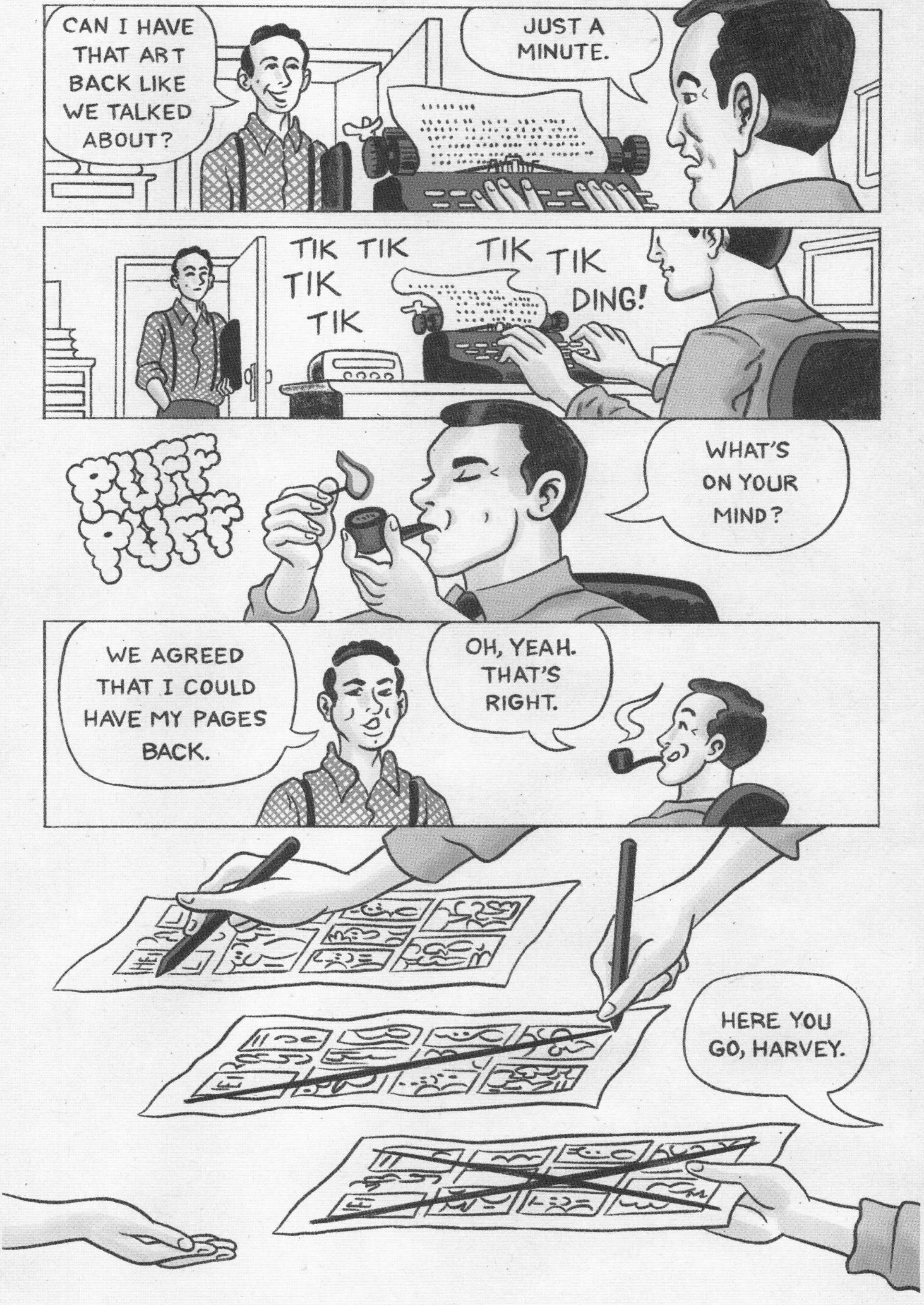

CAN I HAVE THAT ART BACK LIKE WE TALKED ABOUT?
JUST A MINUTE.
TIK TIK TIK TIK TIK TIK
DING!
PUFF PUFF
WHAT'S ON YOUR MIND?
WE AGREED THAT I COULD HAVE MY PAGES BACK.
OH, YEAH. THAT'S RIGHT.
HERE YOU GO, HARVEY.

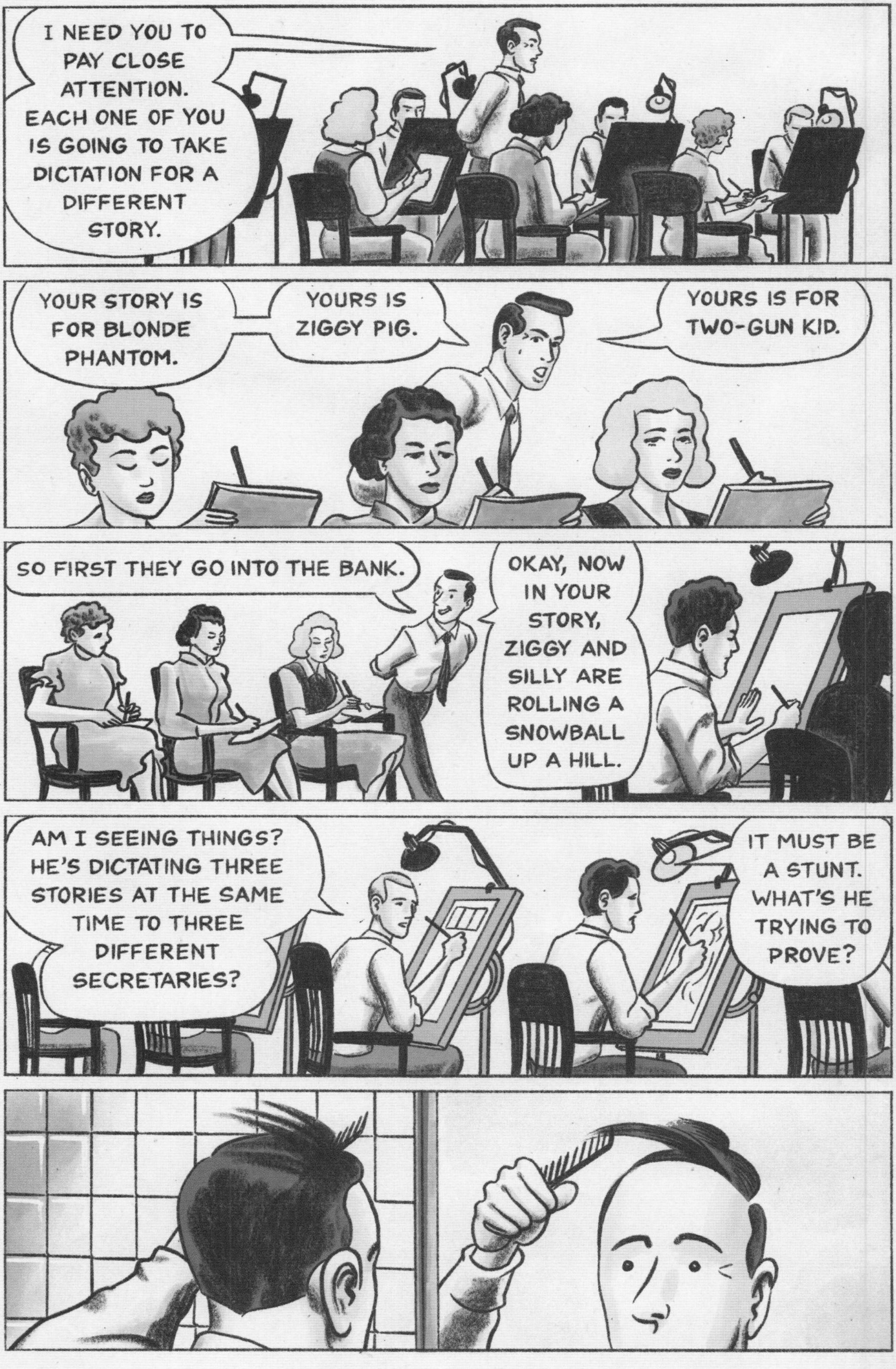
I NEED YOU TO PAY CLOSE ATTENTION. EACH ONE OF YOU IS GOING TO TAKE DICTATION FOR A DIFFERENT STORY.
YOUR STORY IS FOR BLONDE PHANTOM.
YOURS IS ZIGGY PIG.
YOURS IS FOR TWO-GUN KID.
SO FIRST THEY GO INTO THE BANK.
OKAY, NOW IN YOUR STORY, ZIGGY AND SILLY ARE ROLLING A SNOWBALL UP A HILL.
AM I SEEING THINGS? HE'S DICTATING THREE STORIES AT THE SAME TIME TO THREE DIFFERENT SECRETARIES?
IT MUST BE A STUNT. WHAT'S HE TRYING TO PROVE?

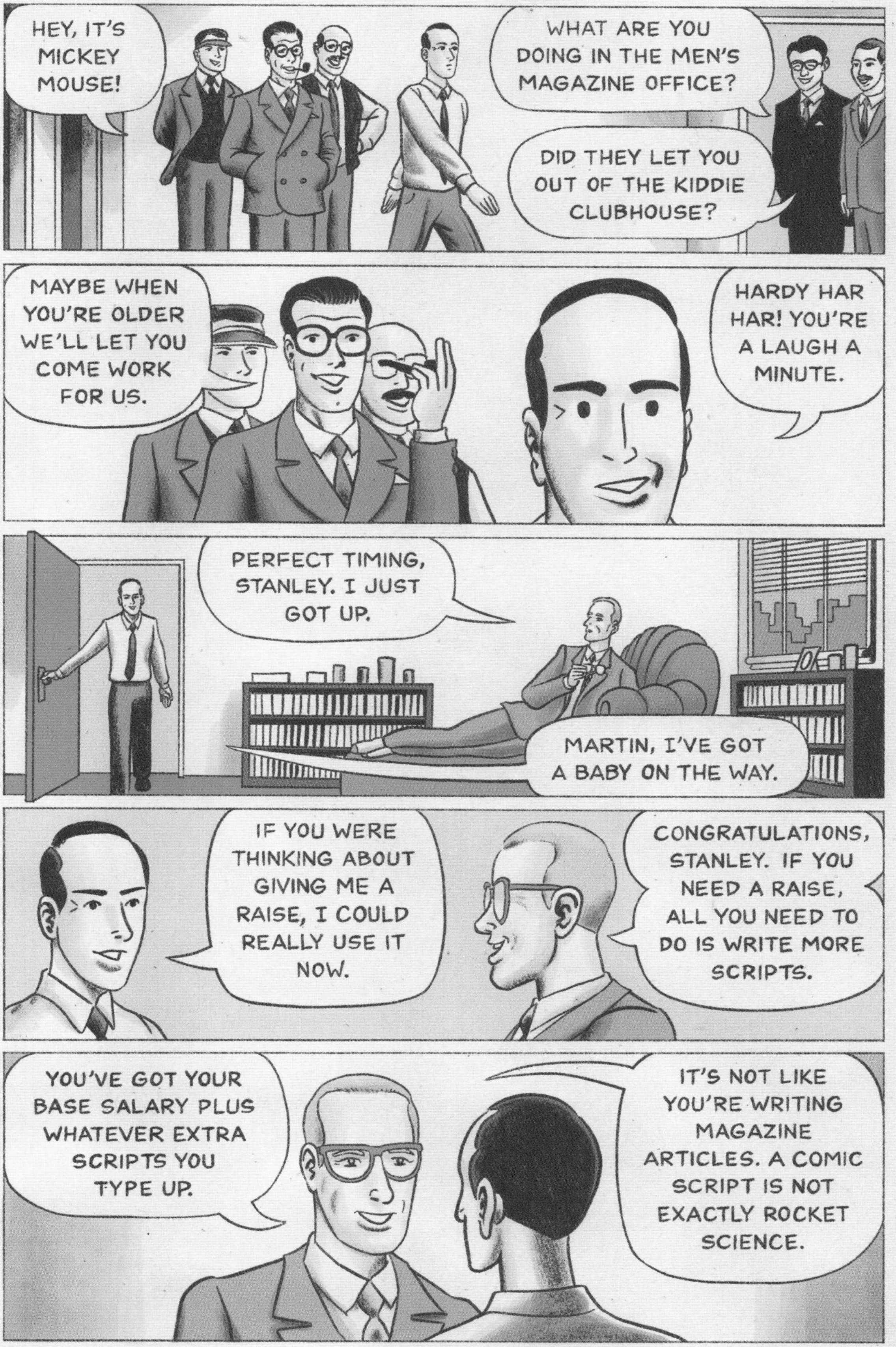
HEY, IT'S MICKEY MOUSE!
WHAT ARE YOU DOING IN THE MEN'S MAGAZINE OFFICE?
DID THEY LET YOU OUT OF THE KIDDIE CLUBHOUSE?
MAYBE WHEN YOU'RE OLDER WE'LL LET YOU COME WORK FOR US.
HARDY HAR HAR! YOU'RE A LAUGH A MINUTE.
PERFECT TIMING, STANLEY. I JUST GOT UP.
MARTIN, I'VE GOT A BABY ON THE WAY.
IF YOU WERE THINKING ABOUT GIVING ME A RAISE, I COULD REALLY USE IT NOW.
CONGRATULATIONS, STANLEY. IF YOU NEED A RAISE, ALL YOU NEED TO DO IS WRITE MORE SCRIPTS.
YOU'VE GOT YOUR BASE SALARY PLUS WHATEVER EXTRA SCRIPTS YOU TYPE UP.
IT'S NOT LIKE YOU'RE WRITING MAGAZINE ARTICLES. A COMIC SCRIPT IS NOT EXACTLY ROCKET SCIENCE.

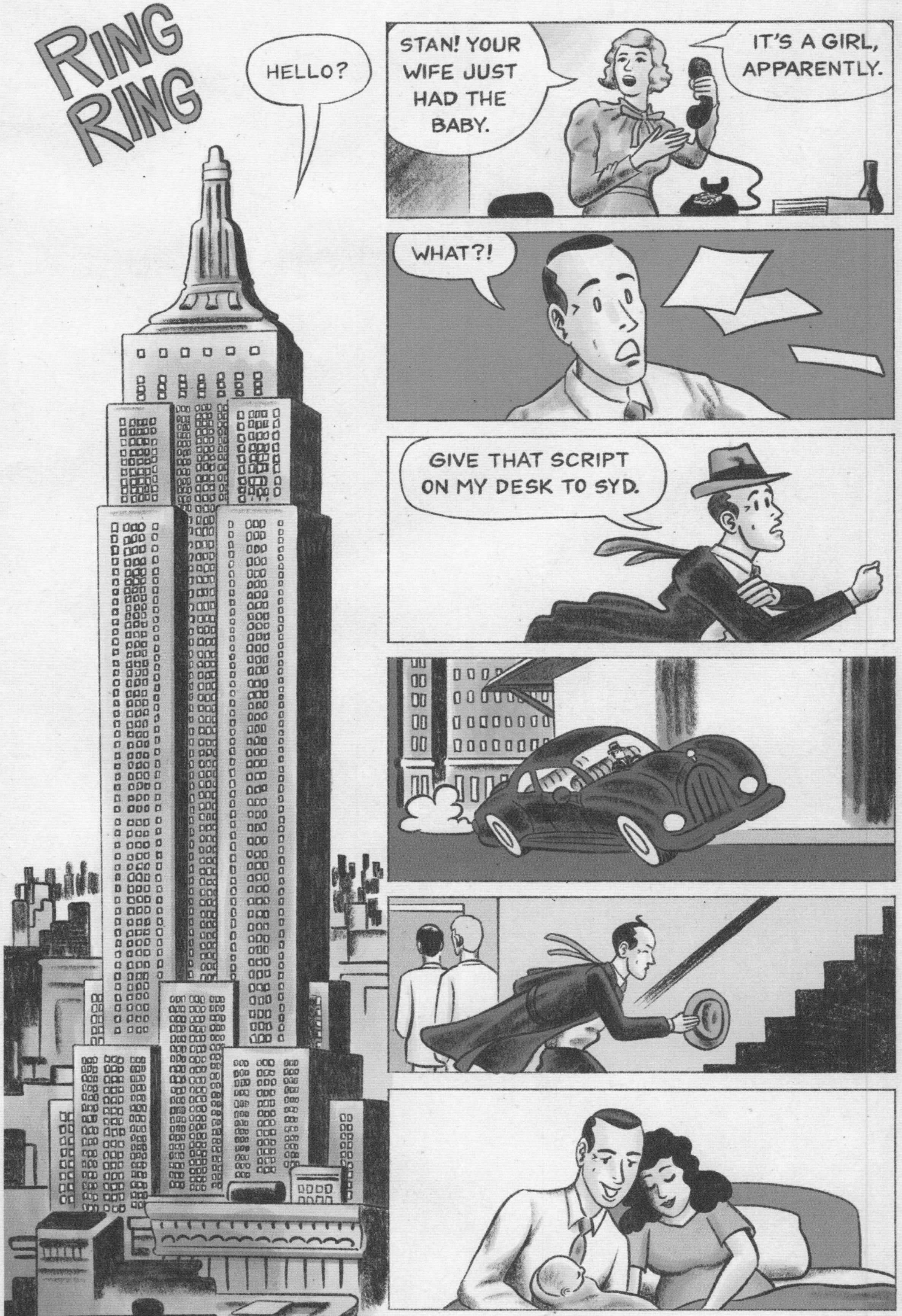
RING RING
HELLO?
STAN! YOUR WIFE JUST HAD THE BABY.
IT'S A GIRL, APPARENTLY.
WHAT?!
GIVE THAT SCRIPT ON MY DESK TO SYD.

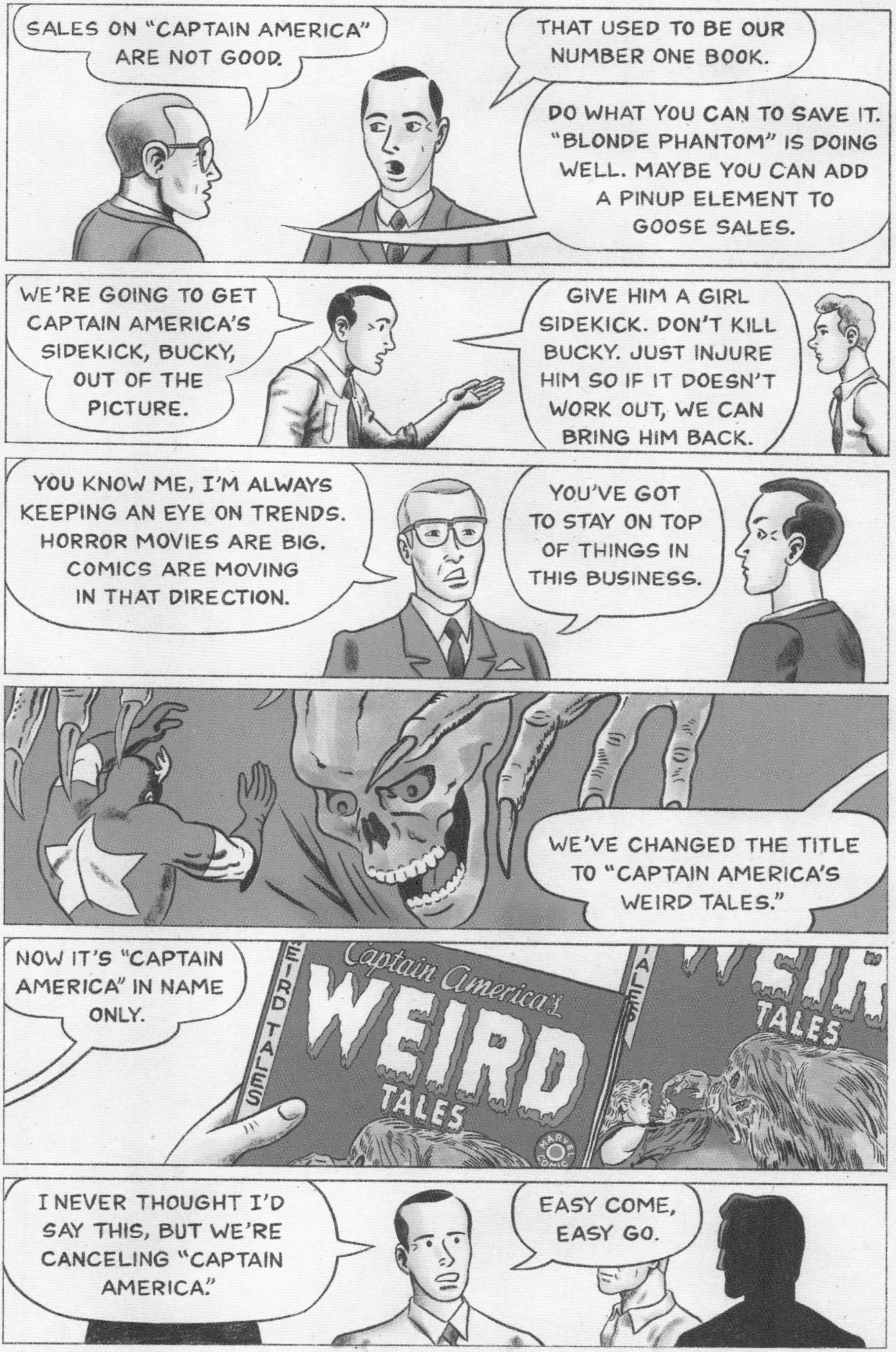
SALES ON "CAPTAIN AMERICA" ARE NOT GOOD.
THAT USED TO BE OUR NUMBER ONE BOOK.
DO WHAT YOU CAN TO SAVE IT. "BLONDE PHANTOM" IS DOING WELL. MAYBE YOU CAN ADD A PINUP ELEMENT TO GOOSE SALES.
WE'RE GOING TO GET CAPTAIN AMERICA'S SIDEKICK, BUCKY, OUT OF THE PICTURE.
GIVE HIM A GIRL SIDEKICK. DON'T KILL BUCKY. JUST INJURE HIM SO IF IT DOESN'T WORK OUT, WE CAN BRING HIM BACK.
YOU KNOW ME, I'M ALWAYS KEEPING AN EYE ON TRENDS. HORROR MOVIES ARE BIG. COMICS ARE MOVING IN THAT DIRECTION.
YOU'VE GOT TO STAY ON TOP OF THINGS IN THIS BUSINESS.
WE'VE CHANGED THE TITLE TO "CAPTAIN AMERICA'S WEIRD TALES."
NOW IT'S "CAPTAIN AMERICA" IN NAME ONLY.
Captain America's
WEIRD
TALES
MARVEL COMIC
I NEVER THOUGHT I'D SAY THIS, BUT WE'RE CANCELING "CAPTAIN AMERICA."
EASY COME, EASY GO.

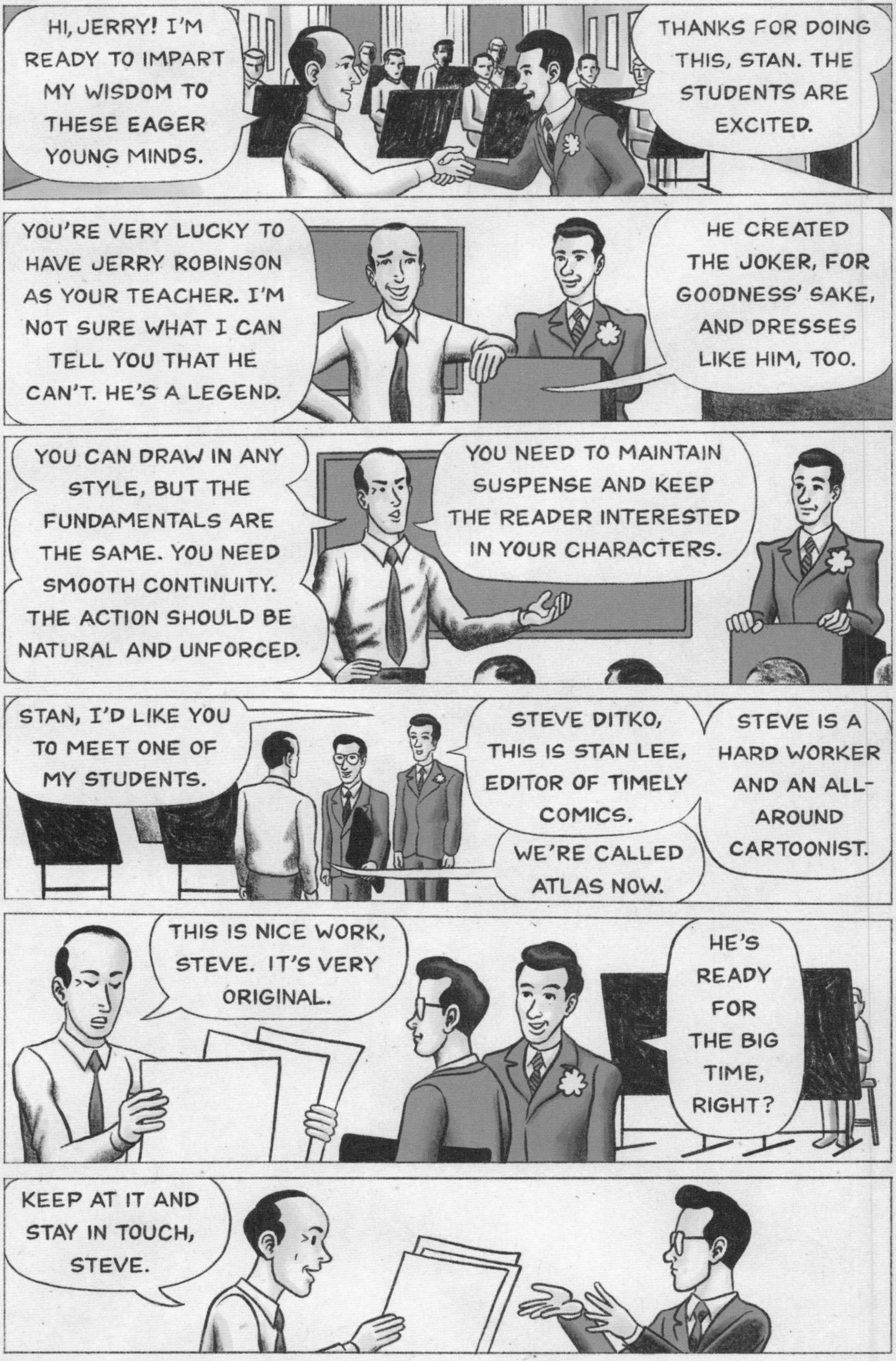
HI, JERRY! I'M READY TO IMPART MY WISDOM TO THESE EAGER YOUNG MINDS.
THANKS FOR DOING THIS, STAN. THE STUDENTS ARE EXCITED.
YOU'RE VERY LUCKY TO HAVE JERRY ROBINSON AS YOUR TEACHER. I'M NOT SURE WHAT I CAN TELL YOU THAT HE CAN'T. HE'S A LEGEND.
HE CREATED THE JOKER, FOR GOODNESS' SAKE, AND DRESSES LIKE HIM, TOO.
YOU CAN DRAW IN ANY STYLE, BUT THE FUNDAMENTALS ARE THE SAME. YOU NEED SMOOTH CONTINUITY. THE ACTION SHOULD BE NATURAL AND UNFORCED.
YOU NEED TO MAINTAIN SUSPENSE AND KEEP THE READER INTERESTED IN YOUR CHARACTERS.
STAN, I'D LIKE YOU TO MEET ONE OF MY STUDENTS.
STEVE DITKO, THIS IS STAN LEE, EDITOR OF TIMELY COMICS.
WE'RE CALLED ATLAS NOW.
STEVE IS A HARD WORKER AND AN ALL-AROUND CARTOONIST.
THIS IS NICE WORK, STEVE. IT'S VERY ORIGINAL.
HE'S READY FOR THE BIG TIME, RIGHT?
KEEP AT IT AND STAY IN TOUCH, STEVE.

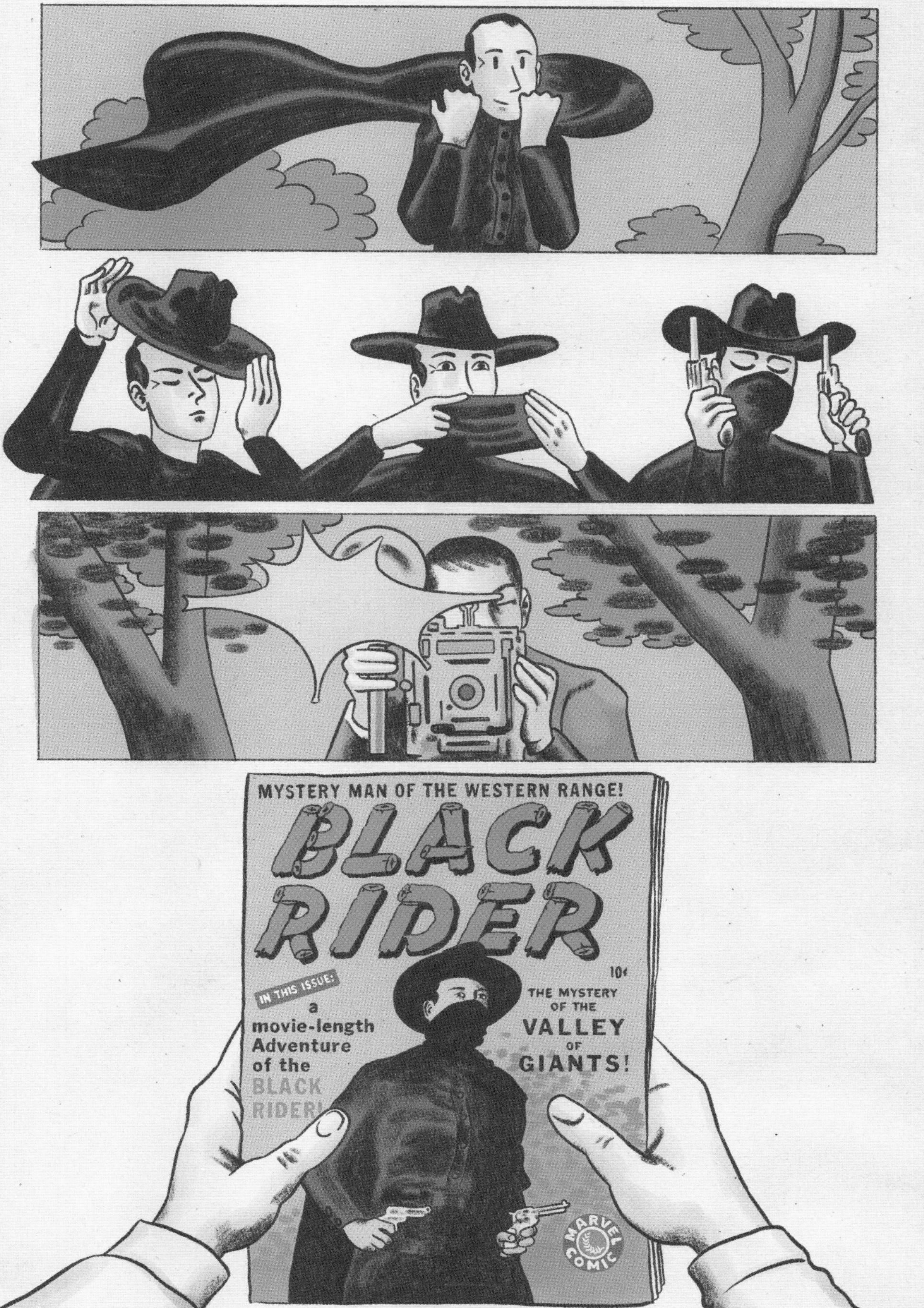
MYSTERY MAN OF THE WESTERN RANGE!
BLACK RIDER
10¢
IN THIS ISSUE:
a movie-length Adventure of the BLACK RIDER!
THE MYSTERY OF THE VALLEY OF GIANTS!
MARVEL COMIC

YOU'RE GOING TO BE A BIG SISTER. THE BABY WILL BE HERE ANY DAY NOW.

HELLO, JAN DARLING. YOU'RE NAMED AFTER YOUR MOMMY AND YOUR DADDY. JOAN PLUS STAN MAKES JAN.

SOMETIMES THIS HAPPENS, MR. LEE. I'M VERY SORRY.

HOSPITAL

NOO! NOOO!

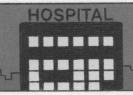

NO! NO! NO! NO! NO! NO! NO! NO! NO! NO! NO! NO! NO!

THIS ISN'T THE END.

WE CAN ADOPT.

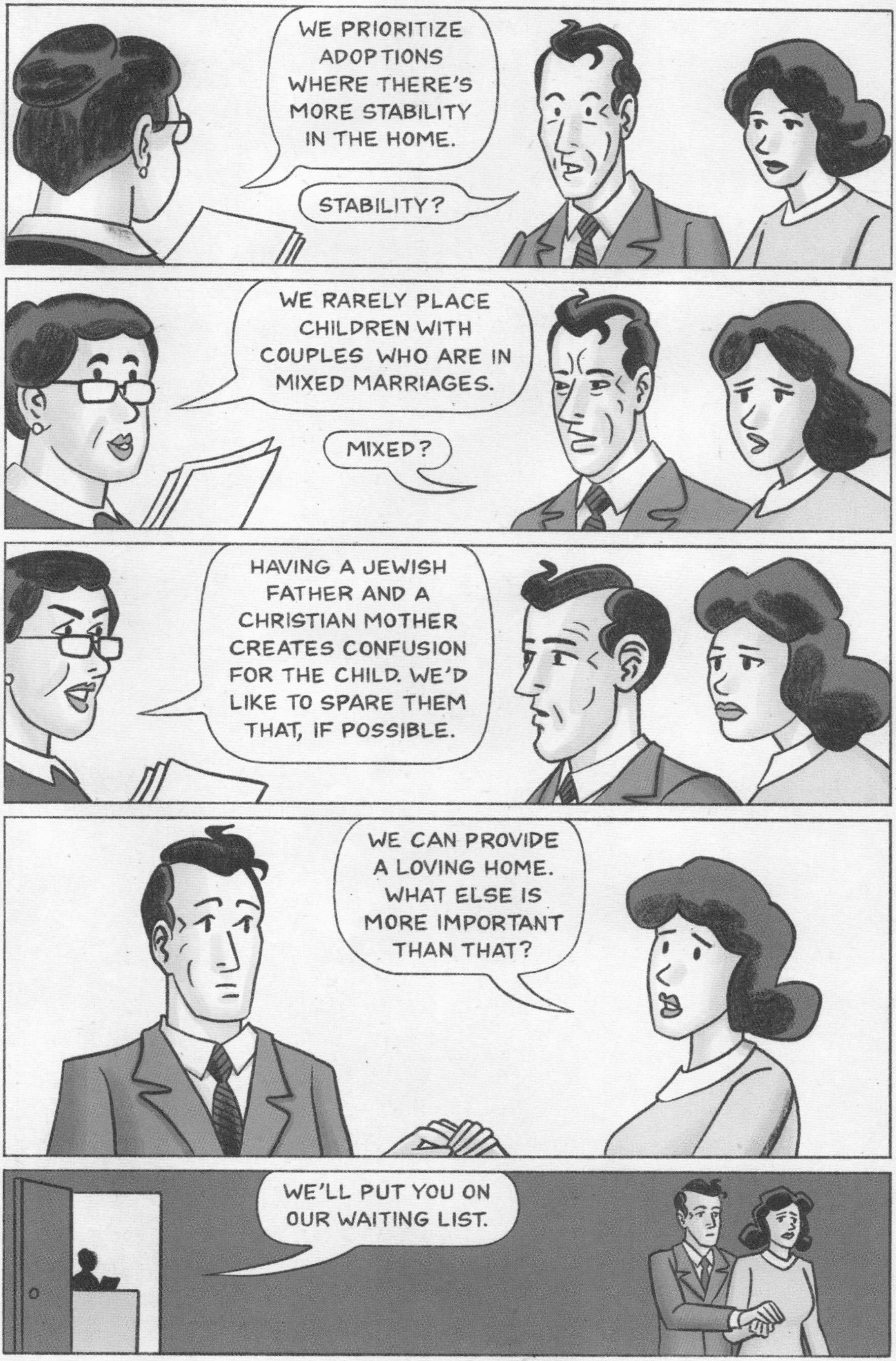
WE PRIORITIZE ADOPTIONS WHERE THERE'S MORE STABILITY IN THE HOME.
STABILITY?
WE RARELY PLACE CHILDREN WITH COUPLES WHO ARE IN MIXED MARRIAGES.
MIXED?
HAVING A JEWISH FATHER AND A CHRISTIAN MOTHER CREATES CONFUSION FOR THE CHILD. WE'D LIKE TO SPARE THEM THAT, IF POSSIBLE.
WE CAN PROVIDE A LOVING HOME. WHAT ELSE IS MORE IMPORTANT THAN THAT?
WE'LL PUT YOU ON OUR WAITING LIST.

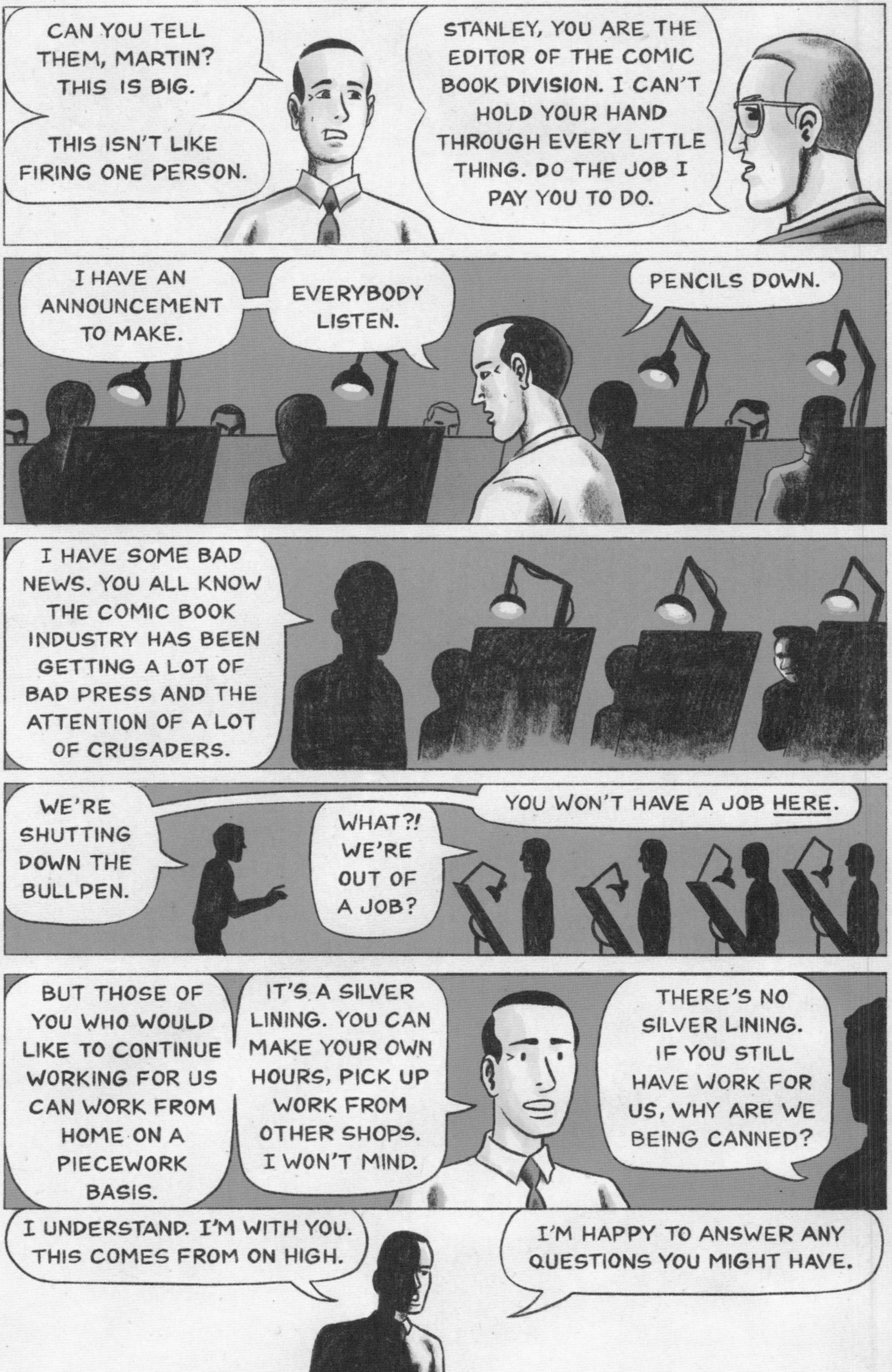
CAN YOU TELL THEM, MARTIN? THIS IS BIG.
THIS ISN'T LIKE FIRING ONE PERSON.
STANLEY, YOU ARE THE EDITOR OF THE COMIC BOOK DIVISION. I CAN'T HOLD YOUR HAND THROUGH EVERY LITTLE THING. DO THE JOB I PAY YOU TO DO.
I HAVE AN ANNOUNCEMENT TO MAKE.
EVERYBODY LISTEN.
PENCILS DOWN.
I HAVE SOME BAD NEWS. YOU ALL KNOW THE COMIC BOOK INDUSTRY HAS BEEN GETTING A LOT OF BAD PRESS AND THE ATTENTION OF A LOT OF CRUSADERS.
WE'RE SHUTTING DOWN THE BULLPEN.
WHAT?! WE'RE OUT OF A JOB?
YOU WON'T HAVE A JOB HERE.
BUT THOSE OF YOU WHO WOULD LIKE TO CONTINUE WORKING FOR US CAN WORK FROM HOME ON A PIECEWORK BASIS.
IT'S A SILVER LINING. YOU CAN MAKE YOUR OWN HOURS, PICK UP WORK FROM OTHER SHOPS. I WON'T MIND.
THERE'S NO SILVER LINING. IF YOU STILL HAVE WORK FOR US, WHY ARE WE BEING CANNED?
I UNDERSTAND. I'M WITH YOU. THIS COMES FROM ON HIGH.
I'M HAPPY TO ANSWER ANY QUESTIONS YOU MIGHT HAVE.

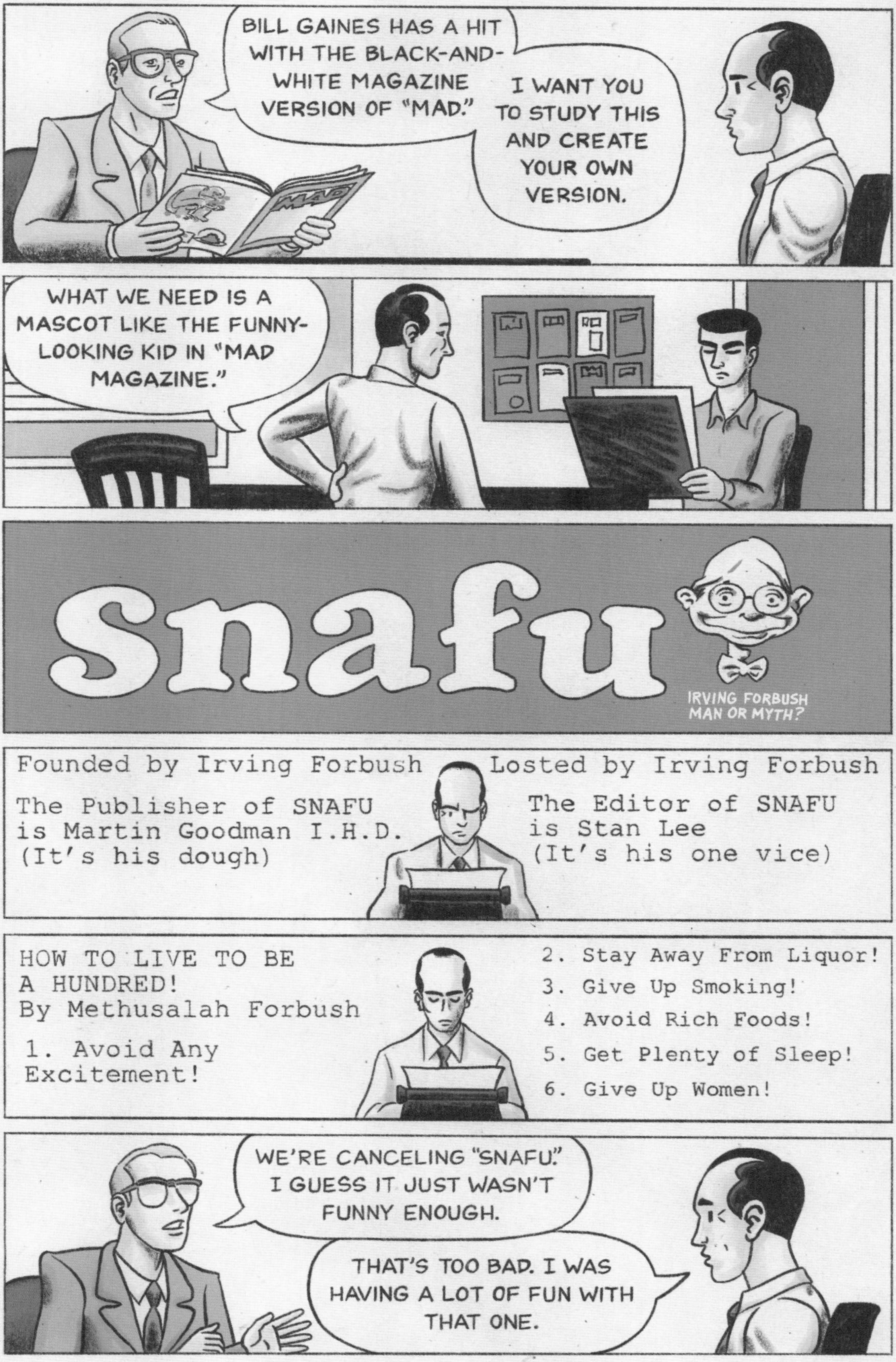
BILL GAINES HAS A HIT WITH THE BLACK-AND-WHITE MAGAZINE VERSION OF "MAD."
I WANT YOU TO STUDY THIS AND CREATE YOUR OWN VERSION.
WHAT WE NEED IS A MASCOT LIKE THE FUNNY-LOOKING KID IN "MAD MAGAZINE."
Snafu
IRVING FORBUSH MAN OR MYTH?
Founded by Irving Forbush
Losted by Irving Forbush
The Publisher of SNAFU is Martin Goodman I.H.D. (It's his dough)
The Editor of SNAFU is Stan Lee (It's his one vice)
HOW TO LIVE TO BE A HUNDRED! By Methusalah Forbush
1. Avoid Any Excitement!
2. Stay Away From Liquor!
3. Give Up Smoking!
4. Avoid Rich Foods!
5. Get Plenty of Sleep!
6. Give Up Women!
WE'RE CANCELING "SNAFU." I GUESS IT JUST WASN'T FUNNY ENOUGH.
THAT'S TOO BAD. I WAS HAVING A LOT OF FUN WITH THAT ONE.

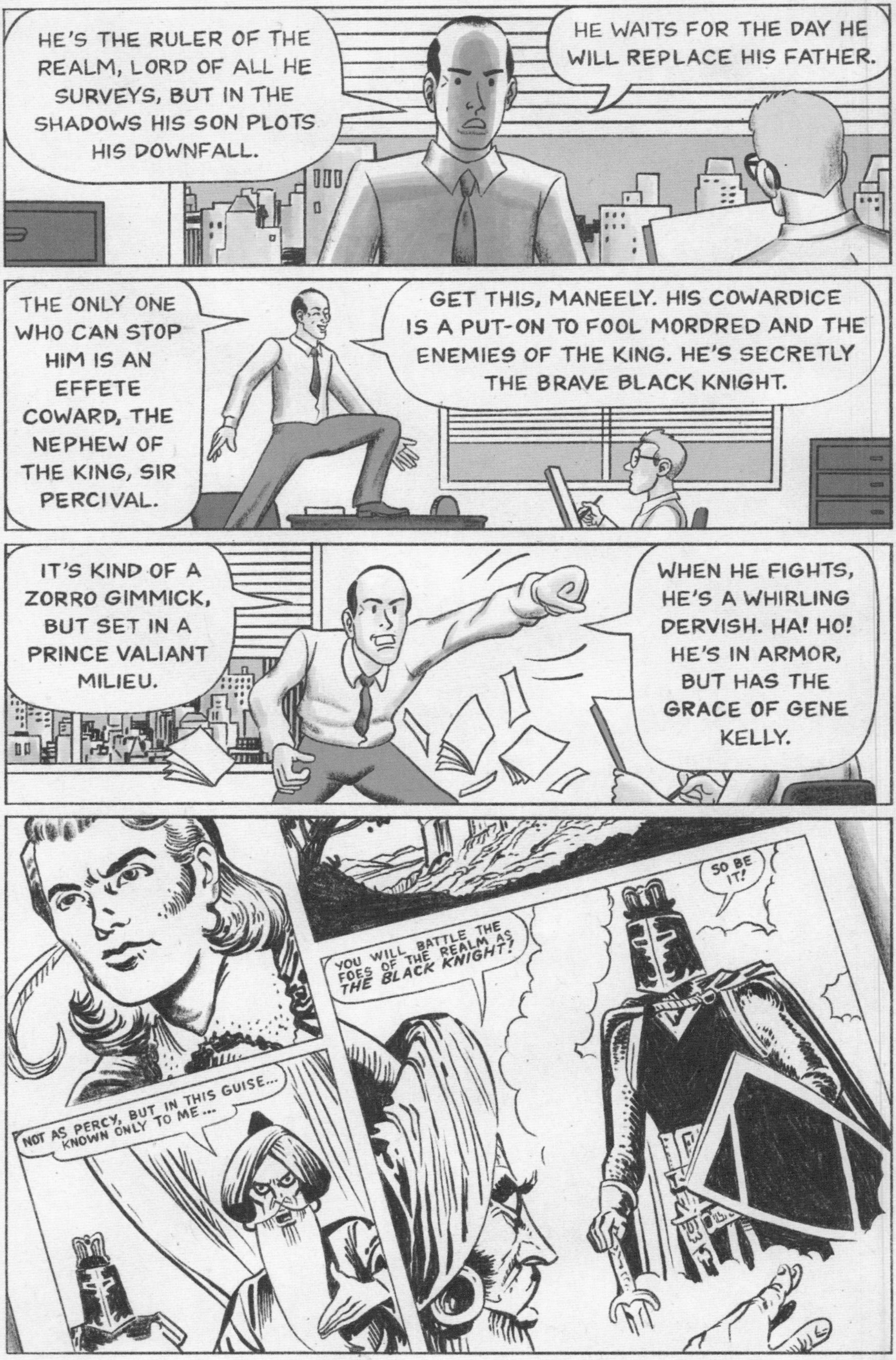
HE'S THE RULER OF THE REALM, LORD OF ALL HE SURVEYS, BUT IN THE SHADOWS HIS SON PLOTS HIS DOWNFALL.
HE WAITS FOR THE DAY HE WILL REPLACE HIS FATHER.
THE ONLY ONE WHO CAN STOP HIM IS AN EFFETE COWARD, THE NEPHEW OF THE KING, SIR PERCIVAL.
GET THIS, MANEELY. HIS COWARDICE IS A PUT-ON TO FOOL MORDRED AND THE ENEMIES OF THE KING. HE'S SECRETLY THE BRAVE BLACK KNIGHT.
IT'S KIND OF A ZORRO GIMMICK, BUT SET IN A PRINCE VALIANT MILIEU.
WHEN HE FIGHTS, HE'S A WHIRLING DERVISH. HA! HO! HE'S IN ARMOR, BUT HAS THE GRACE OF GENE KELLY.
NOT AS PERCY, BUT IN THIS GUISE... KNOWN ONLY TO ME...
YOU WILL BATTLE THE FOES OF THE REALM AS THE BLACK KNIGHT!
SO BE IT!

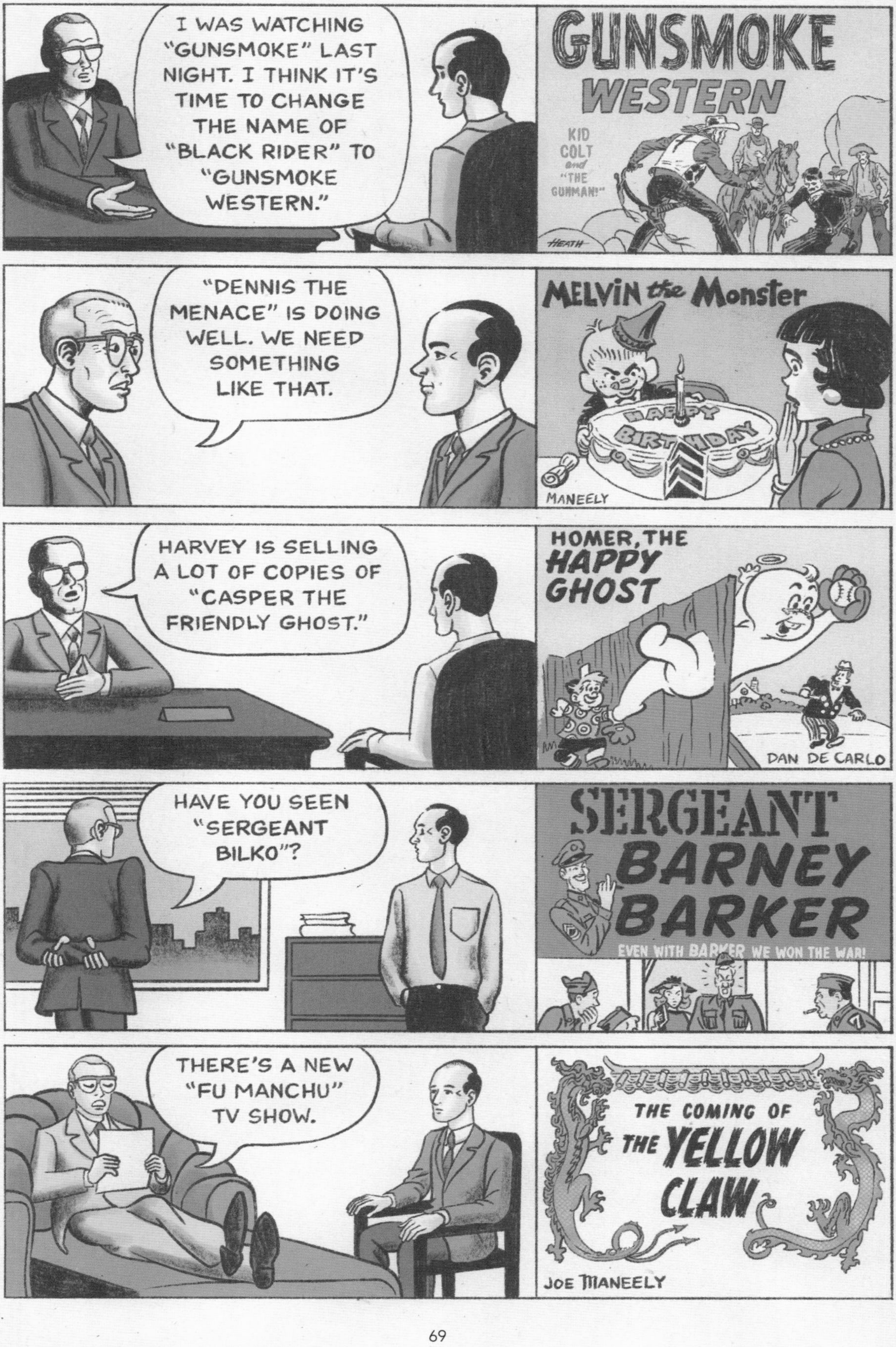
I WAS WATCHING "GUNSMOKE" LAST NIGHT. I THINK IT'S TIME TO CHANGE THE NAME OF "BLACK RIDER" TO "GUNSMOKE WESTERN."
GUNSMOKE WESTERN
KID COLT and "THE GUNMAN!"
HEATH
"DENNIS THE MENACE" IS DOING WELL. WE NEED SOMETHING LIKE THAT.
MELVIN the Monster
HAPPY BIRTHDAY
MANEELY
HARVEY IS SELLING A LOT OF COPIES OF "CASPER THE FRIENDLY GHOST."
HOMER, THE HAPPY GHOST
DAN DE CARLO
HAVE YOU SEEN "SERGEANT BILKO"?
SERGEANT BARNEY BARKER
EVEN WITH BARKER WE WON THE WAR!
THERE'S A NEW "FU MANCHU" TV SHOW.
THE COMING OF THE YELLOW CLAW
JOE MANEELY

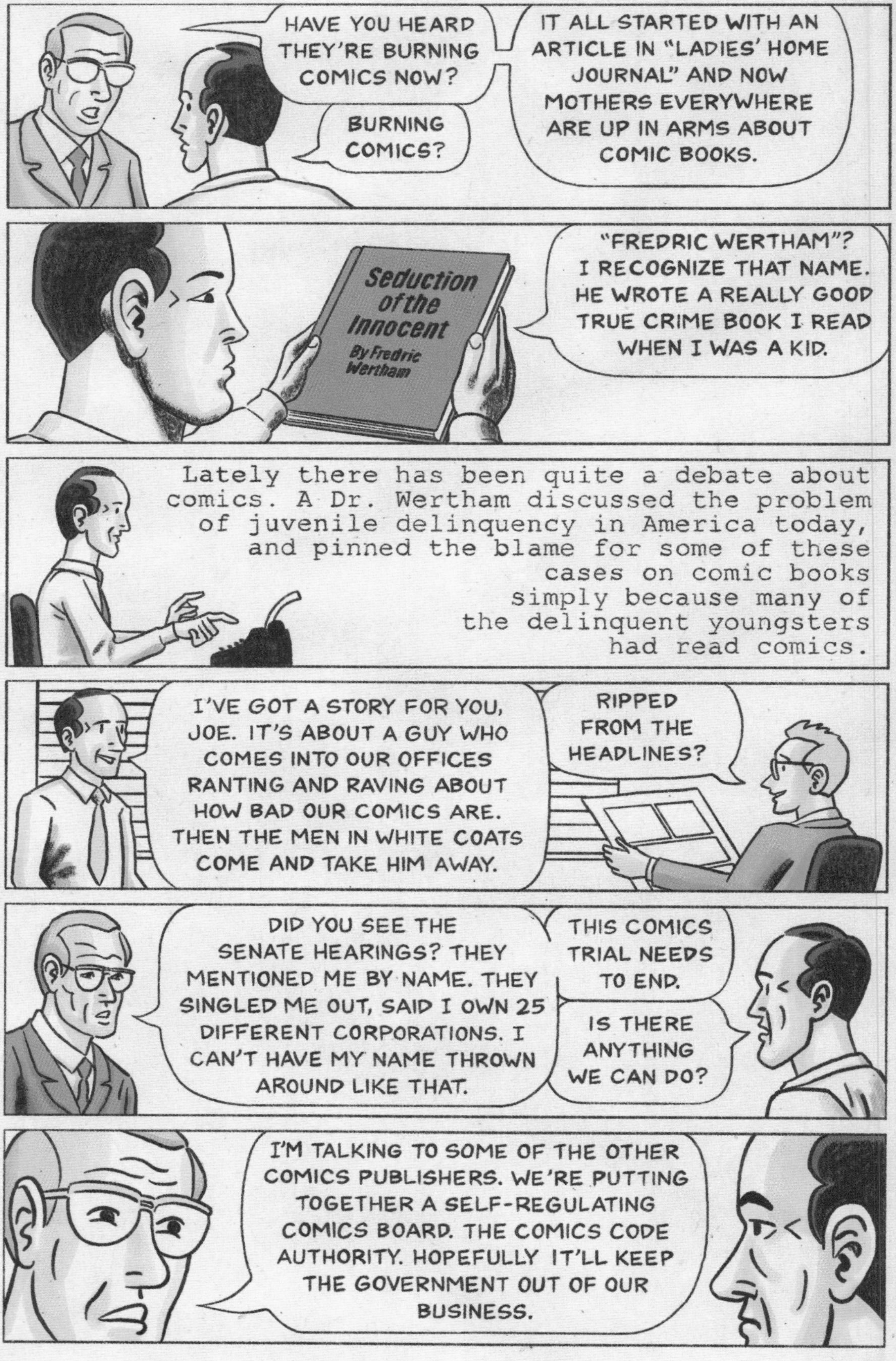
HAVE YOU HEARD THEY'RE BURNING COMICS NOW?
BURNING COMICS?
IT ALL STARTED WITH AN ARTICLE IN "LADIES' HOME JOURNAL" AND NOW MOTHERS EVERYWHERE ARE UP IN ARMS ABOUT COMIC BOOKS.
Seduction of the Innocent By Fredric Wertham
"FREDRIC WERTHAM"? I RECOGNIZE THAT NAME. HE WROTE A REALLY GOOD TRUE CRIME BOOK I READ WHEN I WAS A KID.
Lately there has been quite a debate about comics. A Dr. Wertham discussed the problem of juvenile delinquency in America today, and pinned the blame for some of these cases on comic books simply because many of the delinquent youngsters had read comics.
I'VE GOT A STORY FOR YOU, JOE. IT'S ABOUT A GUY WHO COMES INTO OUR OFFICES RANTING AND RAVING ABOUT HOW BAD OUR COMICS ARE. THEN THE MEN IN WHITE COATS COME AND TAKE HIM AWAY.
RIPPED FROM THE HEADLINES?
DID YOU SEE THE SENATE HEARINGS? THEY MENTIONED ME BY NAME. THEY SINGLED ME OUT, SAID I OWN 25 DIFFERENT CORPORATIONS. I CAN'T HAVE MY NAME THROWN AROUND LIKE THAT.
THIS COMICS TRIAL NEEDS TO END.
IS THERE ANYTHING WE CAN DO?
I'M TALKING TO SOME OF THE OTHER COMICS PUBLISHERS. WE'RE PUTTING TOGETHER A SELF-REGULATING COMICS BOARD. THE COMICS CODE AUTHORITY. HOPEFULLY IT'LL KEEP THE GOVERNMENT OUT OF OUR BUSINESS.

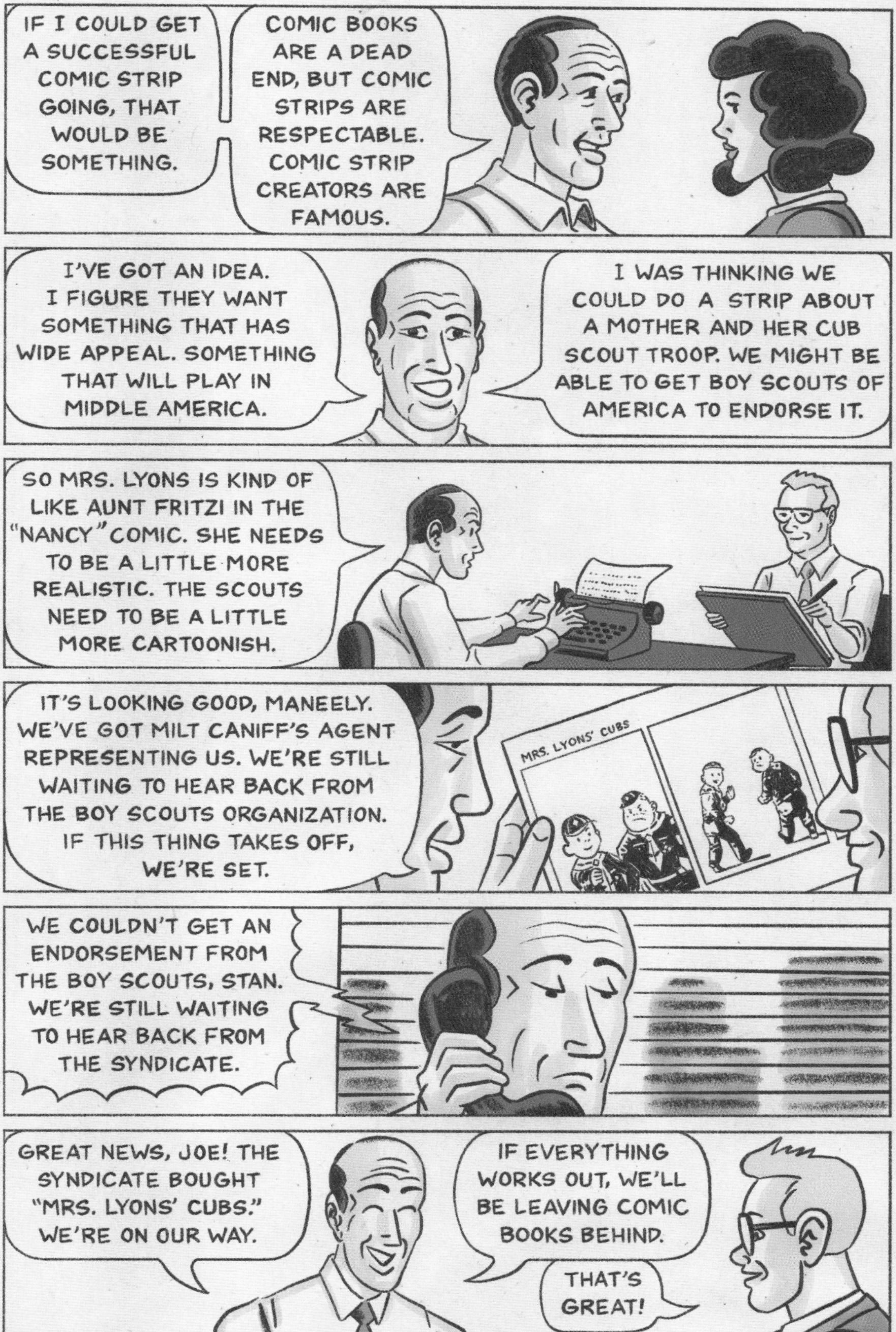
IF I COULD GET A SUCCESSFUL COMIC STRIP GOING, THAT WOULD BE SOMETHING.
COMIC BOOKS ARE A DEAD END, BUT COMIC STRIPS ARE RESPECTABLE. COMIC STRIP CREATORS ARE FAMOUS.
I'VE GOT AN IDEA. I FIGURE THEY WANT SOMETHING THAT HAS WIDE APPEAL. SOMETHING THAT WILL PLAY IN MIDDLE AMERICA.
I WAS THINKING WE COULD DO A STRIP ABOUT A MOTHER AND HER CUB SCOUT TROOP. WE MIGHT BE ABLE TO GET BOY SCOUTS OF AMERICA TO ENDORSE IT.
SO MRS. LYONS IS KIND OF LIKE AUNT FRITZI IN THE "NANCY" COMIC. SHE NEEDS TO BE A LITTLE MORE REALISTIC. THE SCOUTS NEED TO BE A LITTLE MORE CARTOONISH.
IT'S LOOKING GOOD, MANEELY. WE'VE GOT MILT CANIFF'S AGENT REPRESENTING US. WE'RE STILL WAITING TO HEAR BACK FROM THE BOY SCOUTS ORGANIZATION. IF THIS THING TAKES OFF, WE'RE SET.
MRS. LYONS' CUBS
WE COULDN'T GET AN ENDORSEMENT FROM THE BOY SCOUTS, STAN. WE'RE STILL WAITING TO HEAR BACK FROM THE SYNDICATE.
GREAT NEWS, JOE! THE SYNDICATE BOUGHT "MRS. LYONS' CUBS." WE'RE ON OUR WAY.
IF EVERYTHING WORKS OUT, WE'LL BE LEAVING COMIC BOOKS BEHIND.
THAT'S GREAT!

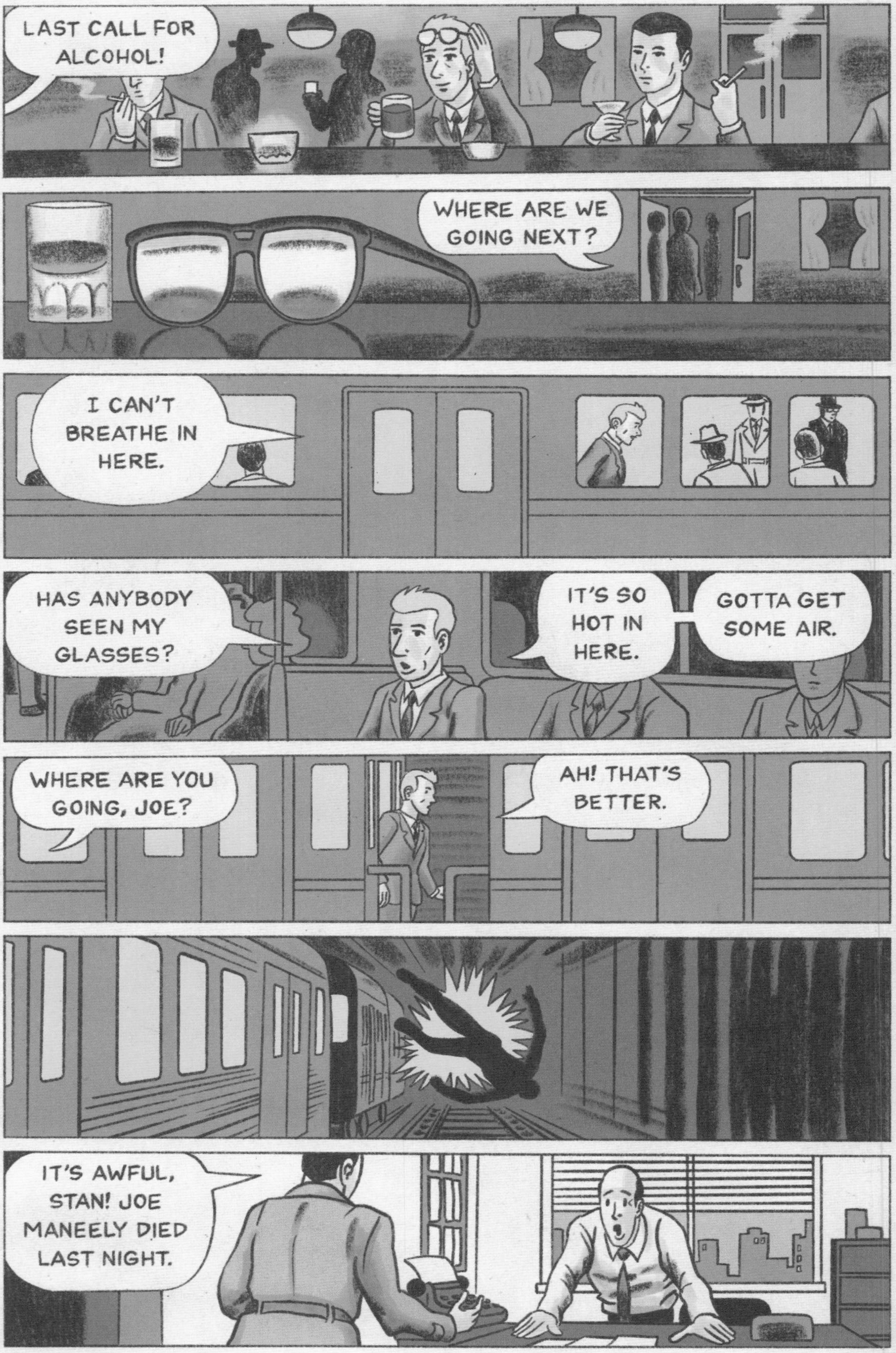
LAST CALL FOR ALCOHOL!
WHERE ARE WE GOING NEXT?
I CAN'T BREATHE IN HERE.
HAS ANYBODY SEEN MY GLASSES?
IT'S SO HOT IN HERE.
GOTTA GET SOME AIR.
WHERE ARE YOU GOING, JOE?
AH! THAT'S BETTER.
IT'S AWFUL, STAN! JOE MANEELY DIED LAST NIGHT.

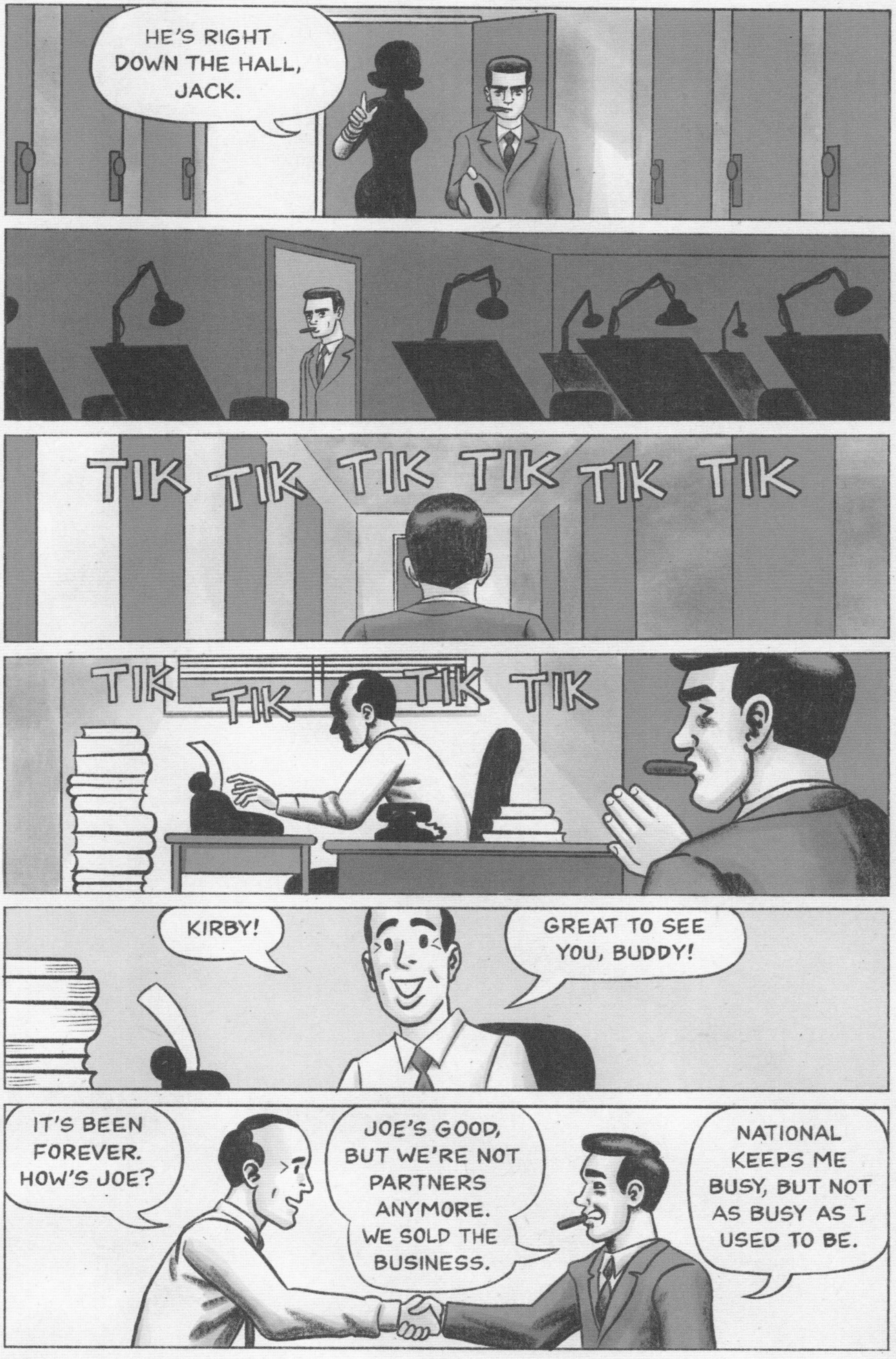
HE'S RIGHT DOWN THE HALL, JACK.
TIK TIK TIK TIK TIK TIK
TIK TIK TIK TIK
KIRBY!
GREAT TO SEE YOU, BUDDY!
IT'S BEEN FOREVER. HOW'S JOE?
JOE'S GOOD, BUT WE'RE NOT PARTNERS ANYMORE. WE SOLD THE BUSINESS.
NATIONAL KEEPS ME BUSY, BUT NOT AS BUSY AS I USED TO BE.

I'M SHUTTING DOWN ATLAS, OUR COMICS DISTRIBUTION COMPANY.

WHAT'S THE THINKING BEHIND THAT?

IT'S GOOD BUSINESS. DISTRIBUTION IS EXPENSIVE AND SUBJECT TO THE WHIMS OF NATURE AND ORGANIZED LABOR. I'LL SAVE A BUNDLE. WITH EVERYTHING GOING ON IN THE SENATE, LET SOMEBODY ELSE DEAL WITH THAT HEADACHE.

Caption: Our calendar is unchanging…predicated on the Earth's fixed orbit through space! Each day has its allotted number of hours. Each month has

STAN, MARTIN WANTS TO TALK TO YOU. IT'S URGENT.

BAD NEWS, STANLEY. THE DISTRIBUTION COMPANY WE JUST SIGNED WITH WENT BELLY-UP.

SO I GUESS WE'LL GO BACK TO DISTRIBUTING OURSELVES?

NO, THAT'S NOT AN OPTION ANYMORE. IT WOULD BE RUINOUS TO START AGAIN FROM THE GROUND UP.

SO HOW ARE WE GOING TO GET OUR BOOKS OUT?

 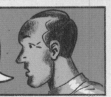

I SIGNED A DEAL WITH NATIONAL. THEY'RE GOING TO DISTRIBUTE OUR COMICS.

NATIONAL? DC COMICS? THEY'RE OUR BIGGEST COMPETITION.

IT DEFINITELY COMES WITH A PRICE.

THEY'RE ONLY LETTING US PUT OUT EIGHT BOOKS.

EIGHT BOOKS?! BUT WE'RE PUBLISHING 30 COMICS A MONTH!

YOU'RE GOING TO HAVE TO CUT 22 OF THEM.

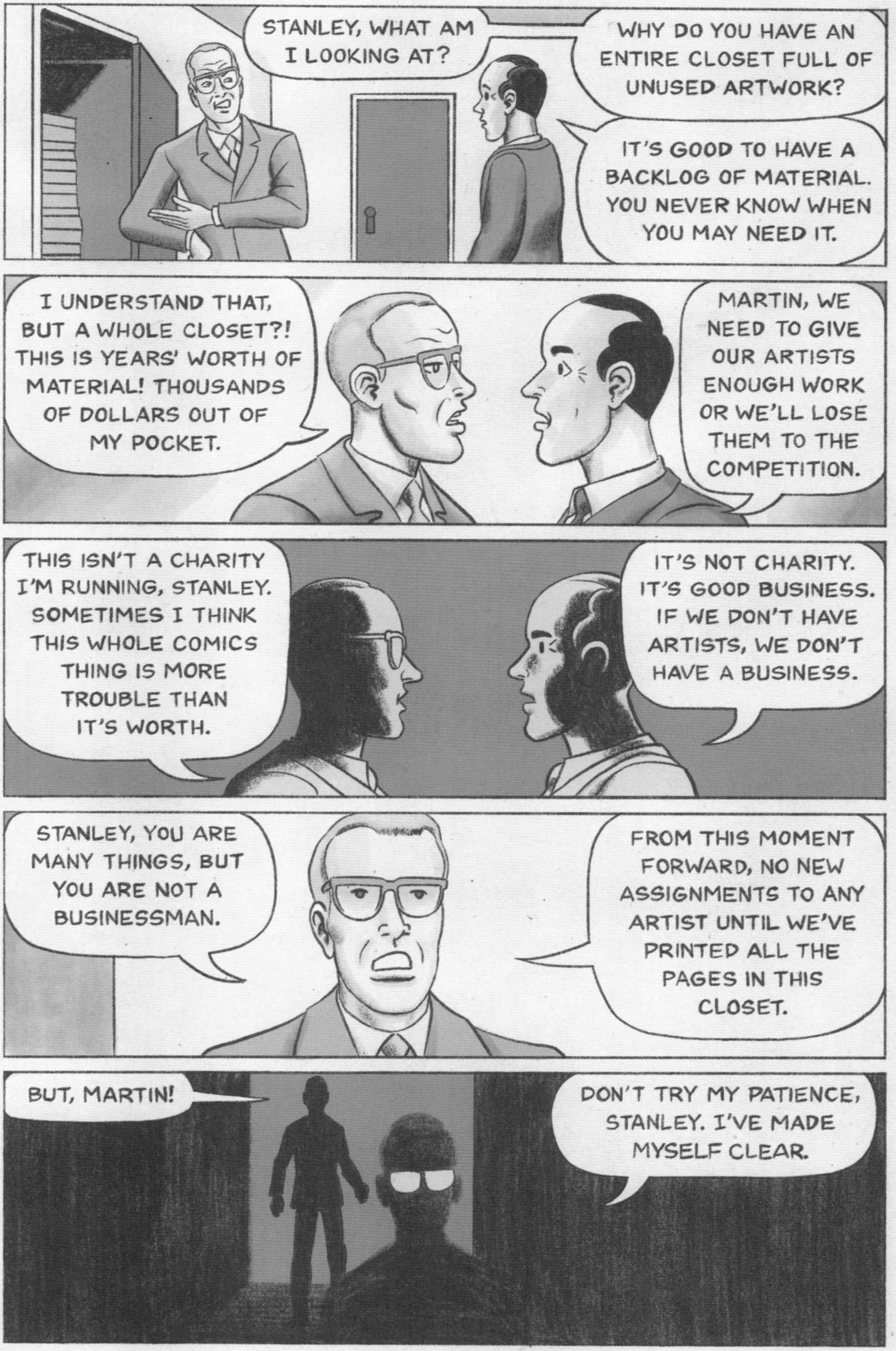
STANLEY, WHAT AM I LOOKING AT?
WHY DO YOU HAVE AN ENTIRE CLOSET FULL OF UNUSED ARTWORK?
IT'S GOOD TO HAVE A BACKLOG OF MATERIAL. YOU NEVER KNOW WHEN YOU MAY NEED IT.
I UNDERSTAND THAT, BUT A WHOLE CLOSET?! THIS IS YEARS' WORTH OF MATERIAL! THOUSANDS OF DOLLARS OUT OF MY POCKET.
MARTIN, WE NEED TO GIVE OUR ARTISTS ENOUGH WORK OR WE'LL LOSE THEM TO THE COMPETITION.
THIS ISN'T A CHARITY I'M RUNNING, STANLEY. SOMETIMES I THINK THIS WHOLE COMICS THING IS MORE TROUBLE THAN IT'S WORTH.
IT'S NOT CHARITY. IT'S GOOD BUSINESS. IF WE DON'T HAVE ARTISTS, WE DON'T HAVE A BUSINESS.
STANLEY, YOU ARE MANY THINGS, BUT YOU ARE NOT A BUSINESSMAN.
FROM THIS MOMENT FORWARD, NO NEW ASSIGNMENTS TO ANY ARTIST UNTIL WE'VE PRINTED ALL THE PAGES IN THIS CLOSET.
BUT, MARTIN!
DON'T TRY MY PATIENCE, STANLEY. I'VE MADE MYSELF CLEAR.

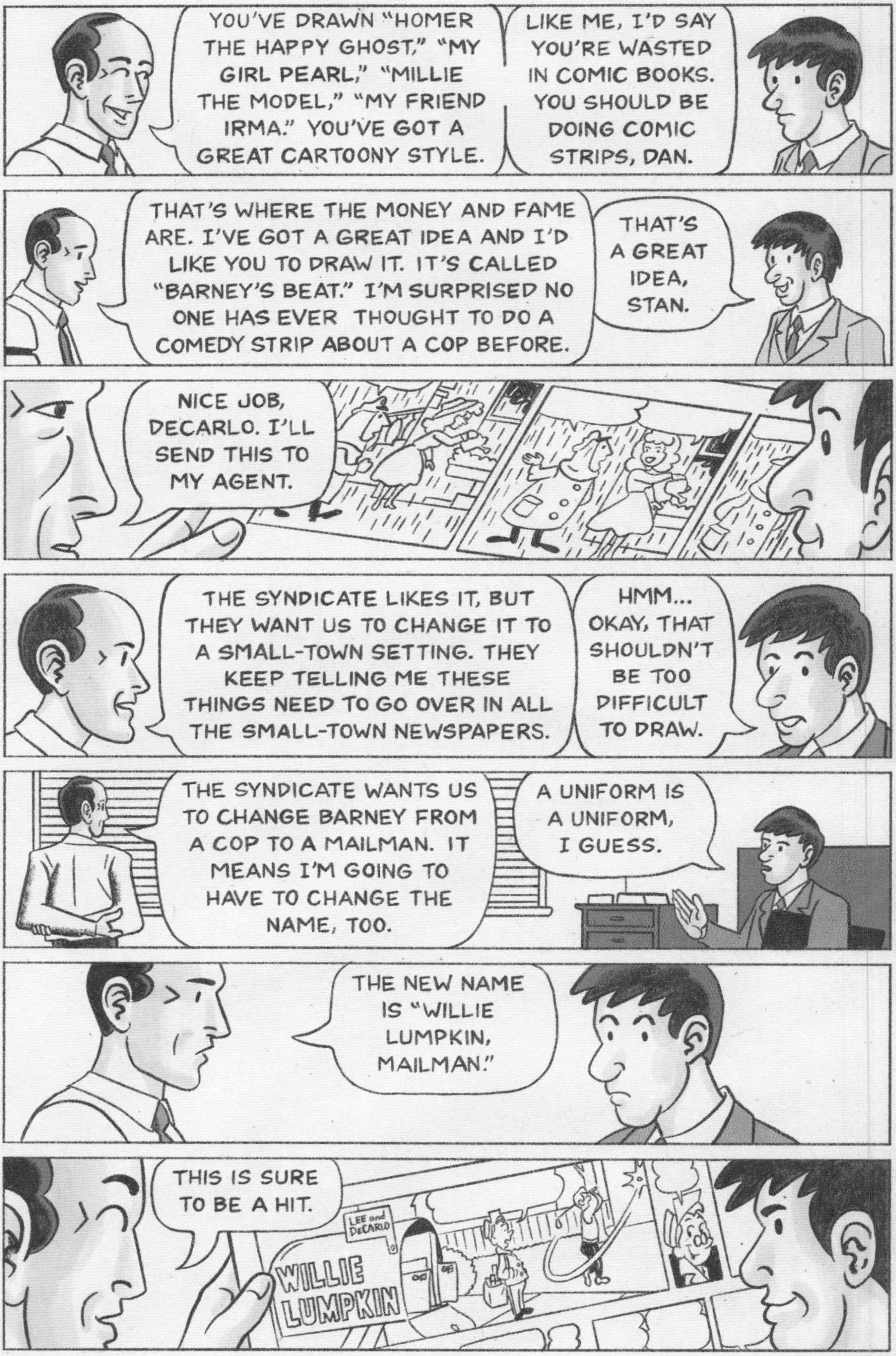
YOU'VE DRAWN "HOMER THE HAPPY GHOST," "MY GIRL PEARL," "MILLIE THE MODEL," "MY FRIEND IRMA." YOU'VE GOT A GREAT CARTOONY STYLE.
LIKE ME, I'D SAY YOU'RE WASTED IN COMIC BOOKS. YOU SHOULD BE DOING COMIC STRIPS, DAN.
THAT'S WHERE THE MONEY AND FAME ARE. I'VE GOT A GREAT IDEA AND I'D LIKE YOU TO DRAW IT. IT'S CALLED "BARNEY'S BEAT." I'M SURPRISED NO ONE HAS EVER THOUGHT TO DO A COMEDY STRIP ABOUT A COP BEFORE.
THAT'S A GREAT IDEA, STAN.
NICE JOB, DECARLO. I'LL SEND THIS TO MY AGENT.
THE SYNDICATE LIKES IT, BUT THEY WANT US TO CHANGE IT TO A SMALL-TOWN SETTING. THEY KEEP TELLING ME THESE THINGS NEED TO GO OVER IN ALL THE SMALL-TOWN NEWSPAPERS.
HMM... OKAY, THAT SHOULDN'T BE TOO DIFFICULT TO DRAW.
THE SYNDICATE WANTS US TO CHANGE BARNEY FROM A COP TO A MAILMAN. IT MEANS I'M GOING TO HAVE TO CHANGE THE NAME, TOO.
A UNIFORM IS A UNIFORM, I GUESS.
THE NEW NAME IS "WILLIE LUMPKIN, MAILMAN."
THIS IS SURE TO BE A HIT.
LEE and DECARLO
WILLIE LUMPKIN

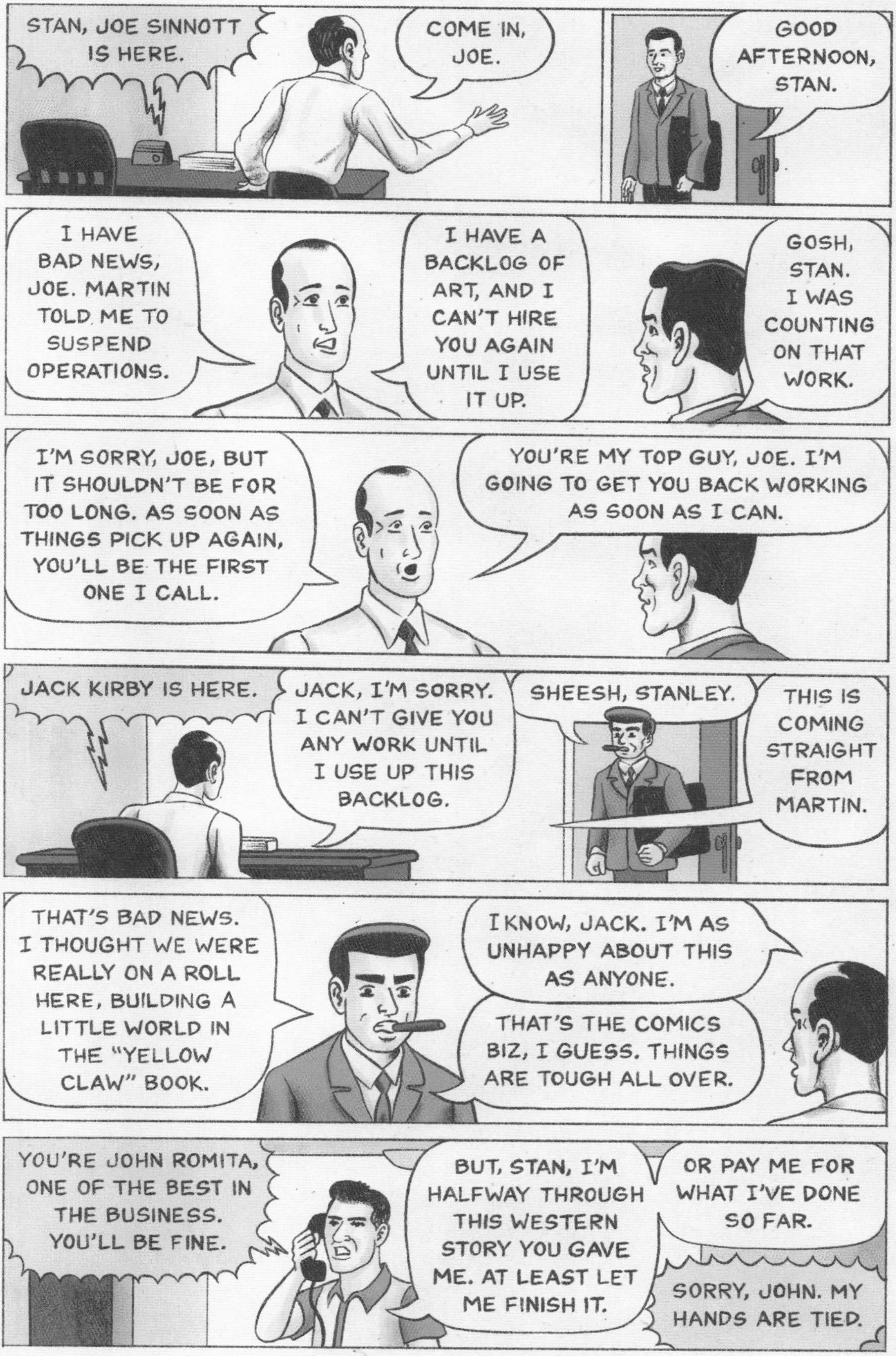

STAN, JOE SINNOTT IS HERE.
COME IN, JOE.
GOOD AFTERNOON, STAN.
I HAVE BAD NEWS, JOE. MARTIN TOLD ME TO SUSPEND OPERATIONS.
I HAVE A BACKLOG OF ART, AND I CAN'T HIRE YOU AGAIN UNTIL I USE IT UP.
GOSH, STAN. I WAS COUNTING ON THAT WORK.
I'M SORRY, JOE, BUT IT SHOULDN'T BE FOR TOO LONG. AS SOON AS THINGS PICK UP AGAIN, YOU'LL BE THE FIRST ONE I CALL.
YOU'RE MY TOP GUY, JOE. I'M GOING TO GET YOU BACK WORKING AS SOON AS I CAN.
JACK KIRBY IS HERE.
JACK, I'M SORRY. I CAN'T GIVE YOU ANY WORK UNTIL I USE UP THIS BACKLOG.
SHEESH, STANLEY.
THIS IS COMING STRAIGHT FROM MARTIN.
THAT'S BAD NEWS. I THOUGHT WE WERE REALLY ON A ROLL HERE, BUILDING A LITTLE WORLD IN THE "YELLOW CLAW" BOOK.
I KNOW, JACK. I'M AS UNHAPPY ABOUT THIS AS ANYONE.
THAT'S THE COMICS BIZ, I GUESS. THINGS ARE TOUGH ALL OVER.
YOU'RE JOHN ROMITA, ONE OF THE BEST IN THE BUSINESS. YOU'LL BE FINE.
BUT, STAN, I'M HALFWAY THROUGH THIS WESTERN STORY YOU GAVE ME. AT LEAST LET ME FINISH IT.
OR PAY ME FOR WHAT I'VE DONE SO FAR.
SORRY, JOHN. MY HANDS ARE TIED.

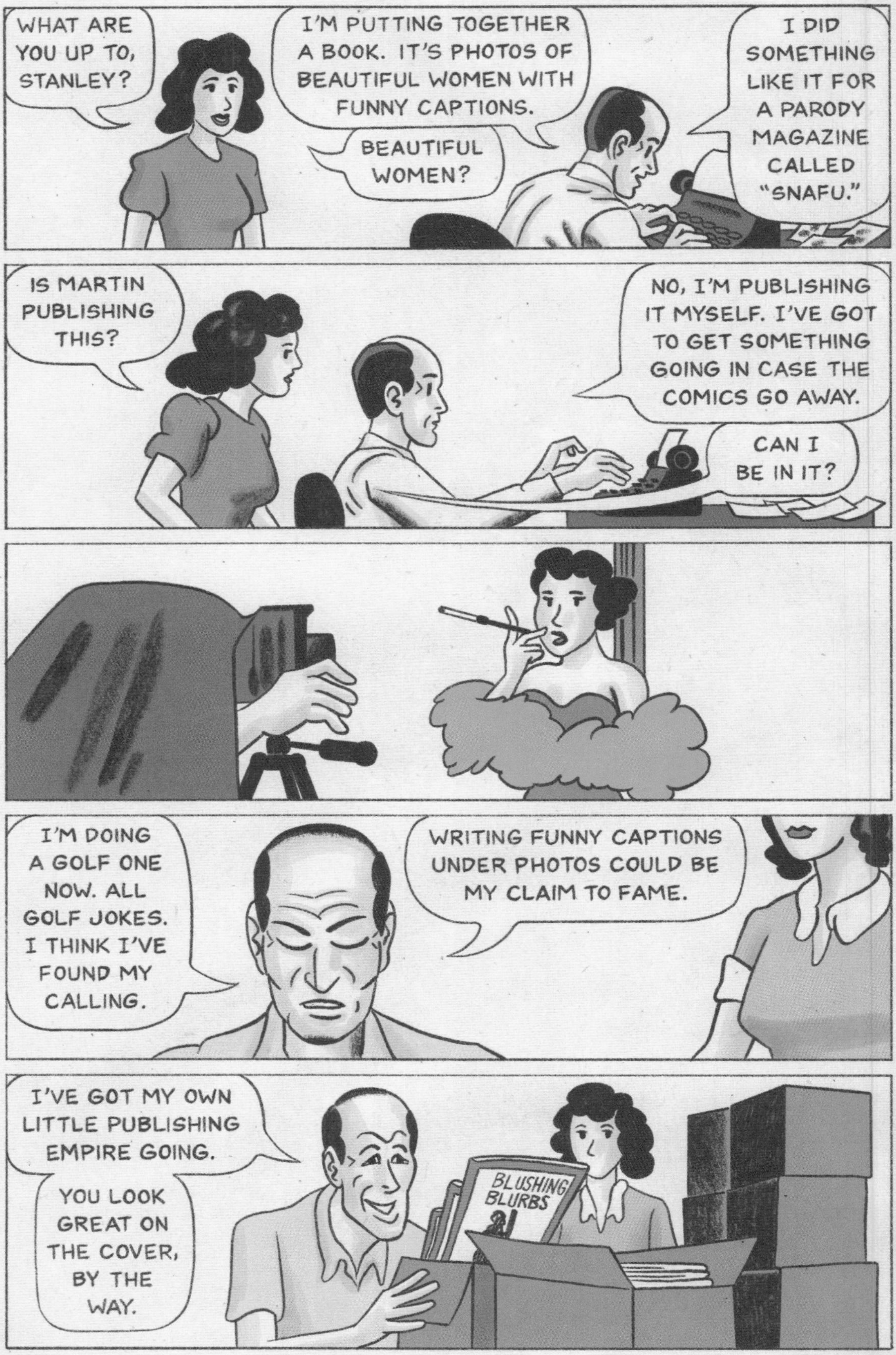
WHAT ARE YOU UP TO, STANLEY?
I'M PUTTING TOGETHER A BOOK. IT'S PHOTOS OF BEAUTIFUL WOMEN WITH FUNNY CAPTIONS.
BEAUTIFUL WOMEN?
I DID SOMETHING LIKE IT FOR A PARODY MAGAZINE CALLED "SNAFU."
IS MARTIN PUBLISHING THIS?
NO, I'M PUBLISHING IT MYSELF. I'VE GOT TO GET SOMETHING GOING IN CASE THE COMICS GO AWAY.
CAN I BE IN IT?
I'M DOING A GOLF ONE NOW. ALL GOLF JOKES. I THINK I'VE FOUND MY CALLING.
WRITING FUNNY CAPTIONS UNDER PHOTOS COULD BE MY CLAIM TO FAME.
I'VE GOT MY OWN LITTLE PUBLISHING EMPIRE GOING.
YOU LOOK GREAT ON THE COVER, BY THE WAY.
BLUSHING BLURBS

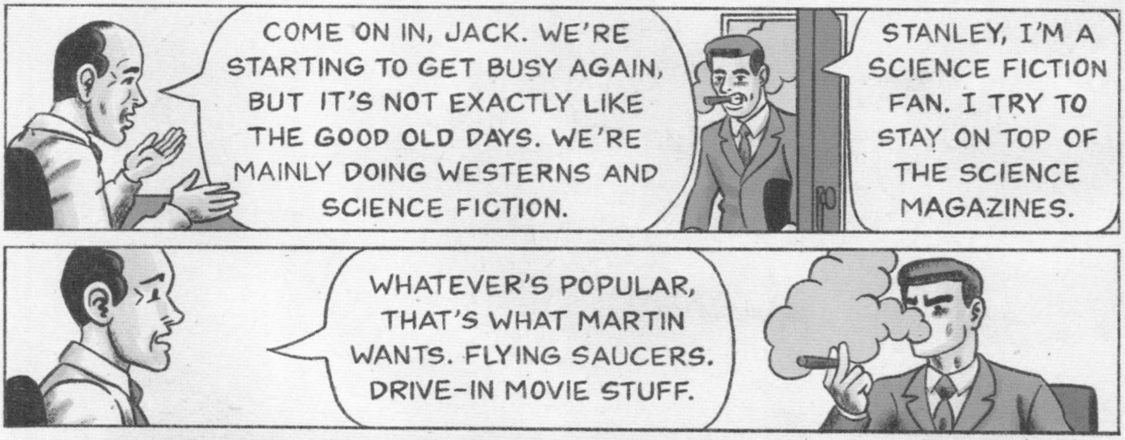
COME ON IN, JACK. WE'RE STARTING TO GET BUSY AGAIN, BUT IT'S NOT EXACTLY LIKE THE GOOD OLD DAYS. WE'RE MAINLY DOING WESTERNS AND SCIENCE FICTION.
STANLEY, I'M A SCIENCE FICTION FAN. I TRY TO STAY ON TOP OF THE SCIENCE MAGAZINES.
WHATEVER'S POPULAR, THAT'S WHAT MARTIN WANTS. FLYING SAUCERS. DRIVE-IN MOVIE STUFF.

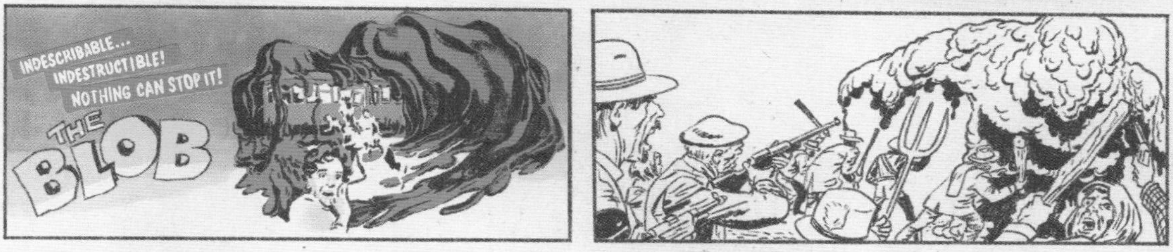
INDESCRIBABLE...
INDESTRUCTIBLE!
NOTHING CAN STOP IT!
THE BLOB

THE GLOP... My very life depended upon my learning its fantastic secret

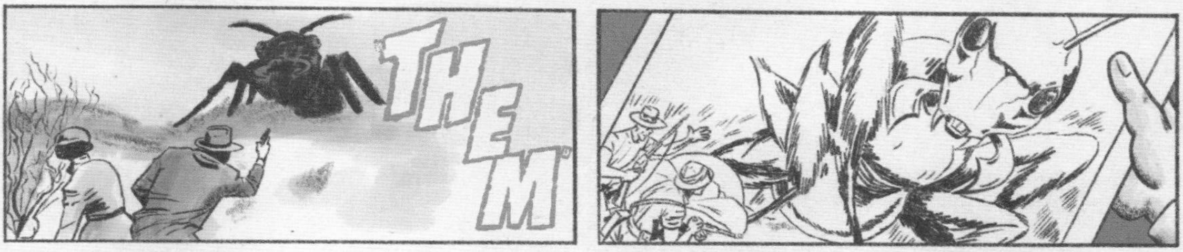
THEM

He was born of the Atomic Age...The menace known as GROTTU, King of the Insects

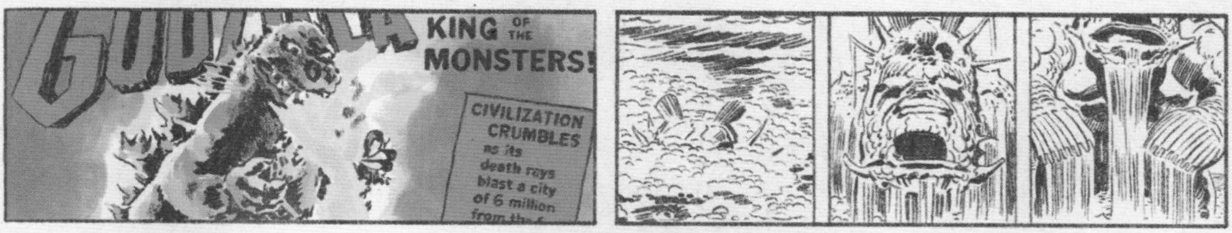
KING OF THE MONSTERS!
CIVILIZATION CRUMBLES as its death rays blast a city of 6 million

Whatever it is, it's rising out of the water! Holy cow!! Wha--What is it?? Run! Run!

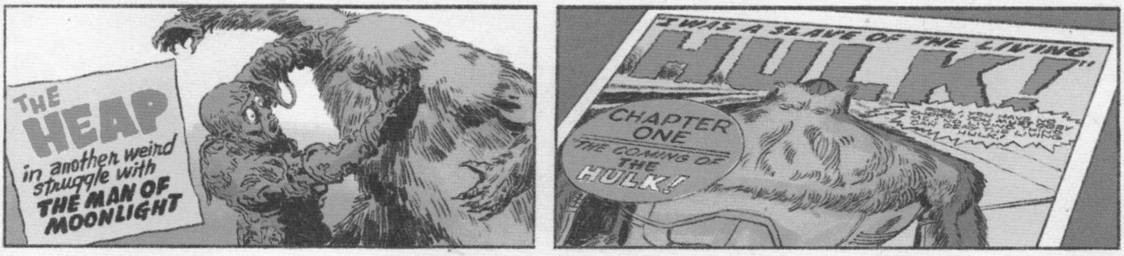
THE HEAP
in another weird struggle with
THE MAN OF MOONLIGHT
"I WAS A SLAVE OF THE LIVING HULK!"
CHAPTER ONE
THE COMING OF THE HULK!

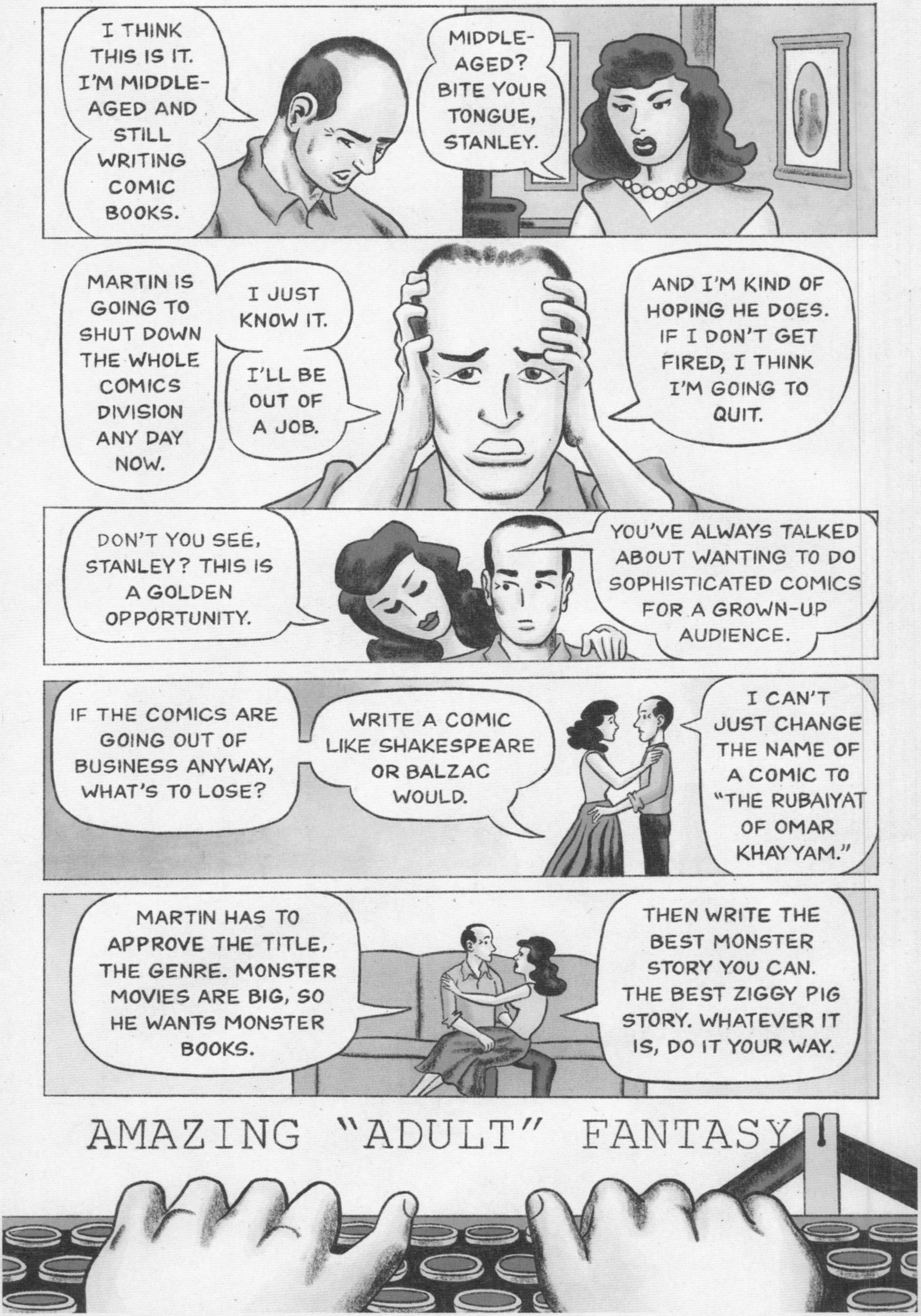
I THINK THIS IS IT. I'M MIDDLE-AGED AND STILL WRITING COMIC BOOKS.
MIDDLE-AGED? BITE YOUR TONGUE, STANLEY.
MARTIN IS GOING TO SHUT DOWN THE WHOLE COMICS DIVISION ANY DAY NOW.
I JUST KNOW IT.
I'LL BE OUT OF A JOB.
AND I'M KIND OF HOPING HE DOES. IF I DON'T GET FIRED, I THINK I'M GOING TO QUIT.
DON'T YOU SEE, STANLEY? THIS IS A GOLDEN OPPORTUNITY.
YOU'VE ALWAYS TALKED ABOUT WANTING TO DO SOPHISTICATED COMICS FOR A GROWN-UP AUDIENCE.
IF THE COMICS ARE GOING OUT OF BUSINESS ANYWAY, WHAT'S TO LOSE?
WRITE A COMIC LIKE SHAKESPEARE OR BALZAC WOULD.
I CAN'T JUST CHANGE THE NAME OF A COMIC TO "THE RUBAIYAT OF OMAR KHAYYAM."
MARTIN HAS TO APPROVE THE TITLE, THE GENRE. MONSTER MOVIES ARE BIG, SO HE WANTS MONSTER BOOKS.
THEN WRITE THE BEST MONSTER STORY YOU CAN. THE BEST ZIGGY PIG STORY. WHATEVER IT IS, DO IT YOUR WAY.
AMAZING "ADULT" FANTASY

 STANLEY, I HEARD THAT NATIONAL IS HAVING SUCCESS WITH THEIR "JUSTICE LEAGUE OF AMERICA." GIVE ME SOMETHING LIKE THAT, ALL THE SUPER CHARACTERS IN ONE BOOK.

LIKE A NEW ALL-WINNERS SQUAD?

SOMETHING LIKE THAT BUT WITH A DIFFERENT NAME.

JACK, YOU'LL BE THRILLED WITH THIS. MARTIN WANTS A NEW SUPERHERO TEAM.

IT'S ABOUT TIME. I'VE BEEN TELLING YOU THEY'RE DUE FOR A COMEBACK.

 WHAT ARE THEY DOING IN THERE, FLO?

THEY'RE HAVING A STORY CONFERENCE. THEY'RE PUTTING TOGETHER A NEW SUPERHERO BOOK.

MARTIN DOESN'T LIKE THE NAME "FABULOUS FOUR." HE'S VERY PARTICULAR ABOUT TITLES.

 COSMIC RAYS.

AN UNDERGROUND KINGDOM OF MONSTERS.

 SURVIVORS OF A ROCKET CRASH.

THIS IS GONNA BE GOOD.  CLACK CLACK CLACK

THE HEAVY IS ACTUALLY PART OF THE TEAM.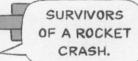

```
1) REED RICHARDS. (Mr. Fantastic) He is young, handsome
              scientist. Leader of the four. Invents a
              space ship to go to Mars. Hopes to be
              first man to reach Mars.
2) SUSAN STORM. (Invisible Girl) She is Reed's girl friend.
              She's an actress. Beautiful, glamorous.
3) BEN GRIMM. (The Thing) Ben is very husky, brutish guy.
              He's a pilot. He falls for Susan also.
4) JOHNNY STORM. (Human Torch) He is Susan's kid brother.
              A teen-ager. 17 years old. High school
              star athlet
```

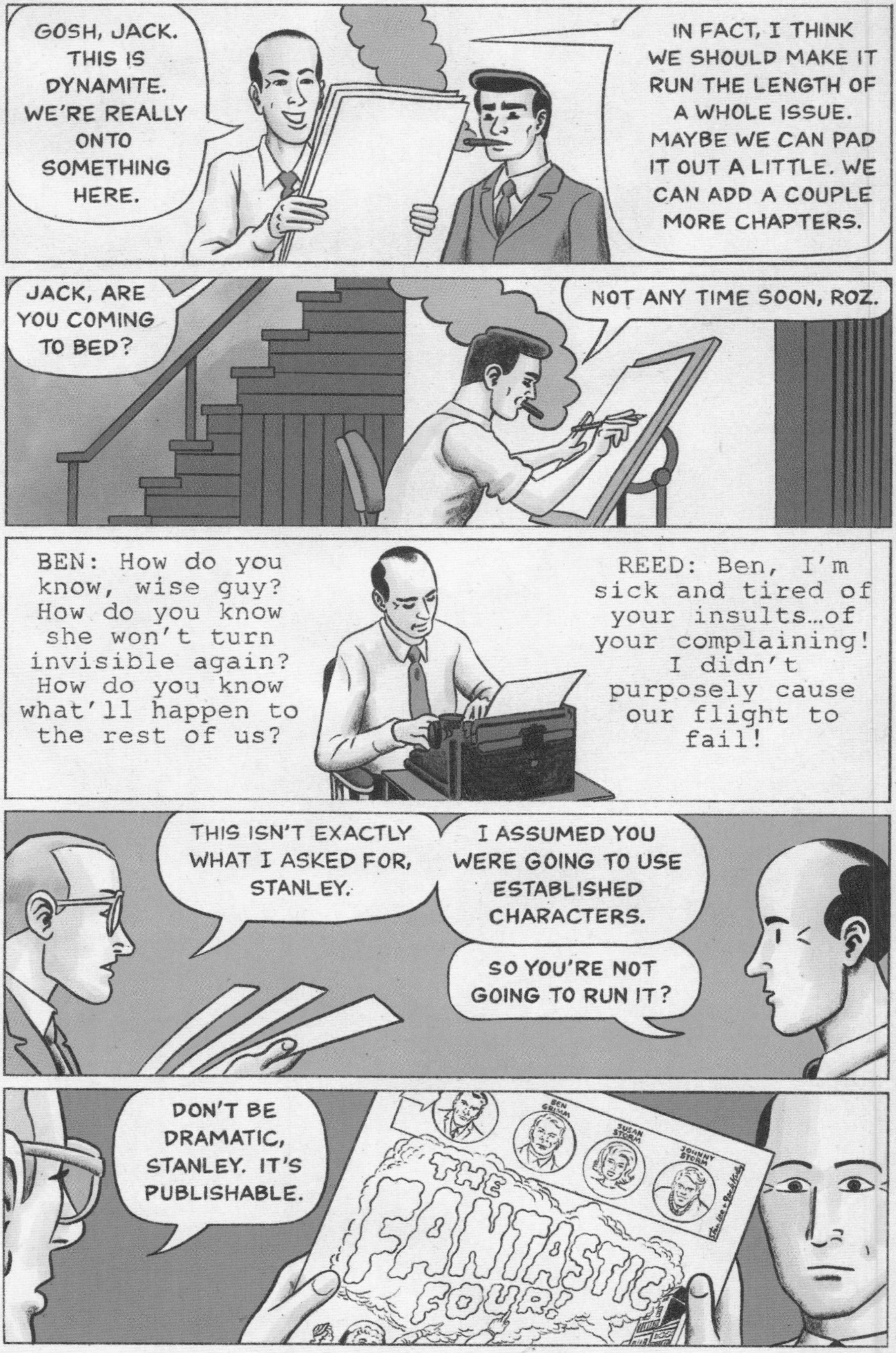
GOSH, JACK. THIS IS DYNAMITE. WE'RE REALLY ONTO SOMETHING HERE.
IN FACT, I THINK WE SHOULD MAKE IT RUN THE LENGTH OF A WHOLE ISSUE. MAYBE WE CAN PAD IT OUT A LITTLE. WE CAN ADD A COUPLE MORE CHAPTERS.
JACK, ARE YOU COMING TO BED?
NOT ANY TIME SOON, ROZ.
BEN: How do you know, wise guy? How do you know she won't turn invisible again? How do you know what'll happen to the rest of us?
REED: Ben, I'm sick and tired of your insults...of your complaining! I didn't purposely cause our flight to fail!
THIS ISN'T EXACTLY WHAT I ASKED FOR, STANLEY.
I ASSUMED YOU WERE GOING TO USE ESTABLISHED CHARACTERS.
SO YOU'RE NOT GOING TO RUN IT?
DON'T BE DRAMATIC, STANLEY. IT'S PUBLISHABLE.
BEN GRIMM
SUSAN STORM
JOHNNY STORM
THE FANTASTIC FOUR!

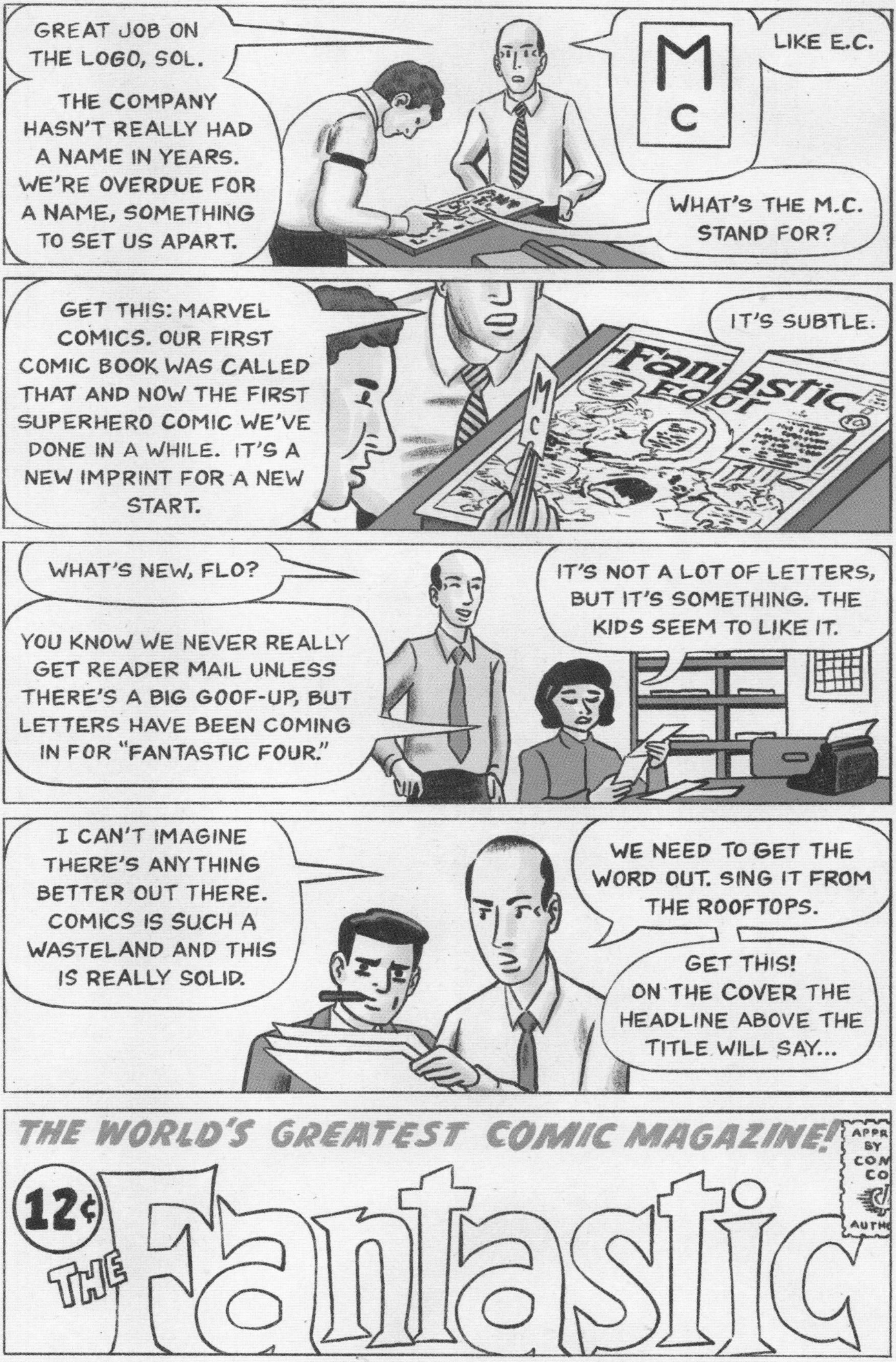
GREAT JOB ON THE LOGO, SOL.
THE COMPANY HASN'T REALLY HAD A NAME IN YEARS. WE'RE OVERDUE FOR A NAME, SOMETHING TO SET US APART.
M C
LIKE E.C.
WHAT'S THE M.C. STAND FOR?
GET THIS: MARVEL COMICS. OUR FIRST COMIC BOOK WAS CALLED THAT AND NOW THE FIRST SUPERHERO COMIC WE'VE DONE IN A WHILE. IT'S A NEW IMPRINT FOR A NEW START.
IT'S SUBTLE.
Fantastic Four
WHAT'S NEW, FLO?
YOU KNOW WE NEVER REALLY GET READER MAIL UNLESS THERE'S A BIG GOOF-UP, BUT LETTERS HAVE BEEN COMING IN FOR "FANTASTIC FOUR."
IT'S NOT A LOT OF LETTERS, BUT IT'S SOMETHING. THE KIDS SEEM TO LIKE IT.
I CAN'T IMAGINE THERE'S ANYTHING BETTER OUT THERE. COMICS IS SUCH A WASTELAND AND THIS IS REALLY SOLID.
WE NEED TO GET THE WORD OUT. SING IT FROM THE ROOFTOPS.
GET THIS! ON THE COVER THE HEADLINE ABOVE THE TITLE WILL SAY...
THE WORLD'S GREATEST COMIC MAGAZINE!
12¢
THE Fantastic

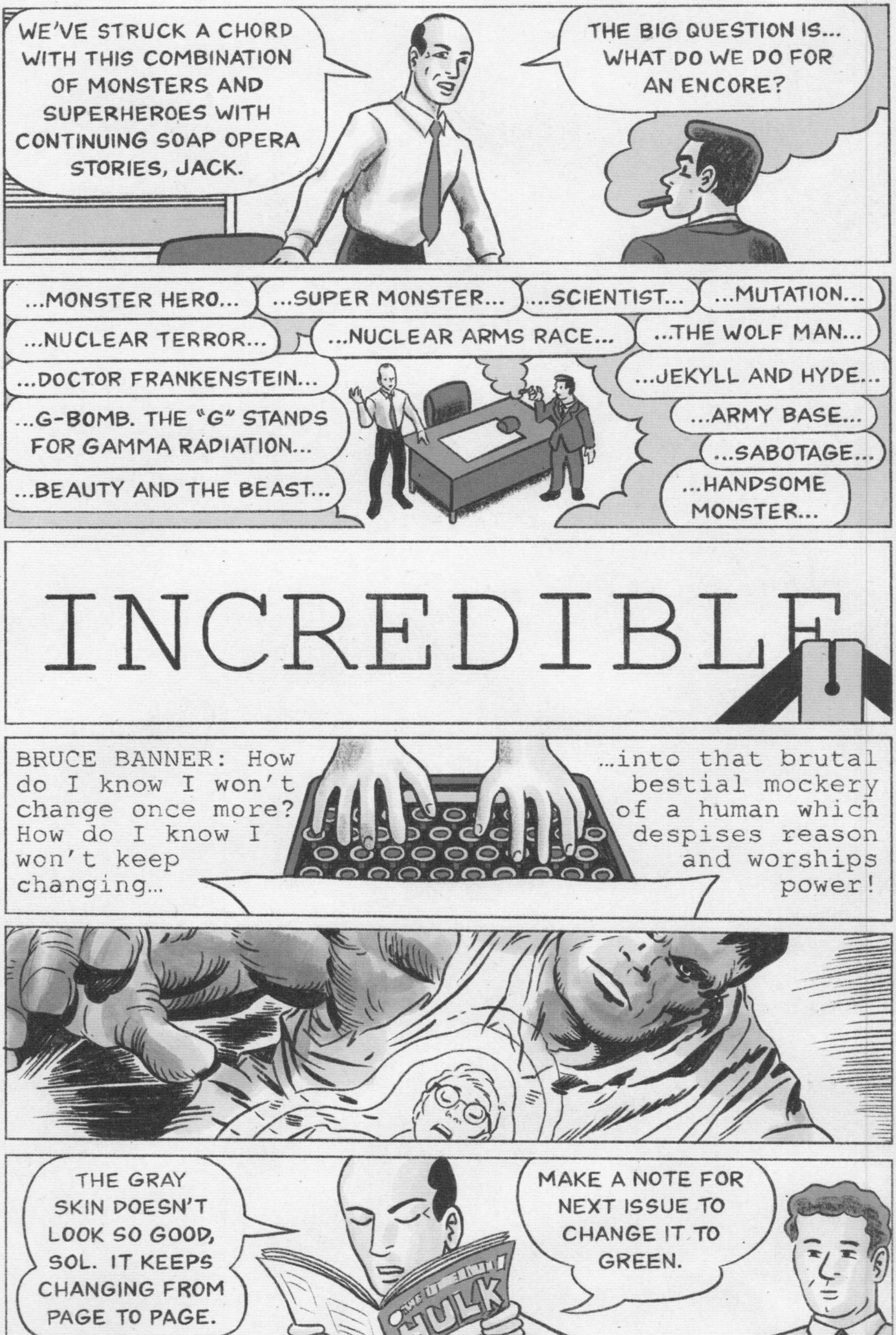
WE'VE STRUCK A CHORD WITH THIS COMBINATION OF MONSTERS AND SUPERHEROES WITH CONTINUING SOAP OPERA STORIES, JACK.
THE BIG QUESTION IS... WHAT DO WE DO FOR AN ENCORE?
...MONSTER HERO...
...SUPER MONSTER...
...SCIENTIST...
...MUTATION...
...NUCLEAR TERROR...
...NUCLEAR ARMS RACE...
...THE WOLF MAN...
...DOCTOR FRANKENSTEIN...
...JEKYLL AND HYDE...
...G-BOMB. THE "G" STANDS FOR GAMMA RADIATION...
...ARMY BASE...
...SABOTAGE...
...BEAUTY AND THE BEAST...
...HANDSOME MONSTER...
INCREDIBLE
BRUCE BANNER: How do I know I won't change once more? How do I know I won't keep changing...
...into that brutal bestial mockery of a human which despises reason and worships power!
THE GRAY SKIN DOESN'T LOOK SO GOOD, SOL. IT KEEPS CHANGING FROM PAGE TO PAGE.
MAKE A NOTE FOR NEXT ISSUE TO CHANGE IT TO GREEN.

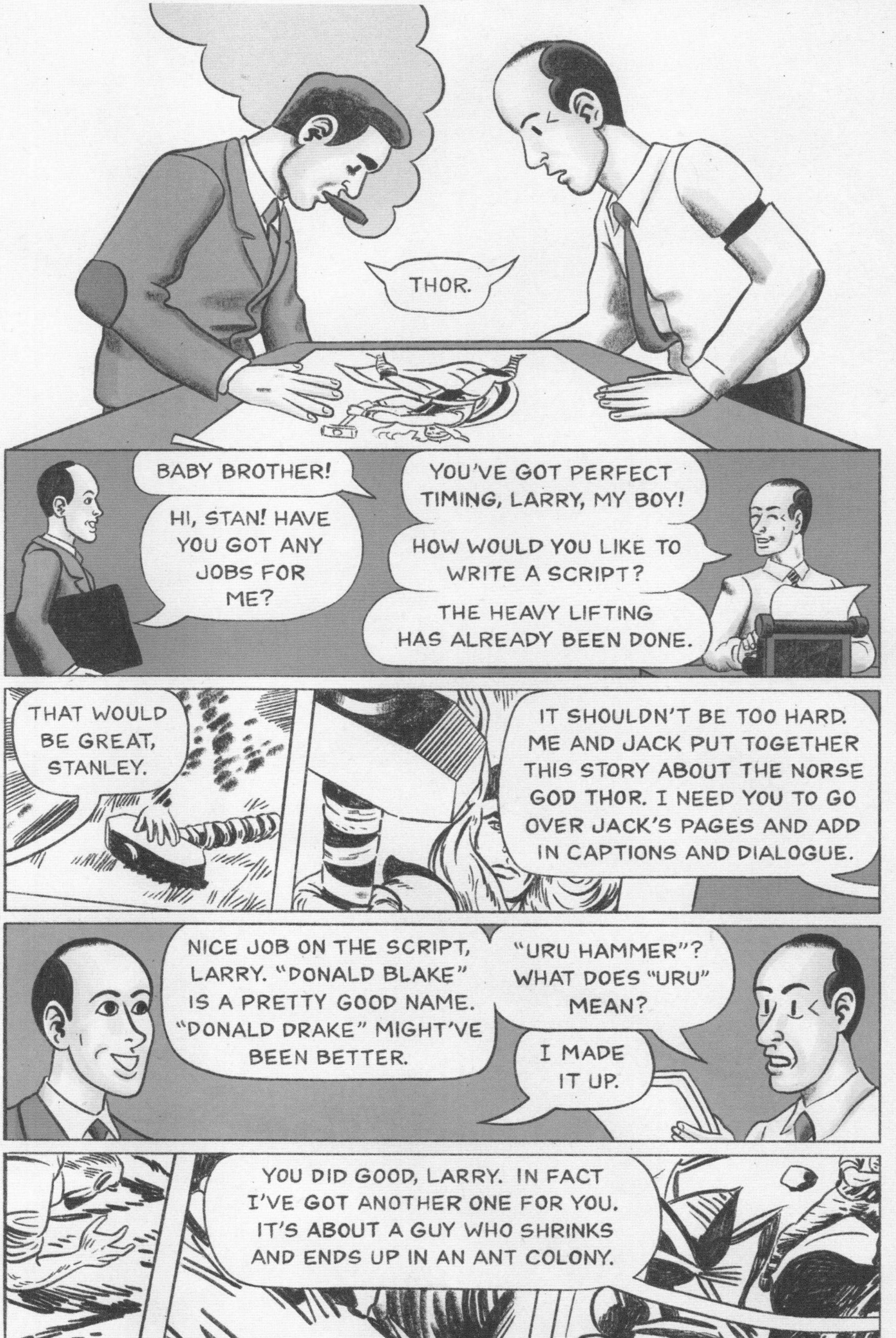
THOR.
BABY BROTHER!
HI, STAN! HAVE YOU GOT ANY JOBS FOR ME?
YOU'VE GOT PERFECT TIMING, LARRY, MY BOY!
HOW WOULD YOU LIKE TO WRITE A SCRIPT?
THE HEAVY LIFTING HAS ALREADY BEEN DONE.
THAT WOULD BE GREAT, STANLEY.
IT SHOULDN'T BE TOO HARD. ME AND JACK PUT TOGETHER THIS STORY ABOUT THE NORSE GOD THOR. I NEED YOU TO GO OVER JACK'S PAGES AND ADD IN CAPTIONS AND DIALOGUE.
NICE JOB ON THE SCRIPT, LARRY. "DONALD BLAKE" IS A PRETTY GOOD NAME. "DONALD DRAKE" MIGHT'VE BEEN BETTER.
"URU HAMMER"? WHAT DOES "URU" MEAN?
I MADE IT UP.
YOU DID GOOD, LARRY. IN FACT I'VE GOT ANOTHER ONE FOR YOU. IT'S ABOUT A GUY WHO SHRINKS AND ENDS UP IN AN ANT COLONY.

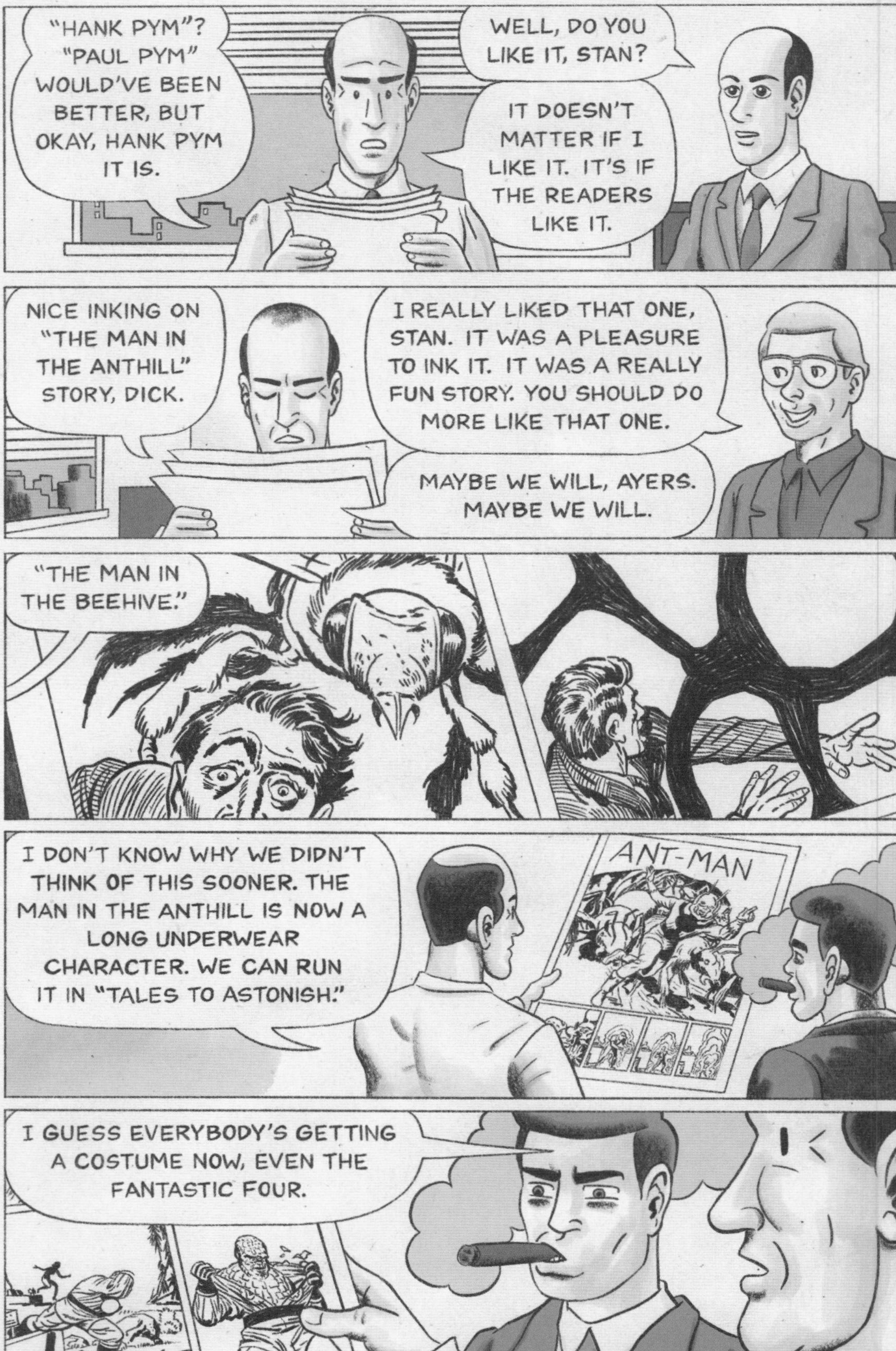
"HANK PYM"? "PAUL PYM" WOULD'VE BEEN BETTER, BUT OKAY, HANK PYM IT IS.
WELL, DO YOU LIKE IT, STAN?
IT DOESN'T MATTER IF I LIKE IT. IT'S IF THE READERS LIKE IT.
NICE INKING ON "THE MAN IN THE ANTHILL" STORY, DICK.
I REALLY LIKED THAT ONE, STAN. IT WAS A PLEASURE TO INK IT. IT WAS A REALLY FUN STORY. YOU SHOULD DO MORE LIKE THAT ONE.
MAYBE WE WILL, AYERS. MAYBE WE WILL.
"THE MAN IN THE BEEHIVE."
I DON'T KNOW WHY WE DIDN'T THINK OF THIS SOONER. THE MAN IN THE ANTHILL IS NOW A LONG UNDERWEAR CHARACTER. WE CAN RUN IT IN "TALES TO ASTONISH."
ANT-MAN
I GUESS EVERYBODY'S GETTING A COSTUME NOW, EVEN THE FANTASTIC FOUR.

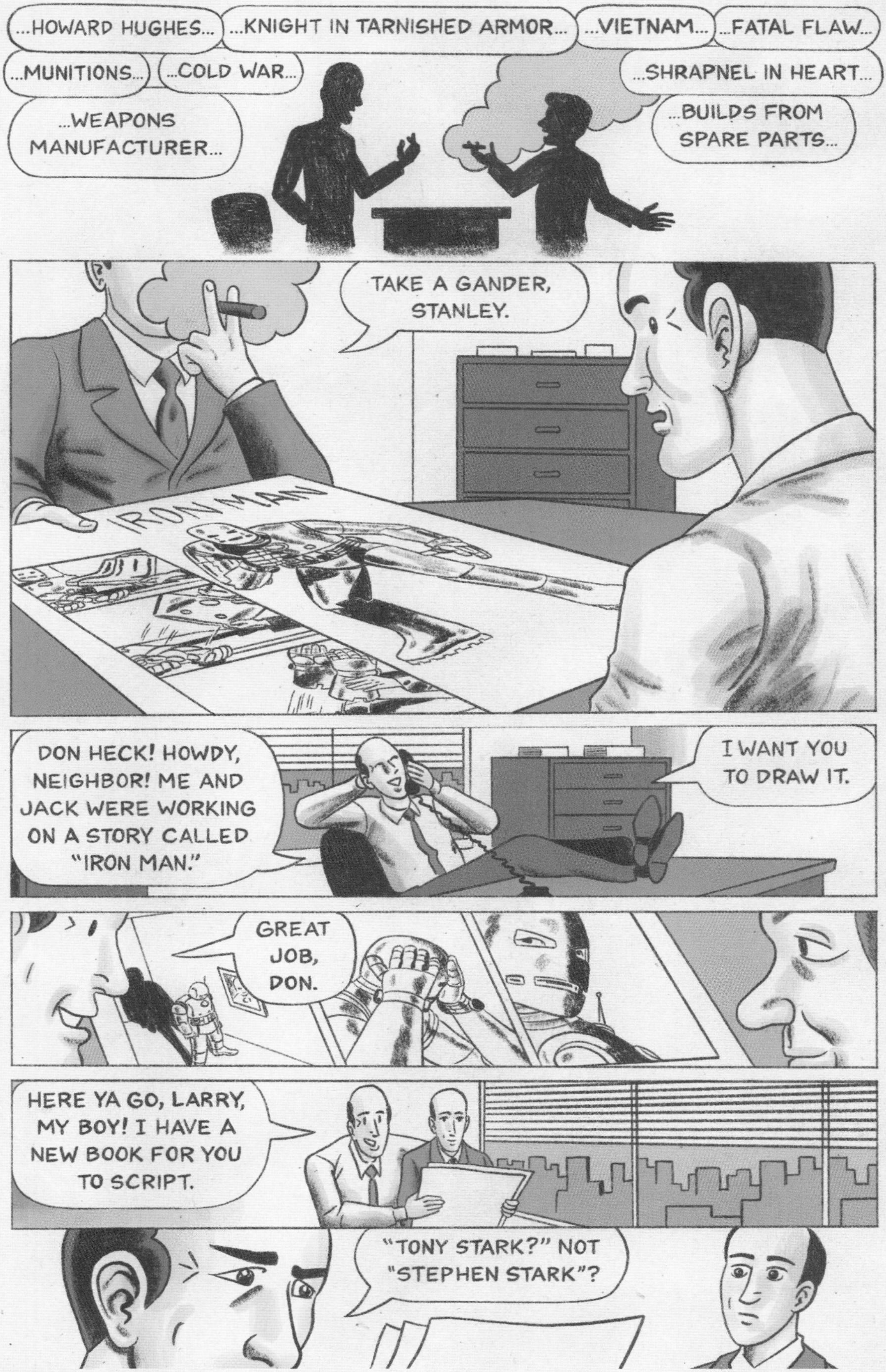

...HOWARD HUGHES...
...KNIGHT IN TARNISHED ARMOR...
...VIETNAM...
...FATAL FLAW...
...MUNITIONS...
...COLD WAR...
...SHRAPNEL IN HEART...
...WEAPONS MANUFACTURER...
...BUILDS FROM SPARE PARTS...
TAKE A GANDER, STANLEY.
IRON MAN
DON HECK! HOWDY, NEIGHBOR! ME AND JACK WERE WORKING ON A STORY CALLED "IRON MAN."
I WANT YOU TO DRAW IT.
GREAT JOB, DON.
HERE YA GO, LARRY, MY BOY! I HAVE A NEW BOOK FOR YOU TO SCRIPT.
"TONY STARK?" NOT "STEPHEN STARK"?

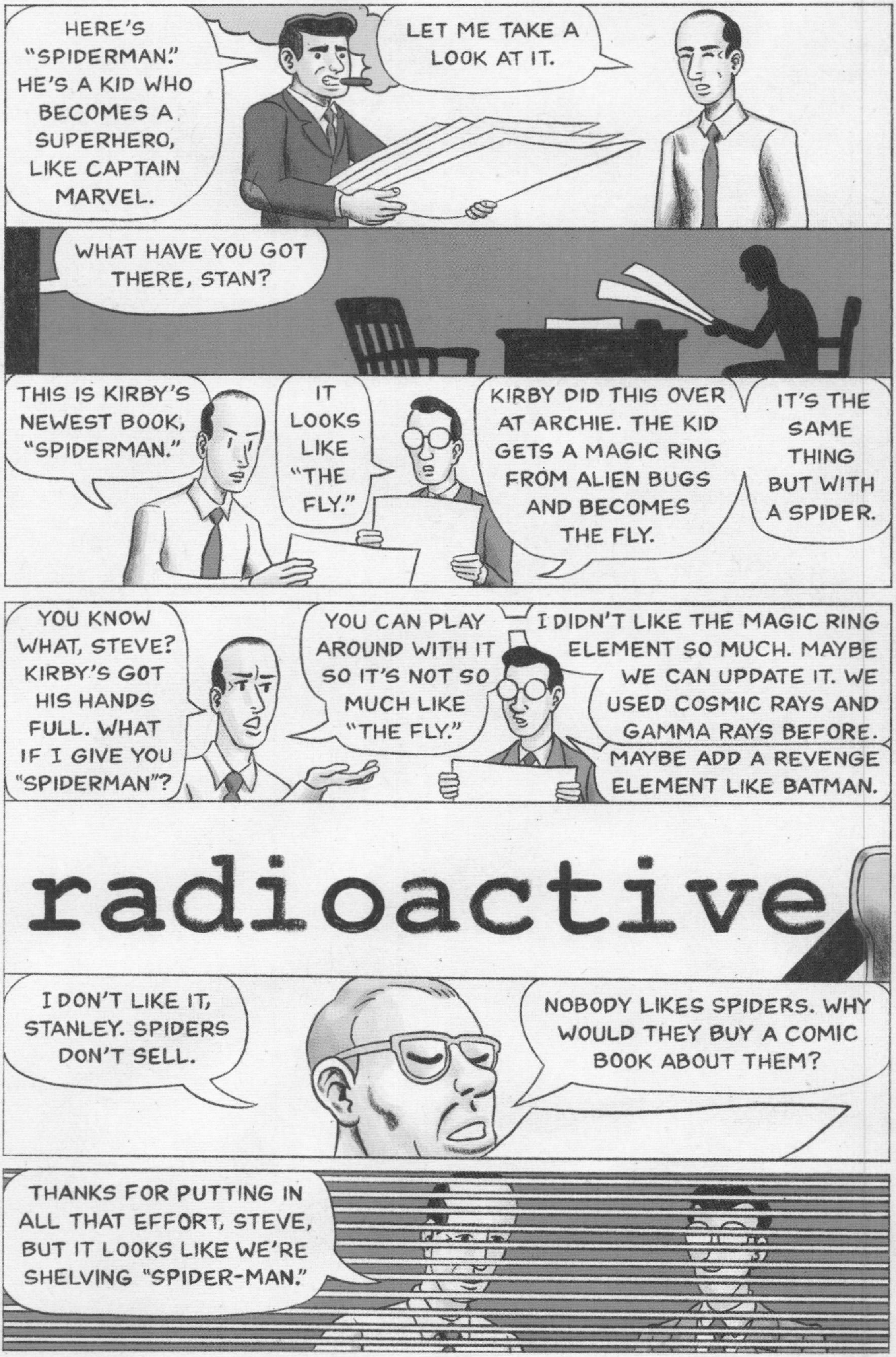
HERE'S "SPIDERMAN." HE'S A KID WHO BECOMES A SUPERHERO, LIKE CAPTAIN MARVEL.
LET ME TAKE A LOOK AT IT.
WHAT HAVE YOU GOT THERE, STAN?
THIS IS KIRBY'S NEWEST BOOK, "SPIDERMAN."
IT LOOKS LIKE "THE FLY."
KIRBY DID THIS OVER AT ARCHIE. THE KID GETS A MAGIC RING FROM ALIEN BUGS AND BECOMES THE FLY.
IT'S THE SAME THING BUT WITH A SPIDER.
YOU KNOW WHAT, STEVE? KIRBY'S GOT HIS HANDS FULL. WHAT IF I GIVE YOU "SPIDERMAN"?
YOU CAN PLAY AROUND WITH IT SO IT'S NOT SO MUCH LIKE "THE FLY."
I DIDN'T LIKE THE MAGIC RING ELEMENT SO MUCH. MAYBE WE CAN UPDATE IT. WE USED COSMIC RAYS AND GAMMA RAYS BEFORE.
MAYBE ADD A REVENGE ELEMENT LIKE BATMAN.
radioactive
I DON'T LIKE IT, STANLEY. SPIDERS DON'T SELL.
NOBODY LIKES SPIDERS. WHY WOULD THEY BUY A COMIC BOOK ABOUT THEM?
THANKS FOR PUTTING IN ALL THAT EFFORT, STEVE, BUT IT LOOKS LIKE WE'RE SHELVING "SPIDER-MAN."

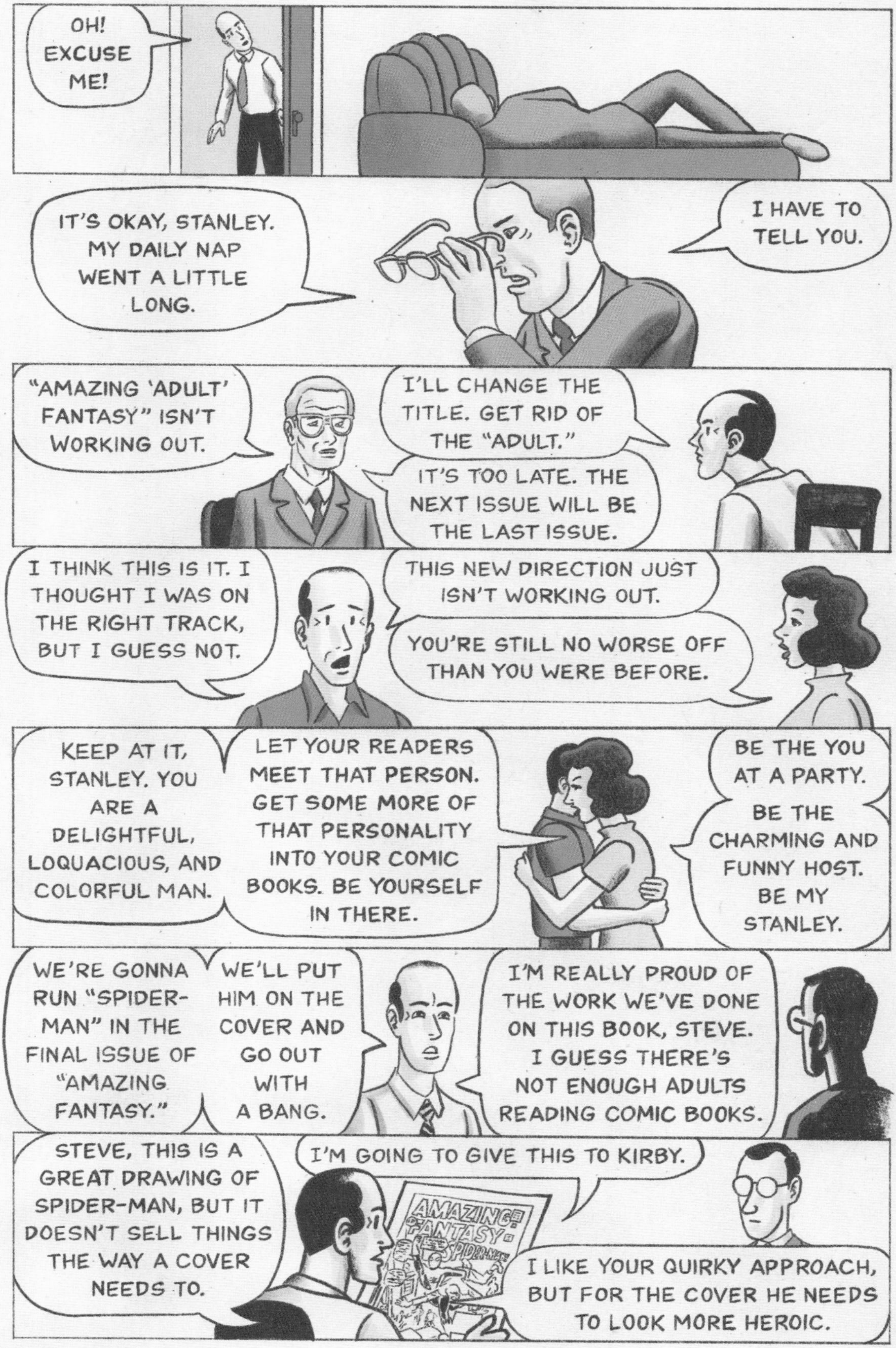
OH! EXCUSE ME!
IT'S OKAY, STANLEY. MY DAILY NAP WENT A LITTLE LONG.
I HAVE TO TELL YOU.
"AMAZING 'ADULT' FANTASY" ISN'T WORKING OUT.
I'LL CHANGE THE TITLE. GET RID OF THE "ADULT."
IT'S TOO LATE. THE NEXT ISSUE WILL BE THE LAST ISSUE.
I THINK THIS IS IT. I THOUGHT I WAS ON THE RIGHT TRACK, BUT I GUESS NOT.
THIS NEW DIRECTION JUST ISN'T WORKING OUT.
YOU'RE STILL NO WORSE OFF THAN YOU WERE BEFORE.
KEEP AT IT, STANLEY. YOU ARE A DELIGHTFUL, LOQUACIOUS, AND COLORFUL MAN.
LET YOUR READERS MEET THAT PERSON. GET SOME MORE OF THAT PERSONALITY INTO YOUR COMIC BOOKS. BE YOURSELF IN THERE.
BE THE YOU AT A PARTY.
BE THE CHARMING AND FUNNY HOST. BE MY STANLEY.
WE'RE GONNA RUN "SPIDER-MAN" IN THE FINAL ISSUE OF "AMAZING FANTASY."
WE'LL PUT HIM ON THE COVER AND GO OUT WITH A BANG.
I'M REALLY PROUD OF THE WORK WE'VE DONE ON THIS BOOK, STEVE. I GUESS THERE'S NOT ENOUGH ADULTS READING COMIC BOOKS.
STEVE, THIS IS A GREAT DRAWING OF SPIDER-MAN, BUT IT DOESN'T SELL THINGS THE WAY A COVER NEEDS TO.
AMAZING FANTASY
SPIDER-MAN
I'M GOING TO GIVE THIS TO KIRBY.
I LIKE YOUR QUIRKY APPROACH, BUT FOR THE COVER HE NEEDS TO LOOK MORE HEROIC.

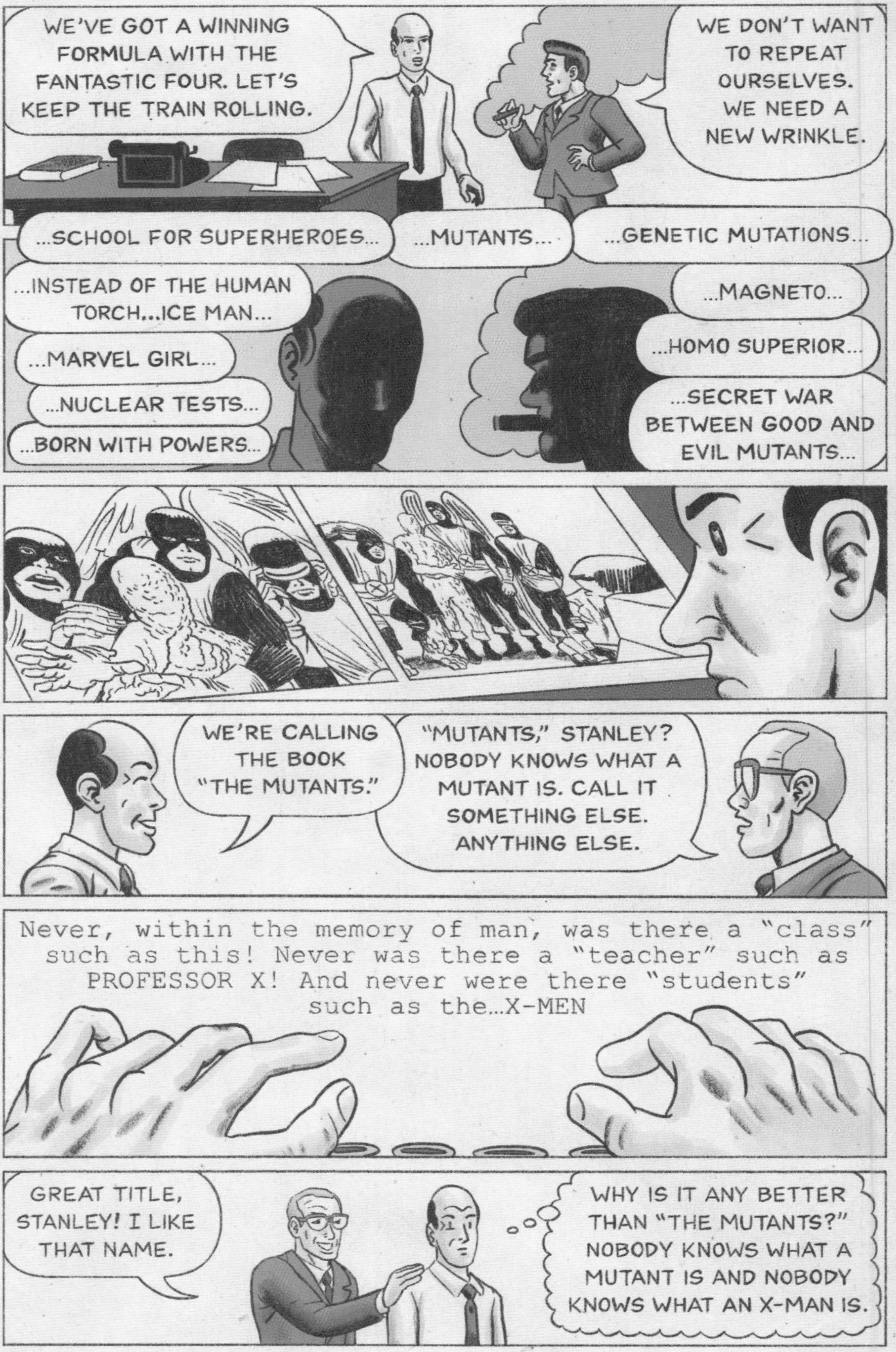

WE'VE GOT A WINNING FORMULA WITH THE FANTASTIC FOUR. LET'S KEEP THE TRAIN ROLLING.
WE DON'T WANT TO REPEAT OURSELVES. WE NEED A NEW WRINKLE.
...SCHOOL FOR SUPERHEROES...
...MUTANTS...
...GENETIC MUTATIONS...
...INSTEAD OF THE HUMAN TORCH...ICE MAN...
...MARVEL GIRL...
...NUCLEAR TESTS...
...BORN WITH POWERS...
...MAGNETO...
...HOMO SUPERIOR...
...SECRET WAR BETWEEN GOOD AND EVIL MUTANTS...
WE'RE CALLING THE BOOK "THE MUTANTS."
"MUTANTS," STANLEY? NOBODY KNOWS WHAT A MUTANT IS. CALL IT SOMETHING ELSE. ANYTHING ELSE.
Never, within the memory of man, was there a "class" such as this! Never was there a "teacher" such as PROFESSOR X! And never were there "students" such as the...X-MEN
GREAT TITLE, STANLEY! I LIKE THAT NAME.
WHY IS IT ANY BETTER THAN "THE MUTANTS?" NOBODY KNOWS WHAT A MUTANT IS AND NOBODY KNOWS WHAT AN X-MAN IS.

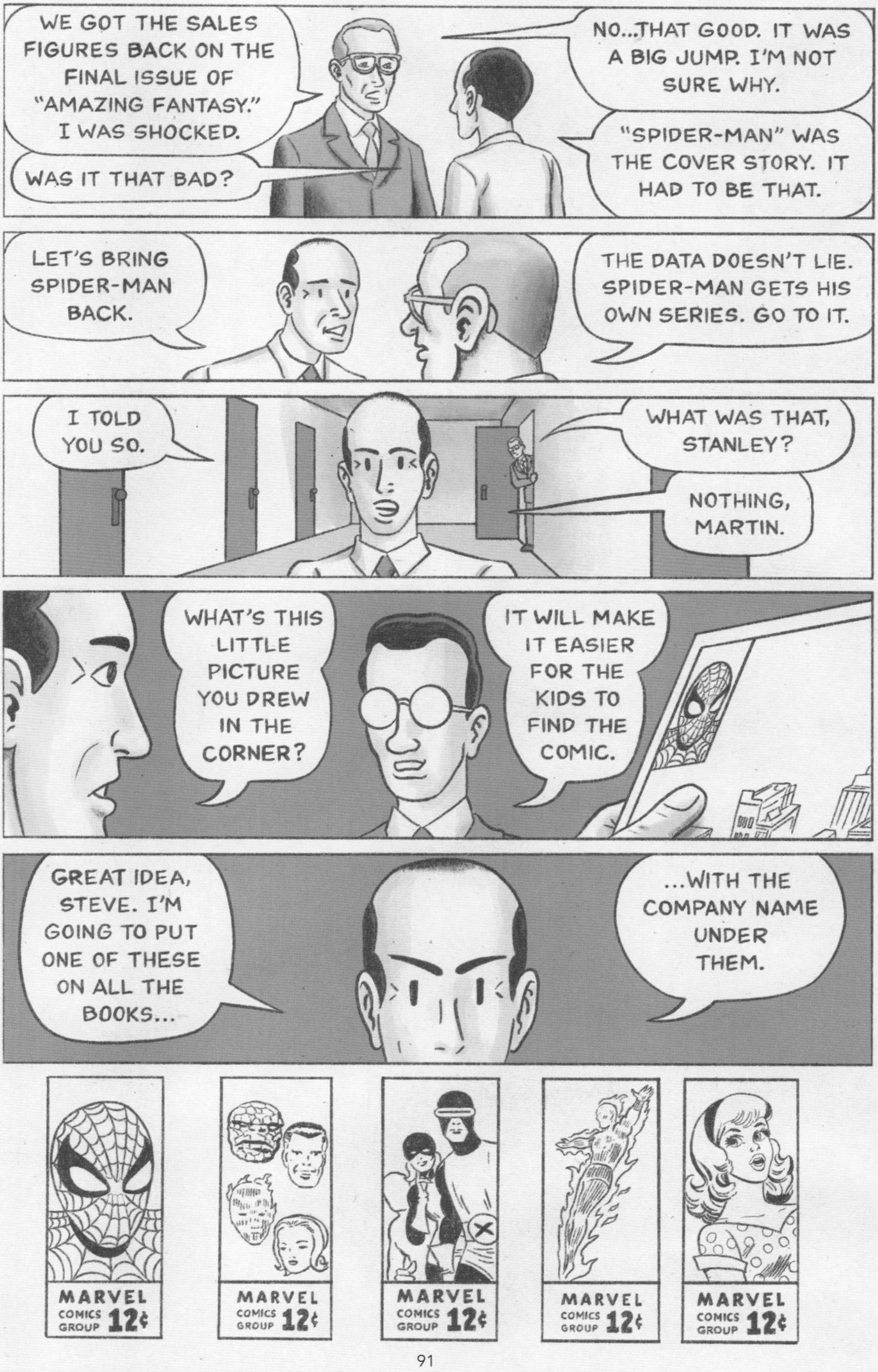
WE GOT THE SALES FIGURES BACK ON THE FINAL ISSUE OF "AMAZING FANTASY." I WAS SHOCKED.
WAS IT THAT BAD?
NO...THAT GOOD. IT WAS A BIG JUMP. I'M NOT SURE WHY.
"SPIDER-MAN" WAS THE COVER STORY. IT HAD TO BE THAT.
LET'S BRING SPIDER-MAN BACK.
THE DATA DOESN'T LIE. SPIDER-MAN GETS HIS OWN SERIES. GO TO IT.
I TOLD YOU SO.
WHAT WAS THAT, STANLEY?
NOTHING, MARTIN.
WHAT'S THIS LITTLE PICTURE YOU DREW IN THE CORNER?
IT WILL MAKE IT EASIER FOR THE KIDS TO FIND THE COMIC.
GREAT IDEA, STEVE. I'M GOING TO PUT ONE OF THESE ON ALL THE BOOKS...
...WITH THE COMPANY NAME UNDER THEM.
MARVEL COMICS GROUP 12¢
MARVEL COMICS GROUP 12¢
MARVEL COMICS GROUP 12¢
MARVEL COMICS GROUP 12¢
MARVEL COMICS GROUP 12¢

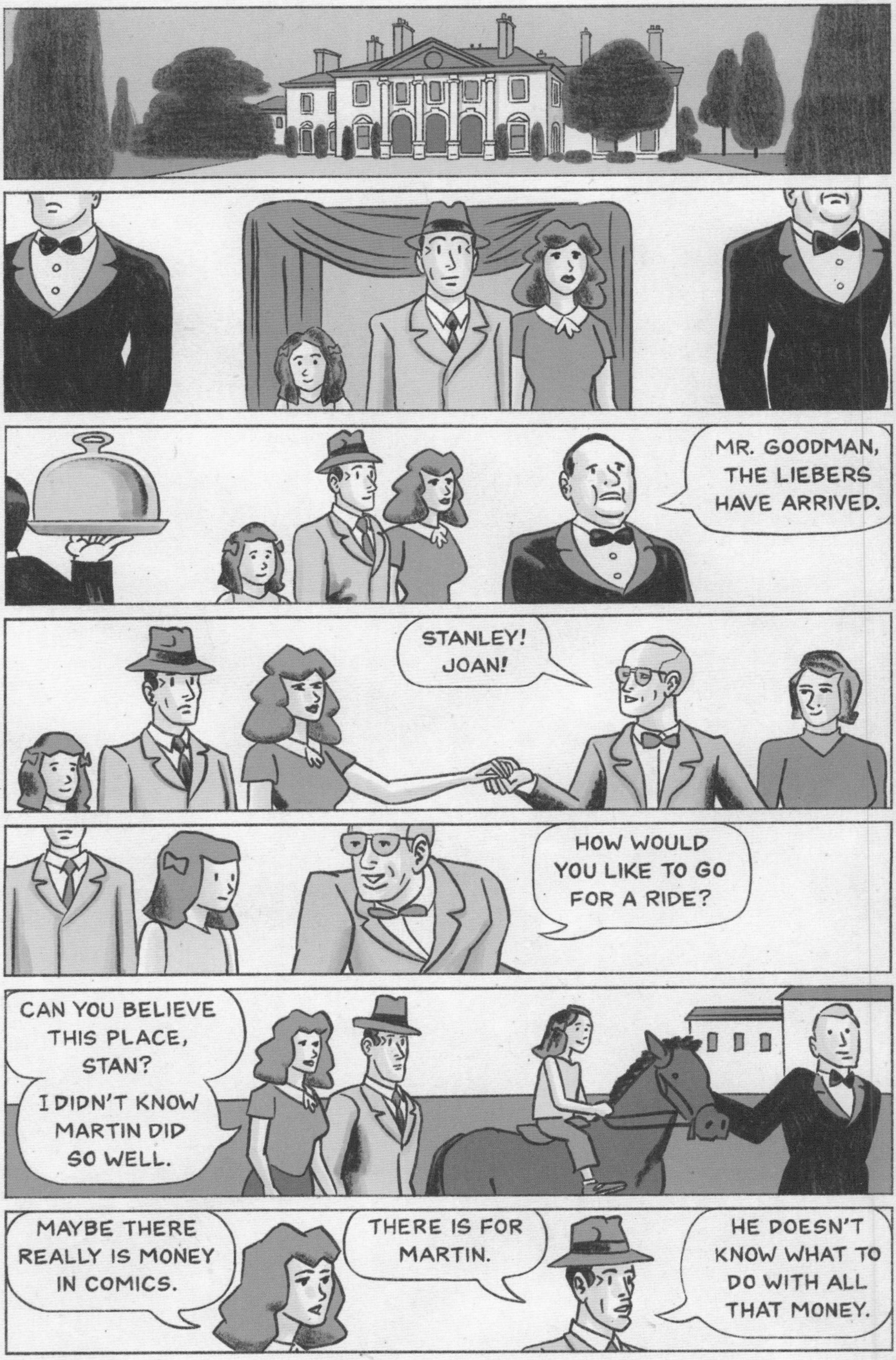
MR. GOODMAN, THE LIEBERS HAVE ARRIVED.
STANLEY! JOAN!
HOW WOULD YOU LIKE TO GO FOR A RIDE?
CAN YOU BELIEVE THIS PLACE, STAN?
I DIDN'T KNOW MARTIN DID SO WELL.
MAYBE THERE REALLY IS MONEY IN COMICS.
THERE IS FOR MARTIN.
HE DOESN'T KNOW WHAT TO DO WITH ALL THAT MONEY.

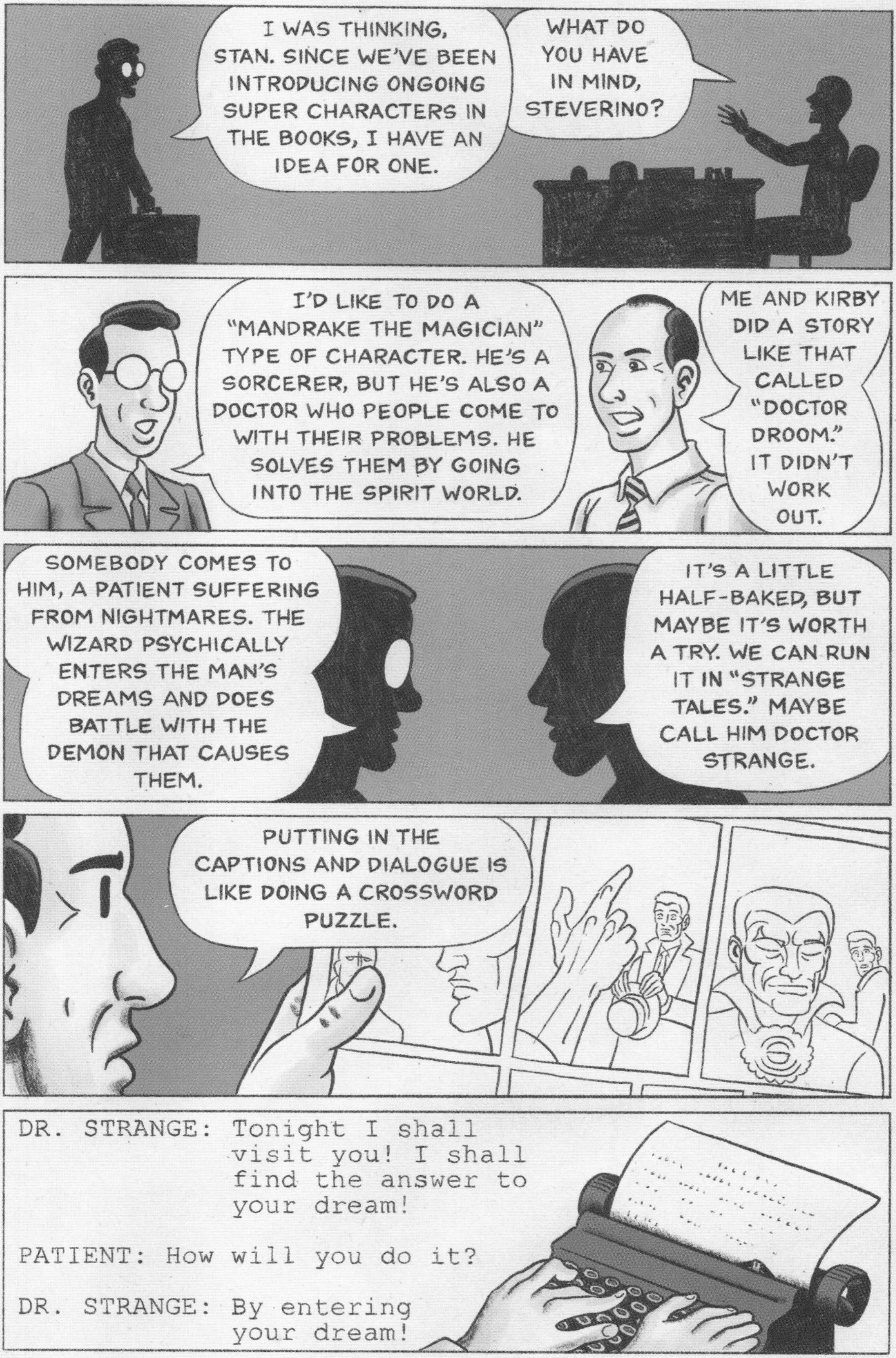
I WAS THINKING, STAN. SINCE WE'VE BEEN INTRODUCING ONGOING SUPER CHARACTERS IN THE BOOKS, I HAVE AN IDEA FOR ONE.
WHAT DO YOU HAVE IN MIND, STEVERINO?
I'D LIKE TO DO A "MANDRAKE THE MAGICIAN" TYPE OF CHARACTER. HE'S A SORCERER, BUT HE'S ALSO A DOCTOR WHO PEOPLE COME TO WITH THEIR PROBLEMS. HE SOLVES THEM BY GOING INTO THE SPIRIT WORLD.
ME AND KIRBY DID A STORY LIKE THAT CALLED "DOCTOR DROOM." IT DIDN'T WORK OUT.
SOMEBODY COMES TO HIM, A PATIENT SUFFERING FROM NIGHTMARES. THE WIZARD PSYCHICALLY ENTERS THE MAN'S DREAMS AND DOES BATTLE WITH THE DEMON THAT CAUSES THEM.
IT'S A LITTLE HALF-BAKED, BUT MAYBE IT'S WORTH A TRY. WE CAN RUN IT IN "STRANGE TALES." MAYBE CALL HIM DOCTOR STRANGE.
PUTTING IN THE CAPTIONS AND DIALOGUE IS LIKE DOING A CROSSWORD PUZZLE.
DR. STRANGE: Tonight I shall visit you! I shall find the answer to your dream!
PATIENT: How will you do it?
DR. STRANGE: By entering your dream!

  WE HAVE A HOLE IN OUR SCHEDULE. CAN YOU COME UP WITH A NEW BOOK FAST?

YOU CAN COUNT ON ME, MARTIN.

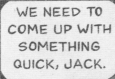 WE NEED TO COME UP WITH SOMETHING QUICK, JACK.

 WELL, MARTIN ALWAYS SAID HE WANTED A "JUSTICE LEAGUE." NOW WE'RE GIVING HIM ONE--A GREAT BIG TEAM-UP.

WHERE'S DOCTOR STRANGE AND SPIDER-MAN?

THOSE ARE DITKO'S GUYS. I WENT WITH MY CHARACTERS.

 I HAVE AN INKING JOB FOR YOU, AYERS. DON'T RUSH IT. DO YOUR USUAL QUALITY JOB...

 ...BUT WE NEED THIS YESTERDAY.

WHAT DO YOU HAVE FOR ME, STAN?

I'M ALMOST DONE, SOL.

I'M PUTTING THE FINISHING TOUCHES ON "YOU DON'T SAY!"

IT'S A FORMULA THAT WORKS—PUTTING FUNNY CAPTIONS ON PHOTOS.

I'M WRITING JOKES FOR JOHN KENNEDY.

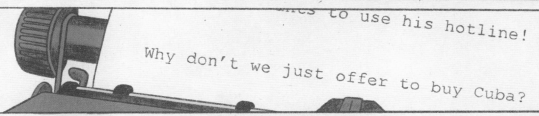

...nes to use his hotline!

Why don't we just offer to buy Cuba?

THESE ONES ARE READY FOR TYPESETTING AND PASTE-UP.

Allow me to introduce myself

Allow me to introduce

"DON'T SAY!"

96 BIG PAGES

MORE "YOU DON'T SAY!"

OVER...

Side-Splits Pictures And C 96 BIG PAG

FROM DALLAS, TEXAS... IT'S APPARENTLY OFFICIAL...

...PRESIDENT KENNEDY DIED AT 1:00 PM CENTRAL STANDARD TIME, SOME 38 MINUTES AGO.

IS THERE ANY WAY WE CAN RECALL THE MAGAZINE? CAN WE PULL IT OFF THE NEWSSTANDS?

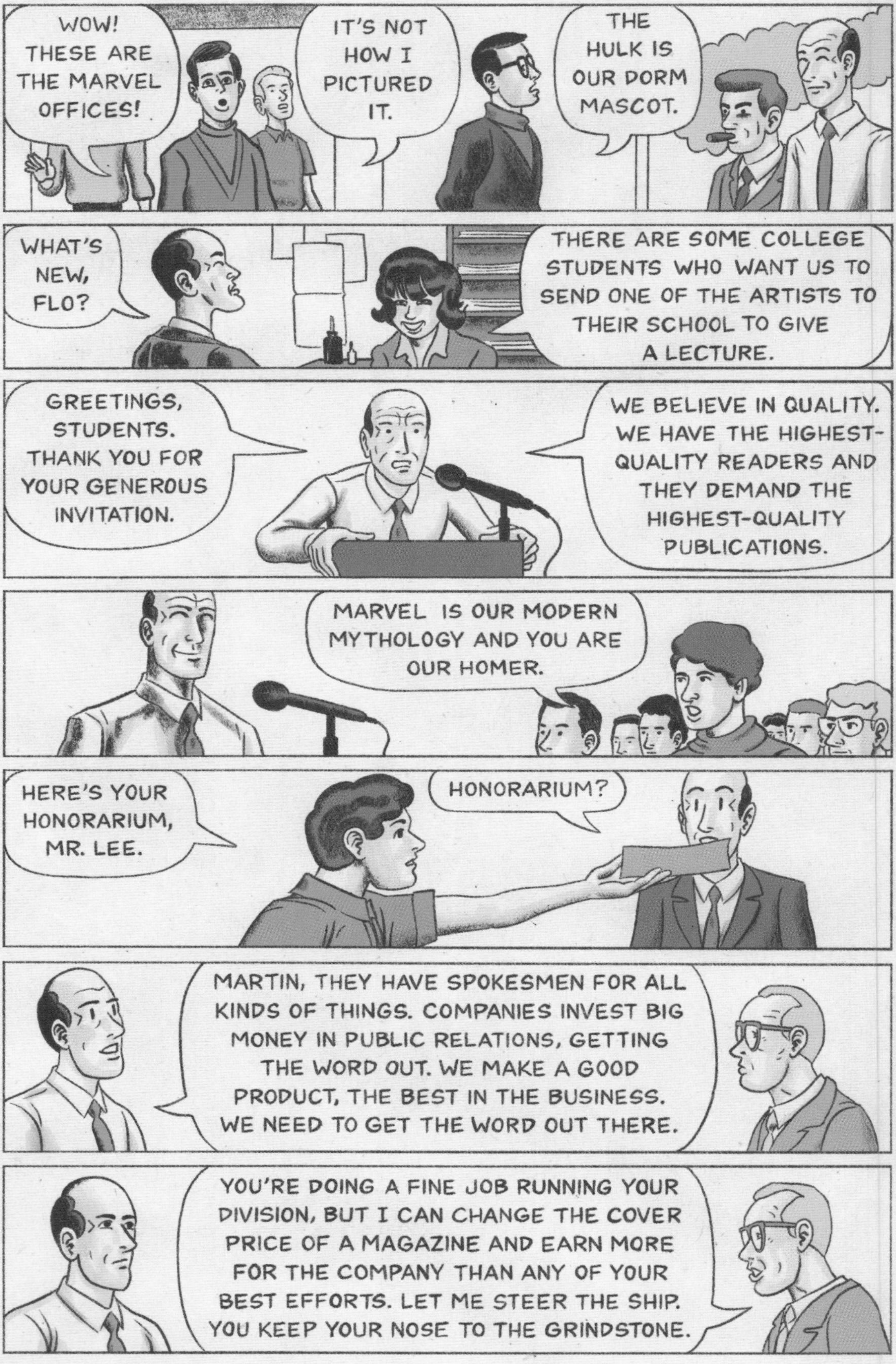
WOW! THESE ARE THE MARVEL OFFICES!
IT'S NOT HOW I PICTURED IT.
THE HULK IS OUR DORM MASCOT.
WHAT'S NEW, FLO?
THERE ARE SOME COLLEGE STUDENTS WHO WANT US TO SEND ONE OF THE ARTISTS TO THEIR SCHOOL TO GIVE A LECTURE.
GREETINGS, STUDENTS. THANK YOU FOR YOUR GENEROUS INVITATION.
WE BELIEVE IN QUALITY. WE HAVE THE HIGHEST-QUALITY READERS AND THEY DEMAND THE HIGHEST-QUALITY PUBLICATIONS.
MARVEL IS OUR MODERN MYTHOLOGY AND YOU ARE OUR HOMER.
HERE'S YOUR HONORARIUM, MR. LEE.
HONORARIUM?
MARTIN, THEY HAVE SPOKESMEN FOR ALL KINDS OF THINGS. COMPANIES INVEST BIG MONEY IN PUBLIC RELATIONS, GETTING THE WORD OUT. WE MAKE A GOOD PRODUCT, THE BEST IN THE BUSINESS. WE NEED TO GET THE WORD OUT THERE.
YOU'RE DOING A FINE JOB RUNNING YOUR DIVISION, BUT I CAN CHANGE THE COVER PRICE OF A MAGAZINE AND EARN MORE FOR THE COMPANY THAN ANY OF YOUR BEST EFFORTS. LET ME STEER THE SHIP. YOU KEEP YOUR NOSE TO THE GRINDSTONE.

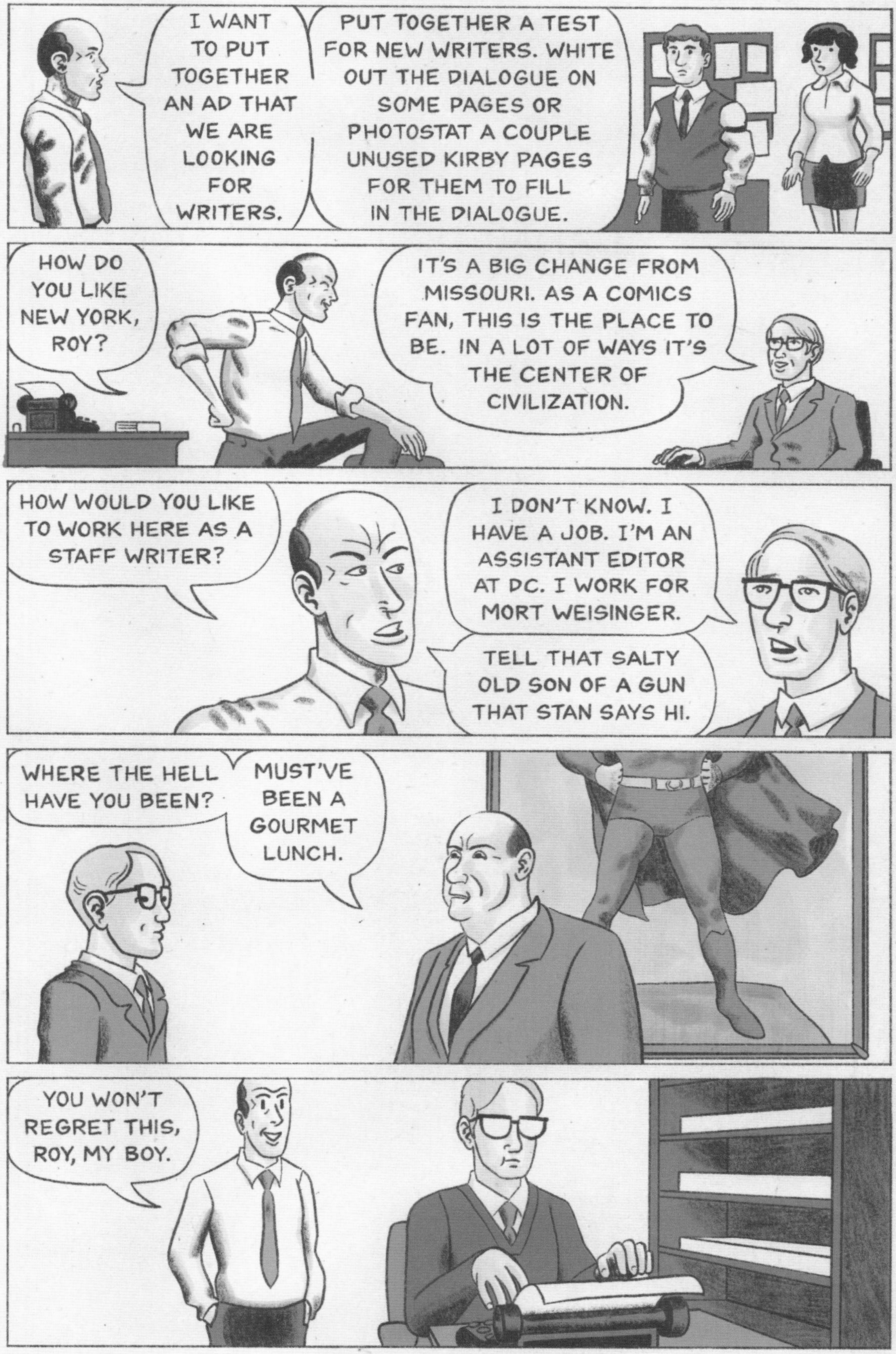
I WANT TO PUT TOGETHER AN AD THAT WE ARE LOOKING FOR WRITERS.
PUT TOGETHER A TEST FOR NEW WRITERS. WHITE OUT THE DIALOGUE ON SOME PAGES OR PHOTOSTAT A COUPLE UNUSED KIRBY PAGES FOR THEM TO FILL IN THE DIALOGUE.
HOW DO YOU LIKE NEW YORK, ROY?
IT'S A BIG CHANGE FROM MISSOURI. AS A COMICS FAN, THIS IS THE PLACE TO BE. IN A LOT OF WAYS IT'S THE CENTER OF CIVILIZATION.
HOW WOULD YOU LIKE TO WORK HERE AS A STAFF WRITER?
I DON'T KNOW. I HAVE A JOB. I'M AN ASSISTANT EDITOR AT DC. I WORK FOR MORT WEISINGER.
TELL THAT SALTY OLD SON OF A GUN THAT STAN SAYS HI.
WHERE THE HELL HAVE YOU BEEN?
MUST'VE BEEN A GOURMET LUNCH.
YOU WON'T REGRET THIS, ROY, MY BOY.

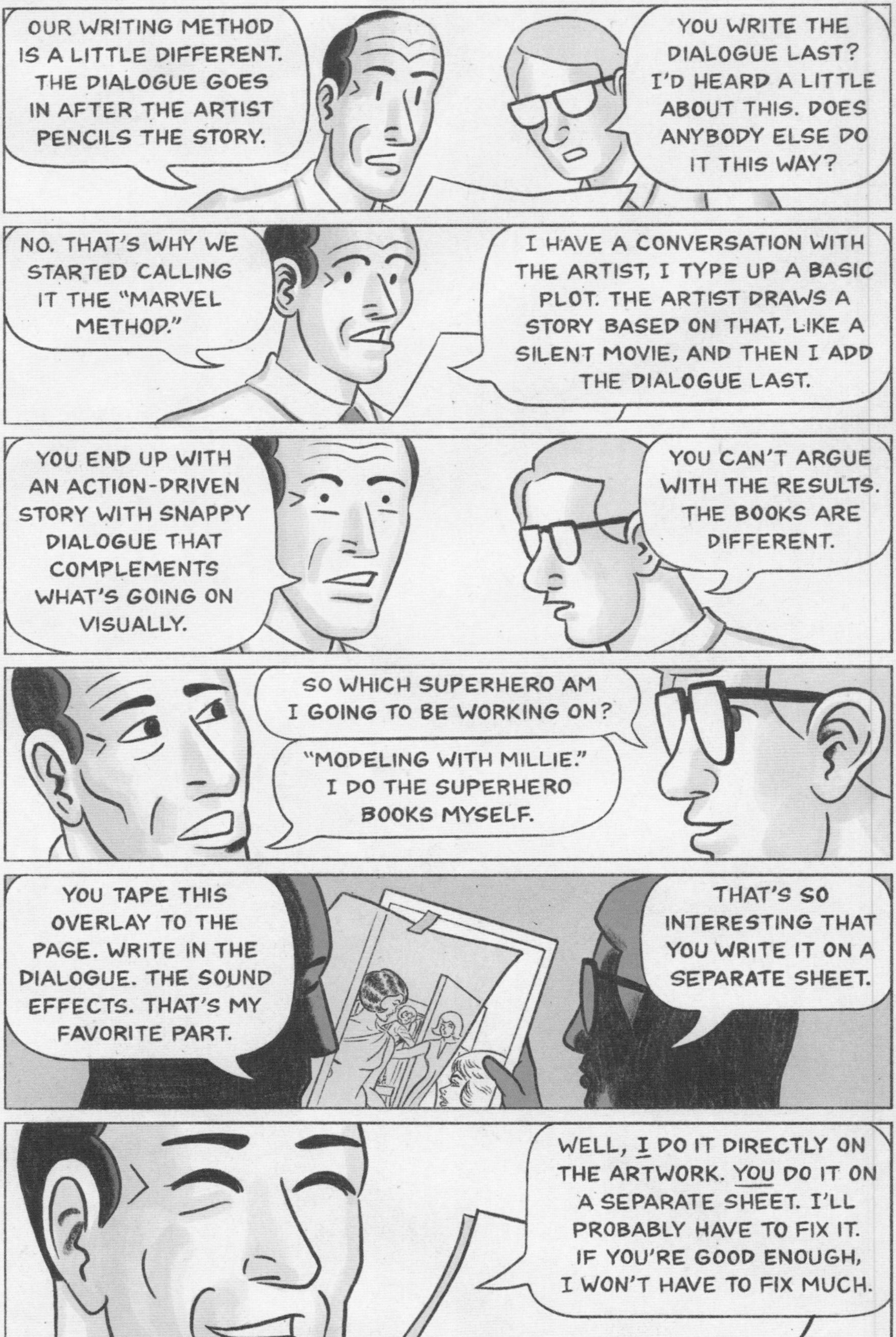
OUR WRITING METHOD IS A LITTLE DIFFERENT. THE DIALOGUE GOES IN AFTER THE ARTIST PENCILS THE STORY.
YOU WRITE THE DIALOGUE LAST? I'D HEARD A LITTLE ABOUT THIS. DOES ANYBODY ELSE DO IT THIS WAY?
NO. THAT'S WHY WE STARTED CALLING IT THE "MARVEL METHOD."
I HAVE A CONVERSATION WITH THE ARTIST, I TYPE UP A BASIC PLOT. THE ARTIST DRAWS A STORY BASED ON THAT, LIKE A SILENT MOVIE, AND THEN I ADD THE DIALOGUE LAST.
YOU END UP WITH AN ACTION-DRIVEN STORY WITH SNAPPY DIALOGUE THAT COMPLEMENTS WHAT'S GOING ON VISUALLY.
YOU CAN'T ARGUE WITH THE RESULTS. THE BOOKS ARE DIFFERENT.
SO WHICH SUPERHERO AM I GOING TO BE WORKING ON?
"MODELING WITH MILLIE." I DO THE SUPERHERO BOOKS MYSELF.
YOU TAPE THIS OVERLAY TO THE PAGE. WRITE IN THE DIALOGUE. THE SOUND EFFECTS. THAT'S MY FAVORITE PART.
THAT'S SO INTERESTING THAT YOU WRITE IT ON A SEPARATE SHEET.
WELL, I DO IT DIRECTLY ON THE ARTWORK. YOU DO IT ON A SEPARATE SHEET. I'LL PROBABLY HAVE TO FIX IT. IF YOU'RE GOOD ENOUGH, I WON'T HAVE TO FIX MUCH.

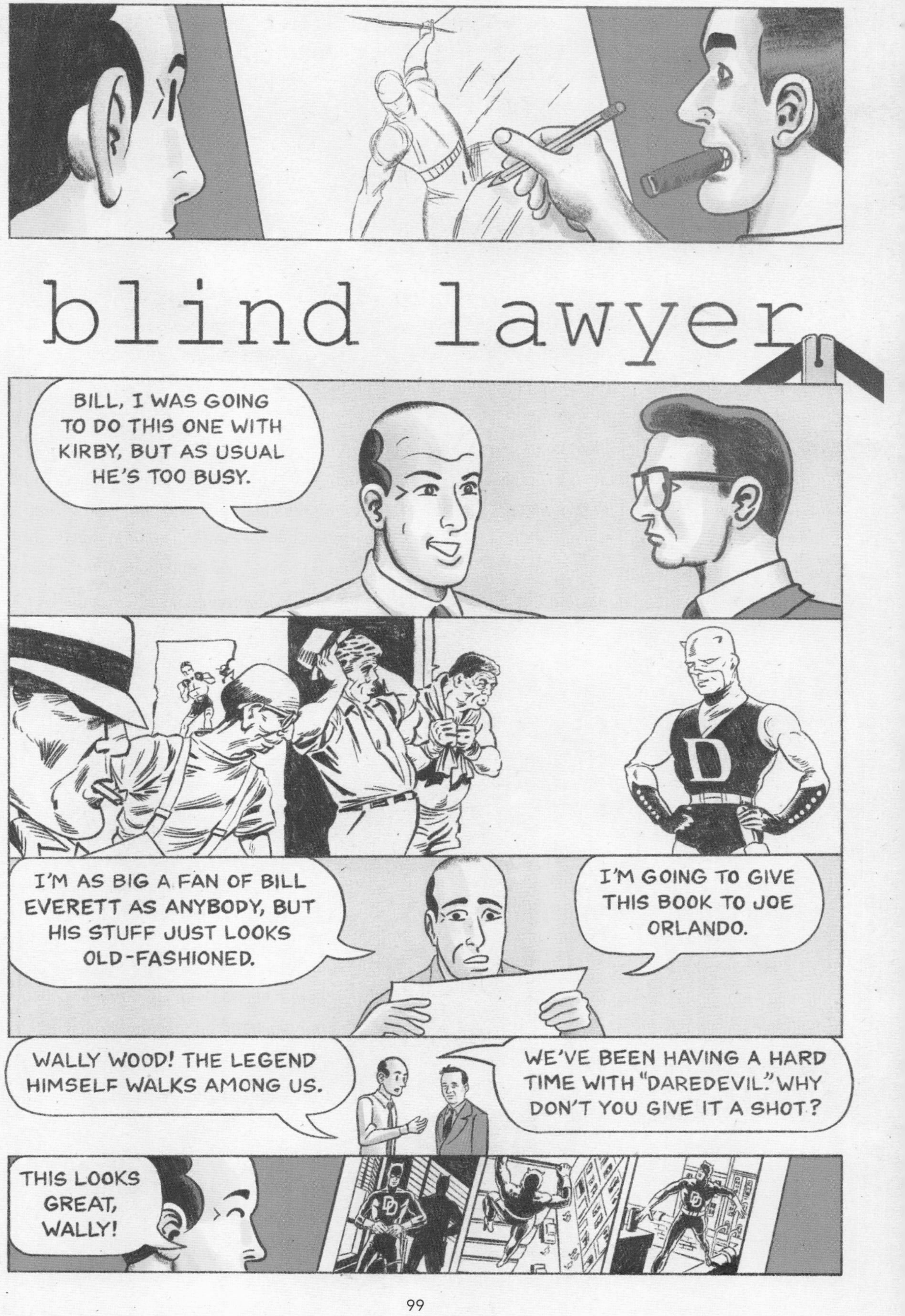
blind lawyer
BILL, I WAS GOING TO DO THIS ONE WITH KIRBY, BUT AS USUAL HE'S TOO BUSY.
D
I'M AS BIG A FAN OF BILL EVERETT AS ANYBODY, BUT HIS STUFF JUST LOOKS OLD-FASHIONED.
I'M GOING TO GIVE THIS BOOK TO JOE ORLANDO.
WALLY WOOD! THE LEGEND HIMSELF WALKS AMONG US.
WE'VE BEEN HAVING A HARD TIME WITH "DAREDEVIL." WHY DON'T YOU GIVE IT A SHOT?
THIS LOOKS GREAT, WALLY!

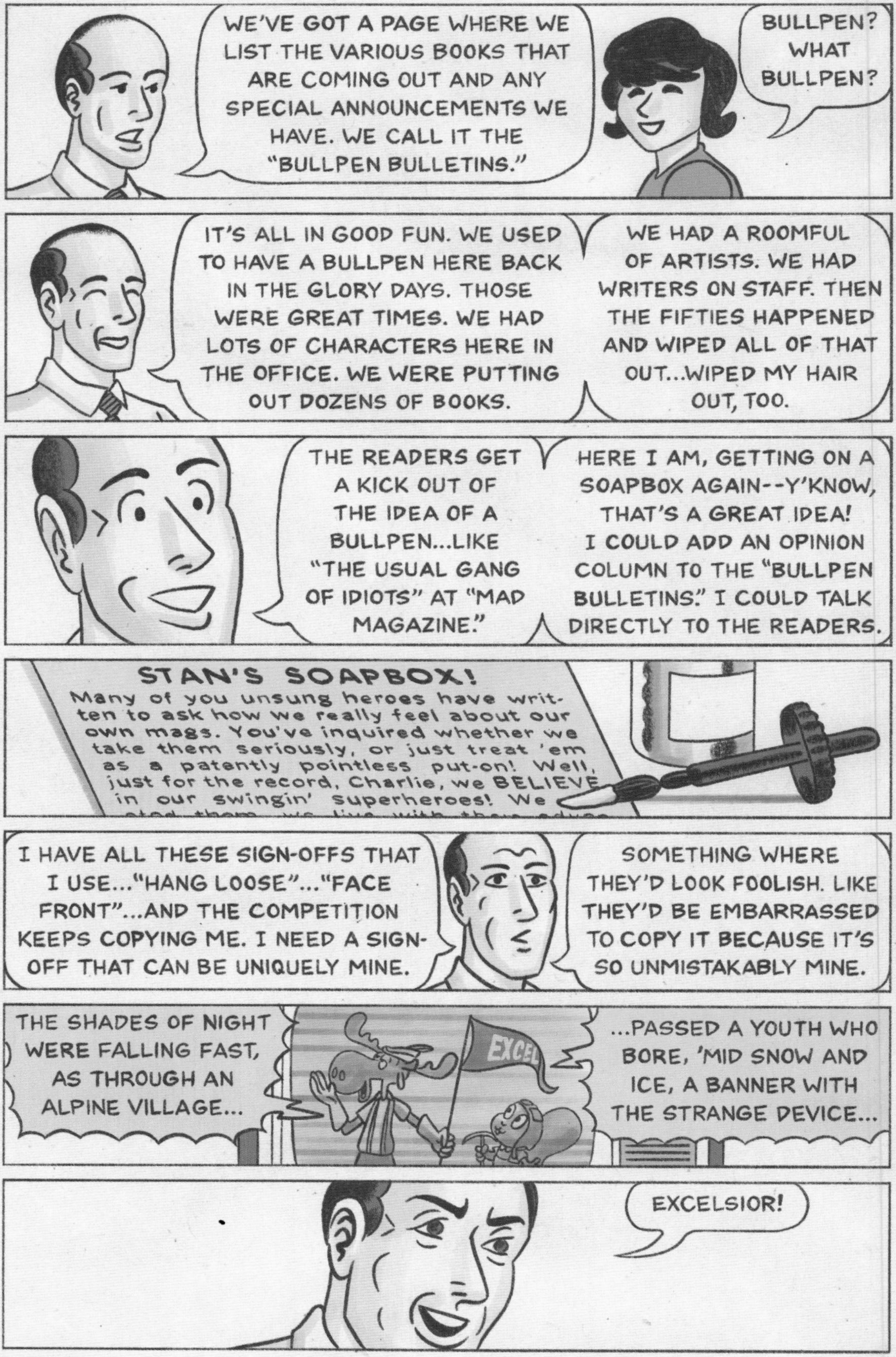
WE'VE GOT A PAGE WHERE WE LIST THE VARIOUS BOOKS THAT ARE COMING OUT AND ANY SPECIAL ANNOUNCEMENTS WE HAVE. WE CALL IT THE "BULLPEN BULLETINS."
BULLPEN? WHAT BULLPEN?
IT'S ALL IN GOOD FUN. WE USED TO HAVE A BULLPEN HERE BACK IN THE GLORY DAYS. THOSE WERE GREAT TIMES. WE HAD LOTS OF CHARACTERS HERE IN THE OFFICE. WE WERE PUTTING OUT DOZENS OF BOOKS.
WE HAD A ROOMFUL OF ARTISTS. WE HAD WRITERS ON STAFF. THEN THE FIFTIES HAPPENED AND WIPED ALL OF THAT OUT...WIPED MY HAIR OUT, TOO.
THE READERS GET A KICK OUT OF THE IDEA OF A BULLPEN...LIKE "THE USUAL GANG OF IDIOTS" AT "MAD MAGAZINE."
HERE I AM, GETTING ON A SOAPBOX AGAIN--Y'KNOW, THAT'S A GREAT IDEA! I COULD ADD AN OPINION COLUMN TO THE "BULLPEN BULLETINS." I COULD TALK DIRECTLY TO THE READERS.
STAN'S SOAPBOX!
Many of you unsung heroes have written to ask how we really feel about our own mags. You've inquired whether we take them seriously, or just treat 'em as a patently pointless put-on! Well, just for the record, Charlie, we BELIEVE in our swingin' superheroes! We
I HAVE ALL THESE SIGN-OFFS THAT I USE..."HANG LOOSE"..."FACE FRONT"...AND THE COMPETITION KEEPS COPYING ME. I NEED A SIGN-OFF THAT CAN BE UNIQUELY MINE.
SOMETHING WHERE THEY'D LOOK FOOLISH. LIKE THEY'D BE EMBARRASSED TO COPY IT BECAUSE IT'S SO UNMISTAKABLY MINE.
THE SHADES OF NIGHT WERE FALLING FAST, AS THROUGH AN ALPINE VILLAGE...
EXCEL
...PASSED A YOUTH WHO BORE, 'MID SNOW AND ICE, A BANNER WITH THE STRANGE DEVICE...
EXCELSIOR!

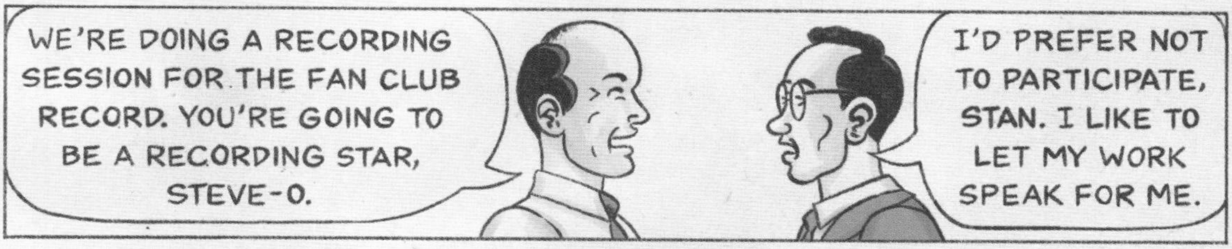
WE'RE DOING A RECORDING SESSION FOR THE FAN CLUB RECORD. YOU'RE GOING TO BE A RECORDING STAR, STEVE-O.
I'D PREFER NOT TO PARTICIPATE, STAN. I LIKE TO LET MY WORK SPEAK FOR ME.

SOL: Why it's shy STEVE DITKO! He heard you're making a record and he's got mic fright. WHOOPS! There he goes!

STAN: Y'know, I'm beginning to think he IS Spider-Man.

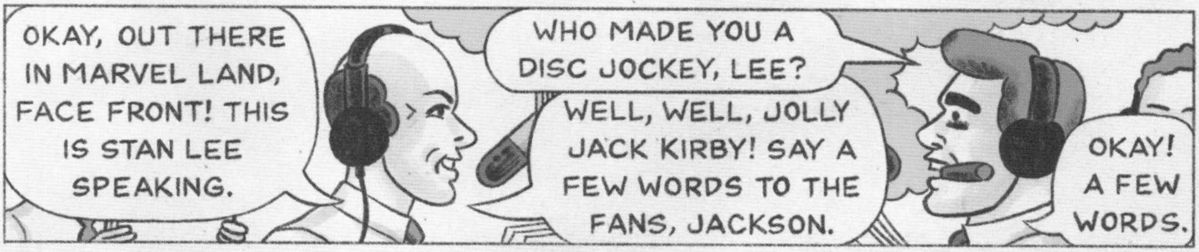
OKAY, OUT THERE IN MARVEL LAND, FACE FRONT! THIS IS STAN LEE SPEAKING.
WHO MADE YOU A DISC JOCKEY, LEE?
WELL, WELL, JOLLY JACK KIRBY! SAY A FEW WORDS TO THE FANS, JACKSON.
OKAY! A FEW WORDS.

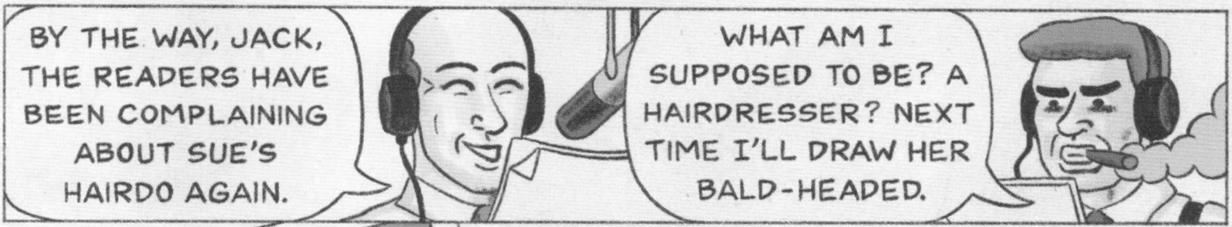
BY THE WAY, JACK, THE READERS HAVE BEEN COMPLAINING ABOUT SUE'S HAIRDO AGAIN.
WHAT AM I SUPPOSED TO BE? A HAIRDRESSER? NEXT TIME I'LL DRAW HER BALD-HEADED.

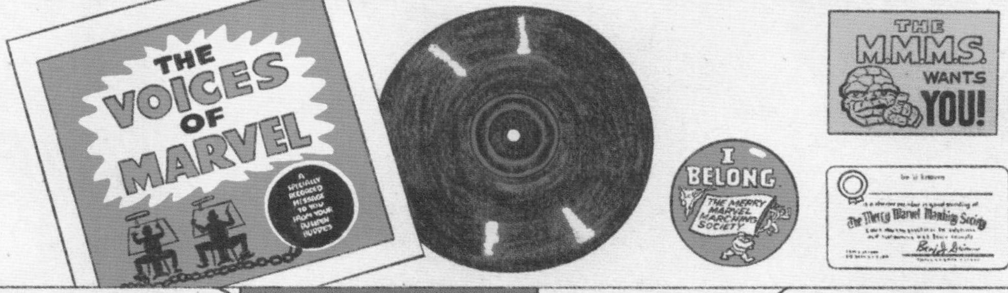
THE VOICES OF MARVEL
THE M.M.M.S. WANTS YOU!
I BELONG
THE MERRY MARVEL MARCHING SOCIETY

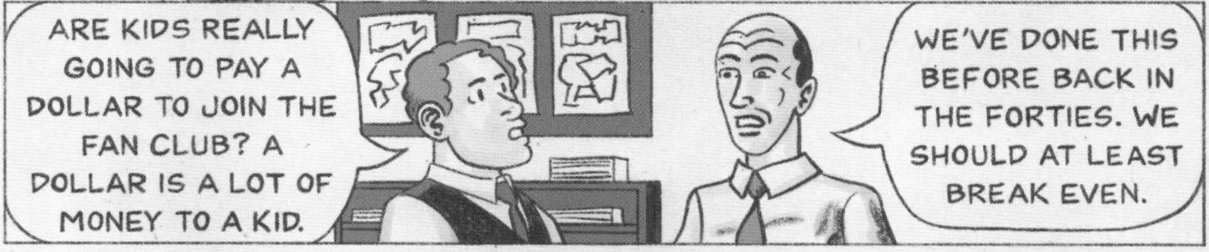
ARE KIDS REALLY GOING TO PAY A DOLLAR TO JOIN THE FAN CLUB? A DOLLAR IS A LOT OF MONEY TO A KID.
WE'VE DONE THIS BEFORE BACK IN THE FORTIES. WE SHOULD AT LEAST BREAK EVEN.

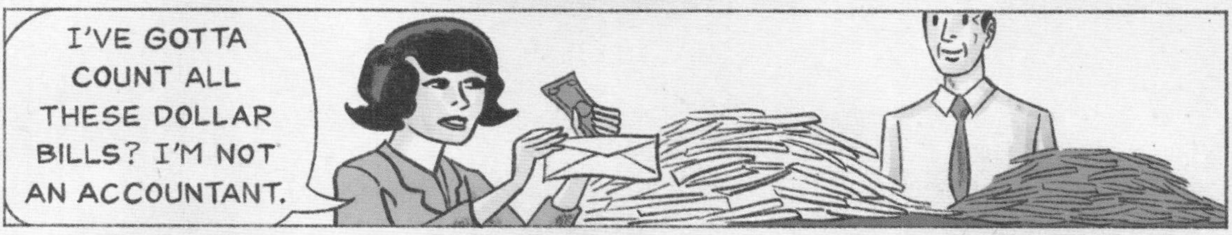
I'VE GOTTA COUNT ALL THESE DOLLAR BILLS? I'M NOT AN ACCOUNTANT.

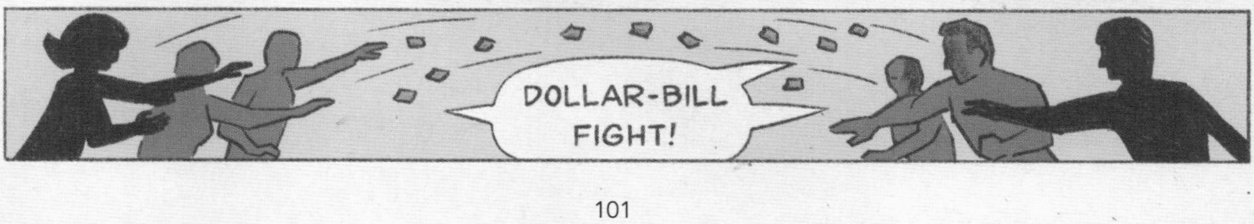
DOLLAR-BILL FIGHT!

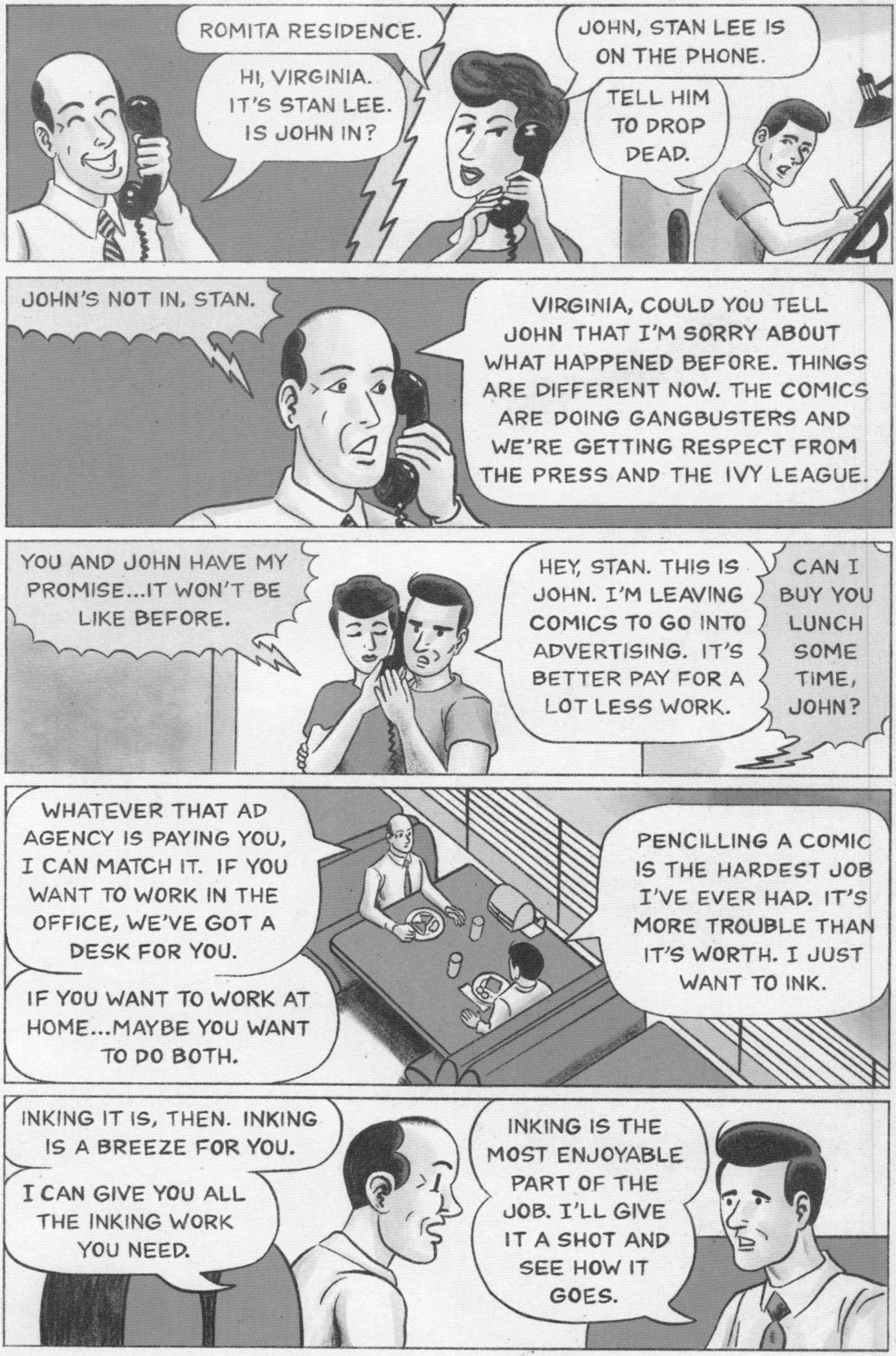
ROMITA RESIDENCE.
HI, VIRGINIA. IT'S STAN LEE. IS JOHN IN?
JOHN, STAN LEE IS ON THE PHONE.
TELL HIM TO DROP DEAD.
JOHN'S NOT IN, STAN.
VIRGINIA, COULD YOU TELL JOHN THAT I'M SORRY ABOUT WHAT HAPPENED BEFORE. THINGS ARE DIFFERENT NOW. THE COMICS ARE DOING GANGBUSTERS AND WE'RE GETTING RESPECT FROM THE PRESS AND THE IVY LEAGUE.
YOU AND JOHN HAVE MY PROMISE...IT WON'T BE LIKE BEFORE.
HEY, STAN. THIS IS JOHN. I'M LEAVING COMICS TO GO INTO ADVERTISING. IT'S BETTER PAY FOR A LOT LESS WORK.
CAN I BUY YOU LUNCH SOME TIME, JOHN?
WHATEVER THAT AD AGENCY IS PAYING YOU, I CAN MATCH IT. IF YOU WANT TO WORK IN THE OFFICE, WE'VE GOT A DESK FOR YOU.
IF YOU WANT TO WORK AT HOME...MAYBE YOU WANT TO DO BOTH.
PENCILLING A COMIC IS THE HARDEST JOB I'VE EVER HAD. IT'S MORE TROUBLE THAN IT'S WORTH. I JUST WANT TO INK.
INKING IT IS, THEN. INKING IS A BREEZE FOR YOU.
I CAN GIVE YOU ALL THE INKING WORK YOU NEED.
INKING IS THE MOST ENJOYABLE PART OF THE JOB. I'LL GIVE IT A SHOT AND SEE HOW IT GOES.

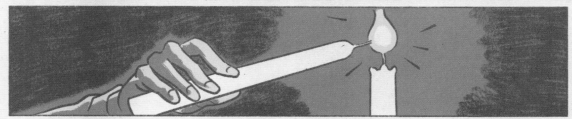

I FOUND SOME MORE CANDLES.

HOW CAN YOU WRITE IN A BLACKOUT?

WHAT ELSE AM I GOING TO DO?

COMICS NEVER STOPS.

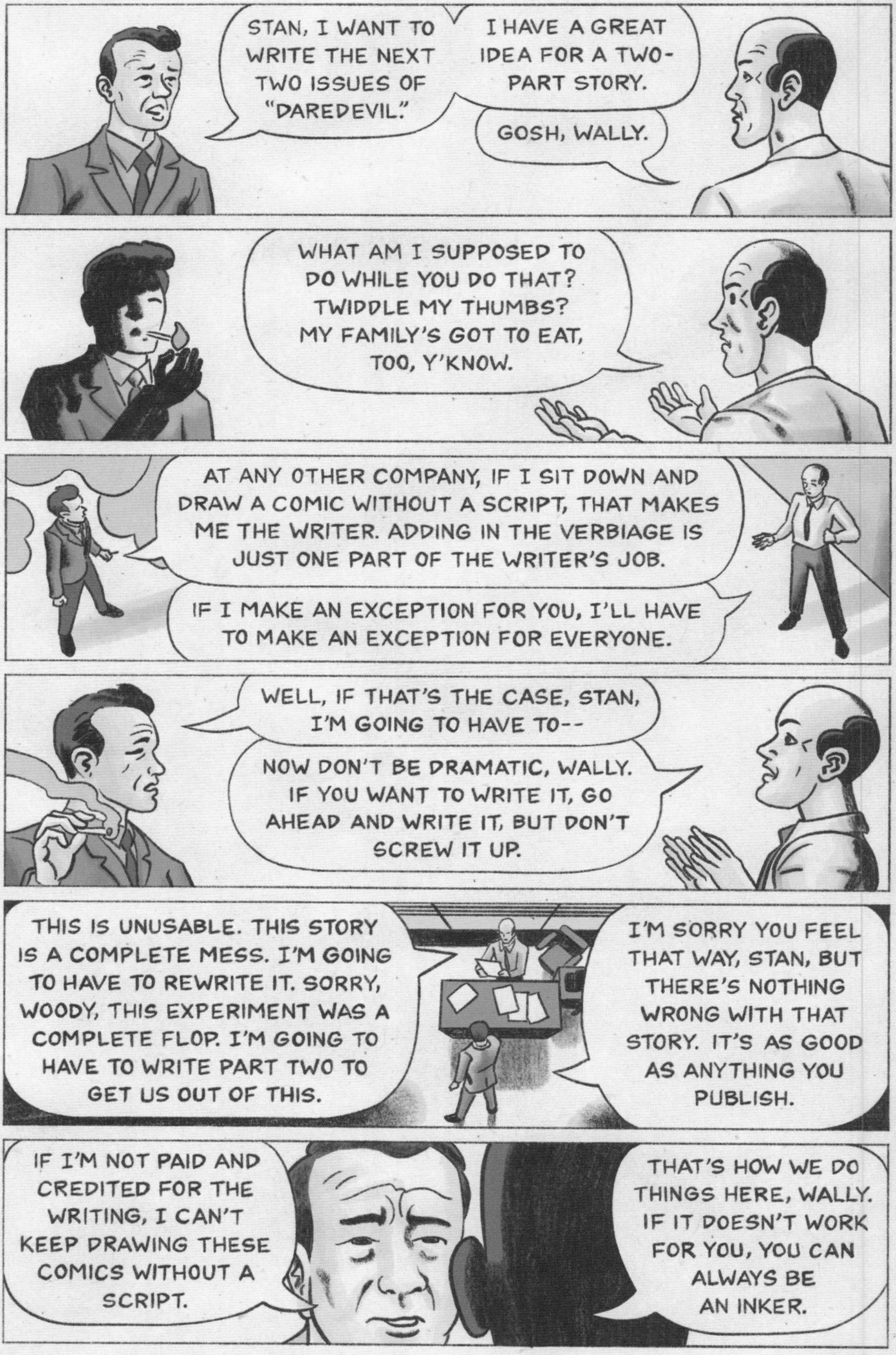
STAN, I WANT TO WRITE THE NEXT TWO ISSUES OF "DAREDEVIL."
I HAVE A GREAT IDEA FOR A TWO-PART STORY.
GOSH, WALLY.
WHAT AM I SUPPOSED TO DO WHILE YOU DO THAT? TWIDDLE MY THUMBS? MY FAMILY'S GOT TO EAT, TOO, Y'KNOW.
AT ANY OTHER COMPANY, IF I SIT DOWN AND DRAW A COMIC WITHOUT A SCRIPT, THAT MAKES ME THE WRITER. ADDING IN THE VERBIAGE IS JUST ONE PART OF THE WRITER'S JOB.
IF I MAKE AN EXCEPTION FOR YOU, I'LL HAVE TO MAKE AN EXCEPTION FOR EVERYONE.
WELL, IF THAT'S THE CASE, STAN, I'M GOING TO HAVE TO--
NOW DON'T BE DRAMATIC, WALLY. IF YOU WANT TO WRITE IT, GO AHEAD AND WRITE IT, BUT DON'T SCREW IT UP.
THIS IS UNUSABLE. THIS STORY IS A COMPLETE MESS. I'M GOING TO HAVE TO REWRITE IT. SORRY, WOODY, THIS EXPERIMENT WAS A COMPLETE FLOP. I'M GOING TO HAVE TO WRITE PART TWO TO GET US OUT OF THIS.
I'M SORRY YOU FEEL THAT WAY, STAN, BUT THERE'S NOTHING WRONG WITH THAT STORY. IT'S AS GOOD AS ANYTHING YOU PUBLISH.
IF I'M NOT PAID AND CREDITED FOR THE WRITING, I CAN'T KEEP DRAWING THESE COMICS WITHOUT A SCRIPT.
THAT'S HOW WE DO THINGS HERE, WALLY. IF IT DOESN'T WORK FOR YOU, YOU CAN ALWAYS BE AN INKER.

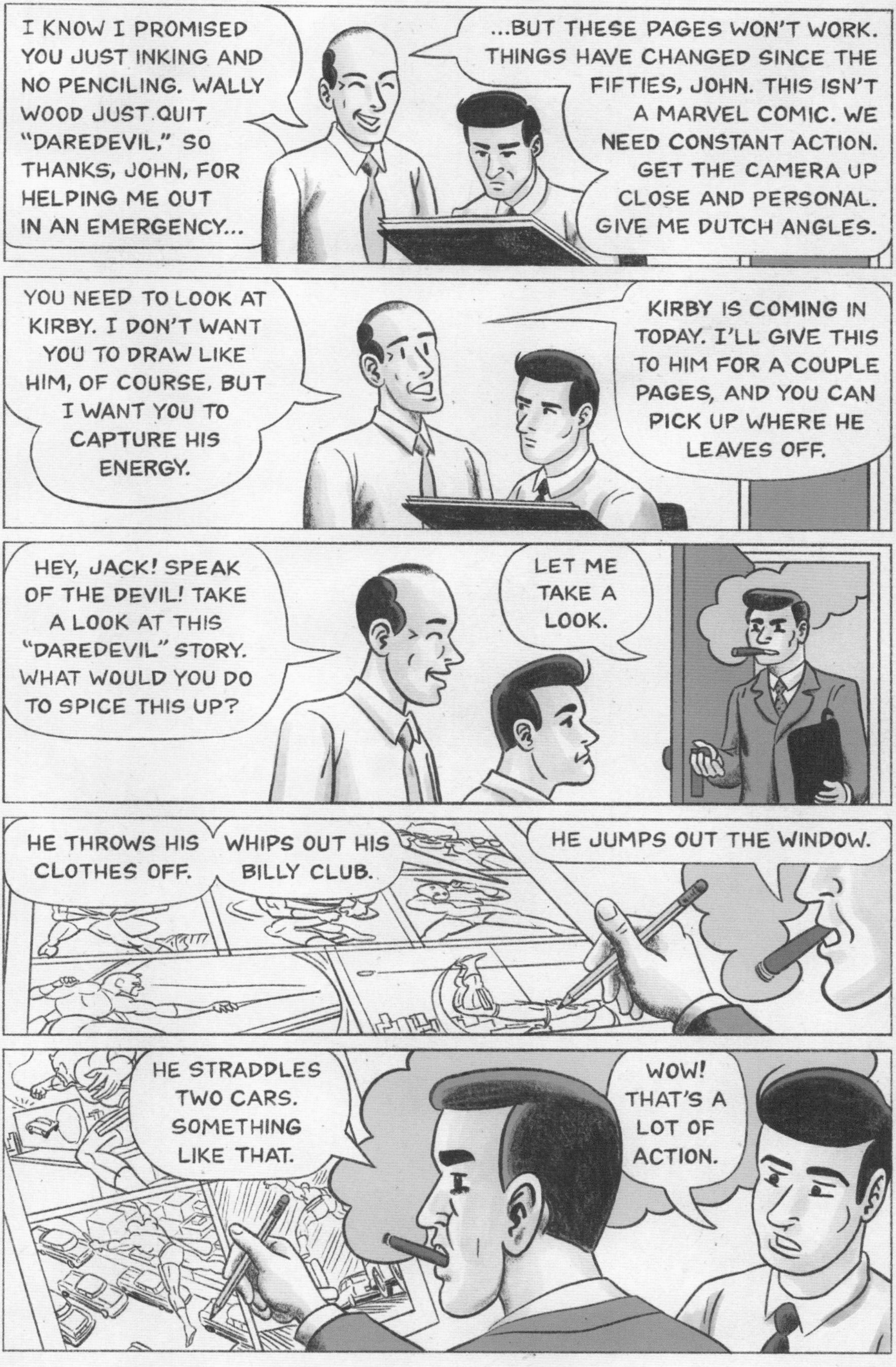
I KNOW I PROMISED YOU JUST INKING AND NO PENCILING. WALLY WOOD JUST QUIT "DAREDEVIL," SO THANKS, JOHN, FOR HELPING ME OUT IN AN EMERGENCY...
...BUT THESE PAGES WON'T WORK. THINGS HAVE CHANGED SINCE THE FIFTIES, JOHN. THIS ISN'T A MARVEL COMIC. WE NEED CONSTANT ACTION. GET THE CAMERA UP CLOSE AND PERSONAL. GIVE ME DUTCH ANGLES.
YOU NEED TO LOOK AT KIRBY. I DON'T WANT YOU TO DRAW LIKE HIM, OF COURSE, BUT I WANT YOU TO CAPTURE HIS ENERGY.
KIRBY IS COMING IN TODAY. I'LL GIVE THIS TO HIM FOR A COUPLE PAGES, AND YOU CAN PICK UP WHERE HE LEAVES OFF.
HEY, JACK! SPEAK OF THE DEVIL! TAKE A LOOK AT THIS "DAREDEVIL" STORY. WHAT WOULD YOU DO TO SPICE THIS UP?
LET ME TAKE A LOOK.
HE THROWS HIS CLOTHES OFF.
WHIPS OUT HIS BILLY CLUB.
HE JUMPS OUT THE WINDOW.
HE STRADDLES TWO CARS. SOMETHING LIKE THAT.
WOW! THAT'S A LOT OF ACTION.

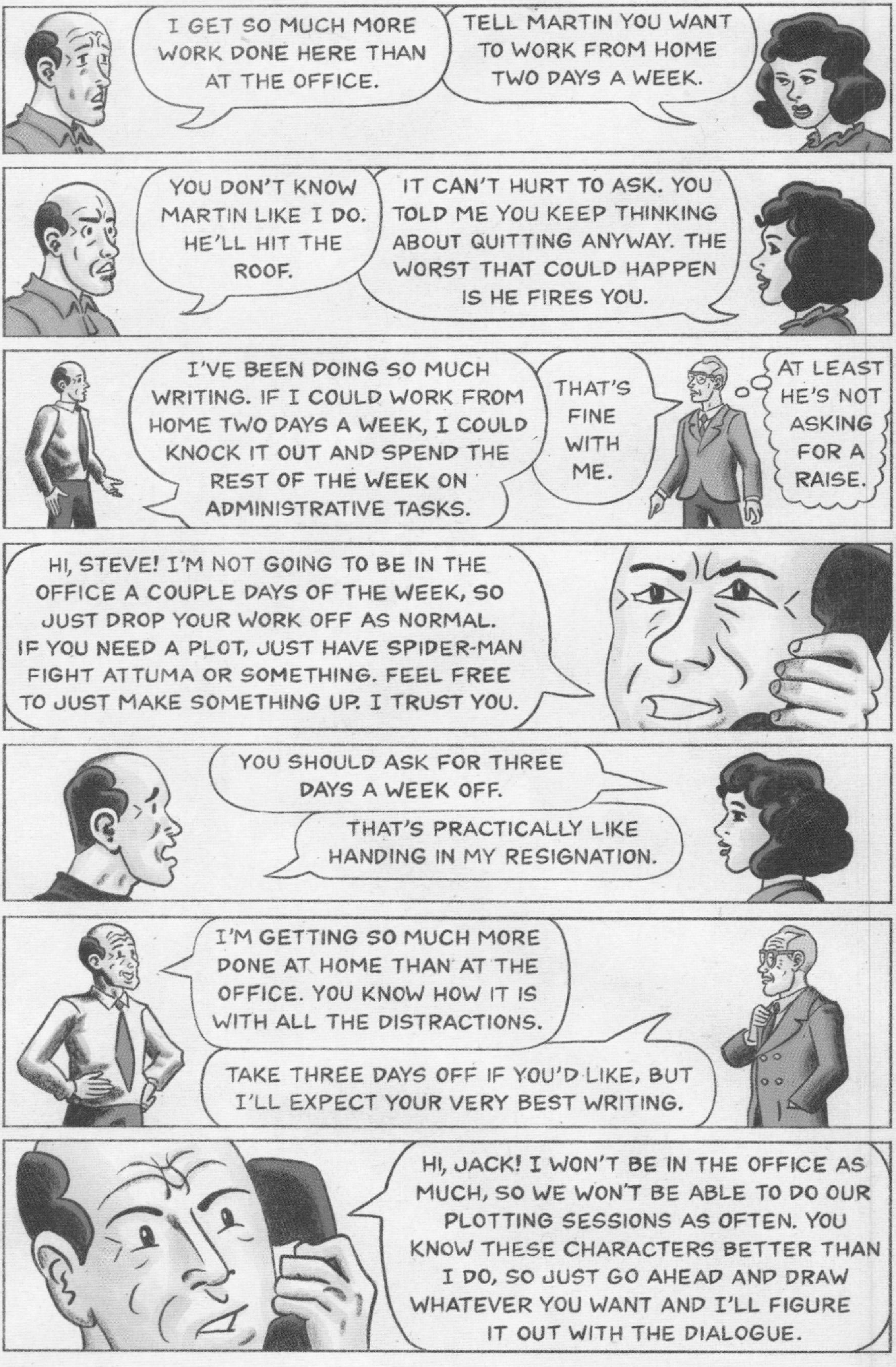
I GET SO MUCH MORE WORK DONE HERE THAN AT THE OFFICE.
TELL MARTIN YOU WANT TO WORK FROM HOME TWO DAYS A WEEK.
YOU DON'T KNOW MARTIN LIKE I DO. HE'LL HIT THE ROOF.
IT CAN'T HURT TO ASK. YOU TOLD ME YOU KEEP THINKING ABOUT QUITTING ANYWAY. THE WORST THAT COULD HAPPEN IS HE FIRES YOU.
I'VE BEEN DOING SO MUCH WRITING. IF I COULD WORK FROM HOME TWO DAYS A WEEK, I COULD KNOCK IT OUT AND SPEND THE REST OF THE WEEK ON ADMINISTRATIVE TASKS.
THAT'S FINE WITH ME.
AT LEAST HE'S NOT ASKING FOR A RAISE.
HI, STEVE! I'M NOT GOING TO BE IN THE OFFICE A COUPLE DAYS OF THE WEEK, SO JUST DROP YOUR WORK OFF AS NORMAL. IF YOU NEED A PLOT, JUST HAVE SPIDER-MAN FIGHT ATTUMA OR SOMETHING. FEEL FREE TO JUST MAKE SOMETHING UP. I TRUST YOU.
YOU SHOULD ASK FOR THREE DAYS A WEEK OFF.
THAT'S PRACTICALLY LIKE HANDING IN MY RESIGNATION.
I'M GETTING SO MUCH MORE DONE AT HOME THAN AT THE OFFICE. YOU KNOW HOW IT IS WITH ALL THE DISTRACTIONS.
TAKE THREE DAYS OFF IF YOU'D LIKE, BUT I'LL EXPECT YOUR VERY BEST WRITING.
HI, JACK! I WON'T BE IN THE OFFICE AS MUCH, SO WE WON'T BE ABLE TO DO OUR PLOTTING SESSIONS AS OFTEN. YOU KNOW THESE CHARACTERS BETTER THAN I DO, SO JUST GO AHEAD AND DRAW WHATEVER YOU WANT AND I'LL FIGURE IT OUT WITH THE DIALOGUE.

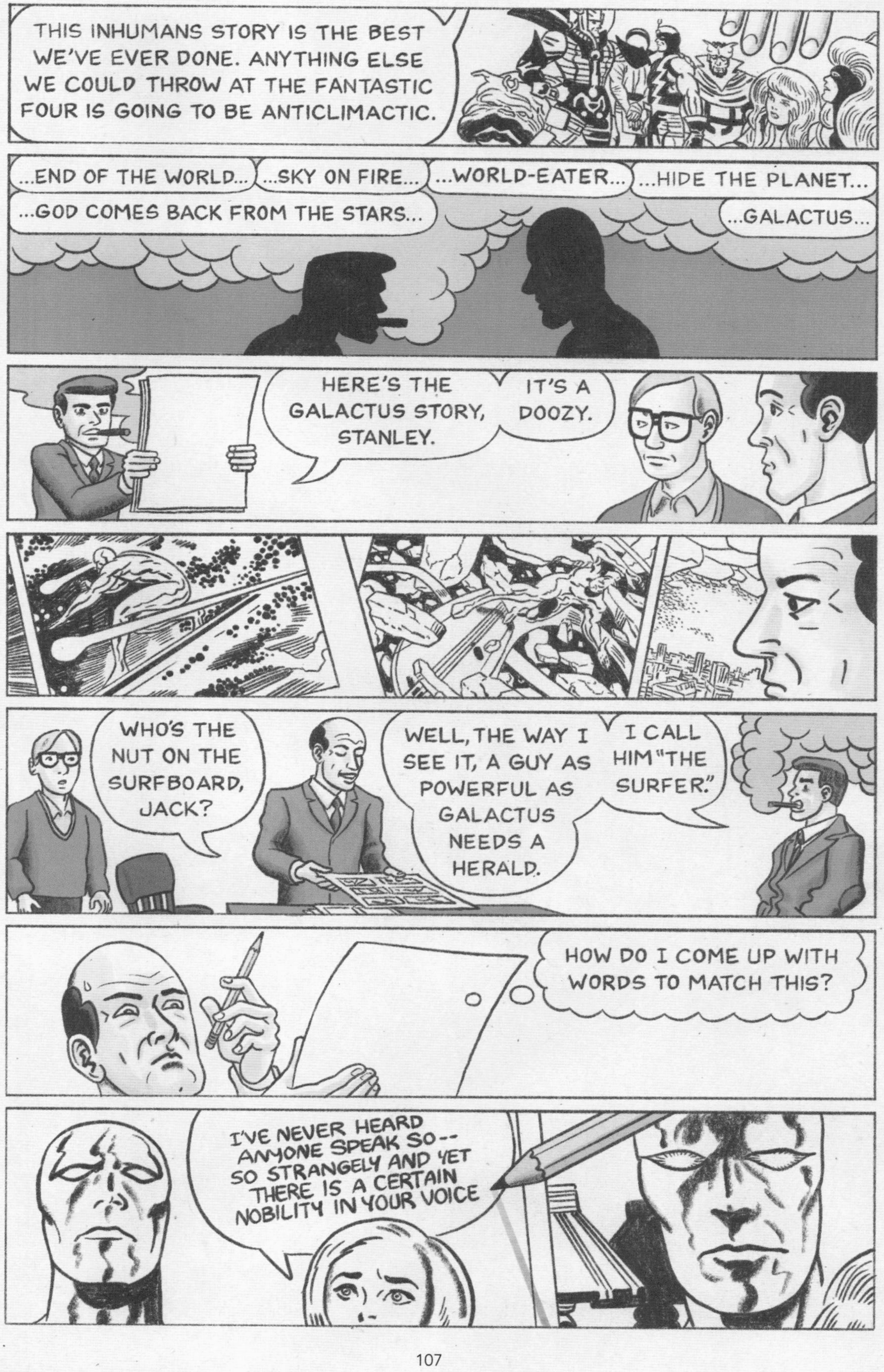
THIS INHUMANS STORY IS THE BEST WE'VE EVER DONE. ANYTHING ELSE WE COULD THROW AT THE FANTASTIC FOUR IS GOING TO BE ANTICLIMACTIC.
...END OF THE WORLD...
...SKY ON FIRE...
...WORLD-EATER...
...HIDE THE PLANET...
...GOD COMES BACK FROM THE STARS...
...GALACTUS...
HERE'S THE GALACTUS STORY, STANLEY.
IT'S A DOOZY.
WHO'S THE NUT ON THE SURFBOARD, JACK?
WELL, THE WAY I SEE IT, A GUY AS POWERFUL AS GALACTUS NEEDS A HERALD.
I CALL HIM "THE SURFER."
HOW DO I COME UP WITH WORDS TO MATCH THIS?
I'VE NEVER HEARD ANYONE SPEAK SO-- SO STRANGELY AND YET THERE IS A CERTAIN NOBILITY IN YOUR VOICE

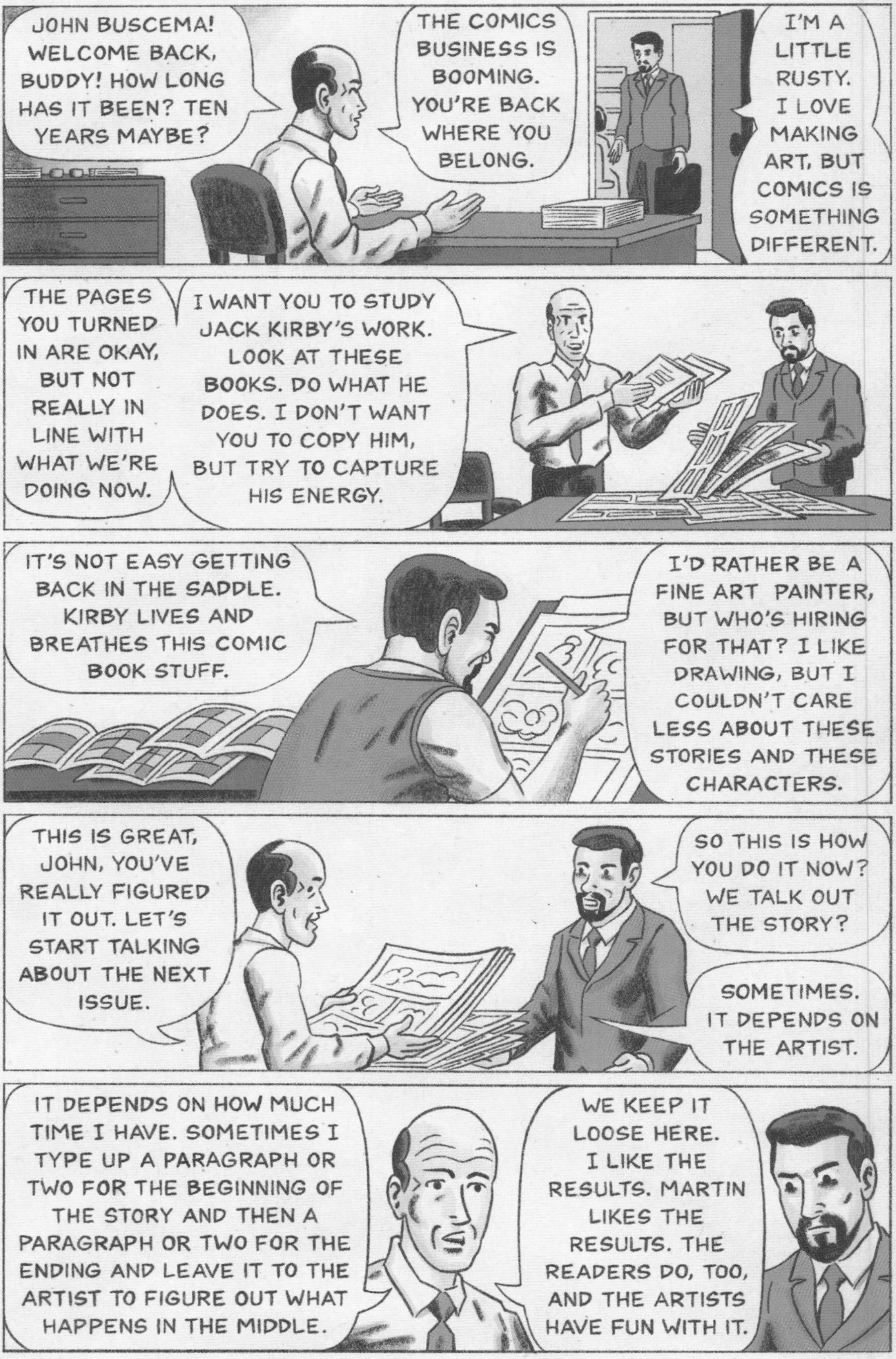
JOHN BUSCEMA! WELCOME BACK, BUDDY! HOW LONG HAS IT BEEN? TEN YEARS MAYBE?
THE COMICS BUSINESS IS BOOMING. YOU'RE BACK WHERE YOU BELONG.
I'M A LITTLE RUSTY. I LOVE MAKING ART, BUT COMICS IS SOMETHING DIFFERENT.
THE PAGES YOU TURNED IN ARE OKAY, BUT NOT REALLY IN LINE WITH WHAT WE'RE DOING NOW.
I WANT YOU TO STUDY JACK KIRBY'S WORK. LOOK AT THESE BOOKS. DO WHAT HE DOES. I DON'T WANT YOU TO COPY HIM, BUT TRY TO CAPTURE HIS ENERGY.
IT'S NOT EASY GETTING BACK IN THE SADDLE. KIRBY LIVES AND BREATHES THIS COMIC BOOK STUFF.
I'D RATHER BE A FINE ART PAINTER, BUT WHO'S HIRING FOR THAT? I LIKE DRAWING, BUT I COULDN'T CARE LESS ABOUT THESE STORIES AND THESE CHARACTERS.
THIS IS GREAT, JOHN, YOU'VE REALLY FIGURED IT OUT. LET'S START TALKING ABOUT THE NEXT ISSUE.
SO THIS IS HOW YOU DO IT NOW? WE TALK OUT THE STORY?
SOMETIMES. IT DEPENDS ON THE ARTIST.
IT DEPENDS ON HOW MUCH TIME I HAVE. SOMETIMES I TYPE UP A PARAGRAPH OR TWO FOR THE BEGINNING OF THE STORY AND THEN A PARAGRAPH OR TWO FOR THE ENDING AND LEAVE IT TO THE ARTIST TO FIGURE OUT WHAT HAPPENS IN THE MIDDLE.
WE KEEP IT LOOSE HERE. I LIKE THE RESULTS. MARTIN LIKES THE RESULTS. THE READERS DO, TOO, AND THE ARTISTS HAVE FUN WITH IT.

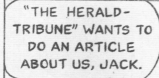 "THE HERALD-TRIBUNE" WANTS TO DO AN ARTICLE ABOUT US, JACK.

 THAT'S SENSATIONAL, STANLEY.

THE THING STARTS A BIG FIGHT WITH THE SURFER AFTER SEEING HIM WITH ALICIA.

  MEANWHILE DOCTOR DOOM'S CAUGHT THE FANTASTIC FOUR AND THEY NEED THE THING'S HELP.

YEAH, OKAY.

"THE HERALD-TRIBUNE" ARTICLE IS OUT.

"STAN LEE, 43, IS A NATIVE NEW YORKER, AN ULTRA-MADISON AVENUE, RANGY LOOK-ALIKE OF REX HARRISON."

"STAN LEE DREW A BIGGER AUDIENCE THAN PRESIDENT EISENHOWER WHEN HE SPOKE LAST YEAR AT BARD, ONE OF THE HIPPER SCHOOLS ON THE EASTERN SEABOARD."

HEY, JACK, YOU SAW THE ARTICLE? PRETTY FABULOUS, RIGHT?

WHAT? DID WE READ THE SAME ARTICLE?

 THIS ARTICLE MAKES ME SOUND LIKE I'M YOUR FLUNKY. IT SAYS YOU'RE A GENIUS AND I'M A DUMPY YES-MAN WHO LOOKS LIKE A GIRDLE FACTORY FOREMAN.

YOU PUT ON A SONG AND DANCE FOR THAT GUY, AND NOW THE WORLD THINKS I JUST SALUTE YOU AND CARRY OUT YOUR ORDERS.

JACK, I DON'T KNOW HOW THIS HAPPENED. I'M AS MAD ABOUT THIS AS ANYBODY. IT SAID I HAVE A HORSE FACE AND THAT I'M LOSING MY HAIR.

  I HOPE YOU DON'T THINK I HAD ANYTHING TO DO WITH THIS.

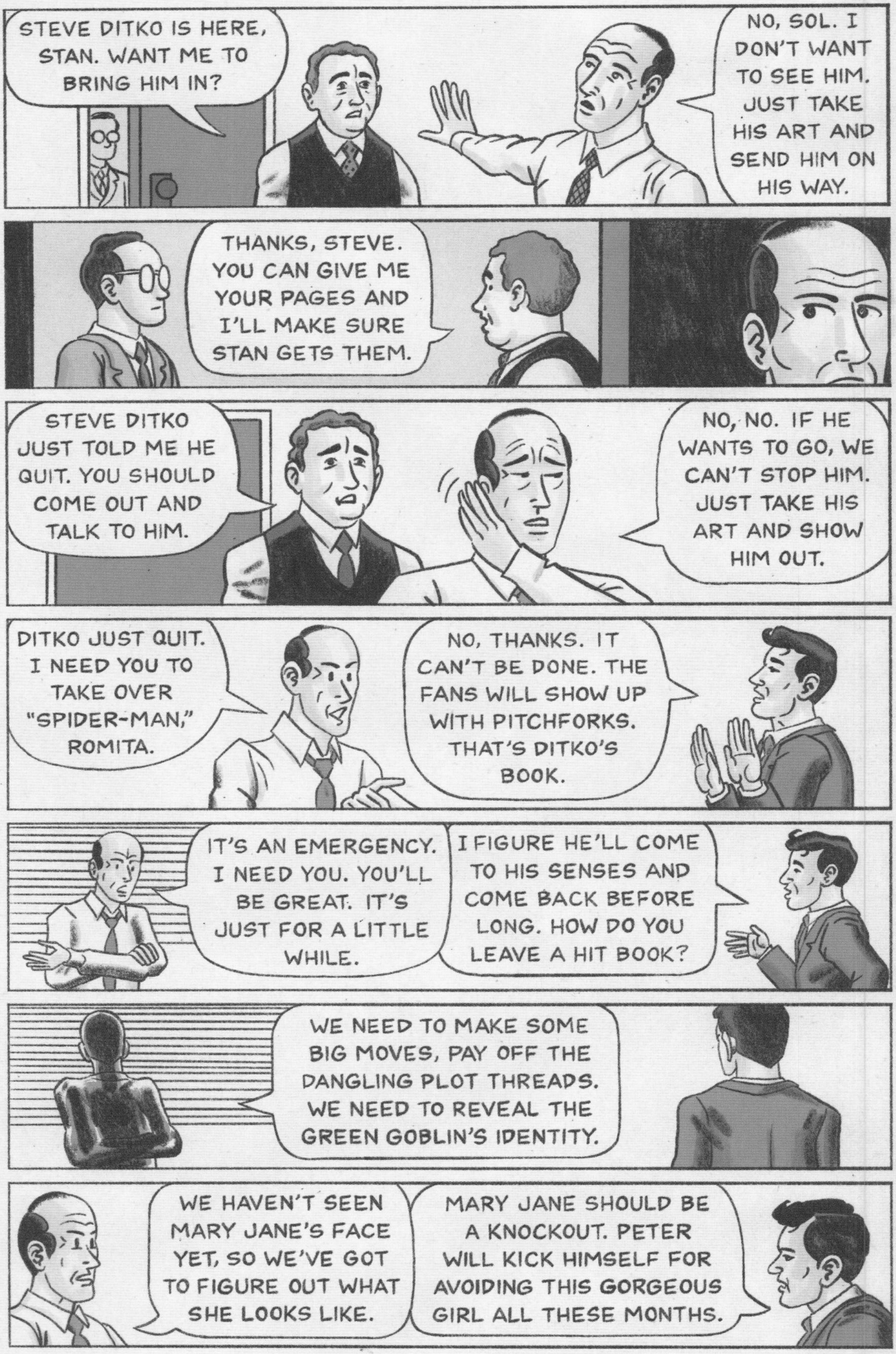

STEVE DITKO IS HERE, STAN. WANT ME TO BRING HIM IN?
NO, SOL. I DON'T WANT TO SEE HIM. JUST TAKE HIS ART AND SEND HIM ON HIS WAY.
THANKS, STEVE. YOU CAN GIVE ME YOUR PAGES AND I'LL MAKE SURE STAN GETS THEM.
STEVE DITKO JUST TOLD ME HE QUIT. YOU SHOULD COME OUT AND TALK TO HIM.
NO, NO. IF HE WANTS TO GO, WE CAN'T STOP HIM. JUST TAKE HIS ART AND SHOW HIM OUT.
DITKO JUST QUIT. I NEED YOU TO TAKE OVER "SPIDER-MAN," ROMITA.
NO, THANKS. IT CAN'T BE DONE. THE FANS WILL SHOW UP WITH PITCHFORKS. THAT'S DITKO'S BOOK.
IT'S AN EMERGENCY. I NEED YOU. YOU'LL BE GREAT. IT'S JUST FOR A LITTLE WHILE.
I FIGURE HE'LL COME TO HIS SENSES AND COME BACK BEFORE LONG. HOW DO YOU LEAVE A HIT BOOK?
WE NEED TO MAKE SOME BIG MOVES, PAY OFF THE DANGLING PLOT THREADS. WE NEED TO REVEAL THE GREEN GOBLIN'S IDENTITY.
WE HAVEN'T SEEN MARY JANE'S FACE YET, SO WE'VE GOT TO FIGURE OUT WHAT SHE LOOKS LIKE.
MARY JANE SHOULD BE A KNOCKOUT. PETER WILL KICK HIMSELF FOR AVOIDING THIS GORGEOUS GIRL ALL THESE MONTHS.

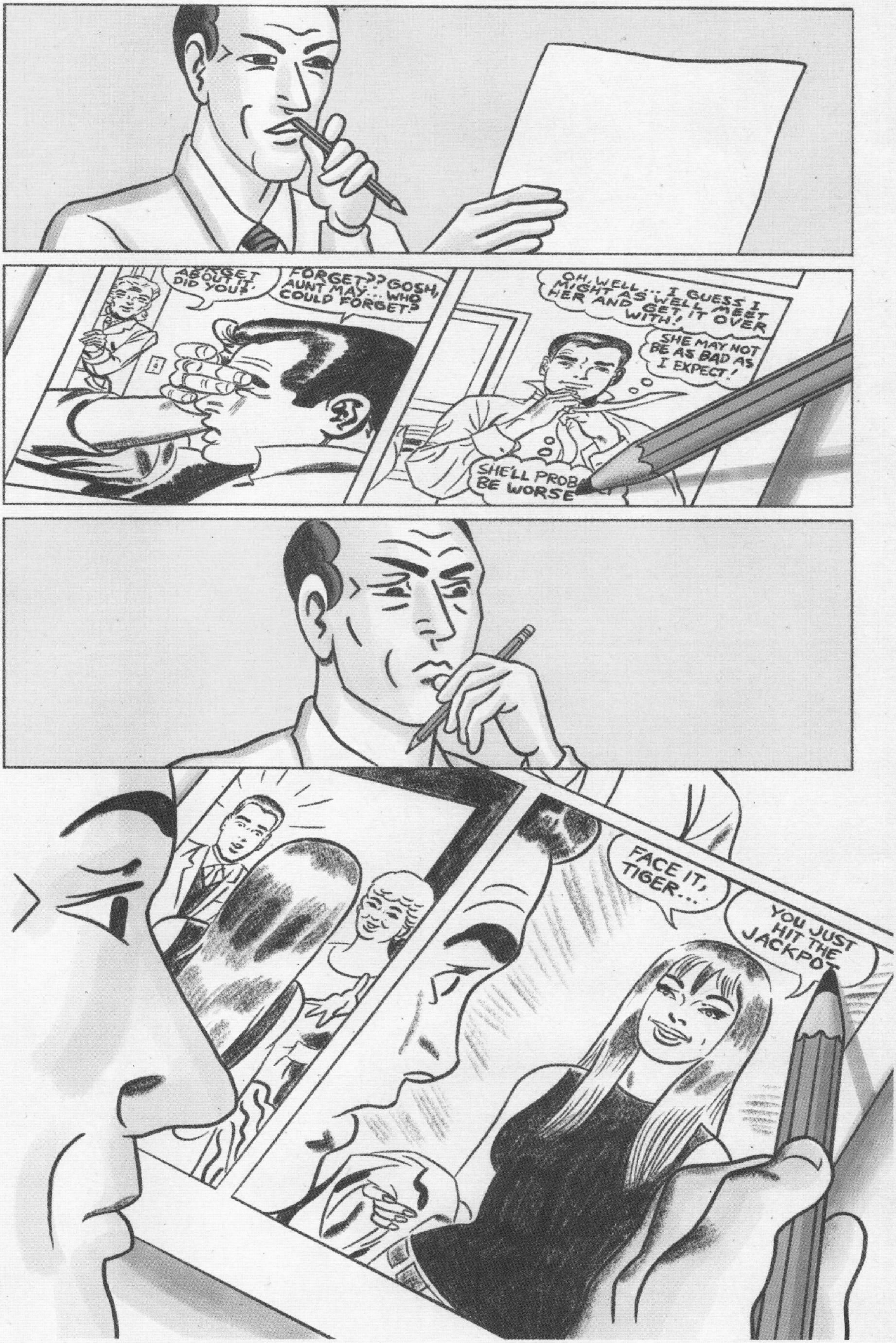
ABOUT IT, DID YOU?
FORGET?? GOSH, AUNT MAY... WHO COULD FORGET?
OH, WELL... I GUESS I MIGHT AS WELL MEET HER AND GET IT OVER WITH!
SHE MAY NOT BE AS BAD AS I EXPECT!
SHE'LL PROB BE WORSE
FACE IT, TIGER...
YOU JUST HIT THE JACKPO

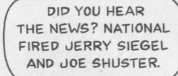

DID YOU HEAR THE NEWS? NATIONAL FIRED JERRY SIEGEL AND JOE SHUSTER.

WHAT FOR?

THEY SUED THE COMPANY TO GET OWNERSHIP OF "SUPERMAN." NOW THEY'RE BOTH OUT OF WORK.

IF THAT CAN HAPPEN TO THE GUYS WHO CREATED "SUPERMAN," IT COULD HAPPEN TO ANYBODY.

THERE'S A JOB APPLICANT--A STRANGE GUY WHO WANTS TO TALK TO YOU.

HELLO, STAN.

DO YOU KNOW WHO THIS IS? THIS IS JERRY SIEGEL. HE CREATED THE WHOLE INDUSTRY.

DO YOU HAVE ANY WRITING WORK?

WE CAN ALWAYS USE A PROOFREADER.

SURE.

COULD I WRITE SOME STORIES, TOO? I'M GLAD TO HELP IN ANY WAY I CAN.

WE'LL SEE IF WE HAVE ANYTHING, BUT IT'S JUST PROOFREADING FOR NOW.

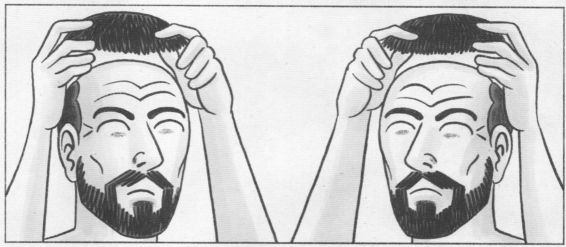

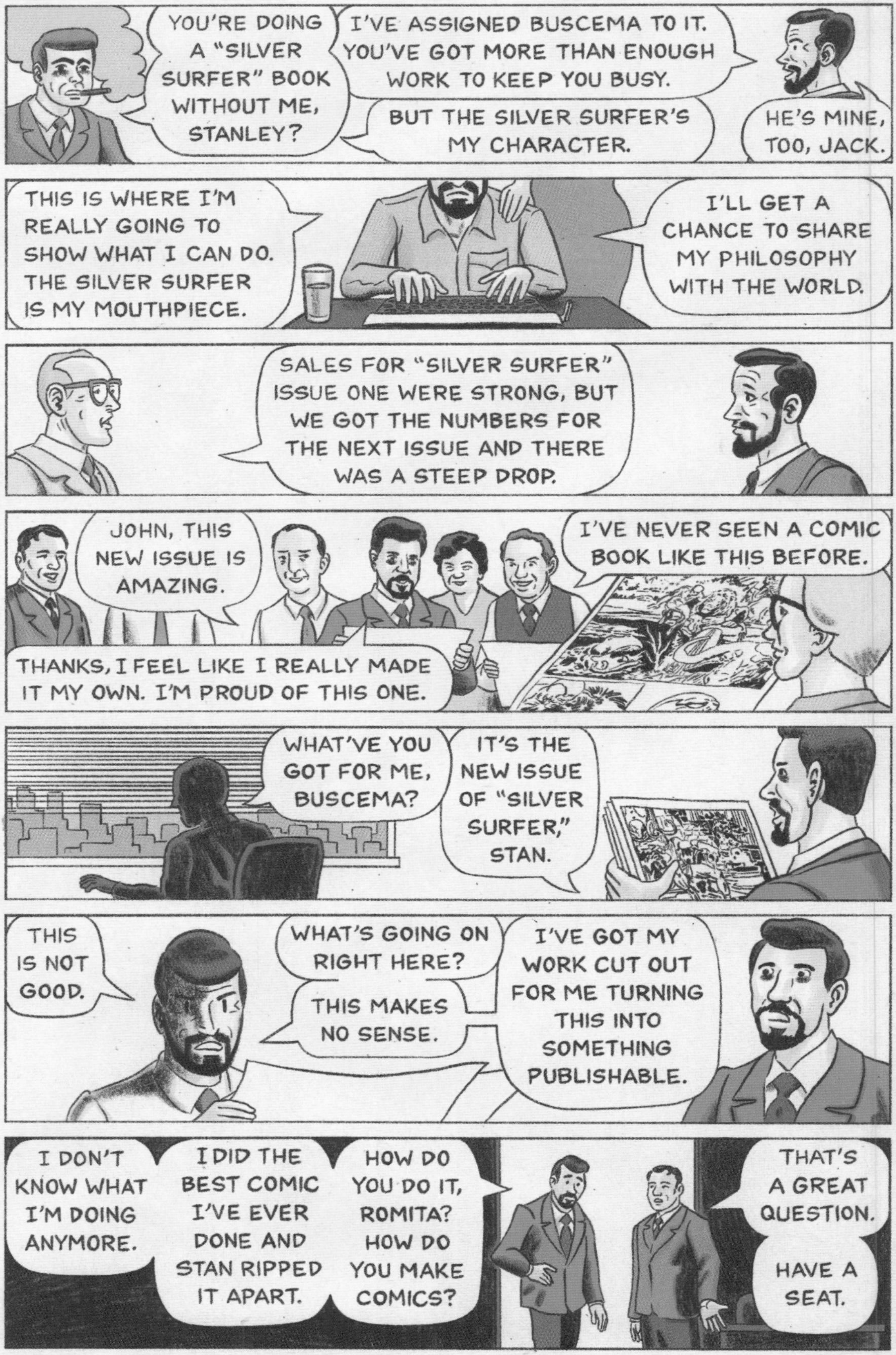
YOU'RE DOING A "SILVER SURFER" BOOK WITHOUT ME, STANLEY?
I'VE ASSIGNED BUSCEMA TO IT. YOU'VE GOT MORE THAN ENOUGH WORK TO KEEP YOU BUSY.
BUT THE SILVER SURFER'S MY CHARACTER.
HE'S MINE, TOO, JACK.
THIS IS WHERE I'M REALLY GOING TO SHOW WHAT I CAN DO. THE SILVER SURFER IS MY MOUTHPIECE.
I'LL GET A CHANCE TO SHARE MY PHILOSOPHY WITH THE WORLD.
SALES FOR "SILVER SURFER" ISSUE ONE WERE STRONG, BUT WE GOT THE NUMBERS FOR THE NEXT ISSUE AND THERE WAS A STEEP DROP.
JOHN, THIS NEW ISSUE IS AMAZING.
I'VE NEVER SEEN A COMIC BOOK LIKE THIS BEFORE.
THANKS, I FEEL LIKE I REALLY MADE IT MY OWN. I'M PROUD OF THIS ONE.
WHAT'VE YOU GOT FOR ME, BUSCEMA?
IT'S THE NEW ISSUE OF "SILVER SURFER," STAN.
THIS IS NOT GOOD.
WHAT'S GOING ON RIGHT HERE?
THIS MAKES NO SENSE.
I'VE GOT MY WORK CUT OUT FOR ME TURNING THIS INTO SOMETHING PUBLISHABLE.
I DON'T KNOW WHAT I'M DOING ANYMORE.
I DID THE BEST COMIC I'VE EVER DONE AND STAN RIPPED IT APART.
HOW DO YOU DO IT, ROMITA? HOW DO YOU MAKE COMICS?
THAT'S A GREAT QUESTION.
HAVE A SEAT.

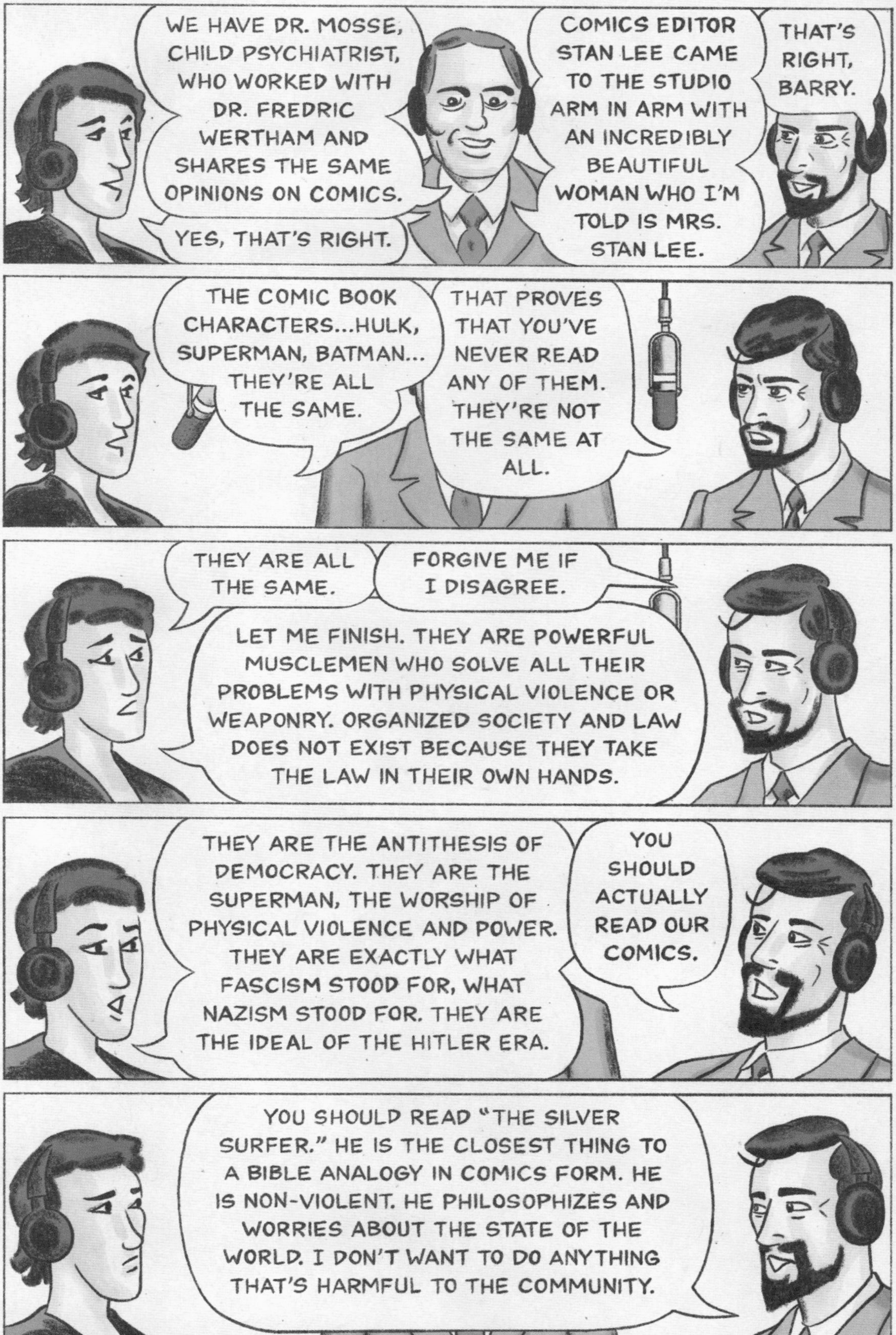
WE HAVE DR. MOSSE, CHILD PSYCHIATRIST, WHO WORKED WITH DR. FREDRIC WERTHAM AND SHARES THE SAME OPINIONS ON COMICS.
YES, THAT'S RIGHT.
COMICS EDITOR STAN LEE CAME TO THE STUDIO ARM IN ARM WITH AN INCREDIBLY BEAUTIFUL WOMAN WHO I'M TOLD IS MRS. STAN LEE.
THAT'S RIGHT, BARRY.
THE COMIC BOOK CHARACTERS...HULK, SUPERMAN, BATMAN... THEY'RE ALL THE SAME.
THAT PROVES THAT YOU'VE NEVER READ ANY OF THEM. THEY'RE NOT THE SAME AT ALL.
THEY ARE ALL THE SAME.
FORGIVE ME IF I DISAGREE.
LET ME FINISH. THEY ARE POWERFUL MUSCLEMEN WHO SOLVE ALL THEIR PROBLEMS WITH PHYSICAL VIOLENCE OR WEAPONRY. ORGANIZED SOCIETY AND LAW DOES NOT EXIST BECAUSE THEY TAKE THE LAW IN THEIR OWN HANDS.
THEY ARE THE ANTITHESIS OF DEMOCRACY. THEY ARE THE SUPERMAN, THE WORSHIP OF PHYSICAL VIOLENCE AND POWER. THEY ARE EXACTLY WHAT FASCISM STOOD FOR, WHAT NAZISM STOOD FOR. THEY ARE THE IDEAL OF THE HITLER ERA.
YOU SHOULD ACTUALLY READ OUR COMICS.
YOU SHOULD READ "THE SILVER SURFER." HE IS THE CLOSEST THING TO A BIBLE ANALOGY IN COMICS FORM. HE IS NON-VIOLENT. HE PHILOSOPHIZES AND WORRIES ABOUT THE STATE OF THE WORLD. I DON'T WANT TO DO ANYTHING THAT'S HARMFUL TO THE COMMUNITY.

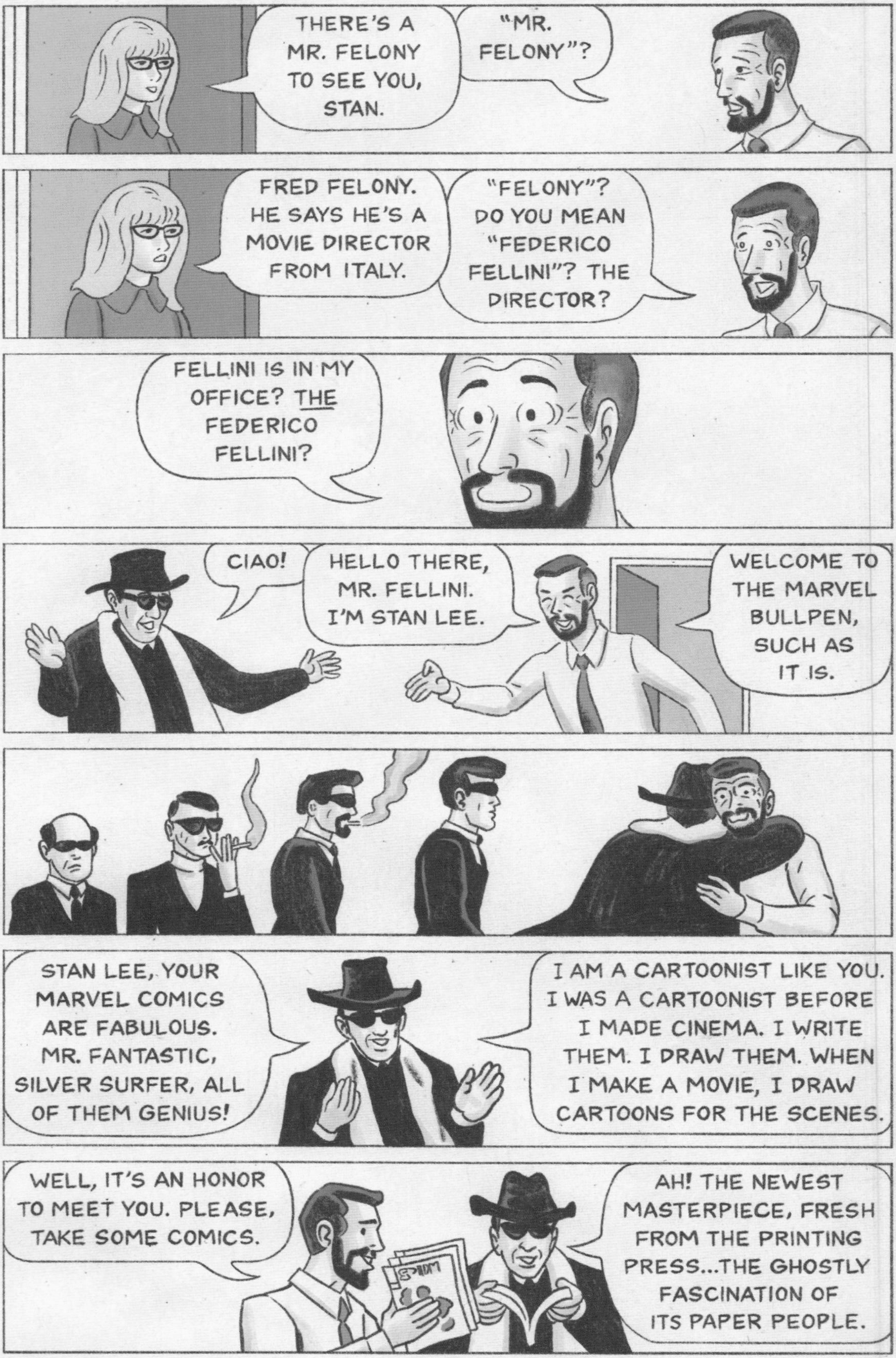
THERE'S A MR. FELONY TO SEE YOU, STAN.
"MR. FELONY"?
FRED FELONY. HE SAYS HE'S A MOVIE DIRECTOR FROM ITALY.
"FELONY"? DO YOU MEAN "FEDERICO FELLINI"? THE DIRECTOR?
FELLINI IS IN MY OFFICE? THE FEDERICO FELLINI?
CIAO!
HELLO THERE, MR. FELLINI. I'M STAN LEE.
WELCOME TO THE MARVEL BULLPEN, SUCH AS IT IS.
STAN LEE, YOUR MARVEL COMICS ARE FABULOUS. MR. FANTASTIC, SILVER SURFER, ALL OF THEM GENIUS!
I AM A CARTOONIST LIKE YOU. I WAS A CARTOONIST BEFORE I MADE CINEMA. I WRITE THEM. I DRAW THEM. WHEN I MAKE A MOVIE, I DRAW CARTOONS FOR THE SCENES.
WELL, IT'S AN HONOR TO MEET YOU. PLEASE, TAKE SOME COMICS.
AH! THE NEWEST MASTERPIECE, FRESH FROM THE PRINTING PRESS...THE GHOSTLY FASCINATION OF ITS PAPER PEOPLE.

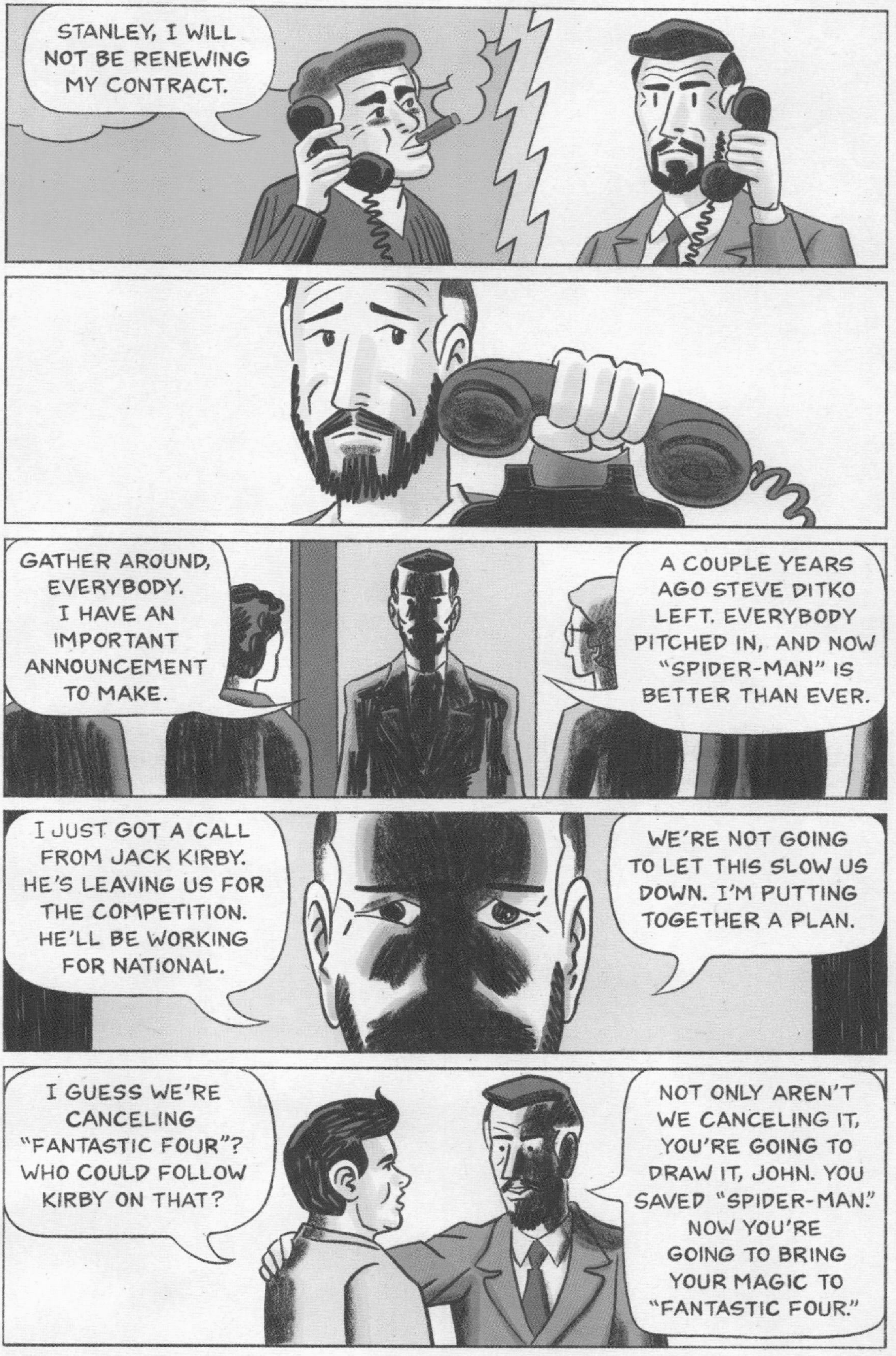
STANLEY, I WILL NOT BE RENEWING MY CONTRACT.
GATHER AROUND, EVERYBODY. I HAVE AN IMPORTANT ANNOUNCEMENT TO MAKE.
A COUPLE YEARS AGO STEVE DITKO LEFT. EVERYBODY PITCHED IN, AND NOW "SPIDER-MAN" IS BETTER THAN EVER.
I JUST GOT A CALL FROM JACK KIRBY. HE'S LEAVING US FOR THE COMPETITION. HE'LL BE WORKING FOR NATIONAL.
WE'RE NOT GOING TO LET THIS SLOW US DOWN. I'M PUTTING TOGETHER A PLAN.
I GUESS WE'RE CANCELING "FANTASTIC FOUR"? WHO COULD FOLLOW KIRBY ON THAT?
NOT ONLY AREN'T WE CANCELING IT, YOU'RE GOING TO DRAW IT, JOHN. YOU SAVED "SPIDER-MAN." NOW YOU'RE GOING TO BRING YOUR MAGIC TO "FANTASTIC FOUR."

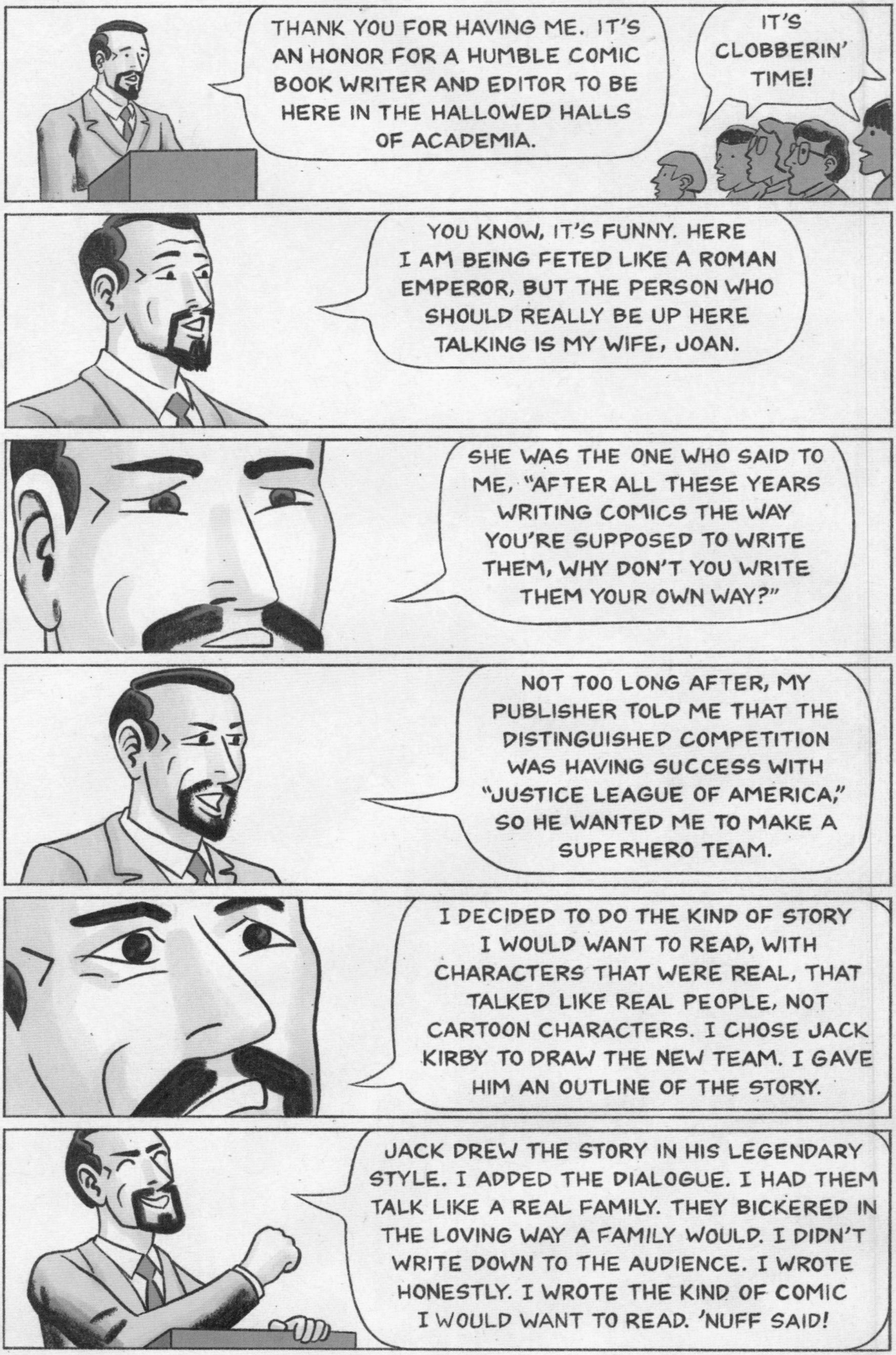
THANK YOU FOR HAVING ME. IT'S AN HONOR FOR A HUMBLE COMIC BOOK WRITER AND EDITOR TO BE HERE IN THE HALLOWED HALLS OF ACADEMIA.
IT'S CLOBBERIN' TIME!
YOU KNOW, IT'S FUNNY. HERE I AM BEING FETED LIKE A ROMAN EMPEROR, BUT THE PERSON WHO SHOULD REALLY BE UP HERE TALKING IS MY WIFE, JOAN.
SHE WAS THE ONE WHO SAID TO ME, "AFTER ALL THESE YEARS WRITING COMICS THE WAY YOU'RE SUPPOSED TO WRITE THEM, WHY DON'T YOU WRITE THEM YOUR OWN WAY?"
NOT TOO LONG AFTER, MY PUBLISHER TOLD ME THAT THE DISTINGUISHED COMPETITION WAS HAVING SUCCESS WITH "JUSTICE LEAGUE OF AMERICA," SO HE WANTED ME TO MAKE A SUPERHERO TEAM.
I DECIDED TO DO THE KIND OF STORY I WOULD WANT TO READ, WITH CHARACTERS THAT WERE REAL, THAT TALKED LIKE REAL PEOPLE, NOT CARTOON CHARACTERS. I CHOSE JACK KIRBY TO DRAW THE NEW TEAM. I GAVE HIM AN OUTLINE OF THE STORY.
JACK DREW THE STORY IN HIS LEGENDARY STYLE. I ADDED THE DIALOGUE. I HAD THEM TALK LIKE A REAL FAMILY. THEY BICKERED IN THE LOVING WAY A FAMILY WOULD. I DIDN'T WRITE DOWN TO THE AUDIENCE. I WROTE HONESTLY. I WROTE THE KIND OF COMIC I WOULD WANT TO READ. 'NUFF SAID!

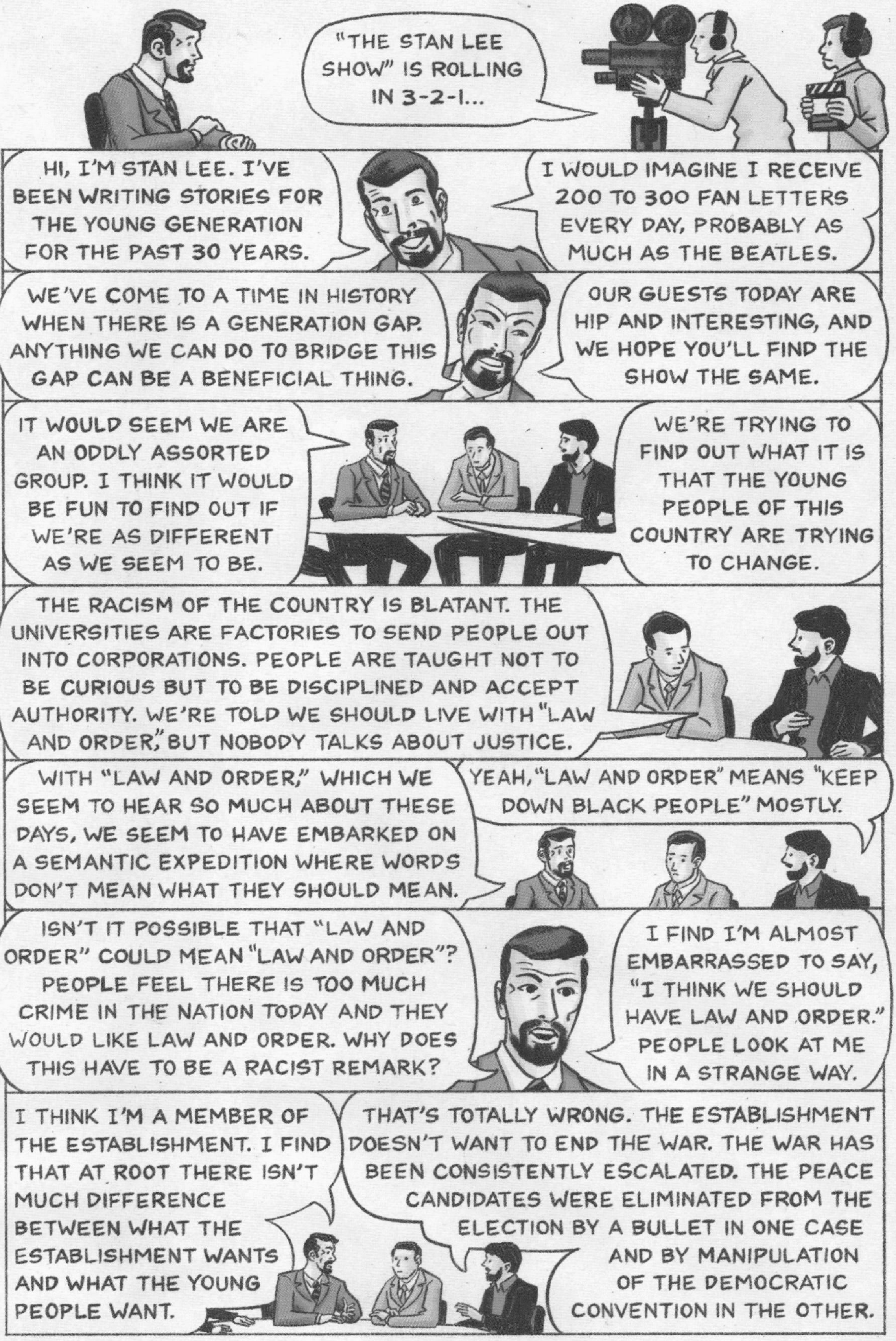

"THE STAN LEE SHOW" IS ROLLING IN 3-2-1...
HI, I'M STAN LEE. I'VE BEEN WRITING STORIES FOR THE YOUNG GENERATION FOR THE PAST 30 YEARS.
I WOULD IMAGINE I RECEIVE 200 TO 300 FAN LETTERS EVERY DAY, PROBABLY AS MUCH AS THE BEATLES.
WE'VE COME TO A TIME IN HISTORY WHEN THERE IS A GENERATION GAP. ANYTHING WE CAN DO TO BRIDGE THIS GAP CAN BE A BENEFICIAL THING.
OUR GUESTS TODAY ARE HIP AND INTERESTING, AND WE HOPE YOU'LL FIND THE SHOW THE SAME.
IT WOULD SEEM WE ARE AN ODDLY ASSORTED GROUP. I THINK IT WOULD BE FUN TO FIND OUT IF WE'RE AS DIFFERENT AS WE SEEM TO BE.
WE'RE TRYING TO FIND OUT WHAT IT IS THAT THE YOUNG PEOPLE OF THIS COUNTRY ARE TRYING TO CHANGE.
THE RACISM OF THE COUNTRY IS BLATANT. THE UNIVERSITIES ARE FACTORIES TO SEND PEOPLE OUT INTO CORPORATIONS. PEOPLE ARE TAUGHT NOT TO BE CURIOUS BUT TO BE DISCIPLINED AND ACCEPT AUTHORITY. WE'RE TOLD WE SHOULD LIVE WITH "LAW AND ORDER," BUT NOBODY TALKS ABOUT JUSTICE.
WITH "LAW AND ORDER," WHICH WE SEEM TO HEAR SO MUCH ABOUT THESE DAYS, WE SEEM TO HAVE EMBARKED ON A SEMANTIC EXPEDITION WHERE WORDS DON'T MEAN WHAT THEY SHOULD MEAN.
YEAH, "LAW AND ORDER" MEANS "KEEP DOWN BLACK PEOPLE" MOSTLY.
ISN'T IT POSSIBLE THAT "LAW AND ORDER" COULD MEAN "LAW AND ORDER"? PEOPLE FEEL THERE IS TOO MUCH CRIME IN THE NATION TODAY AND THEY WOULD LIKE LAW AND ORDER. WHY DOES THIS HAVE TO BE A RACIST REMARK?
I FIND I'M ALMOST EMBARRASSED TO SAY, "I THINK WE SHOULD HAVE LAW AND ORDER." PEOPLE LOOK AT ME IN A STRANGE WAY.
I THINK I'M A MEMBER OF THE ESTABLISHMENT. I FIND THAT AT ROOT THERE ISN'T MUCH DIFFERENCE BETWEEN WHAT THE ESTABLISHMENT WANTS AND WHAT THE YOUNG PEOPLE WANT.
THAT'S TOTALLY WRONG. THE ESTABLISHMENT DOESN'T WANT TO END THE WAR. THE WAR HAS BEEN CONSISTENTLY ESCALATED. THE PEACE CANDIDATES WERE ELIMINATED FROM THE ELECTION BY A BULLET IN ONE CASE AND BY MANIPULATION OF THE DEMOCRATIC CONVENTION IN THE OTHER.

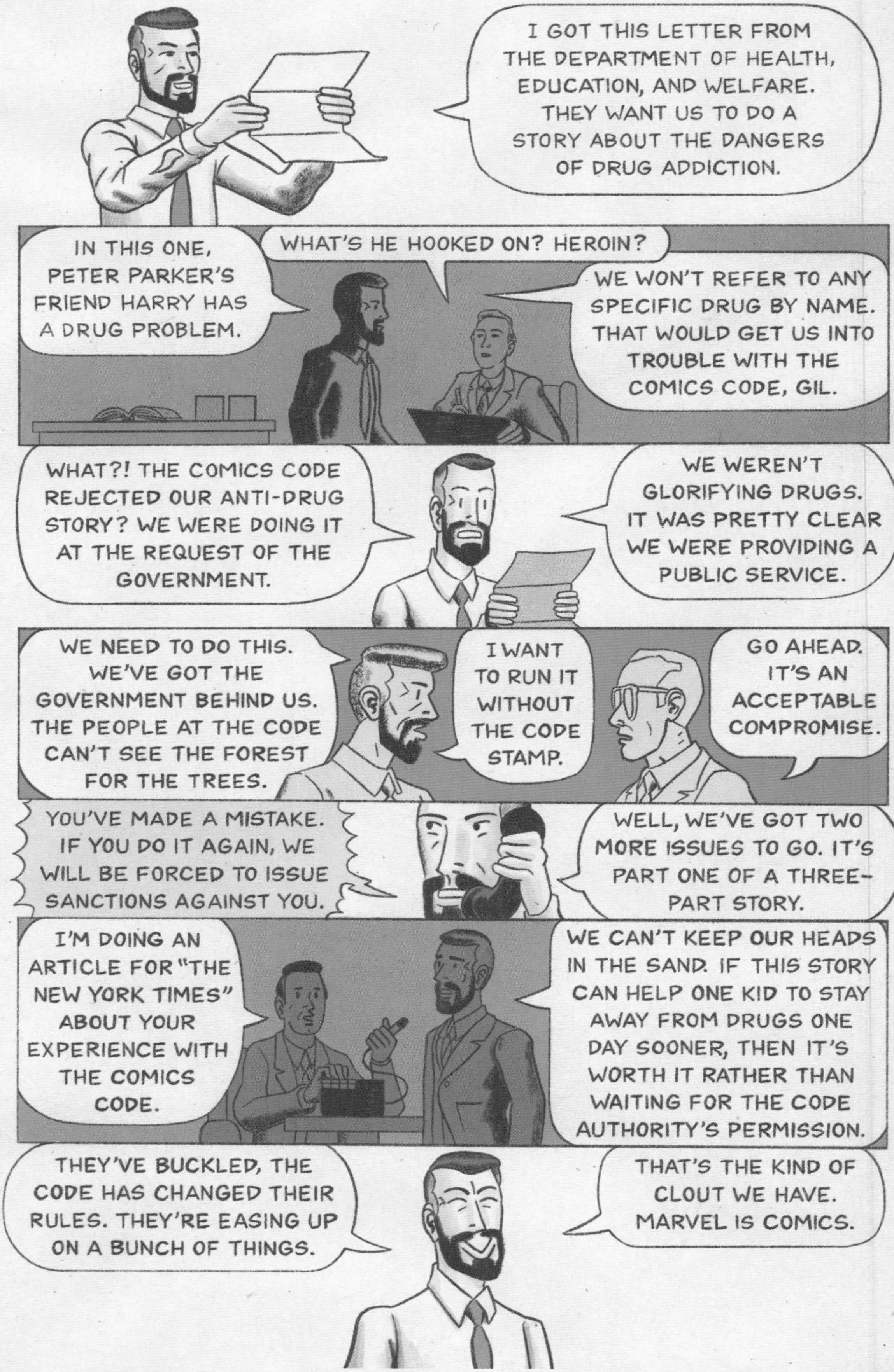
I GOT THIS LETTER FROM THE DEPARTMENT OF HEALTH, EDUCATION, AND WELFARE. THEY WANT US TO DO A STORY ABOUT THE DANGERS OF DRUG ADDICTION.
IN THIS ONE, PETER PARKER'S FRIEND HARRY HAS A DRUG PROBLEM.
WHAT'S HE HOOKED ON? HEROIN?
WE WON'T REFER TO ANY SPECIFIC DRUG BY NAME. THAT WOULD GET US INTO TROUBLE WITH THE COMICS CODE, GIL.
WHAT?! THE COMICS CODE REJECTED OUR ANTI-DRUG STORY? WE WERE DOING IT AT THE REQUEST OF THE GOVERNMENT.
WE WEREN'T GLORIFYING DRUGS. IT WAS PRETTY CLEAR WE WERE PROVIDING A PUBLIC SERVICE.
WE NEED TO DO THIS. WE'VE GOT THE GOVERNMENT BEHIND US. THE PEOPLE AT THE CODE CAN'T SEE THE FOREST FOR THE TREES.
I WANT TO RUN IT WITHOUT THE CODE STAMP.
GO AHEAD. IT'S AN ACCEPTABLE COMPROMISE.
YOU'VE MADE A MISTAKE. IF YOU DO IT AGAIN, WE WILL BE FORCED TO ISSUE SANCTIONS AGAINST YOU.
WELL, WE'VE GOT TWO MORE ISSUES TO GO. IT'S PART ONE OF A THREE-PART STORY.
I'M DOING AN ARTICLE FOR "THE NEW YORK TIMES" ABOUT YOUR EXPERIENCE WITH THE COMICS CODE.
WE CAN'T KEEP OUR HEADS IN THE SAND. IF THIS STORY CAN HELP ONE KID TO STAY AWAY FROM DRUGS ONE DAY SOONER, THEN IT'S WORTH IT RATHER THAN WAITING FOR THE CODE AUTHORITY'S PERMISSION.
THEY'VE BUCKLED, THE CODE HAS CHANGED THEIR RULES. THEY'RE EASING UP ON A BUNCH OF THINGS.
THAT'S THE KIND OF CLOUT WE HAVE. MARVEL IS COMICS.

 I SAID TO MYSELF, I MUST MEET THE GENIUS WHO CREATED THESE COMIC BOOKS. I MUST MEET STAN LEE!

 I HOPE I'M NOT A DISAPPOINTMENT.

 AH! THE STAN LEE SELF-DEPRECATING WIT. YOU ARE EXACTLY AS I PICTURED YOU.

MEET ALAIN RESNAIS. HE'S A FAMOUS FILMMAKER.

 HE'S GOING TO BE STAYING IN THE GUESTHOUSE.

STAN, WE SHOULD MAKE A MOVIE TOGETHER. SOMETHING IMPORTANT. ABOUT POLLUTION.

 YOU WRITE. I DIRECT.

THE MONSTER MAKER

Written by Stan Lee
For a film by Alain Resnais

THE POLLUTION IN THE EAST RIVER TURNS INTO A MONSTER AND GOES ON A RAMPAGE.

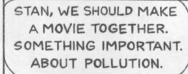

THERE'S A LOVE TRIANGLE. THERE'S A ROGER CORMAN-TYPE B-MOVIE DIRECTOR AND AN ART FILM DIRECTOR FROM LONDON.

THEY'RE ROMANTIC RIVALS.

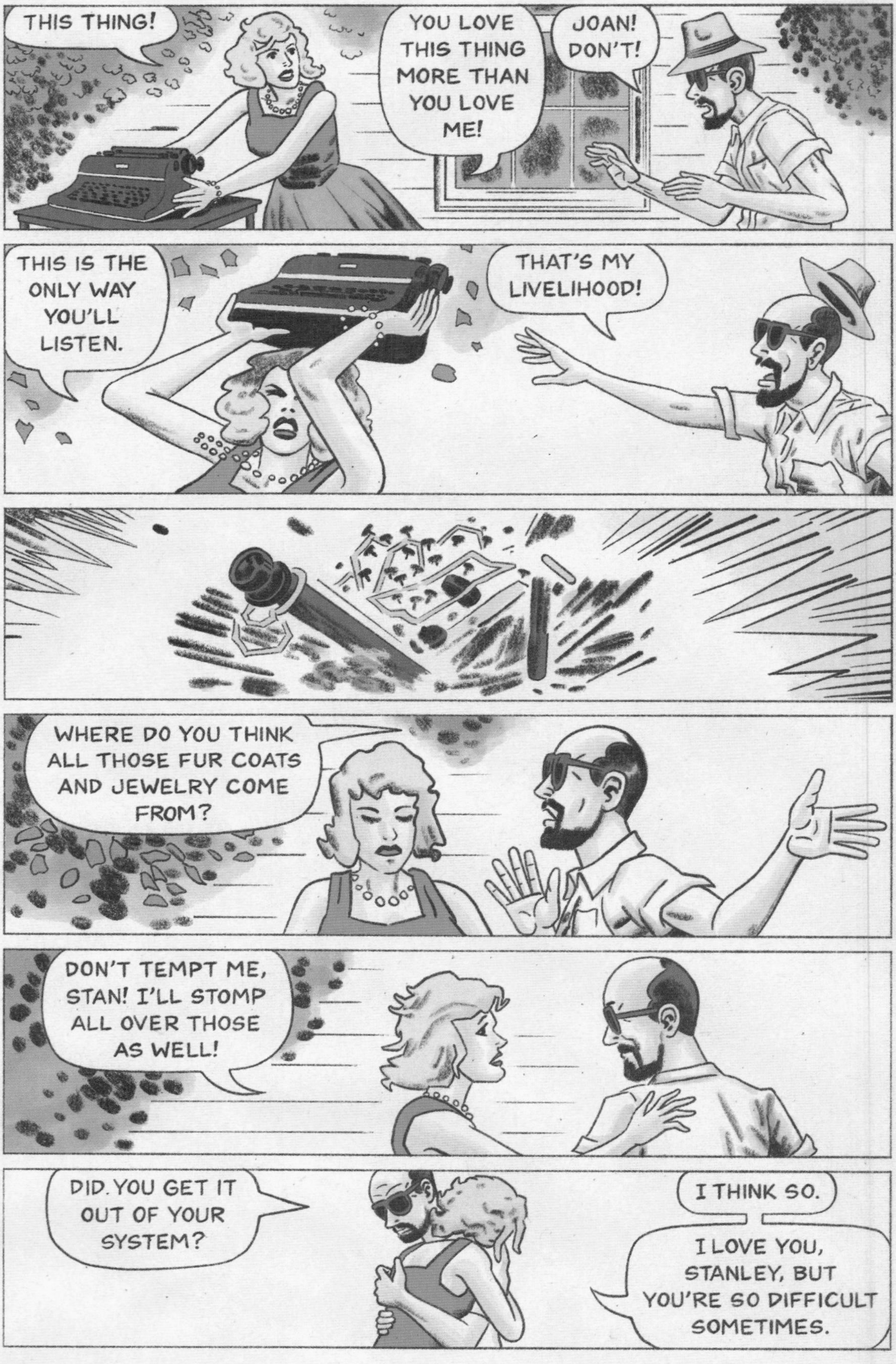
THIS THING!
YOU LOVE THIS THING MORE THAN YOU LOVE ME!
JOAN! DON'T!
THIS IS THE ONLY WAY YOU'LL LISTEN.
THAT'S MY LIVELIHOOD!
WHERE DO YOU THINK ALL THOSE FUR COATS AND JEWELRY COME FROM?
DON'T TEMPT ME, STAN! I'LL STOMP ALL OVER THOSE AS WELL!
DID. YOU GET IT OUT OF YOUR SYSTEM?
I THINK SO.
I LOVE YOU, STANLEY, BUT YOU'RE SO DIFFICULT SOMETIMES.

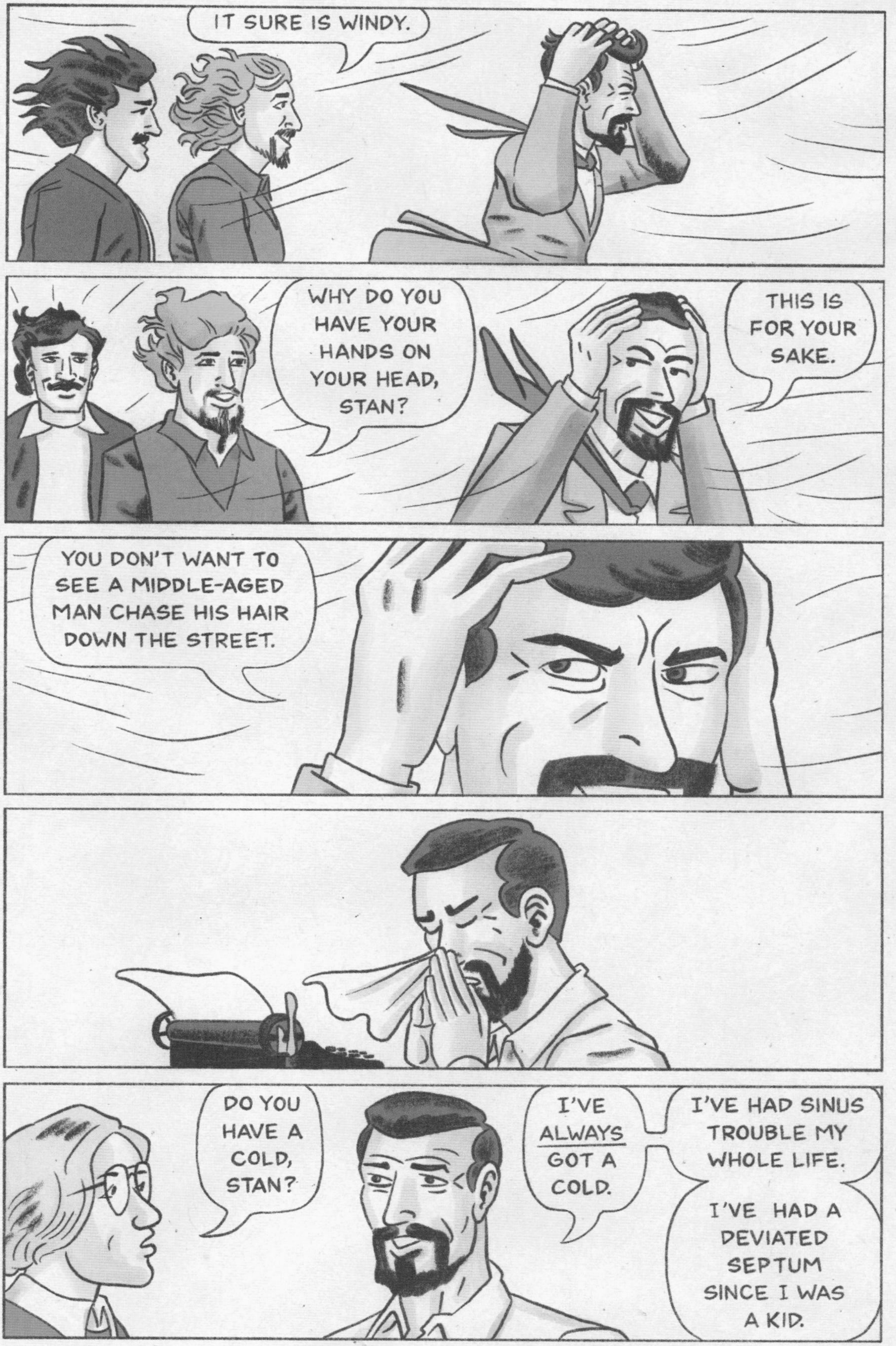
IT SURE IS WINDY.
WHY DO YOU HAVE YOUR HANDS ON YOUR HEAD, STAN?
THIS IS FOR YOUR SAKE.
YOU DON'T WANT TO SEE A MIDDLE-AGED MAN CHASE HIS HAIR DOWN THE STREET.
DO YOU HAVE A COLD, STAN?
I'VE ALWAYS GOT A COLD.
I'VE HAD SINUS TROUBLE MY WHOLE LIFE.
I'VE HAD A DEVIATED SEPTUM SINCE I WAS A KID.

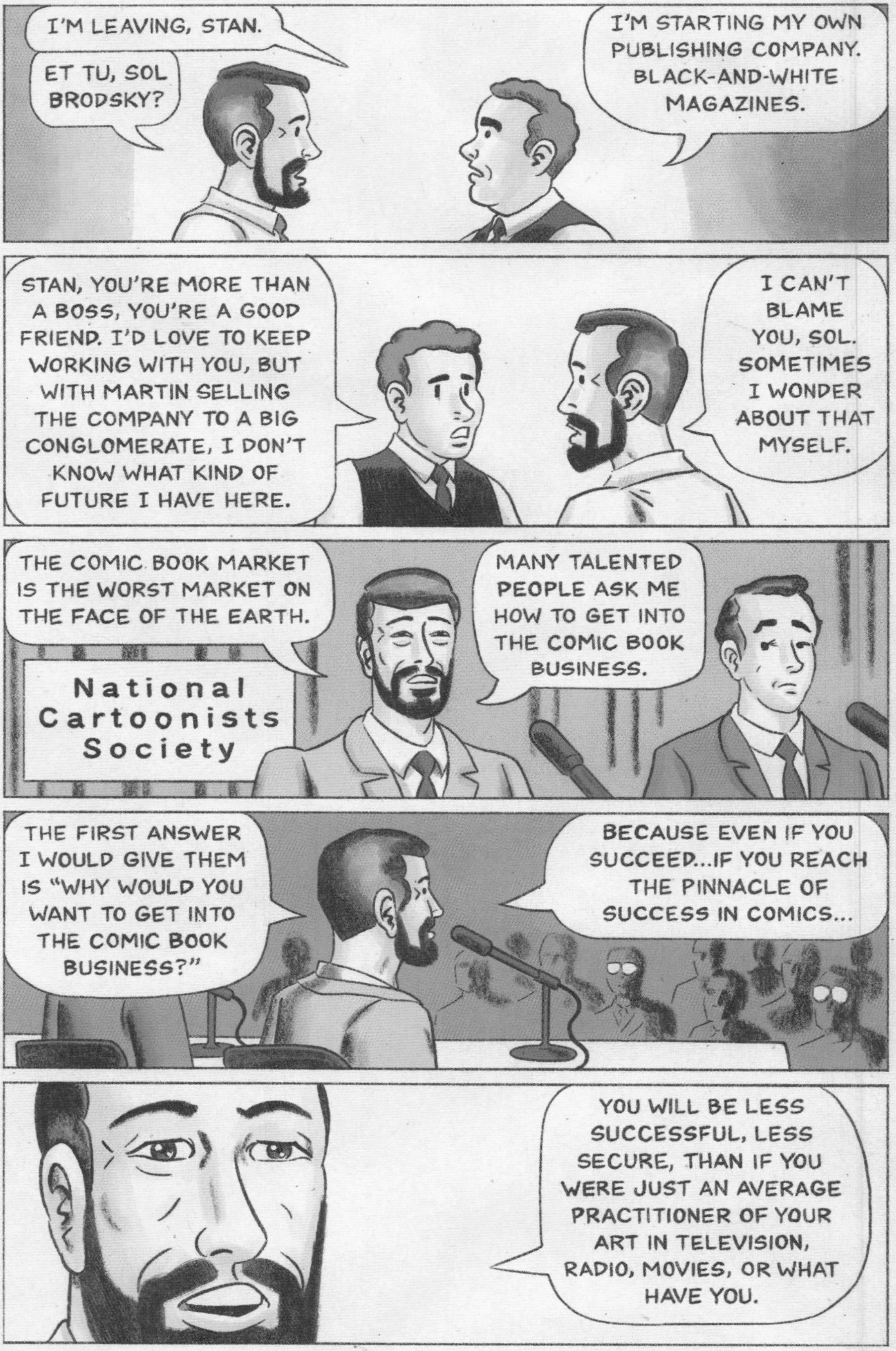
I'M LEAVING, STAN.
ET TU, SOL BRODSKY?
I'M STARTING MY OWN PUBLISHING COMPANY. BLACK-AND-WHITE MAGAZINES.
STAN, YOU'RE MORE THAN A BOSS, YOU'RE A GOOD FRIEND. I'D LOVE TO KEEP WORKING WITH YOU, BUT WITH MARTIN SELLING THE COMPANY TO A BIG CONGLOMERATE, I DON'T KNOW WHAT KIND OF FUTURE I HAVE HERE.
I CAN'T BLAME YOU, SOL. SOMETIMES I WONDER ABOUT THAT MYSELF.
THE COMIC BOOK MARKET IS THE WORST MARKET ON THE FACE OF THE EARTH.
National Cartoonists Society
MANY TALENTED PEOPLE ASK ME HOW TO GET INTO THE COMIC BOOK BUSINESS.
THE FIRST ANSWER I WOULD GIVE THEM IS "WHY WOULD YOU WANT TO GET INTO THE COMIC BOOK BUSINESS?"
BECAUSE EVEN IF YOU SUCCEED...IF YOU REACH THE PINNACLE OF SUCCESS IN COMICS...
YOU WILL BE LESS SUCCESSFUL, LESS SECURE, THAN IF YOU WERE JUST AN AVERAGE PRACTITIONER OF YOUR ART IN TELEVISION, RADIO, MOVIES, OR WHAT HAVE YOU.

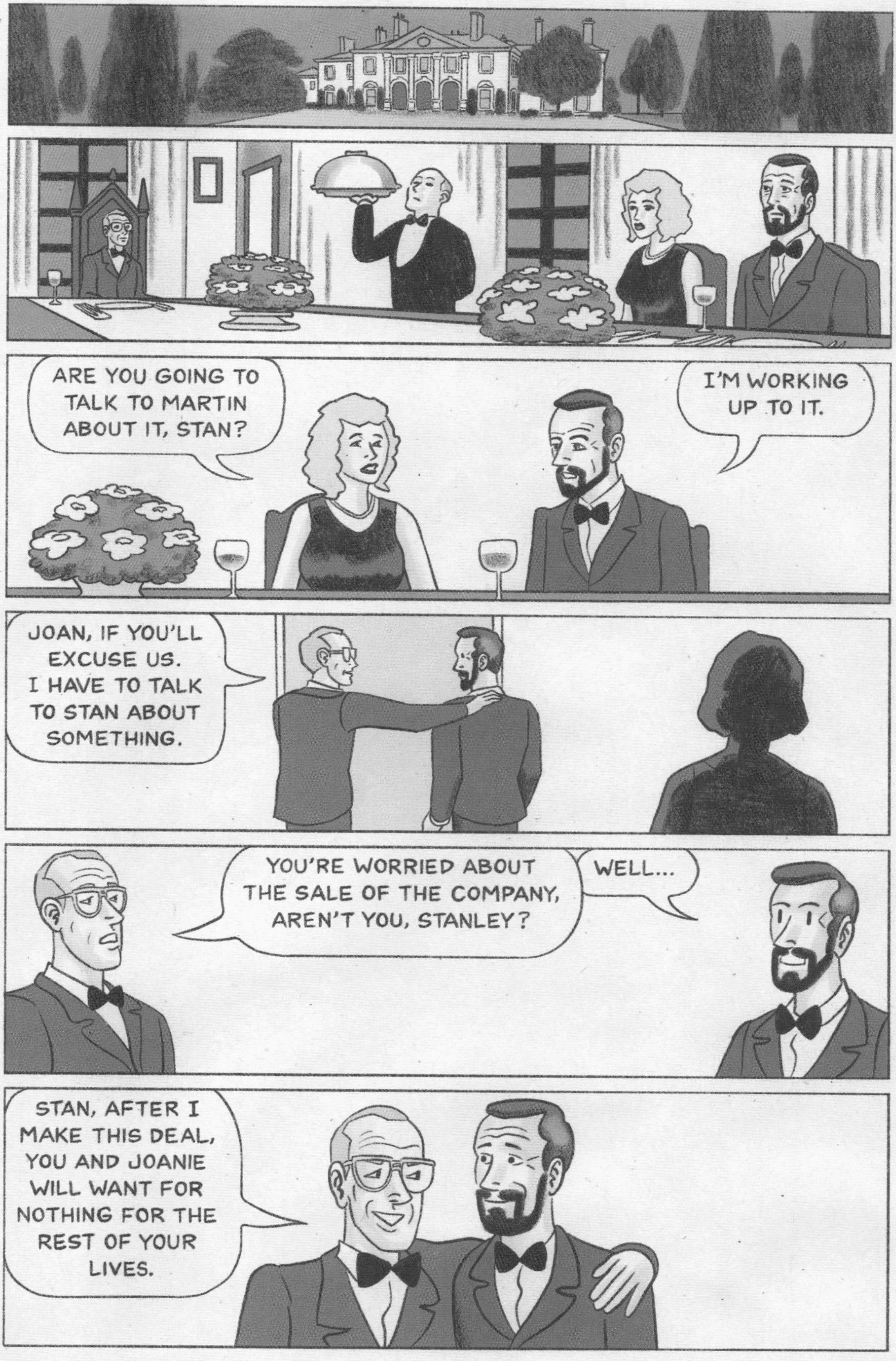
ARE YOU GOING TO TALK TO MARTIN ABOUT IT, STAN?
I'M WORKING UP TO IT.
JOAN, IF YOU'LL EXCUSE US. I HAVE TO TALK TO STAN ABOUT SOMETHING.
YOU'RE WORRIED ABOUT THE SALE OF THE COMPANY, AREN'T YOU, STANLEY?
WELL...
STAN, AFTER I MAKE THIS DEAL, YOU AND JOANIE WILL WANT FOR NOTHING FOR THE REST OF YOUR LIVES.

CARMINE, I CAN'T BELIEVE I'M SAYING THIS, BUT MAYBE I COULD COME WORK AT DC.

WE'D LOVE TO HAVE YOU HERE, STAN. WE'VE GOT KIRBY. WE COULD TEAM YOU GUYS UP AGAIN.

I'LL HAVE TO THINK ABOUT IT. IT'S A BIG STEP. I'VE WORKED AT MARVEL MY WHOLE LIFE.

LET ME KNOW WHEN YOU MAKE UP YOUR MIND. THE DOOR IS ALWAYS OPEN.

WE'RE BUYING THE COMPANY. IT'S NO SECRET. WE WANT YOU RUNNING MARVEL COMICS, BUT MARTIN HAS US LOCKED INTO CHIP GOODMAN AS YOUR BOSS.

I'D LIKE TO STAY. I'VE SPENT MY WHOLE CAREER HERE, BUT I DON'T WANT TO HAVE TO RUN EVERYTHING PAST MY OLD BOSS'S LITTLE BOY.

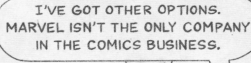

I'VE GOT OTHER OPTIONS. MARVEL ISN'T THE ONLY COMPANY IN THE COMICS BUSINESS.

AND WHO SAYS I'M GOING TO STAY IN COMICS? I'VE BEEN APPROACHED BY HOLLYWOOD DIRECTORS LOOKING TO COLLABORATE WITH ME.

CHIP GOODMAN IS OUT AT MARVEL. YOU'RE IN, STAN.

YOU WON'T REGRET IT.

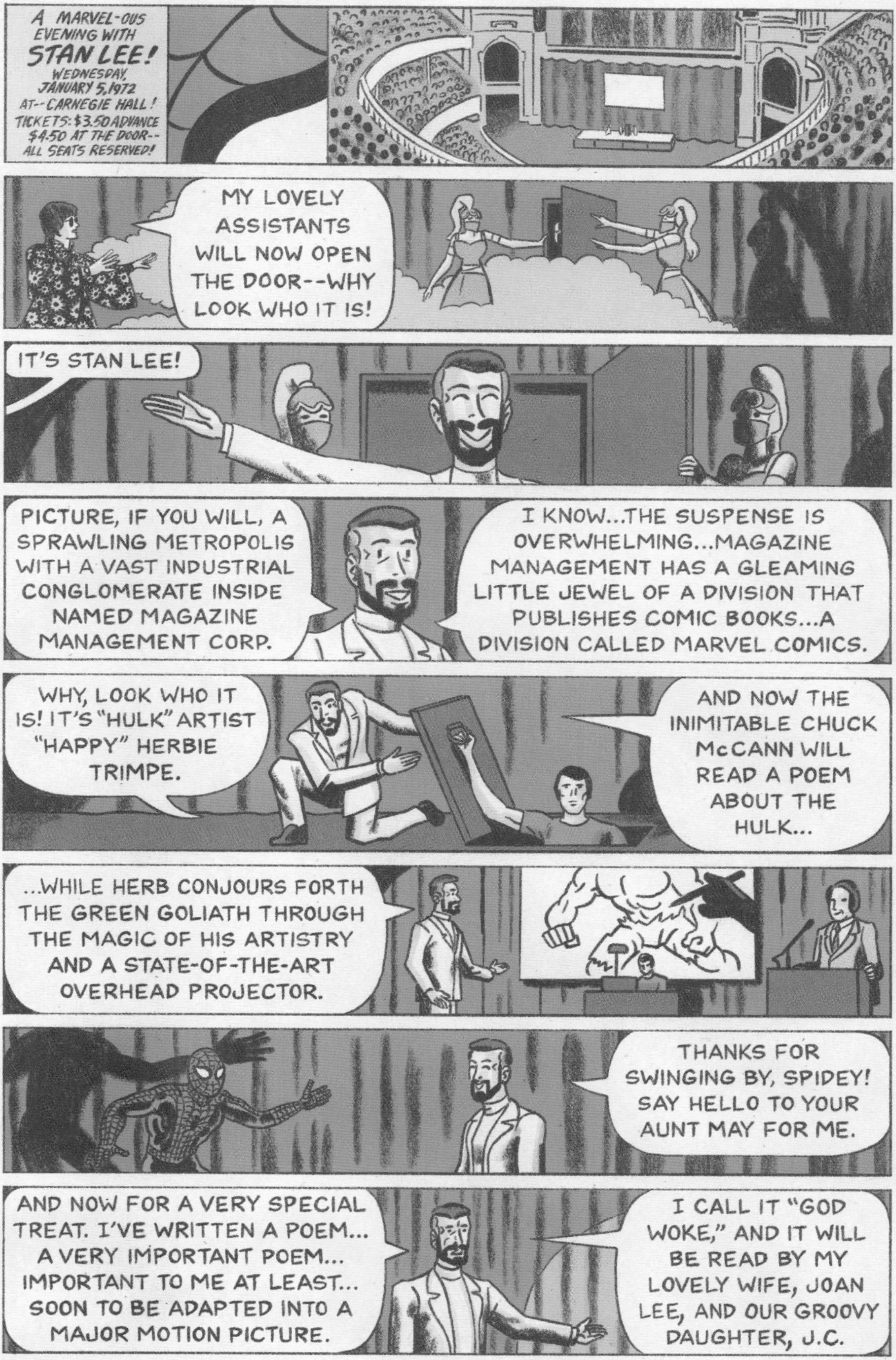
A MARVEL-OUS EVENING WITH STAN LEE! WEDNESDAY, JANUARY 5, 1972 AT--CARNEGIE HALL! TICKETS: $3.50 ADVANCE $4.50 AT THE DOOR-- ALL SEATS RESERVED!
MY LOVELY ASSISTANTS WILL NOW OPEN THE DOOR--WHY LOOK WHO IT IS!
IT'S STAN LEE!
PICTURE, IF YOU WILL, A SPRAWLING METROPOLIS WITH A VAST INDUSTRIAL CONGLOMERATE INSIDE NAMED MAGAZINE MANAGEMENT CORP.
I KNOW...THE SUSPENSE IS OVERWHELMING...MAGAZINE MANAGEMENT HAS A GLEAMING LITTLE JEWEL OF A DIVISION THAT PUBLISHES COMIC BOOKS...A DIVISION CALLED MARVEL COMICS.
WHY, LOOK WHO IT IS! IT'S "HULK" ARTIST "HAPPY" HERBIE TRIMPE.
AND NOW THE INIMITABLE CHUCK McCANN WILL READ A POEM ABOUT THE HULK...
...WHILE HERB CONJOURS FORTH THE GREEN GOLIATH THROUGH THE MAGIC OF HIS ARTISTRY AND A STATE-OF-THE-ART OVERHEAD PROJECTOR.
THANKS FOR SWINGING BY, SPIDEY! SAY HELLO TO YOUR AUNT MAY FOR ME.
AND NOW FOR A VERY SPECIAL TREAT. I'VE WRITTEN A POEM... A VERY IMPORTANT POEM... IMPORTANT TO ME AT LEAST... SOON TO BE ADAPTED INTO A MAJOR MOTION PICTURE.
I CALL IT "GOD WOKE," AND IT WILL BE READ BY MY LOVELY WIFE, JOAN LEE, AND OUR GROOVY DAUGHTER, J.C.

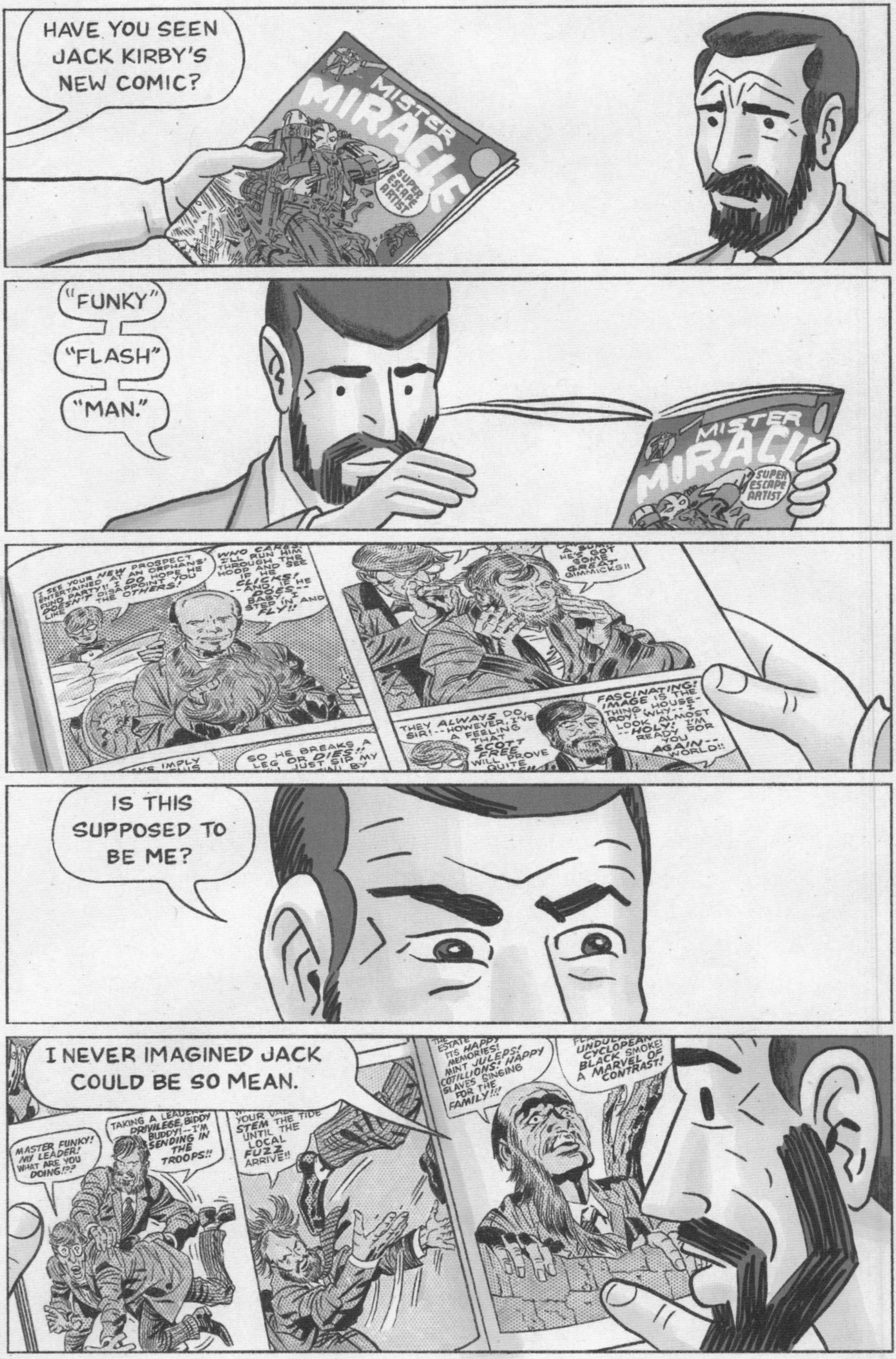
HAVE YOU SEEN JACK KIRBY'S NEW COMIC?
MISTER MIRACLE
SUPER ESCAPE ARTIST
"FUNKY"
"FLASH"
"MAN."
IS THIS SUPPOSED TO BE ME?
I NEVER IMAGINED JACK COULD BE SO MEAN.

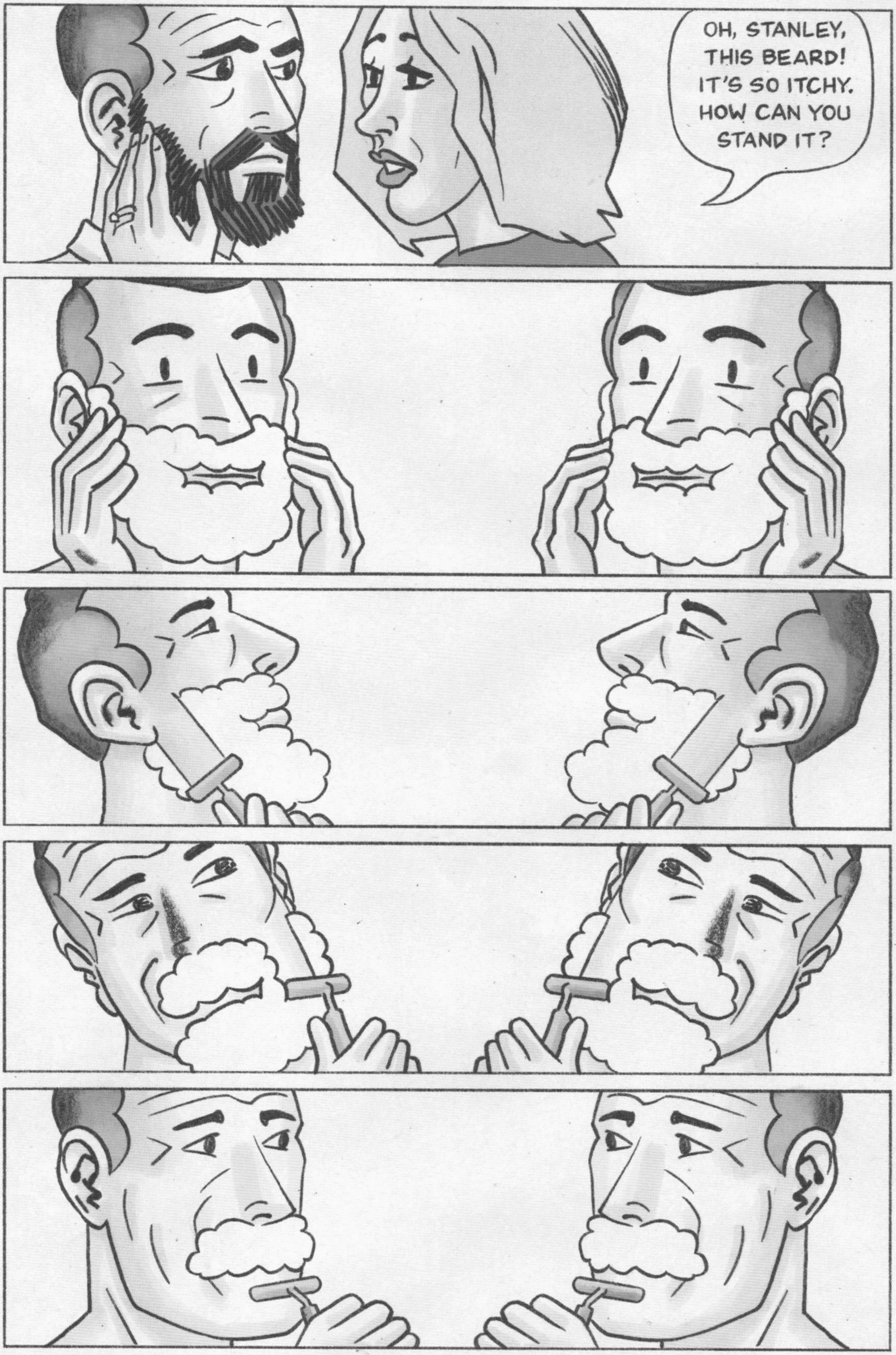
OH, STANLEY, THIS BEARD! IT'S SO ITCHY. HOW CAN YOU STAND IT?

I'VE HIRED AN AGENT TO GET ME MORE SPEAKING ENGAGEMENTS ON THE COLLEGE CIRCUIT. IT'S THE MOST VALUABLE USE OF MY TIME, EVEN MORE THAN MY WRITING.

YOU WERE BORN FOR THE STAGE, DARLING.

THIS IS WHAT WE'LL BE SENDING OUT TO THE SCHOOLS. IT'S KIND OF CORNY, BUT IT'S EFFECTIVE.

THIS IS GREAT!

THEY'RE READING COMIC BOOKS!

WHAT IS IT?

IT IS I— STAN LEE OF MARVEL COMICS!

—BETTER KNOWN AS SPEAKER-MAN!

BUT WHO IS THIS STRANGE

OUR CHARACTERS ARE UNLIKE ANY OTHERS. THEY HAVE MORE IN COMMON WITH REAL PEOPLE THAN WITH OTHER COMIC CHARACTERS. THEY HAVE PERSONAL PROBLEMS LIKE YOU OR ME.

WHY CAN'T A SUPERHERO HAVE DANDRUFF OR ATHLETE'S FOOT LIKE THE REST OF US? JUST BECAUSE YOU HAVE SUPERPOWERS DOESN'T MAKE YOU IMMUNE TO THE HUMAN CONDITION.

AND IN CLOSING, LET ME LEAVE YOU WITH THIS...

EXCELSIOR!

SPEAKING TONIGHT MARVEL COMICS EDITOR STAN LEE

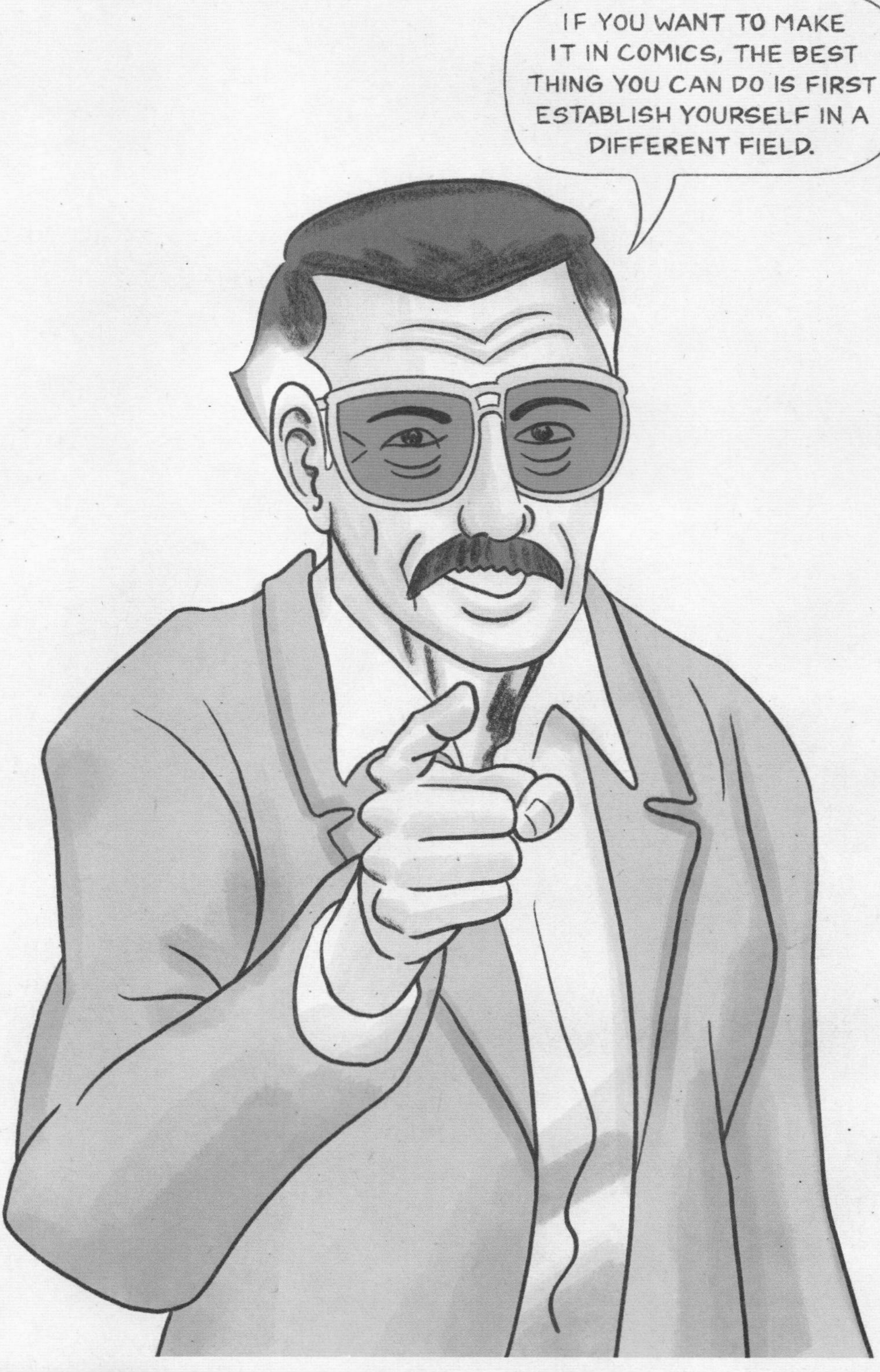
IF YOU WANT TO MAKE IT IN COMICS, THE BEST THING YOU CAN DO IS FIRST ESTABLISH YOURSELF IN A DIFFERENT FIELD.

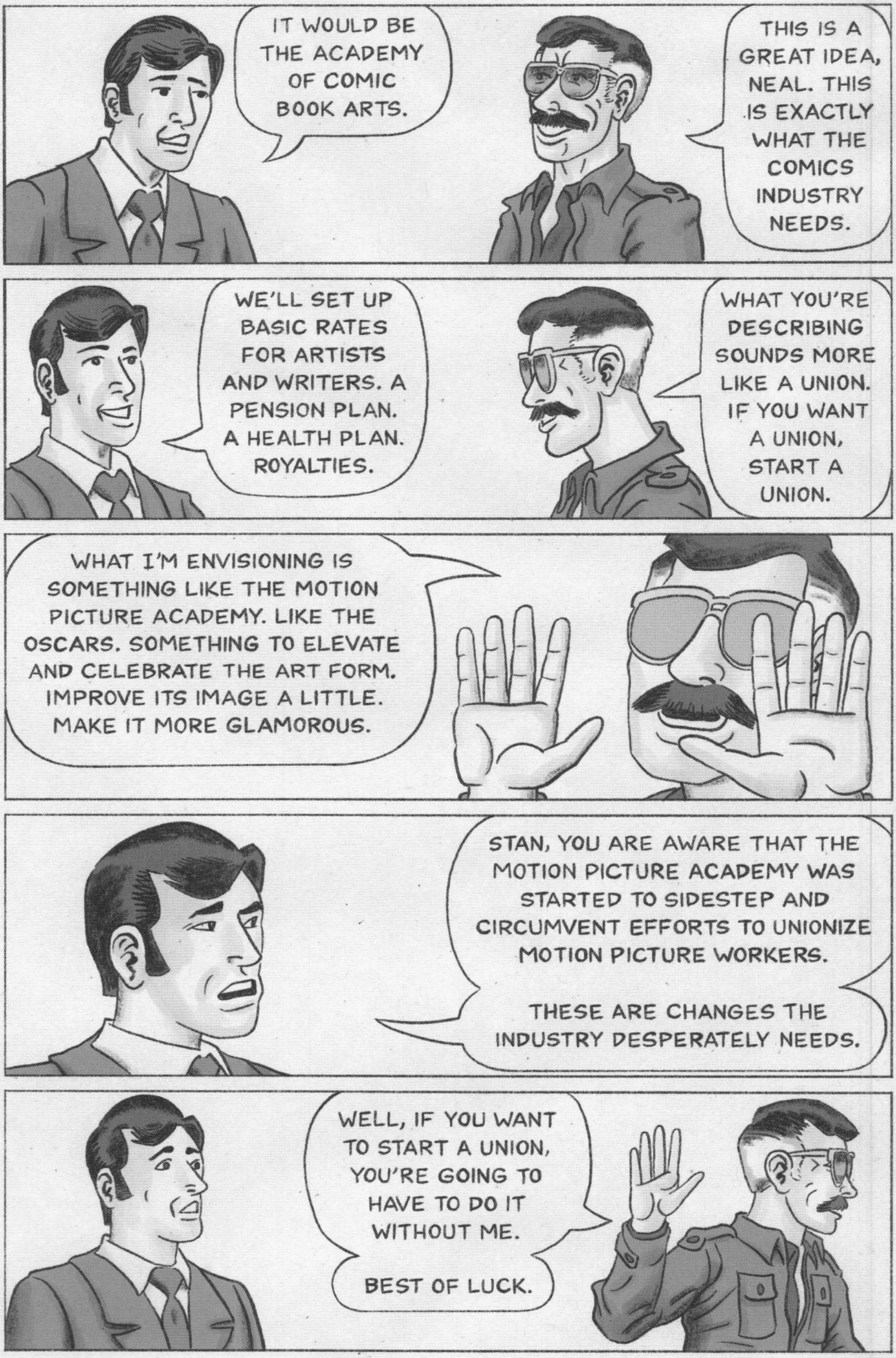
IT WOULD BE THE ACADEMY OF COMIC BOOK ARTS.
THIS IS A GREAT IDEA, NEAL. THIS IS EXACTLY WHAT THE COMICS INDUSTRY NEEDS.
WE'LL SET UP BASIC RATES FOR ARTISTS AND WRITERS. A PENSION PLAN. A HEALTH PLAN. ROYALTIES.
WHAT YOU'RE DESCRIBING SOUNDS MORE LIKE A UNION. IF YOU WANT A UNION, START A UNION.
WHAT I'M ENVISIONING IS SOMETHING LIKE THE MOTION PICTURE ACADEMY. LIKE THE OSCARS. SOMETHING TO ELEVATE AND CELEBRATE THE ART FORM. IMPROVE ITS IMAGE A LITTLE. MAKE IT MORE GLAMOROUS.
STAN, YOU ARE AWARE THAT THE MOTION PICTURE ACADEMY WAS STARTED TO SIDESTEP AND CIRCUMVENT EFFORTS TO UNIONIZE MOTION PICTURE WORKERS.
THESE ARE CHANGES THE INDUSTRY DESPERATELY NEEDS.
WELL, IF YOU WANT TO START A UNION, YOU'RE GOING TO HAVE TO DO IT WITHOUT ME.
BEST OF LUCK.

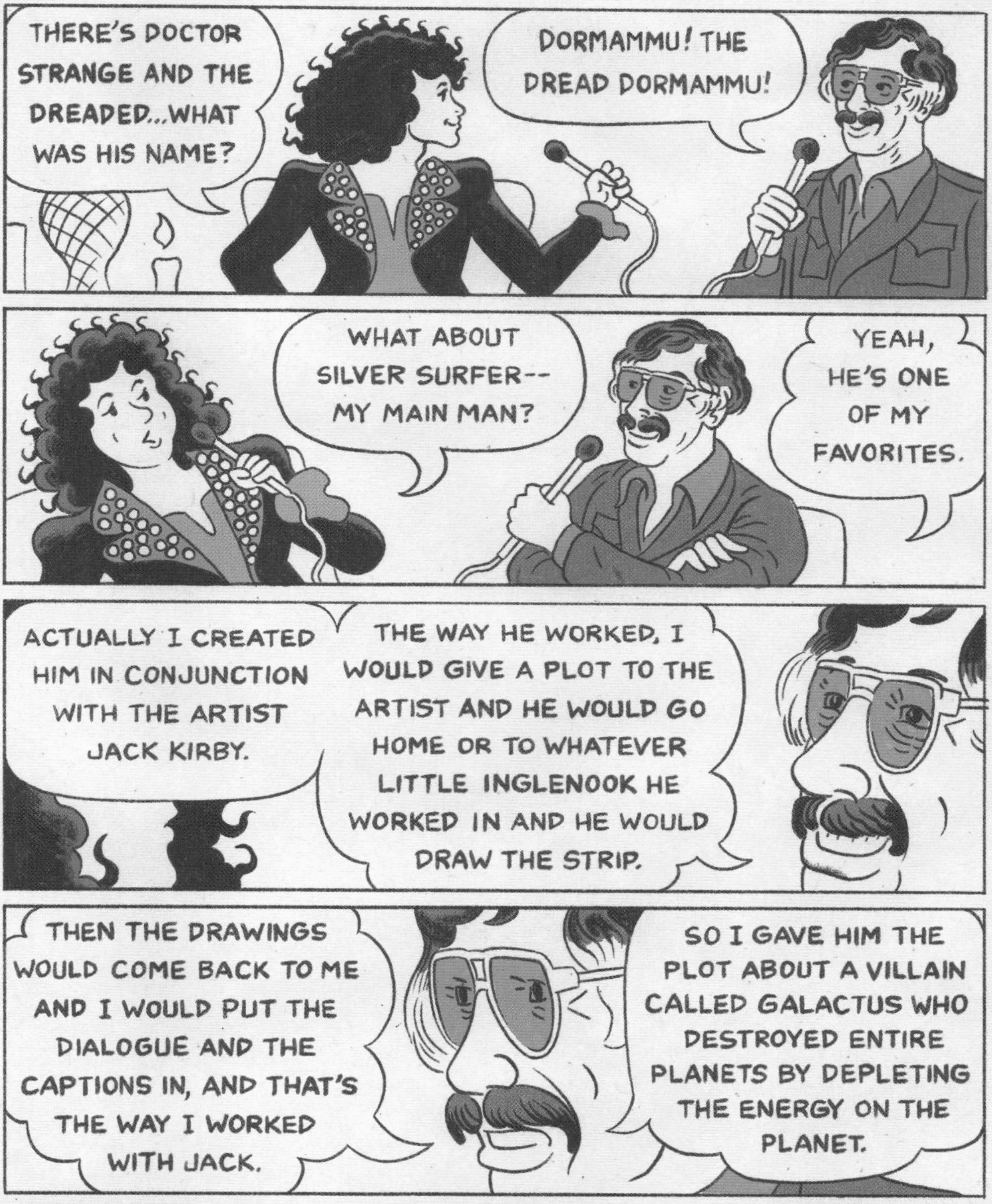
THERE'S DOCTOR STRANGE AND THE DREADED...WHAT WAS HIS NAME?
DORMAMMU! THE DREAD DORMAMMU!
WHAT ABOUT SILVER SURFER-- MY MAIN MAN?
YEAH, HE'S ONE OF MY FAVORITES.
ACTUALLY I CREATED HIM IN CONJUNCTION WITH THE ARTIST JACK KIRBY.
THE WAY HE WORKED, I WOULD GIVE A PLOT TO THE ARTIST AND HE WOULD GO HOME OR TO WHATEVER LITTLE INGLENOOK HE WORKED IN AND HE WOULD DRAW THE STRIP.
THEN THE DRAWINGS WOULD COME BACK TO ME AND I WOULD PUT THE DIALOGUE AND THE CAPTIONS IN, AND THAT'S THE WAY I WORKED WITH JACK.
SO I GAVE HIM THE PLOT ABOUT A VILLAIN CALLED GALACTUS WHO DESTROYED ENTIRE PLANETS BY DEPLETING THE ENERGY ON THE PLANET.
WELL, WHEN JACK GAVE ME THE DRAWINGS I SAW THIS NUT ON A FLYING SURFBOARD IN THE STORY--
HAHA!
I SAID, "WHO'S THAT GUY?"

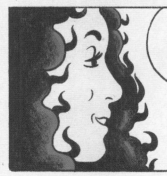

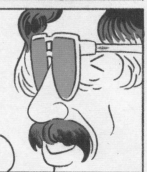

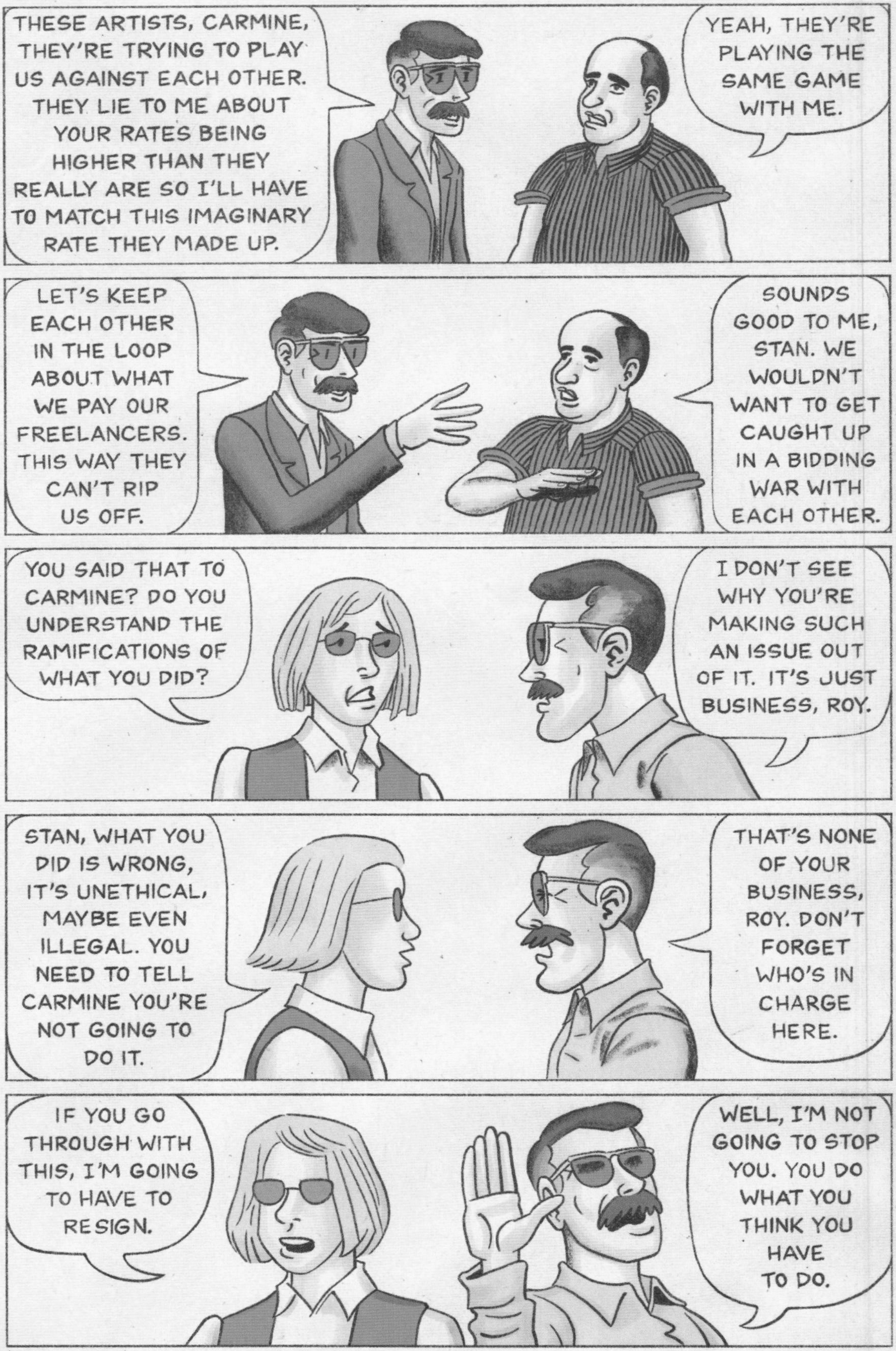
THESE ARTISTS, CARMINE, THEY'RE TRYING TO PLAY US AGAINST EACH OTHER. THEY LIE TO ME ABOUT YOUR RATES BEING HIGHER THAN THEY REALLY ARE SO I'LL HAVE TO MATCH THIS IMAGINARY RATE THEY MADE UP.
YEAH, THEY'RE PLAYING THE SAME GAME WITH ME.
LET'S KEEP EACH OTHER IN THE LOOP ABOUT WHAT WE PAY OUR FREELANCERS. THIS WAY THEY CAN'T RIP US OFF.
SOUNDS GOOD TO ME, STAN. WE WOULDN'T WANT TO GET CAUGHT UP IN A BIDDING WAR WITH EACH OTHER.
YOU SAID THAT TO CARMINE? DO YOU UNDERSTAND THE RAMIFICATIONS OF WHAT YOU DID?
I DON'T SEE WHY YOU'RE MAKING SUCH AN ISSUE OUT OF IT. IT'S JUST BUSINESS, ROY.
STAN, WHAT YOU DID IS WRONG, IT'S UNETHICAL, MAYBE EVEN ILLEGAL. YOU NEED TO TELL CARMINE YOU'RE NOT GOING TO DO IT.
THAT'S NONE OF YOUR BUSINESS, ROY. DON'T FORGET WHO'S IN CHARGE HERE.
IF YOU GO THROUGH WITH THIS, I'M GOING TO HAVE TO RESIGN.
WELL, I'M NOT GOING TO STOP YOU. YOU DO WHAT YOU THINK YOU HAVE TO DO.

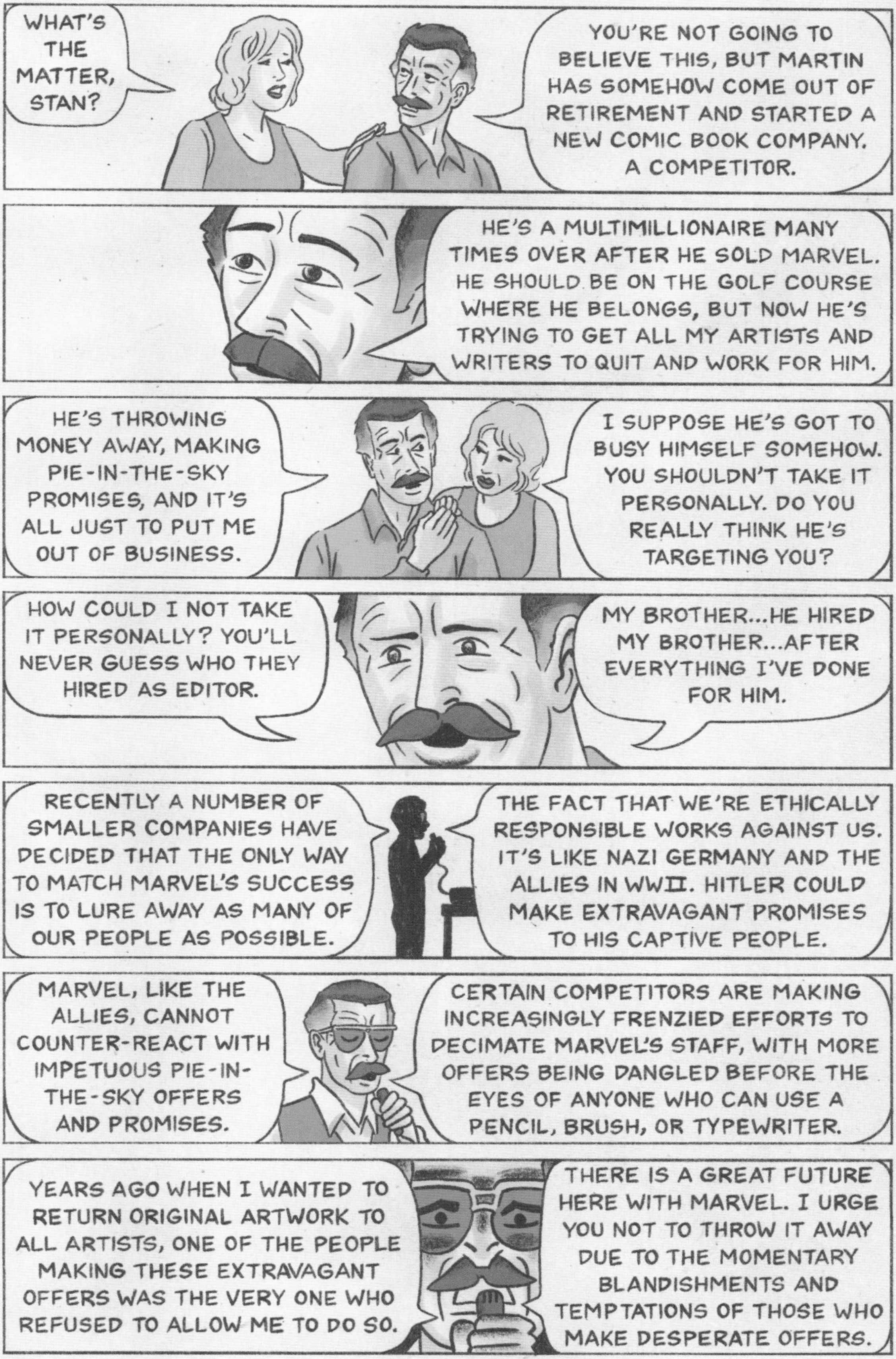
WHAT'S THE MATTER, STAN?
YOU'RE NOT GOING TO BELIEVE THIS, BUT MARTIN HAS SOMEHOW COME OUT OF RETIREMENT AND STARTED A NEW COMIC BOOK COMPANY. A COMPETITOR.
HE'S A MULTIMILLIONAIRE MANY TIMES OVER AFTER HE SOLD MARVEL. HE SHOULD BE ON THE GOLF COURSE WHERE HE BELONGS, BUT NOW HE'S TRYING TO GET ALL MY ARTISTS AND WRITERS TO QUIT AND WORK FOR HIM.
HE'S THROWING MONEY AWAY, MAKING PIE-IN-THE-SKY PROMISES, AND IT'S ALL JUST TO PUT ME OUT OF BUSINESS.
I SUPPOSE HE'S GOT TO BUSY HIMSELF SOMEHOW. YOU SHOULDN'T TAKE IT PERSONALLY. DO YOU REALLY THINK HE'S TARGETING YOU?
HOW COULD I NOT TAKE IT PERSONALLY? YOU'LL NEVER GUESS WHO THEY HIRED AS EDITOR.
MY BROTHER...HE HIRED MY BROTHER...AFTER EVERYTHING I'VE DONE FOR HIM.
RECENTLY A NUMBER OF SMALLER COMPANIES HAVE DECIDED THAT THE ONLY WAY TO MATCH MARVEL'S SUCCESS IS TO LURE AWAY AS MANY OF OUR PEOPLE AS POSSIBLE.
THE FACT THAT WE'RE ETHICALLY RESPONSIBLE WORKS AGAINST US. IT'S LIKE NAZI GERMANY AND THE ALLIES IN WWII. HITLER COULD MAKE EXTRAVAGANT PROMISES TO HIS CAPTIVE PEOPLE.
MARVEL, LIKE THE ALLIES, CANNOT COUNTER-REACT WITH IMPETUOUS PIE-IN-THE-SKY OFFERS AND PROMISES.
CERTAIN COMPETITORS ARE MAKING INCREASINGLY FRENZIED EFFORTS TO DECIMATE MARVEL'S STAFF, WITH MORE OFFERS BEING DANGLED BEFORE THE EYES OF ANYONE WHO CAN USE A PENCIL, BRUSH, OR TYPEWRITER.
YEARS AGO WHEN I WANTED TO RETURN ORIGINAL ARTWORK TO ALL ARTISTS, ONE OF THE PEOPLE MAKING THESE EXTRAVAGANT OFFERS WAS THE VERY ONE WHO REFUSED TO ALLOW ME TO DO SO.
THERE IS A GREAT FUTURE HERE WITH MARVEL. I URGE YOU NOT TO THROW IT AWAY DUE TO THE MOMENTARY BLANDISHMENTS AND TEMPTATIONS OF THOSE WHO MAKE DESPERATE OFFERS.

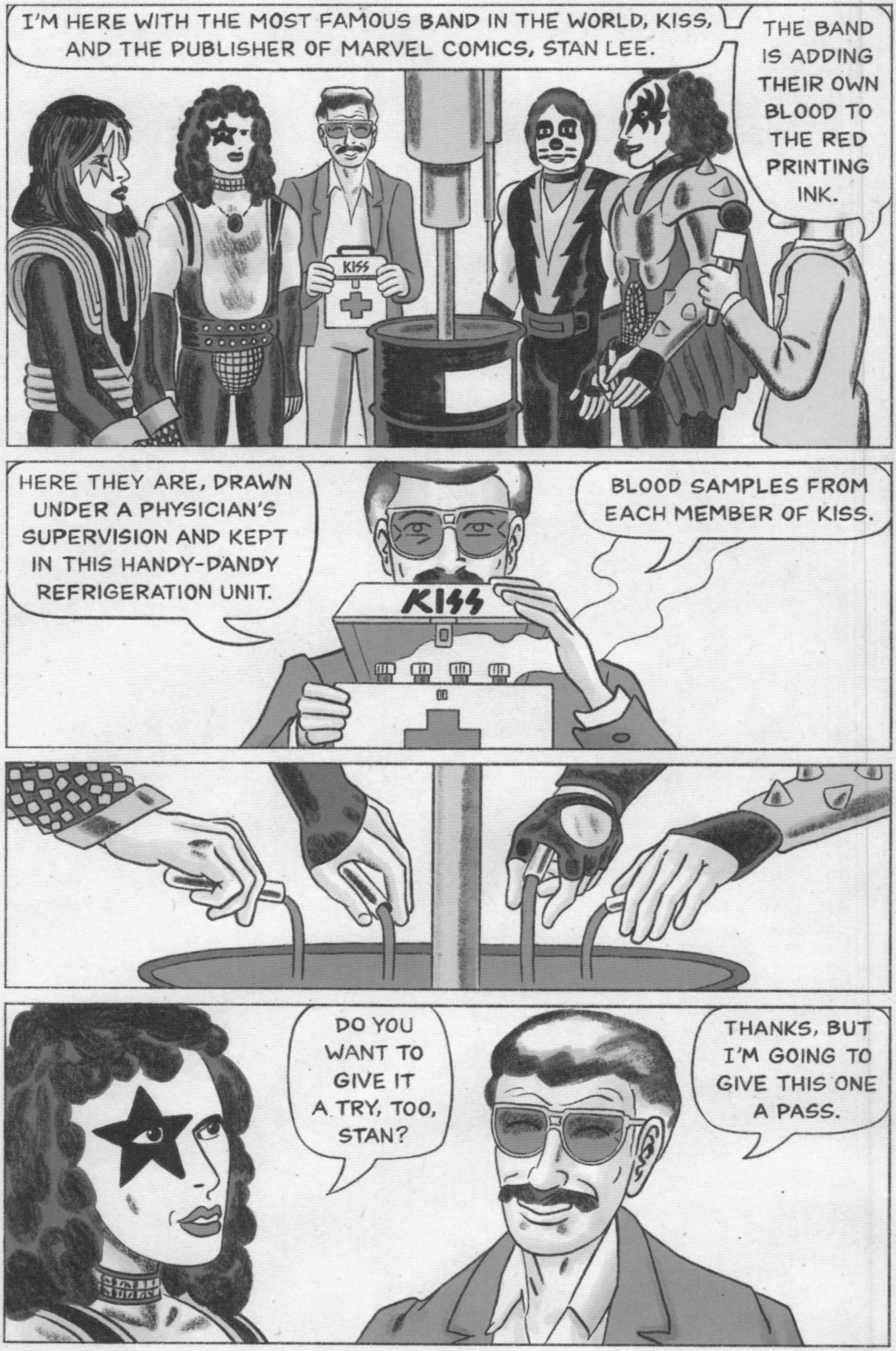
I'M HERE WITH THE MOST FAMOUS BAND IN THE WORLD, KISS, AND THE PUBLISHER OF MARVEL COMICS, STAN LEE.
THE BAND IS ADDING THEIR OWN BLOOD TO THE RED PRINTING INK.
KISS
HERE THEY ARE, DRAWN UNDER A PHYSICIAN'S SUPERVISION AND KEPT IN THIS HANDY-DANDY REFRIGERATION UNIT.
BLOOD SAMPLES FROM EACH MEMBER OF KISS.
KISS
DO YOU WANT TO GIVE IT A TRY, TOO, STAN?
THANKS, BUT I'M GOING TO GIVE THIS ONE A PASS.

THAT'S SUPPOSED TO BE SPIDER-MAN'S WEB? IT DOESN'T LOOK VERY STRONG. IT LOOKS LIKE A DOILY GENTLY LAID UPON THE BAD GUYS.

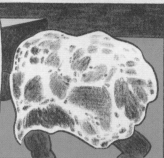

HOW'S THAT SUPPOSED TO HOLD ANYBODY?

I'M SORRY TO SAY THE ACTION IS THE BEST THING ABOUT THE SHOW. THE SUCCESS OF THE COMIC CAME FROM THE HUMOR AND WIT. THERE'S NONE OF THAT HERE.

THERE'S NO PERSONALITY--NO CHARACTERIZATION. THE DIALOGUE IS FLAT. IT HAS NO COLOR.

THIS IS TELEVISION. THIS ISN'T COMIC BOOKS, STAN. YOU DON'T HAVE TO HAVE CONSTANT TALK.

YOU NEED TO LEAVE ROOM FOR THINGS TO BREATHE.

IT'S NOT TELEVISION VERSUS COMICS. IT'S GOOD WRITING VERSUS BAD WRITING.

THIS IS JUST BAD WRITING.

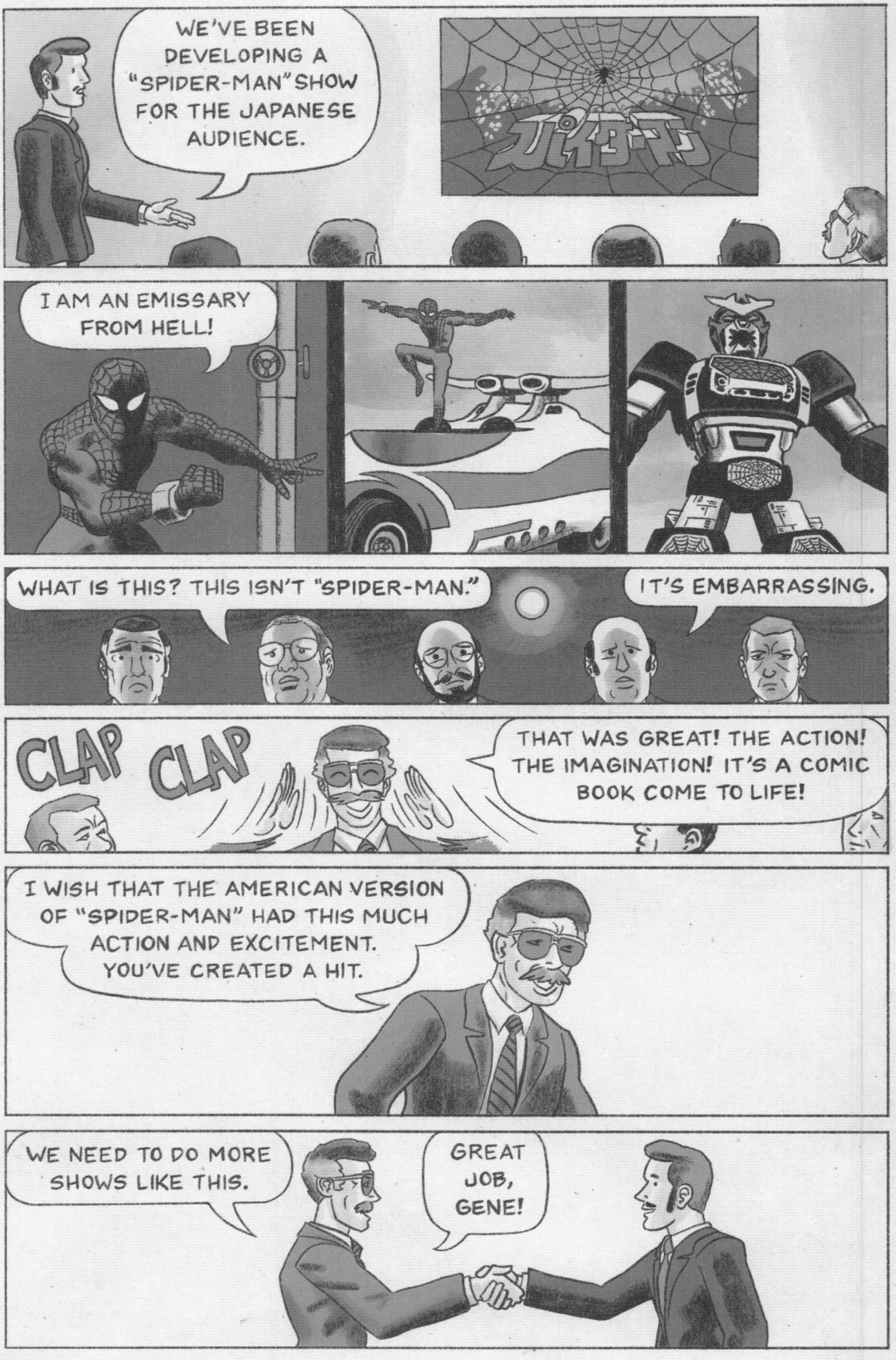
WE'VE BEEN DEVELOPING A "SPIDER-MAN" SHOW FOR THE JAPANESE AUDIENCE.
スパイダーマン
I AM AN EMISSARY FROM HELL!
WHAT IS THIS? THIS ISN'T "SPIDER-MAN."
IT'S EMBARRASSING.
CLAP
CLAP
THAT WAS GREAT! THE ACTION! THE IMAGINATION! IT'S A COMIC BOOK COME TO LIFE!
I WISH THAT THE AMERICAN VERSION OF "SPIDER-MAN" HAD THIS MUCH ACTION AND EXCITEMENT. YOU'VE CREATED A HIT.
WE NEED TO DO MORE SHOWS LIKE THIS.
GREAT JOB, GENE!

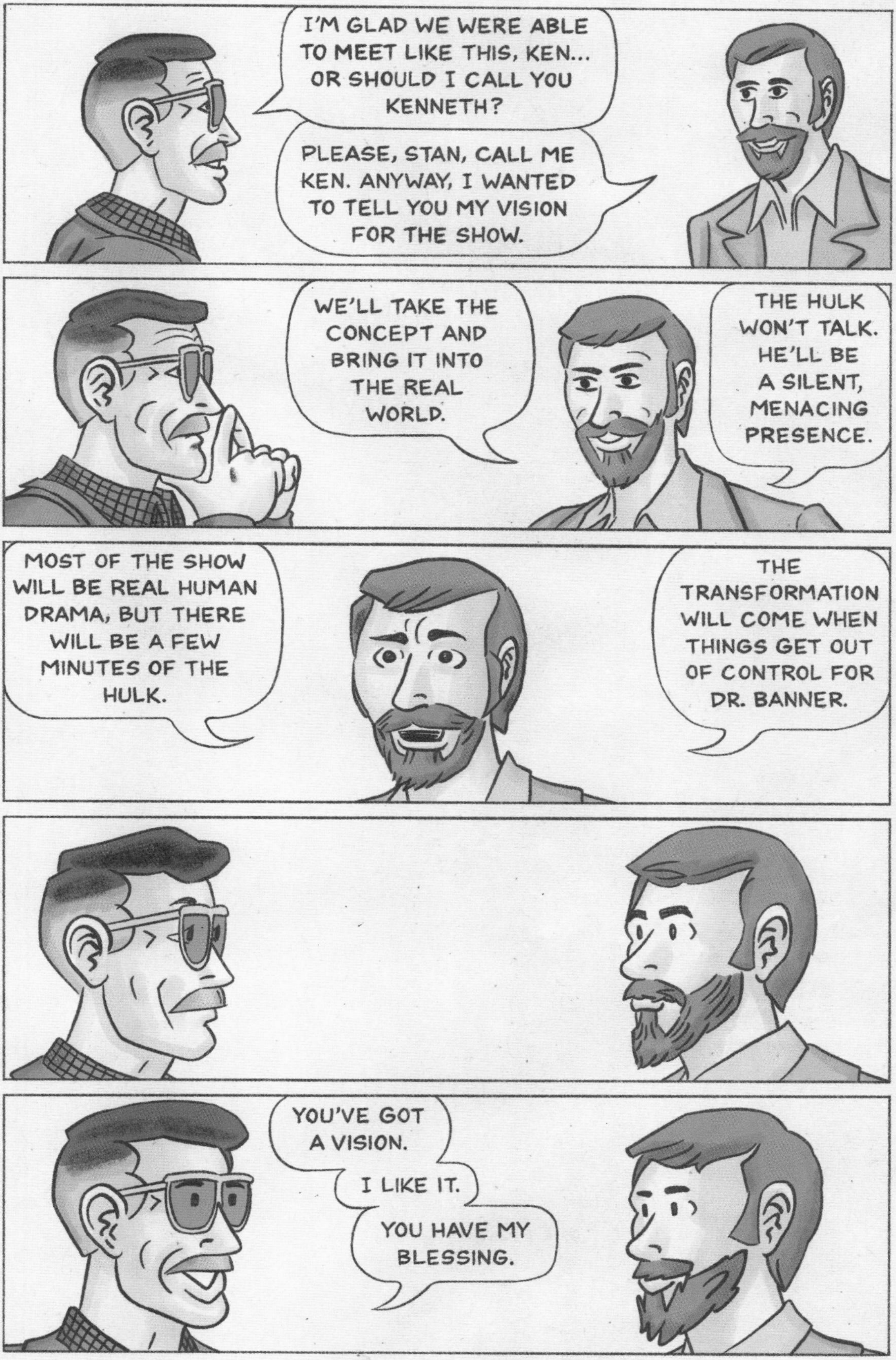
I'M GLAD WE WERE ABLE TO MEET LIKE THIS, KEN... OR SHOULD I CALL YOU KENNETH?
PLEASE, STAN, CALL ME KEN. ANYWAY, I WANTED TO TELL YOU MY VISION FOR THE SHOW.
WE'LL TAKE THE CONCEPT AND BRING IT INTO THE REAL WORLD.
THE HULK WON'T TALK. HE'LL BE A SILENT, MENACING PRESENCE.
MOST OF THE SHOW WILL BE REAL HUMAN DRAMA, BUT THERE WILL BE A FEW MINUTES OF THE HULK.
THE TRANSFORMATION WILL COME WHEN THINGS GET OUT OF CONTROL FOR DR. BANNER.
YOU'VE GOT A VISION.
I LIKE IT.
YOU HAVE MY BLESSING.

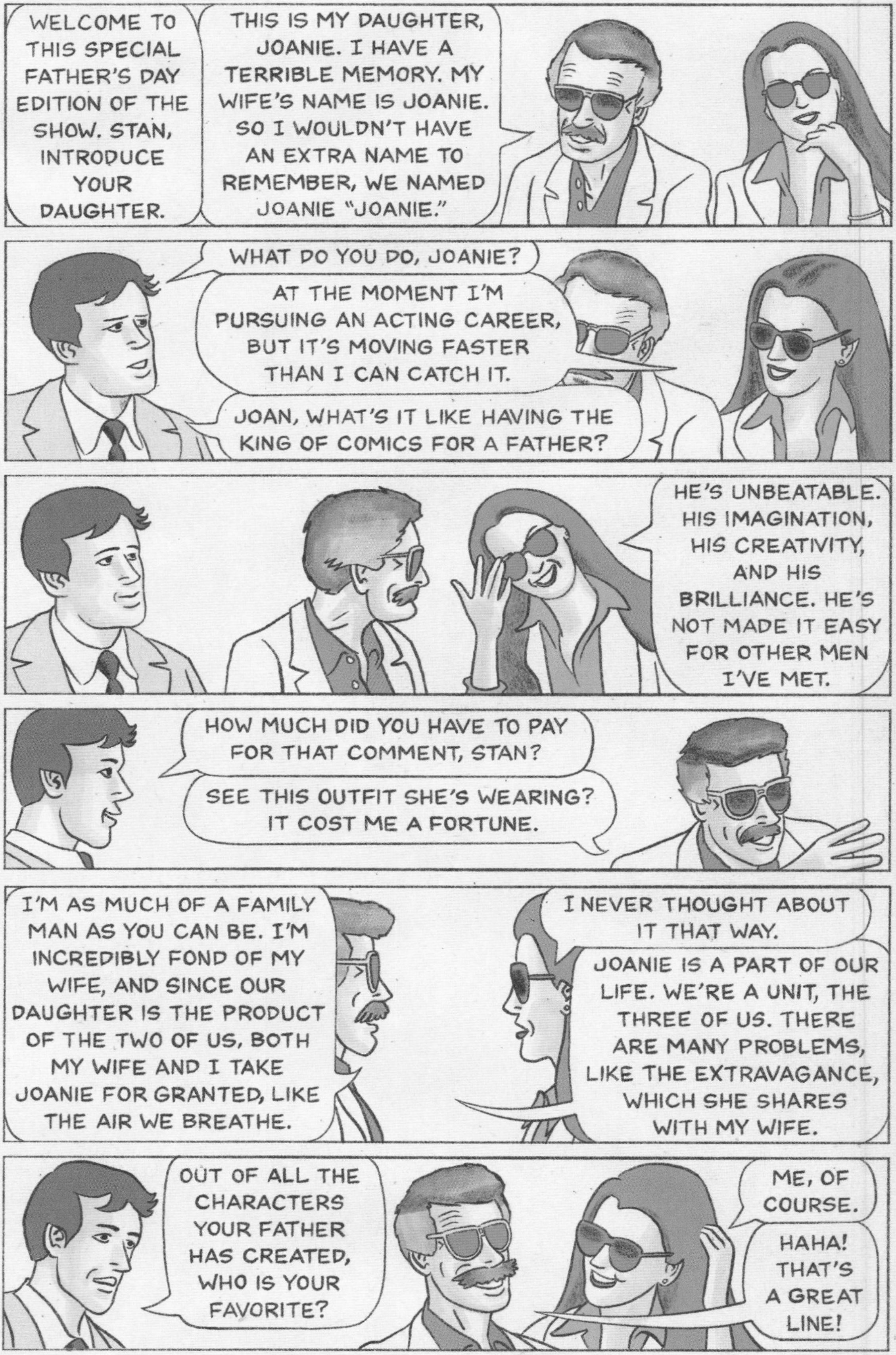

WELCOME TO THIS SPECIAL FATHER'S DAY EDITION OF THE SHOW. STAN, INTRODUCE YOUR DAUGHTER.
THIS IS MY DAUGHTER, JOANIE. I HAVE A TERRIBLE MEMORY. MY WIFE'S NAME IS JOANIE. SO I WOULDN'T HAVE AN EXTRA NAME TO REMEMBER, WE NAMED JOANIE "JOANIE."
WHAT DO YOU DO, JOANIE?
AT THE MOMENT I'M PURSUING AN ACTING CAREER, BUT IT'S MOVING FASTER THAN I CAN CATCH IT.
JOAN, WHAT'S IT LIKE HAVING THE KING OF COMICS FOR A FATHER?
HE'S UNBEATABLE. HIS IMAGINATION, HIS CREATIVITY, AND HIS BRILLIANCE. HE'S NOT MADE IT EASY FOR OTHER MEN I'VE MET.
HOW MUCH DID YOU HAVE TO PAY FOR THAT COMMENT, STAN?
SEE THIS OUTFIT SHE'S WEARING? IT COST ME A FORTUNE.
I'M AS MUCH OF A FAMILY MAN AS YOU CAN BE. I'M INCREDIBLY FOND OF MY WIFE, AND SINCE OUR DAUGHTER IS THE PRODUCT OF THE TWO OF US, BOTH MY WIFE AND I TAKE JOANIE FOR GRANTED, LIKE THE AIR WE BREATHE.
I NEVER THOUGHT ABOUT IT THAT WAY.
JOANIE IS A PART OF OUR LIFE. WE'RE A UNIT, THE THREE OF US. THERE ARE MANY PROBLEMS, LIKE THE EXTRAVAGANCE, WHICH SHE SHARES WITH MY WIFE.
OUT OF ALL THE CHARACTERS YOUR FATHER HAS CREATED, WHO IS YOUR FAVORITE?
ME, OF COURSE.
HAHA! THAT'S A GREAT LINE!

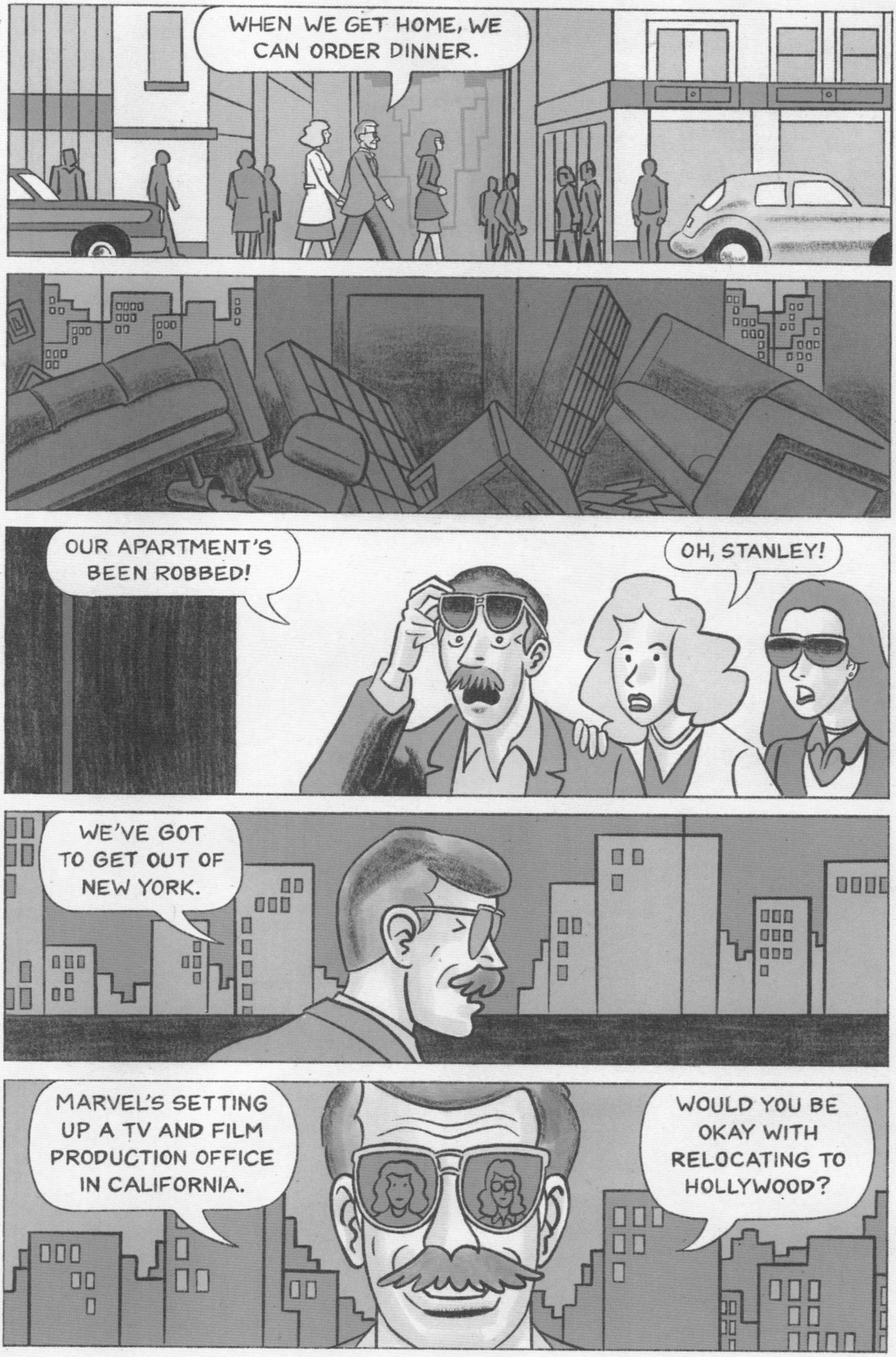
WHEN WE GET HOME, WE CAN ORDER DINNER.
OUR APARTMENT'S BEEN ROBBED!
OH, STANLEY!
WE'VE GOT TO GET OUT OF NEW YORK.
MARVEL'S SETTING UP A TV AND FILM PRODUCTION OFFICE IN CALIFORNIA.
WOULD YOU BE OKAY WITH RELOCATING TO HOLLYWOOD?

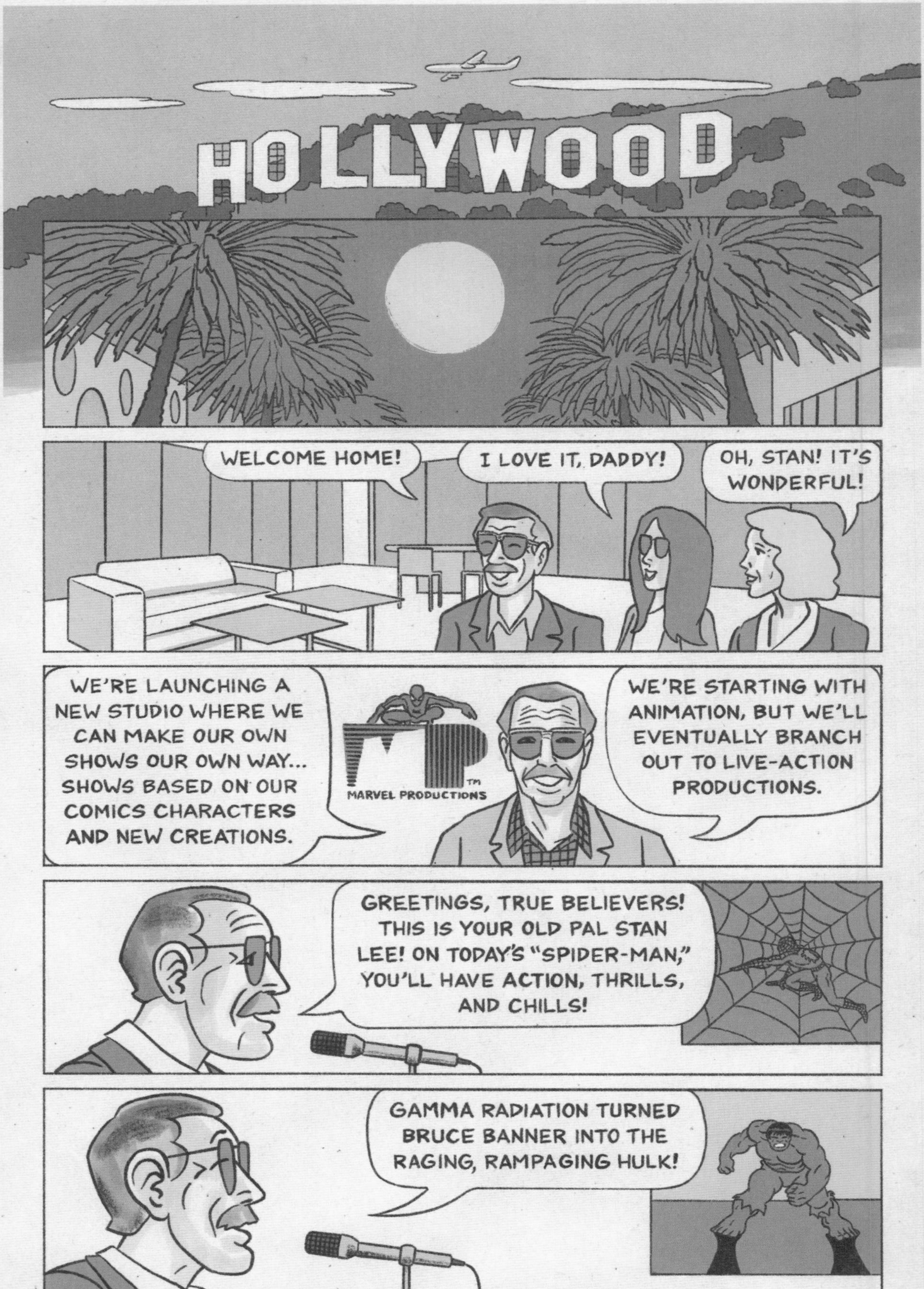
HOLLYWOOD
WELCOME HOME!
I LOVE IT, DADDY!
OH, STAN! IT'S WONDERFUL!
WE'RE LAUNCHING A NEW STUDIO WHERE WE CAN MAKE OUR OWN SHOWS OUR OWN WAY... SHOWS BASED ON OUR COMICS CHARACTERS AND NEW CREATIONS.
MARVEL PRODUCTIONS
WE'RE STARTING WITH ANIMATION, BUT WE'LL EVENTUALLY BRANCH OUT TO LIVE-ACTION PRODUCTIONS.
GREETINGS, TRUE BELIEVERS! THIS IS YOUR OLD PAL STAN LEE! ON TODAY'S "SPIDER-MAN," YOU'LL HAVE ACTION, THRILLS, AND CHILLS!
GAMMA RADIATION TURNED BRUCE BANNER INTO THE RAGING, RAMPAGING HULK!

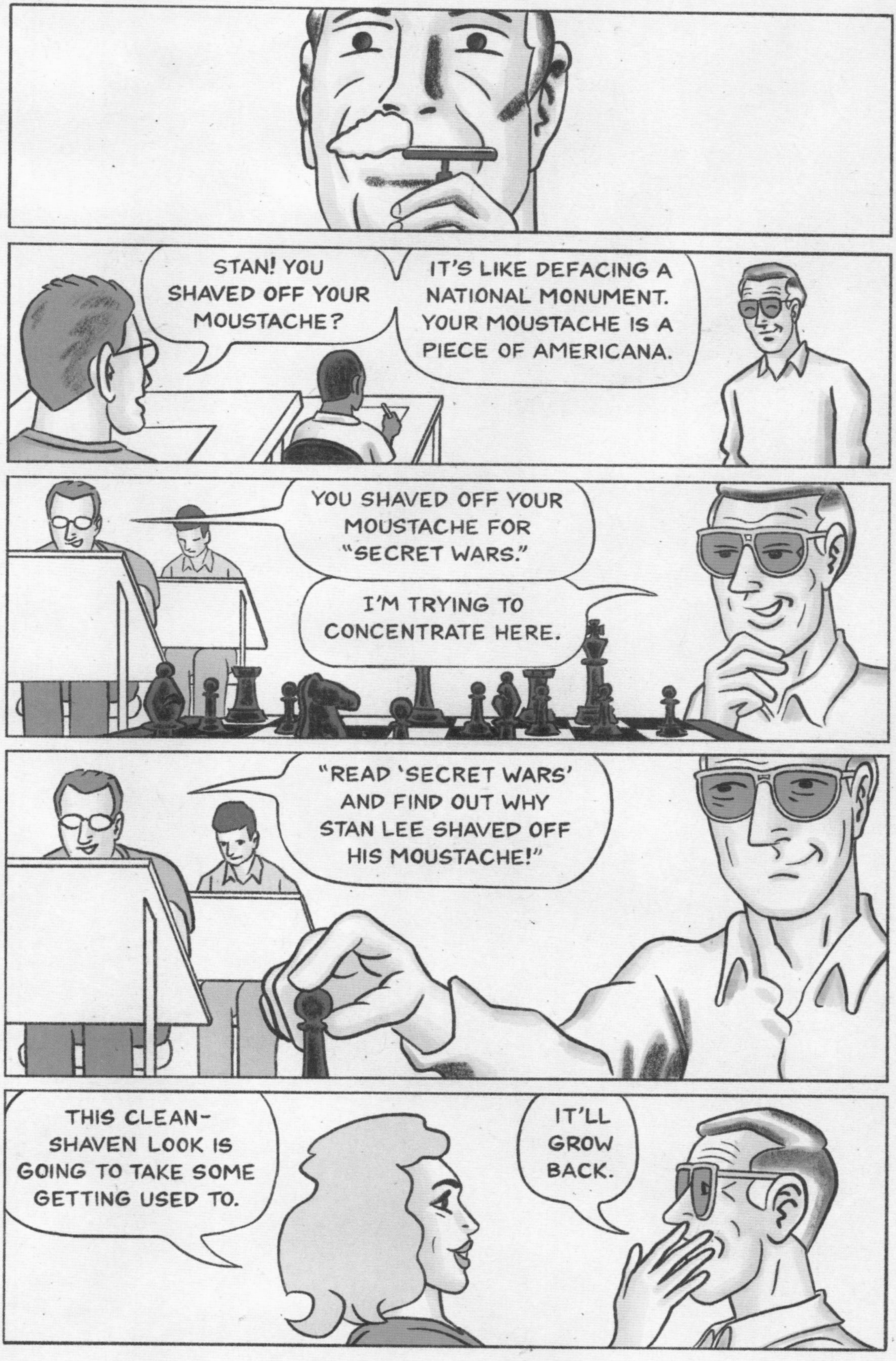
STAN! YOU SHAVED OFF YOUR MOUSTACHE?
IT'S LIKE DEFACING A NATIONAL MONUMENT. YOUR MOUSTACHE IS A PIECE OF AMERICANA.
YOU SHAVED OFF YOUR MOUSTACHE FOR "SECRET WARS."
I'M TRYING TO CONCENTRATE HERE.
"READ 'SECRET WARS' AND FIND OUT WHY STAN LEE SHAVED OFF HIS MOUSTACHE!"
THIS CLEAN-SHAVEN LOOK IS GOING TO TAKE SOME GETTING USED TO.
IT'LL GROW BACK.

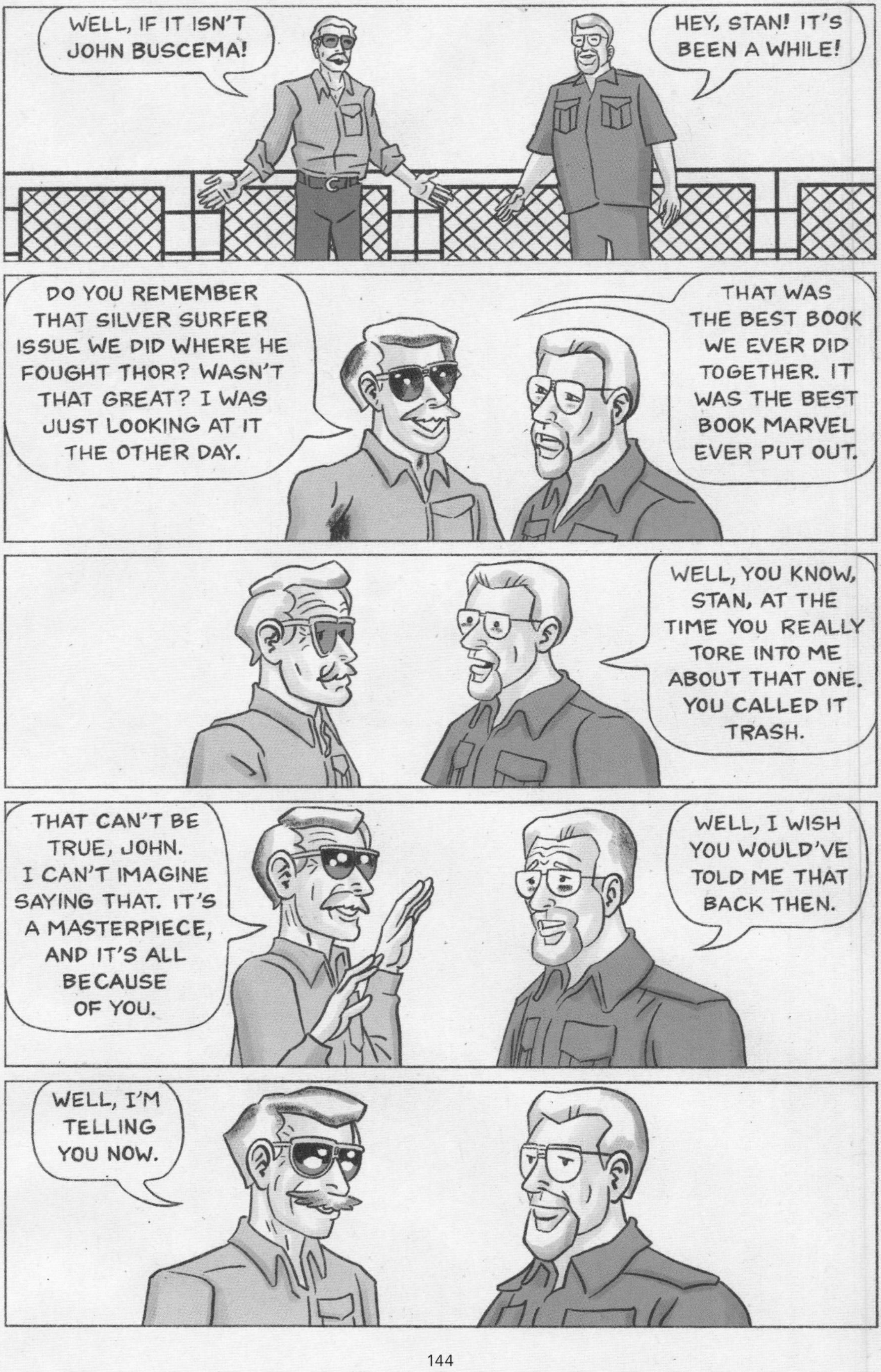
WELL, IF IT ISN'T JOHN BUSCEMA!
HEY, STAN! IT'S BEEN A WHILE!
DO YOU REMEMBER THAT SILVER SURFER ISSUE WE DID WHERE HE FOUGHT THOR? WASN'T THAT GREAT? I WAS JUST LOOKING AT IT THE OTHER DAY.
THAT WAS THE BEST BOOK WE EVER DID TOGETHER. IT WAS THE BEST BOOK MARVEL EVER PUT OUT.
WELL, YOU KNOW, STAN, AT THE TIME YOU REALLY TORE INTO ME ABOUT THAT ONE. YOU CALLED IT TRASH.
THAT CAN'T BE TRUE, JOHN. I CAN'T IMAGINE SAYING THAT. IT'S A MASTERPIECE, AND IT'S ALL BECAUSE OF YOU.
WELL, I WISH YOU WOULD'VE TOLD ME THAT BACK THEN.
WELL, I'M TELLING YOU NOW.

THIS IS THE TOP SHOW FOR KIDS IN JAPAN. IT'S A MASSIVE HIT.

WE WANT TO BRING IT TO AMERICA. WE PARTNERED WITH THIS STUDIO FOR THE JAPANESE "SPIDER-MAN" SERIES A FEW YEARS BACK.

WE'LL TAKE THE EFFECTS FOOTAGE AND FIGHT SCENES FROM THE JAPANESE SHOW.

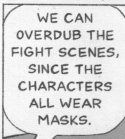

WE CAN OVERDUB THE FIGHT SCENES, SINCE THE CHARACTERS ALL WEAR MASKS.

AND FILM NEW PLAINCLOTHES SEGMENTS WITH ENGLISH-SPEAKING ACTORS.

LOOK OUT!

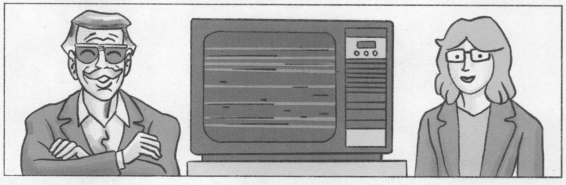

WHAT IS THIS? IT'S CHEESY. IT'S VIOLENT. IT'S STUPID.

WHY ARE YOU WASTING OUR TIME WITH THIS?

IF WE AIRED THIS, WE'D BE LAUGHED OUT OF THE BUSINESS.

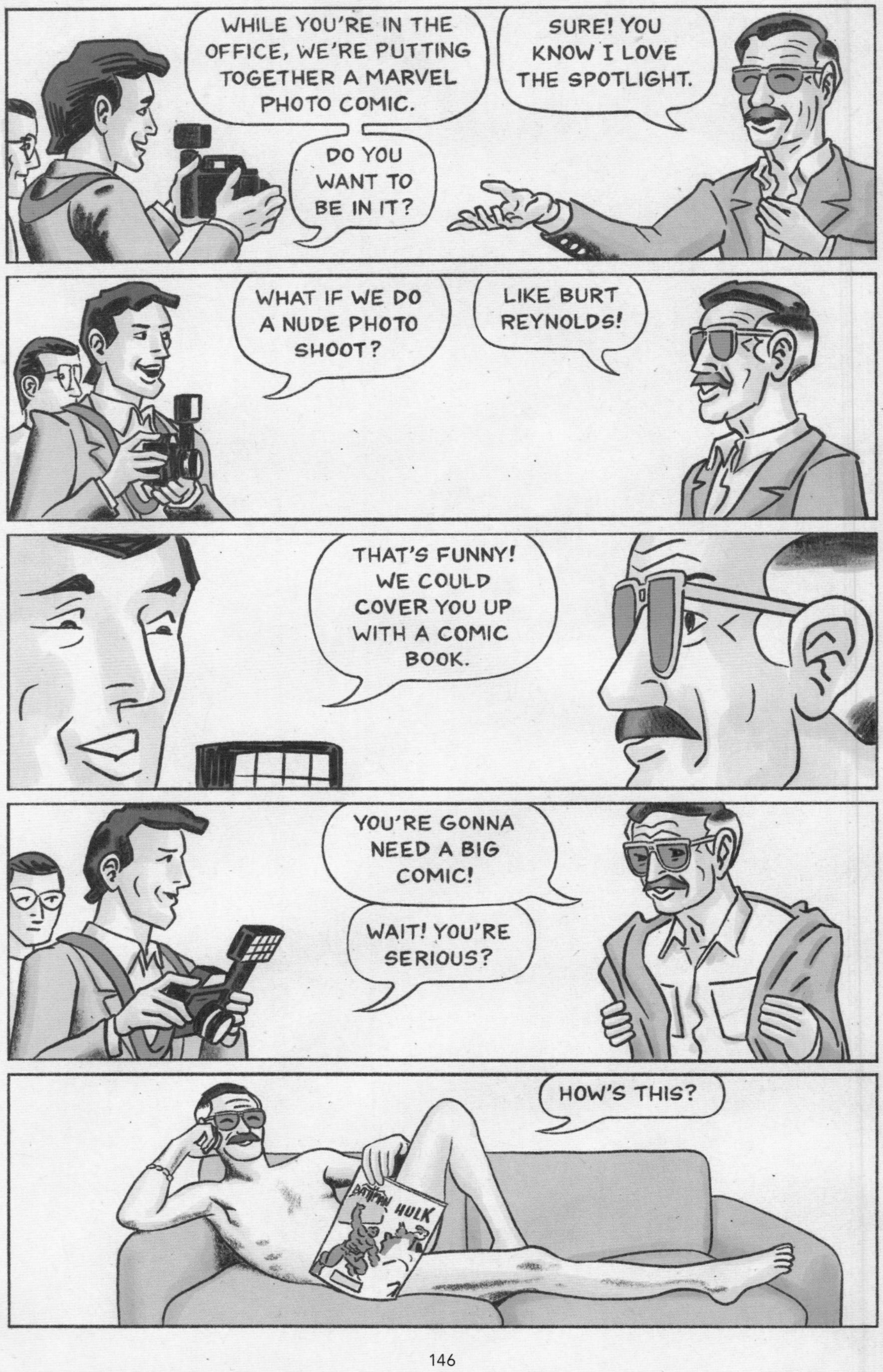
WHILE YOU'RE IN THE OFFICE, WE'RE PUTTING TOGETHER A MARVEL PHOTO COMIC.
DO YOU WANT TO BE IN IT?
SURE! YOU KNOW I LOVE THE SPOTLIGHT.
WHAT IF WE DO A NUDE PHOTO SHOOT?
LIKE BURT REYNOLDS!
THAT'S FUNNY! WE COULD COVER YOU UP WITH A COMIC BOOK.
YOU'RE GONNA NEED A BIG COMIC!
WAIT! YOU'RE SERIOUS?
HOW'S THIS?
HULK

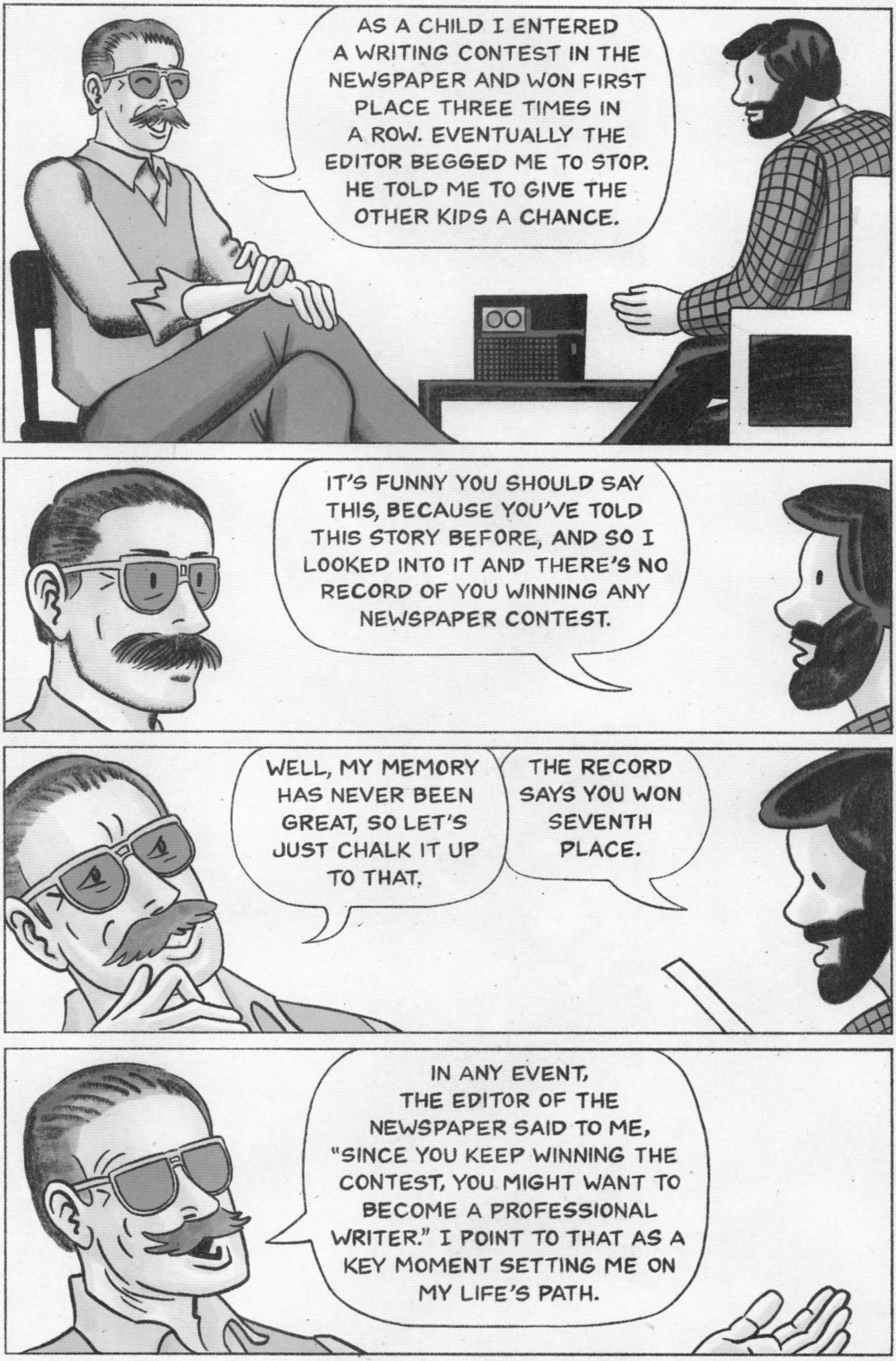

AS A CHILD I ENTERED A WRITING CONTEST IN THE NEWSPAPER AND WON FIRST PLACE THREE TIMES IN A ROW. EVENTUALLY THE EDITOR BEGGED ME TO STOP. HE TOLD ME TO GIVE THE OTHER KIDS A CHANCE.
IT'S FUNNY YOU SHOULD SAY THIS, BECAUSE YOU'VE TOLD THIS STORY BEFORE, AND SO I LOOKED INTO IT AND THERE'S NO RECORD OF YOU WINNING ANY NEWSPAPER CONTEST.
WELL, MY MEMORY HAS NEVER BEEN GREAT, SO LET'S JUST CHALK IT UP TO THAT.
THE RECORD SAYS YOU WON SEVENTH PLACE.
IN ANY EVENT, THE EDITOR OF THE NEWSPAPER SAID TO ME, "SINCE YOU KEEP WINNING THE CONTEST, YOU MIGHT WANT TO BECOME A PROFESSIONAL WRITER." I POINT TO THAT AS A KEY MOMENT SETTING ME ON MY LIFE'S PATH.

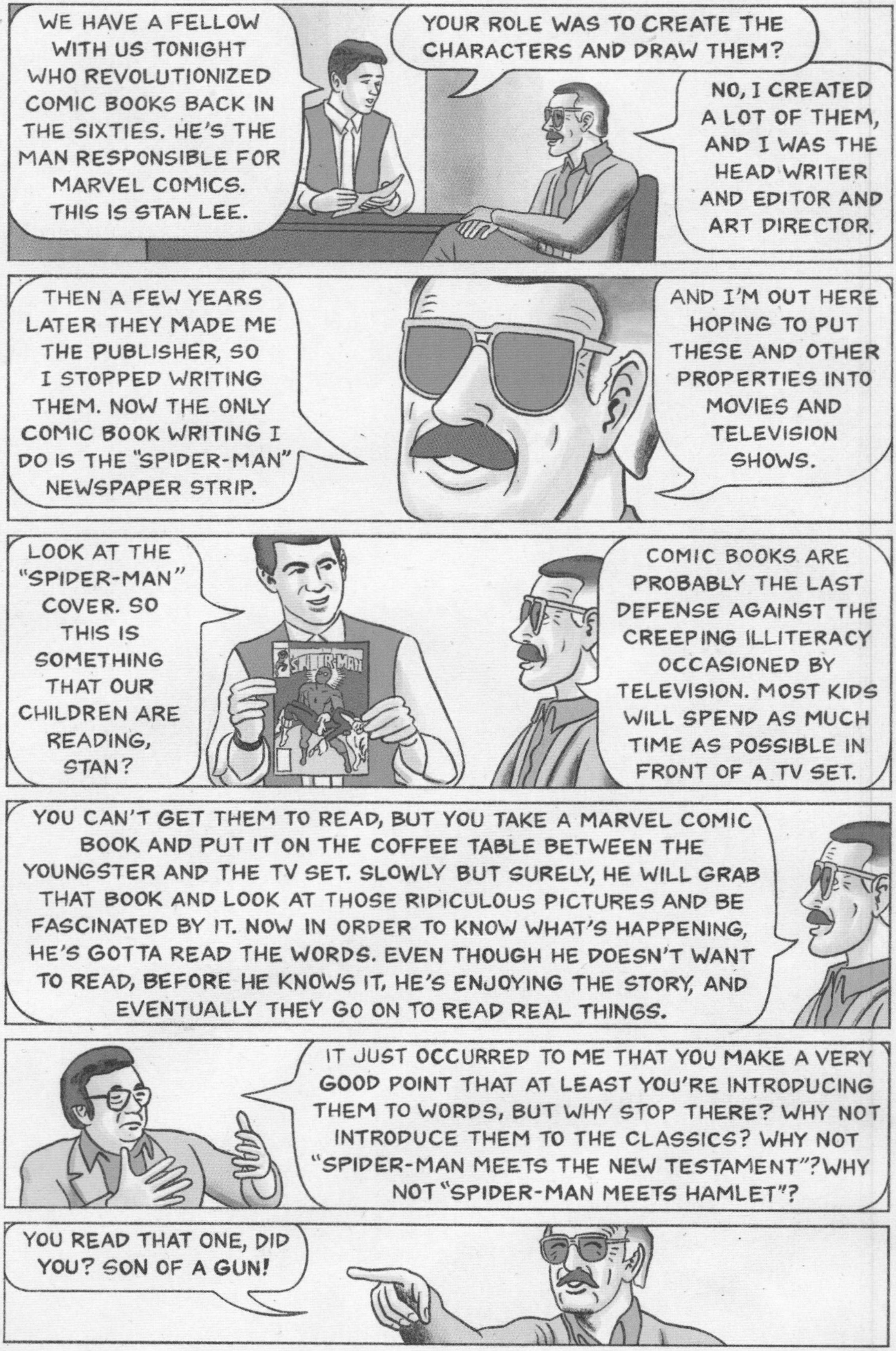
WE HAVE A FELLOW WITH US TONIGHT WHO REVOLUTIONIZED COMIC BOOKS BACK IN THE SIXTIES. HE'S THE MAN RESPONSIBLE FOR MARVEL COMICS. THIS IS STAN LEE.
YOUR ROLE WAS TO CREATE THE CHARACTERS AND DRAW THEM?
NO, I CREATED A LOT OF THEM, AND I WAS THE HEAD WRITER AND EDITOR AND ART DIRECTOR.
THEN A FEW YEARS LATER THEY MADE ME THE PUBLISHER, SO I STOPPED WRITING THEM. NOW THE ONLY COMIC BOOK WRITING I DO IS THE "SPIDER-MAN" NEWSPAPER STRIP.
AND I'M OUT HERE HOPING TO PUT THESE AND OTHER PROPERTIES INTO MOVIES AND TELEVISION SHOWS.
LOOK AT THE "SPIDER-MAN" COVER. SO THIS IS SOMETHING THAT OUR CHILDREN ARE READING, STAN?
COMIC BOOKS ARE PROBABLY THE LAST DEFENSE AGAINST THE CREEPING ILLITERACY OCCASIONED BY TELEVISION. MOST KIDS WILL SPEND AS MUCH TIME AS POSSIBLE IN FRONT OF A TV SET.
YOU CAN'T GET THEM TO READ, BUT YOU TAKE A MARVEL COMIC BOOK AND PUT IT ON THE COFFEE TABLE BETWEEN THE YOUNGSTER AND THE TV SET. SLOWLY BUT SURELY, HE WILL GRAB THAT BOOK AND LOOK AT THOSE RIDICULOUS PICTURES AND BE FASCINATED BY IT. NOW IN ORDER TO KNOW WHAT'S HAPPENING, HE'S GOTTA READ THE WORDS. EVEN THOUGH HE DOESN'T WANT TO READ, BEFORE HE KNOWS IT, HE'S ENJOYING THE STORY, AND EVENTUALLY THEY GO ON TO READ REAL THINGS.
IT JUST OCCURRED TO ME THAT YOU MAKE A VERY GOOD POINT THAT AT LEAST YOU'RE INTRODUCING THEM TO WORDS, BUT WHY STOP THERE? WHY NOT INTRODUCE THEM TO THE CLASSICS? WHY NOT "SPIDER-MAN MEETS THE NEW TESTAMENT"? WHY NOT "SPIDER-MAN MEETS HAMLET"?
YOU READ THAT ONE, DID YOU? SON OF A GUN!

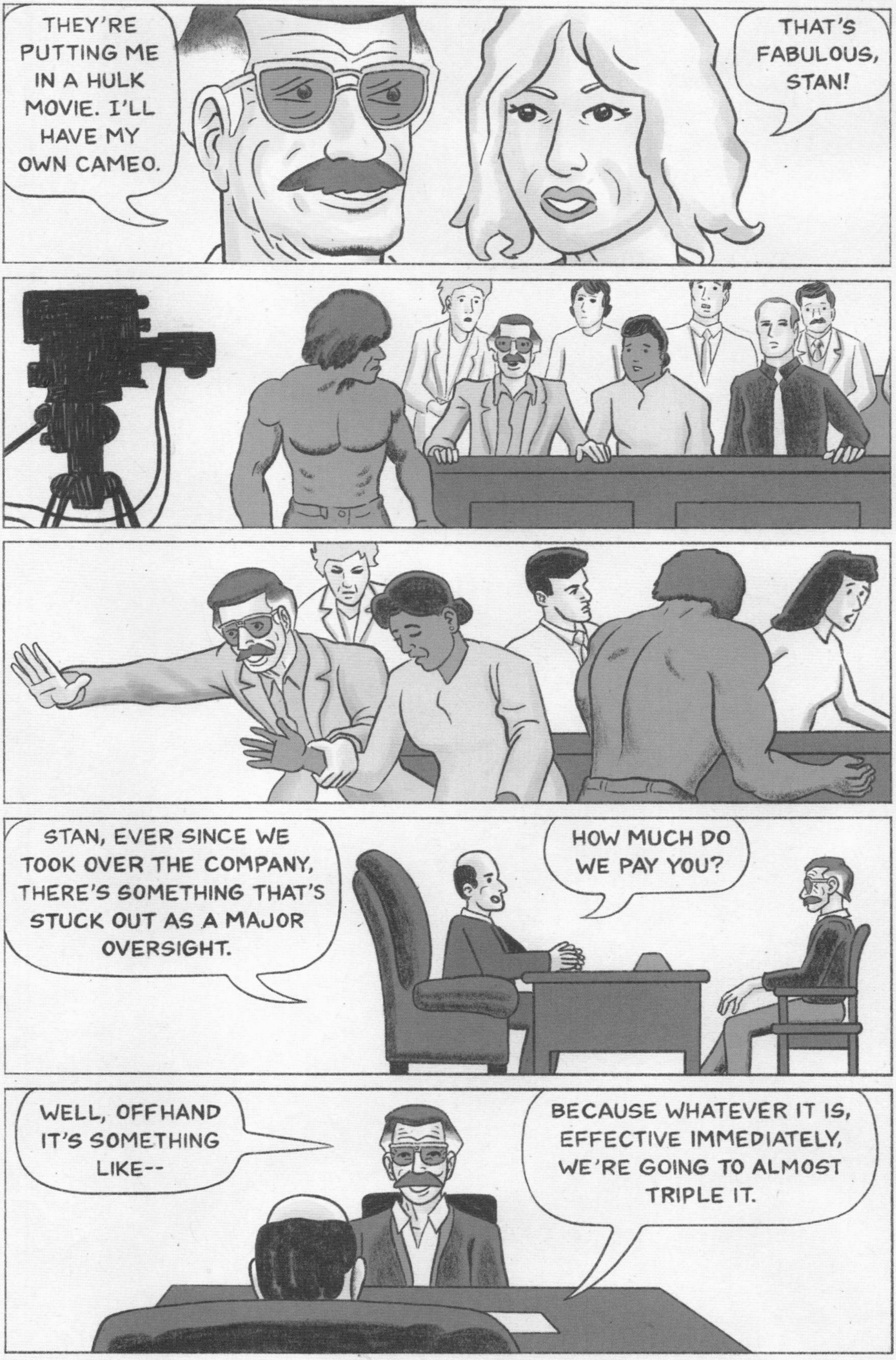
THEY'RE PUTTING ME IN A HULK MOVIE. I'LL HAVE MY OWN CAMEO.
THAT'S FABULOUS, STAN!
STAN, EVER SINCE WE TOOK OVER THE COMPANY, THERE'S SOMETHING THAT'S STUCK OUT AS A MAJOR OVERSIGHT.
HOW MUCH DO WE PAY YOU?
WELL, OFFHAND IT'S SOMETHING LIKE--
BECAUSE WHATEVER IT IS, EFFECTIVE IMMEDIATELY, WE'RE GOING TO ALMOST TRIPLE IT.

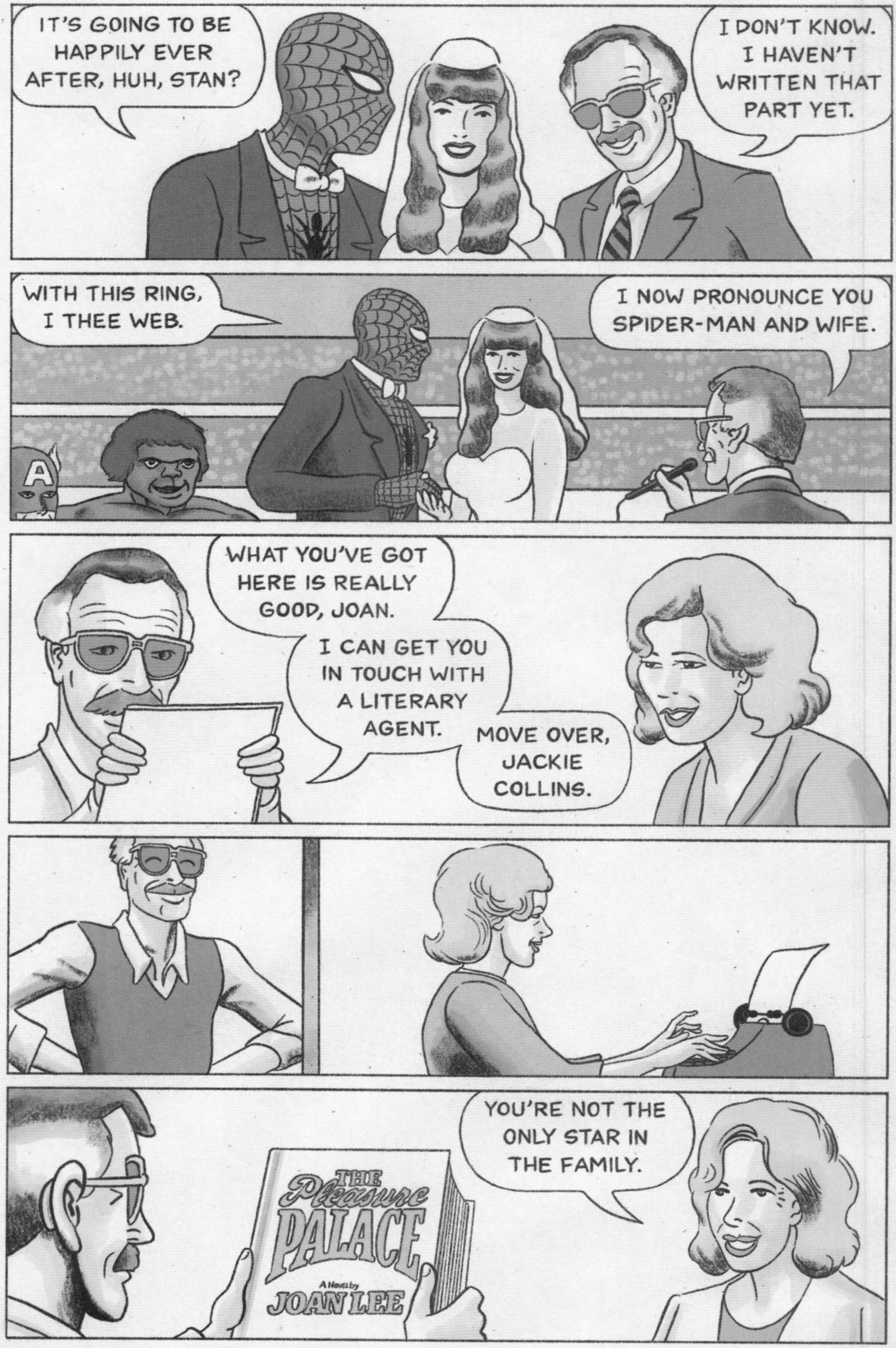

IT'S GOING TO BE HAPPILY EVER AFTER, HUH, STAN?
I DON'T KNOW. I HAVEN'T WRITTEN THAT PART YET.
WITH THIS RING, I THEE WEB.
I NOW PRONOUNCE YOU SPIDER-MAN AND WIFE.
WHAT YOU'VE GOT HERE IS REALLY GOOD, JOAN.
I CAN GET YOU IN TOUCH WITH A LITERARY AGENT.
MOVE OVER, JACKIE COLLINS.
THE Pleasure PALACE
A Novel by
JOAN LEE
YOU'RE NOT THE ONLY STAR IN THE FAMILY.

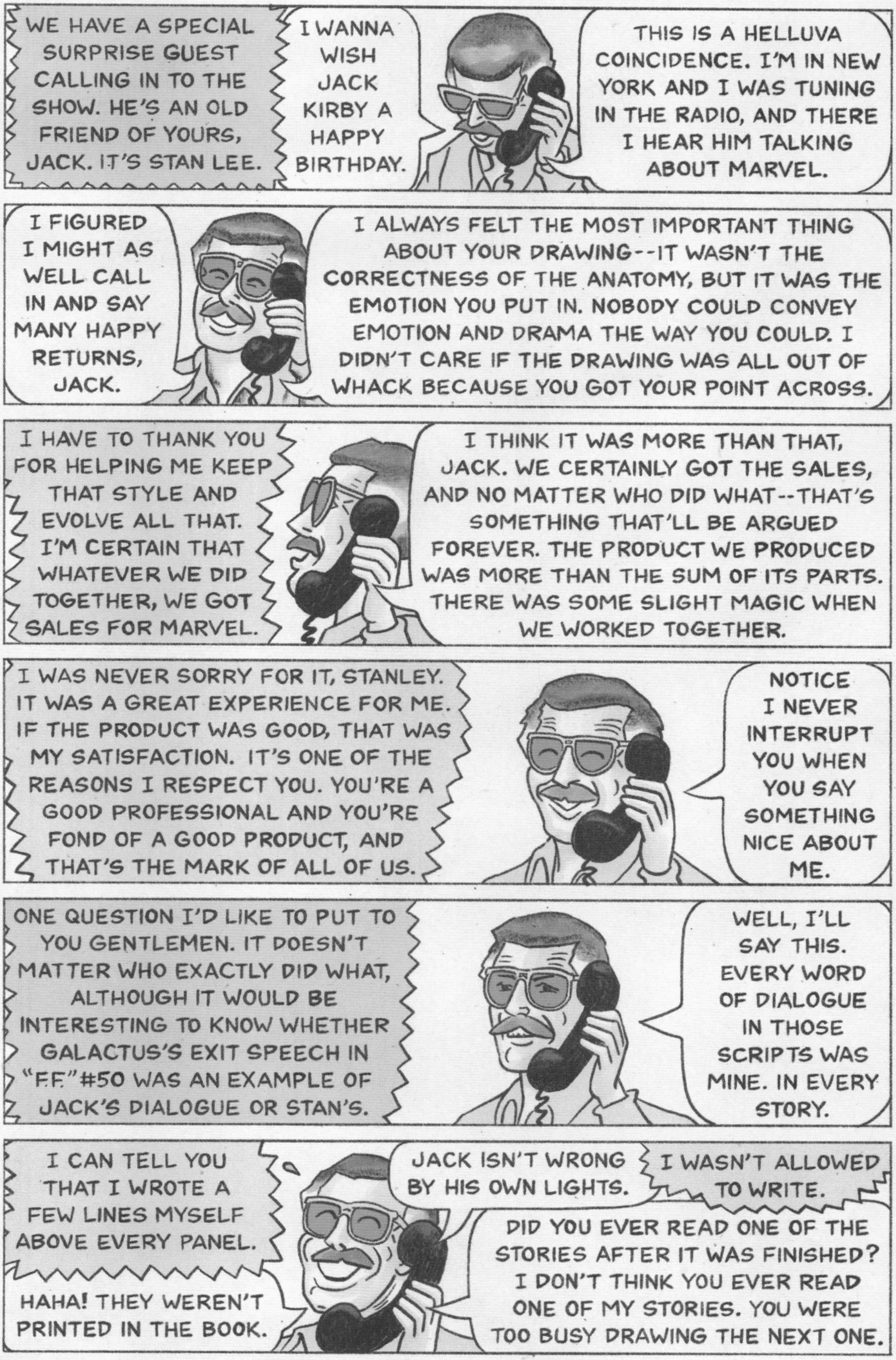
WE HAVE A SPECIAL SURPRISE GUEST CALLING IN TO THE SHOW. HE'S AN OLD FRIEND OF YOURS, JACK. IT'S STAN LEE.
I WANNA WISH JACK KIRBY A HAPPY BIRTHDAY.
THIS IS A HELLUVA COINCIDENCE. I'M IN NEW YORK AND I WAS TUNING IN THE RADIO, AND THERE I HEAR HIM TALKING ABOUT MARVEL.
I FIGURED I MIGHT AS WELL CALL IN AND SAY MANY HAPPY RETURNS, JACK.
I ALWAYS FELT THE MOST IMPORTANT THING ABOUT YOUR DRAWING--IT WASN'T THE CORRECTNESS OF THE ANATOMY, BUT IT WAS THE EMOTION YOU PUT IN. NOBODY COULD CONVEY EMOTION AND DRAMA THE WAY YOU COULD. I DIDN'T CARE IF THE DRAWING WAS ALL OUT OF WHACK BECAUSE YOU GOT YOUR POINT ACROSS.
I HAVE TO THANK YOU FOR HELPING ME KEEP THAT STYLE AND EVOLVE ALL THAT. I'M CERTAIN THAT WHATEVER WE DID TOGETHER, WE GOT SALES FOR MARVEL.
I THINK IT WAS MORE THAN THAT, JACK. WE CERTAINLY GOT THE SALES, AND NO MATTER WHO DID WHAT--THAT'S SOMETHING THAT'LL BE ARGUED FOREVER. THE PRODUCT WE PRODUCED WAS MORE THAN THE SUM OF ITS PARTS. THERE WAS SOME SLIGHT MAGIC WHEN WE WORKED TOGETHER.
I WAS NEVER SORRY FOR IT, STANLEY. IT WAS A GREAT EXPERIENCE FOR ME. IF THE PRODUCT WAS GOOD, THAT WAS MY SATISFACTION. IT'S ONE OF THE REASONS I RESPECT YOU. YOU'RE A GOOD PROFESSIONAL AND YOU'RE FOND OF A GOOD PRODUCT, AND THAT'S THE MARK OF ALL OF US.
NOTICE I NEVER INTERRUPT YOU WHEN YOU SAY SOMETHING NICE ABOUT ME.
ONE QUESTION I'D LIKE TO PUT TO YOU GENTLEMEN. IT DOESN'T MATTER WHO EXACTLY DID WHAT, ALTHOUGH IT WOULD BE INTERESTING TO KNOW WHETHER GALACTUS'S EXIT SPEECH IN "F.F." #50 WAS AN EXAMPLE OF JACK'S DIALOGUE OR STAN'S.
WELL, I'LL SAY THIS. EVERY WORD OF DIALOGUE IN THOSE SCRIPTS WAS MINE. IN EVERY STORY.
I CAN TELL YOU THAT I WROTE A FEW LINES MYSELF ABOVE EVERY PANEL.
HAHA! THEY WEREN'T PRINTED IN THE BOOK.
JACK ISN'T WRONG BY HIS OWN LIGHTS.
I WASN'T ALLOWED TO WRITE.
DID YOU EVER READ ONE OF THE STORIES AFTER IT WAS FINISHED? I DON'T THINK YOU EVER READ ONE OF MY STORIES. YOU WERE TOO BUSY DRAWING THE NEXT ONE.

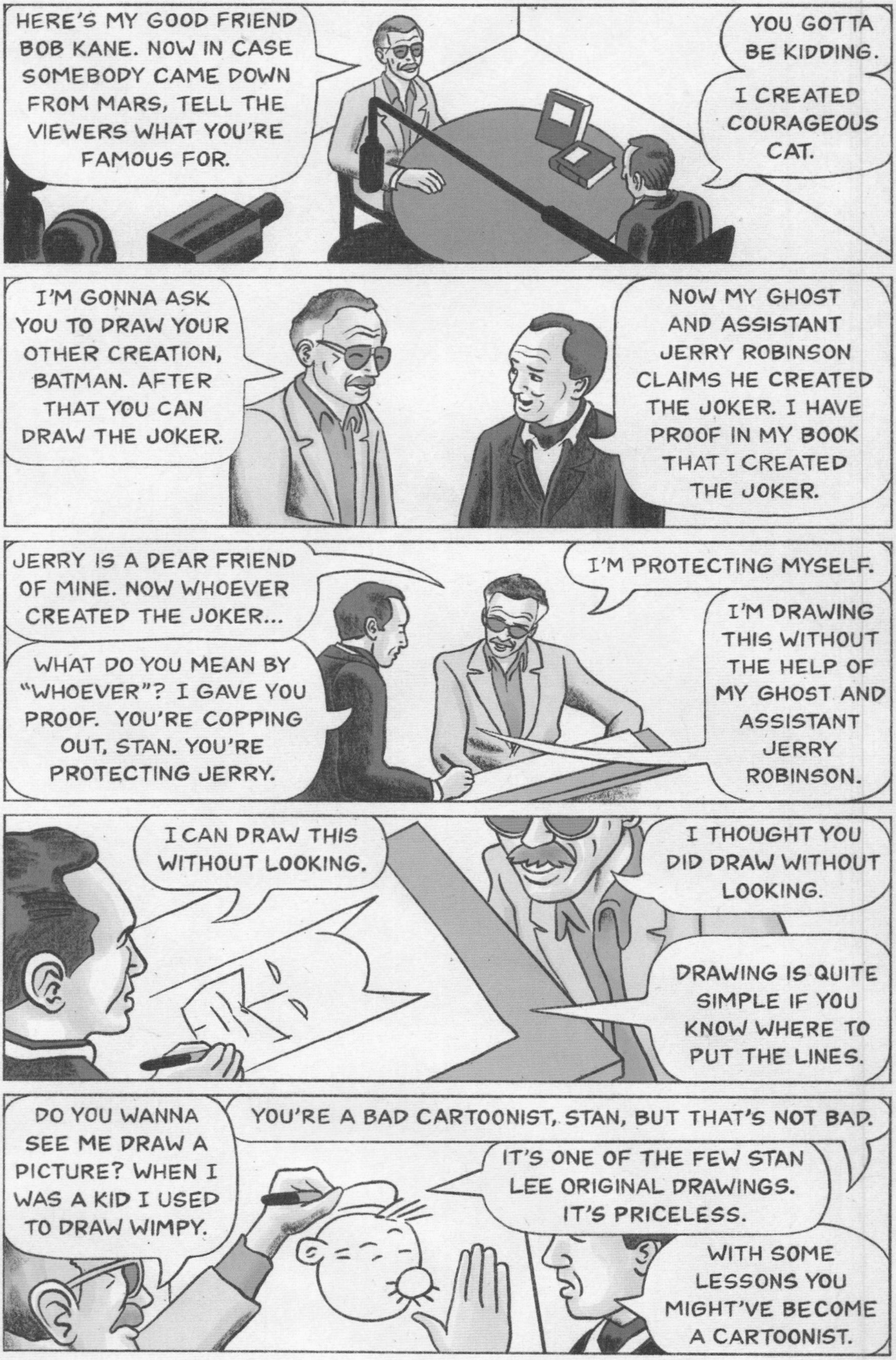
HERE'S MY GOOD FRIEND BOB KANE. NOW IN CASE SOMEBODY CAME DOWN FROM MARS, TELL THE VIEWERS WHAT YOU'RE FAMOUS FOR.
YOU GOTTA BE KIDDING.
I CREATED COURAGEOUS CAT.
I'M GONNA ASK YOU TO DRAW YOUR OTHER CREATION, BATMAN. AFTER THAT YOU CAN DRAW THE JOKER.
NOW MY GHOST AND ASSISTANT JERRY ROBINSON CLAIMS HE CREATED THE JOKER. I HAVE PROOF IN MY BOOK THAT I CREATED THE JOKER.
JERRY IS A DEAR FRIEND OF MINE. NOW WHOEVER CREATED THE JOKER...
I'M PROTECTING MYSELF.
WHAT DO YOU MEAN BY "WHOEVER"? I GAVE YOU PROOF. YOU'RE COPPING OUT, STAN. YOU'RE PROTECTING JERRY.
I'M DRAWING THIS WITHOUT THE HELP OF MY GHOST AND ASSISTANT JERRY ROBINSON.
I CAN DRAW THIS WITHOUT LOOKING.
I THOUGHT YOU DID DRAW WITHOUT LOOKING.
DRAWING IS QUITE SIMPLE IF YOU KNOW WHERE TO PUT THE LINES.
DO YOU WANNA SEE ME DRAW A PICTURE? WHEN I WAS A KID I USED TO DRAW WIMPY.
YOU'RE A BAD CARTOONIST, STAN, BUT THAT'S NOT BAD.
IT'S ONE OF THE FEW STAN LEE ORIGINAL DRAWINGS. IT'S PRICELESS.
WITH SOME LESSONS YOU MIGHT'VE BECOME A CARTOONIST.

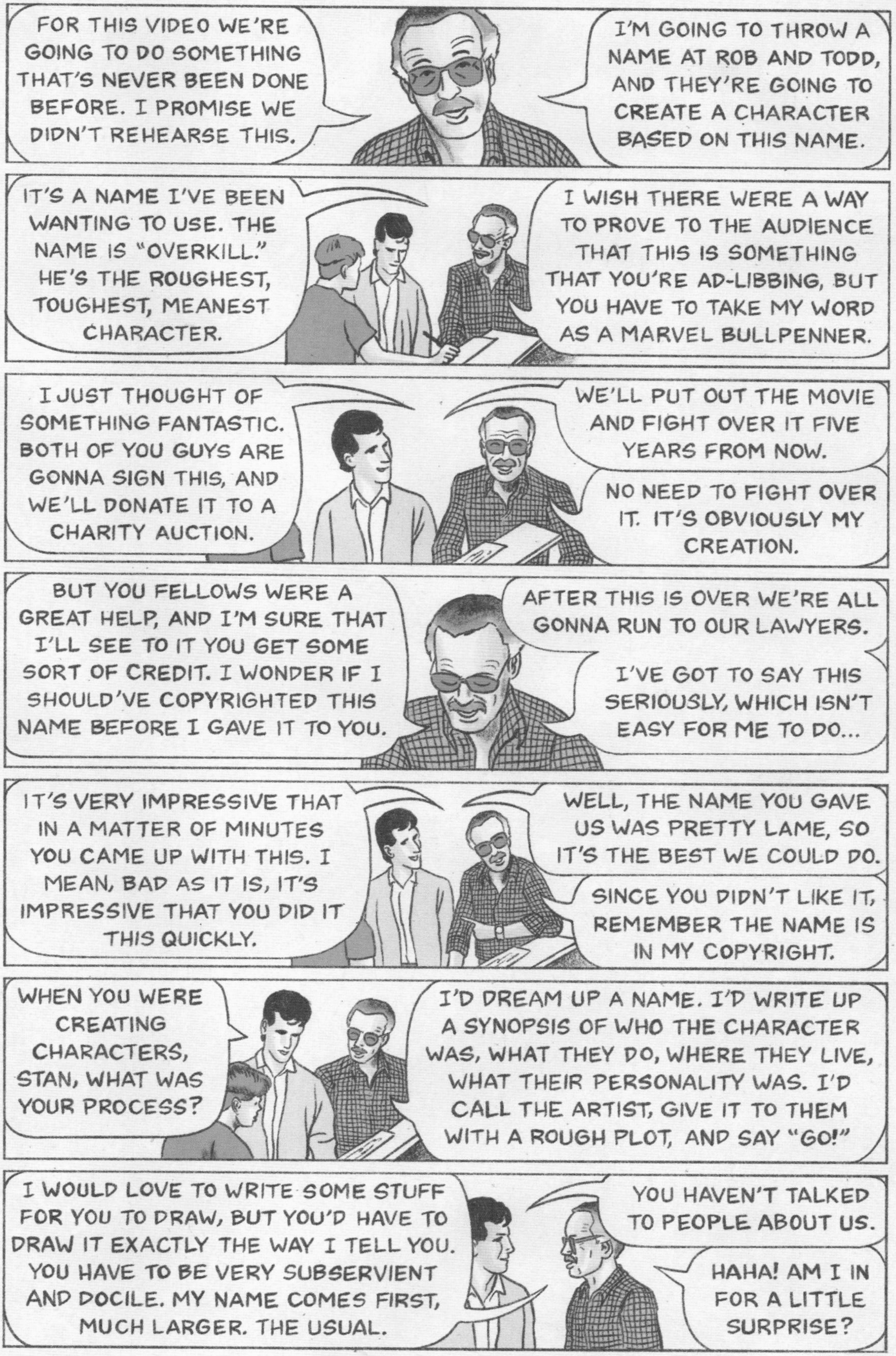
FOR THIS VIDEO WE'RE GOING TO DO SOMETHING THAT'S NEVER BEEN DONE BEFORE. I PROMISE WE DIDN'T REHEARSE THIS.
I'M GOING TO THROW A NAME AT ROB AND TODD, AND THEY'RE GOING TO CREATE A CHARACTER BASED ON THIS NAME.
IT'S A NAME I'VE BEEN WANTING TO USE. THE NAME IS "OVERKILL." HE'S THE ROUGHEST, TOUGHEST, MEANEST CHARACTER.
I WISH THERE WERE A WAY TO PROVE TO THE AUDIENCE THAT THIS IS SOMETHING THAT YOU'RE AD-LIBBING, BUT YOU HAVE TO TAKE MY WORD AS A MARVEL BULLPENNER.
I JUST THOUGHT OF SOMETHING FANTASTIC. BOTH OF YOU GUYS ARE GONNA SIGN THIS, AND WE'LL DONATE IT TO A CHARITY AUCTION.
WE'LL PUT OUT THE MOVIE AND FIGHT OVER IT FIVE YEARS FROM NOW.
NO NEED TO FIGHT OVER IT. IT'S OBVIOUSLY MY CREATION.
BUT YOU FELLOWS WERE A GREAT HELP, AND I'M SURE THAT I'LL SEE TO IT YOU GET SOME SORT OF CREDIT. I WONDER IF I SHOULD'VE COPYRIGHTED THIS NAME BEFORE I GAVE IT TO YOU.
AFTER THIS IS OVER WE'RE ALL GONNA RUN TO OUR LAWYERS.
I'VE GOT TO SAY THIS SERIOUSLY, WHICH ISN'T EASY FOR ME TO DO...
IT'S VERY IMPRESSIVE THAT IN A MATTER OF MINUTES YOU CAME UP WITH THIS. I MEAN, BAD AS IT IS, IT'S IMPRESSIVE THAT YOU DID IT THIS QUICKLY.
WELL, THE NAME YOU GAVE US WAS PRETTY LAME, SO IT'S THE BEST WE COULD DO.
SINCE YOU DIDN'T LIKE IT, REMEMBER THE NAME IS IN MY COPYRIGHT.
WHEN YOU WERE CREATING CHARACTERS, STAN, WHAT WAS YOUR PROCESS?
I'D DREAM UP A NAME. I'D WRITE UP A SYNOPSIS OF WHO THE CHARACTER WAS, WHAT THEY DO, WHERE THEY LIVE, WHAT THEIR PERSONALITY WAS. I'D CALL THE ARTIST, GIVE IT TO THEM WITH A ROUGH PLOT, AND SAY "GO!"
I WOULD LOVE TO WRITE SOME STUFF FOR YOU TO DRAW, BUT YOU'D HAVE TO DRAW IT EXACTLY THE WAY I TELL YOU. YOU HAVE TO BE VERY SUBSERVIENT AND DOCILE. MY NAME COMES FIRST, MUCH LARGER. THE USUAL.
YOU HAVEN'T TALKED TO PEOPLE ABOUT US.
HAHA! AM I IN FOR A LITTLE SURPRISE?

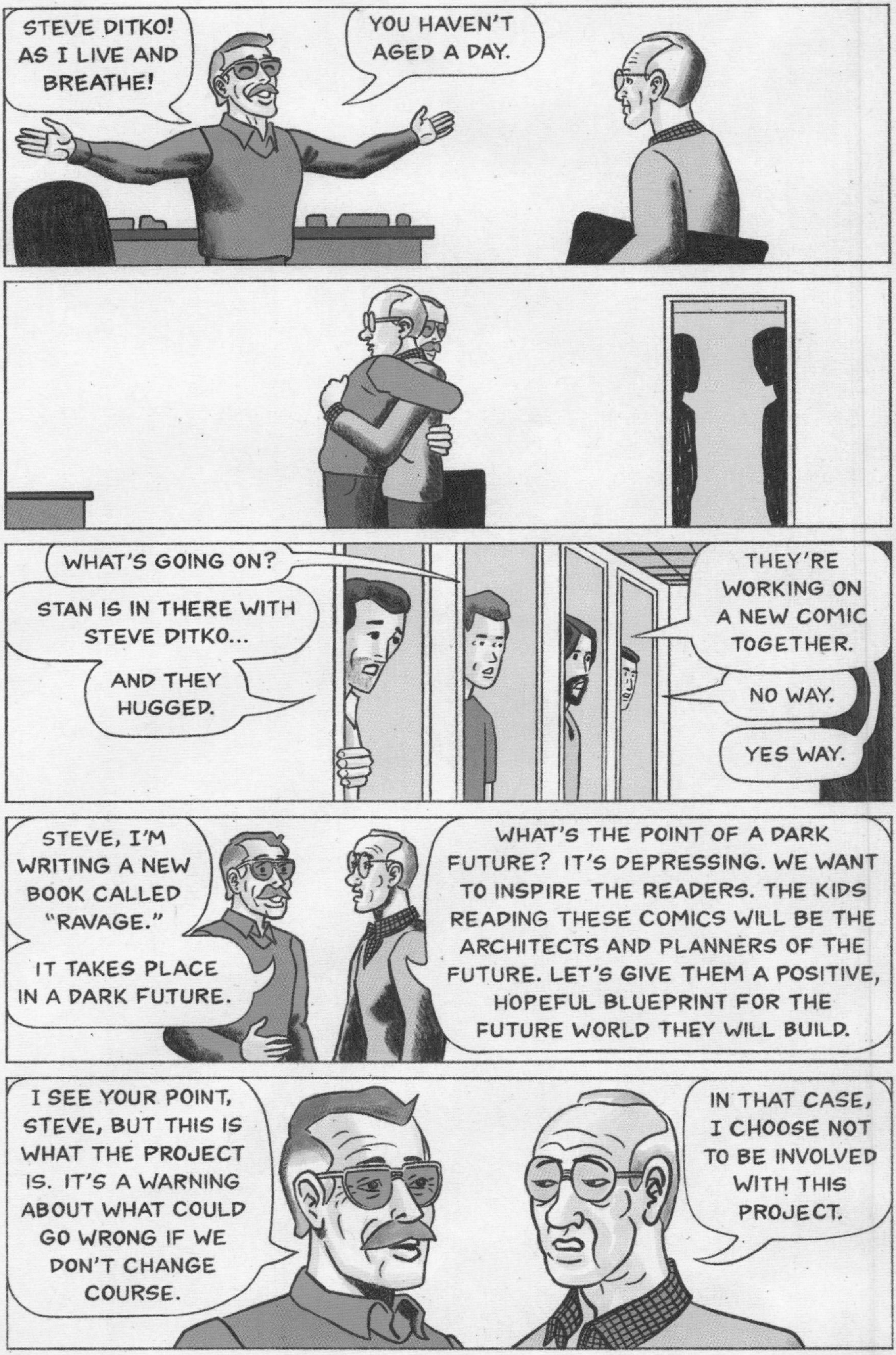

STEVE DITKO! AS I LIVE AND BREATHE!
YOU HAVEN'T AGED A DAY.
WHAT'S GOING ON?
STAN IS IN THERE WITH STEVE DITKO...
AND THEY HUGGED.
THEY'RE WORKING ON A NEW COMIC TOGETHER.
NO WAY.
YES WAY.
STEVE, I'M WRITING A NEW BOOK CALLED "RAVAGE."
IT TAKES PLACE IN A DARK FUTURE.
WHAT'S THE POINT OF A DARK FUTURE? IT'S DEPRESSING. WE WANT TO INSPIRE THE READERS. THE KIDS READING THESE COMICS WILL BE THE ARCHITECTS AND PLANNERS OF THE FUTURE. LET'S GIVE THEM A POSITIVE, HOPEFUL BLUEPRINT FOR THE FUTURE WORLD THEY WILL BUILD.
I SEE YOUR POINT, STEVE, BUT THIS IS WHAT THE PROJECT IS. IT'S A WARNING ABOUT WHAT COULD GO WRONG IF WE DON'T CHANGE COURSE.
IN THAT CASE, I CHOOSE NOT TO BE INVOLVED WITH THIS PROJECT.

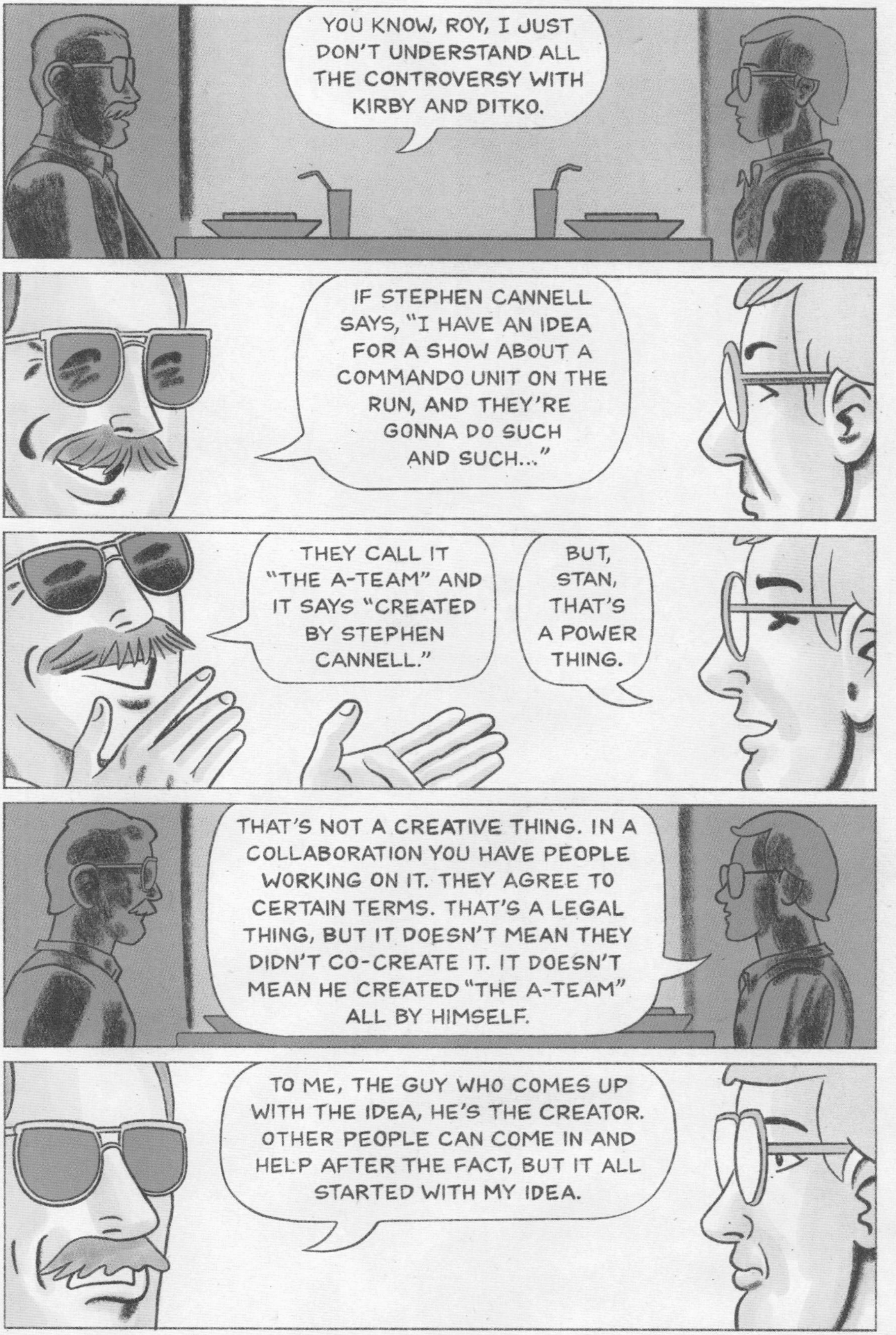
YOU KNOW, ROY, I JUST DON'T UNDERSTAND ALL THE CONTROVERSY WITH KIRBY AND DITKO.
IF STEPHEN CANNELL SAYS, "I HAVE AN IDEA FOR A SHOW ABOUT A COMMANDO UNIT ON THE RUN, AND THEY'RE GONNA DO SUCH AND SUCH..."
THEY CALL IT "THE A-TEAM" AND IT SAYS "CREATED BY STEPHEN CANNELL."
BUT, STAN, THAT'S A POWER THING.
THAT'S NOT A CREATIVE THING. IN A COLLABORATION YOU HAVE PEOPLE WORKING ON IT. THEY AGREE TO CERTAIN TERMS. THAT'S A LEGAL THING, BUT IT DOESN'T MEAN THEY DIDN'T CO-CREATE IT. IT DOESN'T MEAN HE CREATED "THE A-TEAM" ALL BY HIMSELF.
TO ME, THE GUY WHO COMES UP WITH THE IDEA, HE'S THE CREATOR. OTHER PEOPLE CAN COME IN AND HELP AFTER THE FACT, BUT IT ALL STARTED WITH MY IDEA.

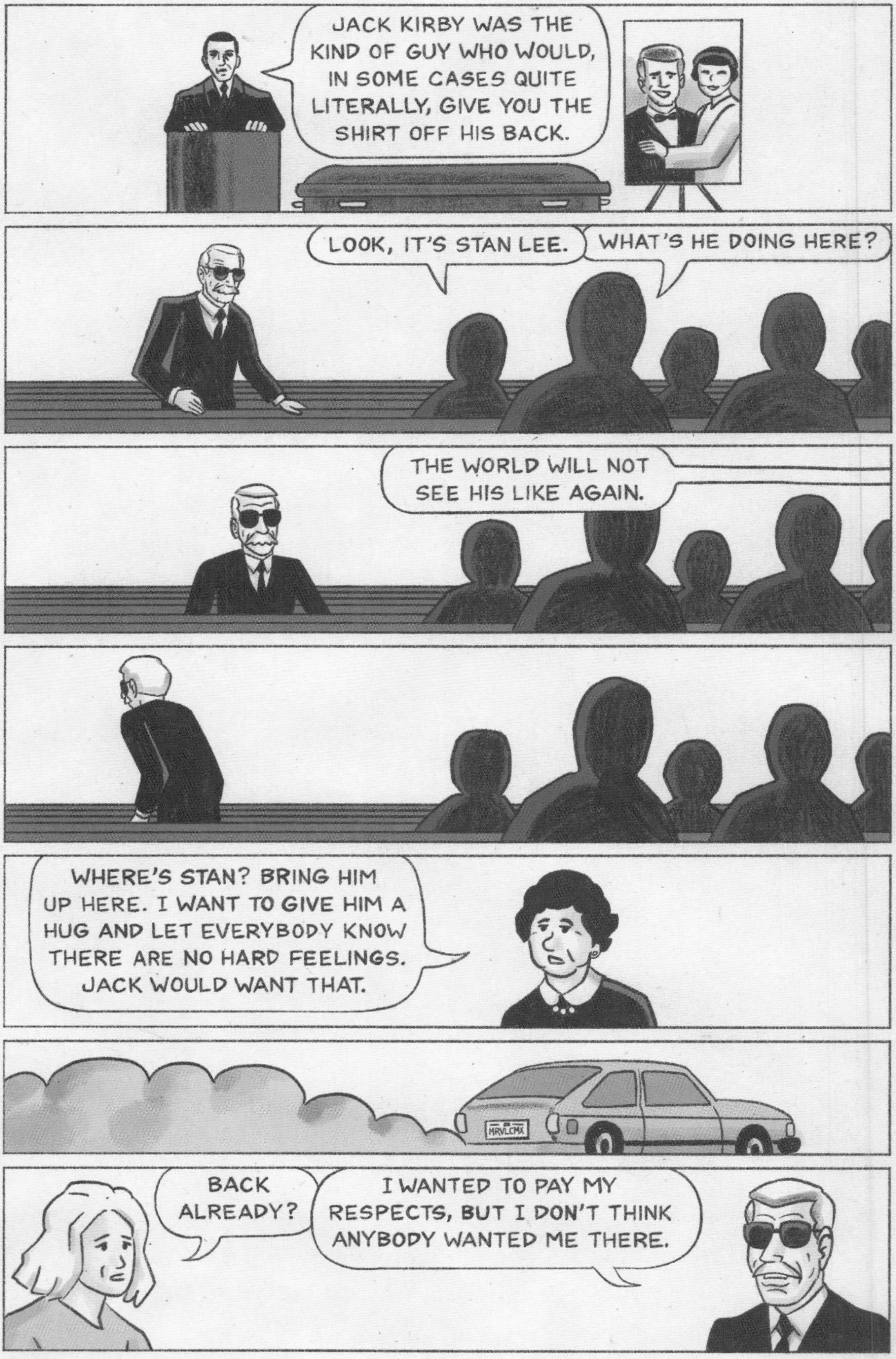

JACK KIRBY WAS THE KIND OF GUY WHO WOULD, IN SOME CASES QUITE LITERALLY, GIVE YOU THE SHIRT OFF HIS BACK.
LOOK, IT'S STAN LEE.
WHAT'S HE DOING HERE?
THE WORLD WILL NOT SEE HIS LIKE AGAIN.
WHERE'S STAN? BRING HIM UP HERE. I WANT TO GIVE HIM A HUG AND LET EVERYBODY KNOW THERE ARE NO HARD FEELINGS. JACK WOULD WANT THAT.
MRVLCMX
BACK ALREADY?
I WANTED TO PAY MY RESPECTS, BUT I DON'T THINK ANYBODY WANTED ME THERE.

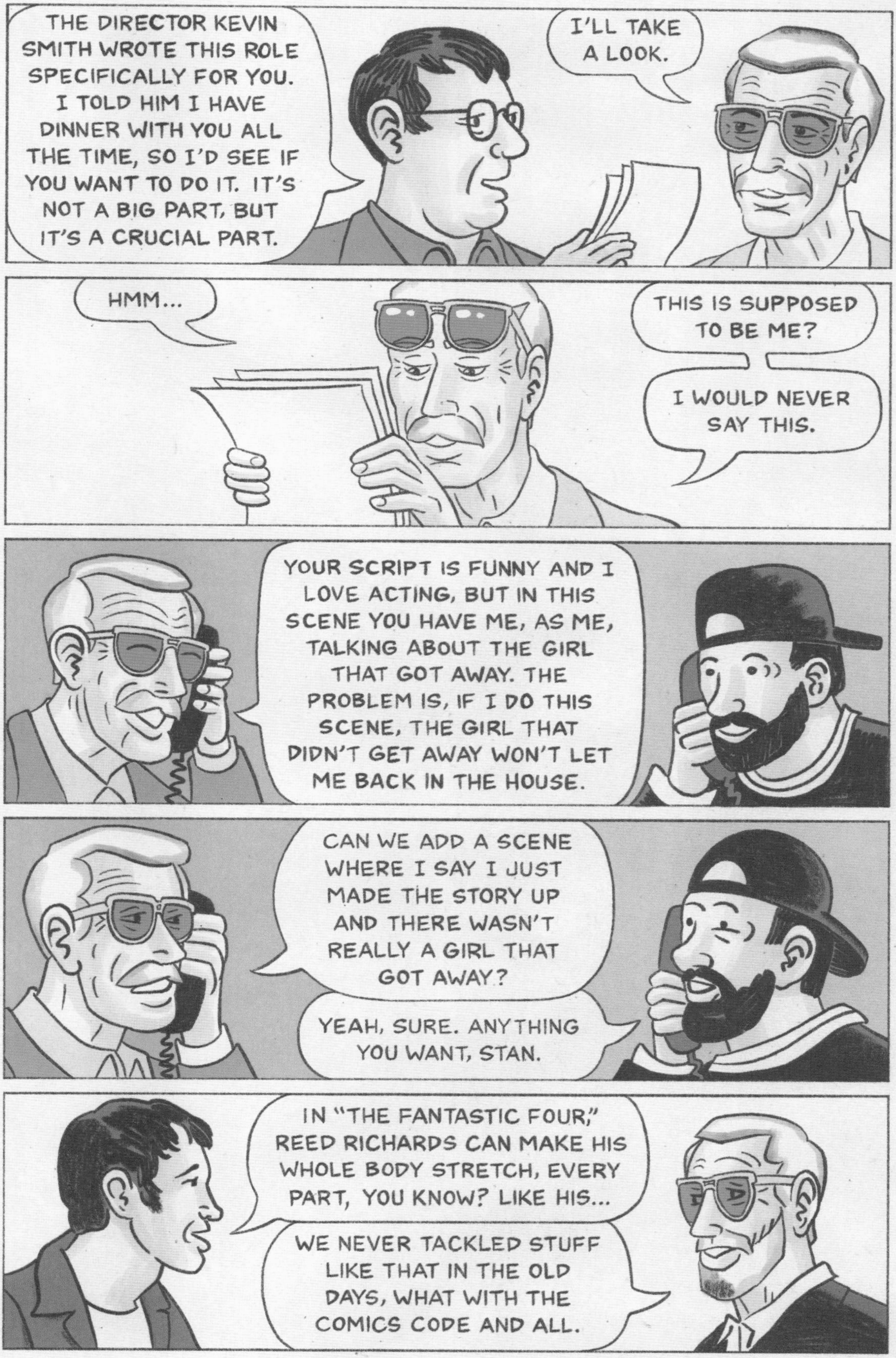
THE DIRECTOR KEVIN SMITH WROTE THIS ROLE SPECIFICALLY FOR YOU. I TOLD HIM I HAVE DINNER WITH YOU ALL THE TIME, SO I'D SEE IF YOU WANT TO DO IT. IT'S NOT A BIG PART, BUT IT'S A CRUCIAL PART.
I'LL TAKE A LOOK.
HMM...
THIS IS SUPPOSED TO BE ME?
I WOULD NEVER SAY THIS.
YOUR SCRIPT IS FUNNY AND I LOVE ACTING, BUT IN THIS SCENE YOU HAVE ME, AS ME, TALKING ABOUT THE GIRL THAT GOT AWAY. THE PROBLEM IS, IF I DO THIS SCENE, THE GIRL THAT DIDN'T GET AWAY WON'T LET ME BACK IN THE HOUSE.
CAN WE ADD A SCENE WHERE I SAY I JUST MADE THE STORY UP AND THERE WASN'T REALLY A GIRL THAT GOT AWAY?
YEAH, SURE. ANYTHING YOU WANT, STAN.
IN "THE FANTASTIC FOUR," REED RICHARDS CAN MAKE HIS WHOLE BODY STRETCH, EVERY PART, YOU KNOW? LIKE HIS...
WE NEVER TACKLED STUFF LIKE THAT IN THE OLD DAYS, WHAT WITH THE COMICS CODE AND ALL.

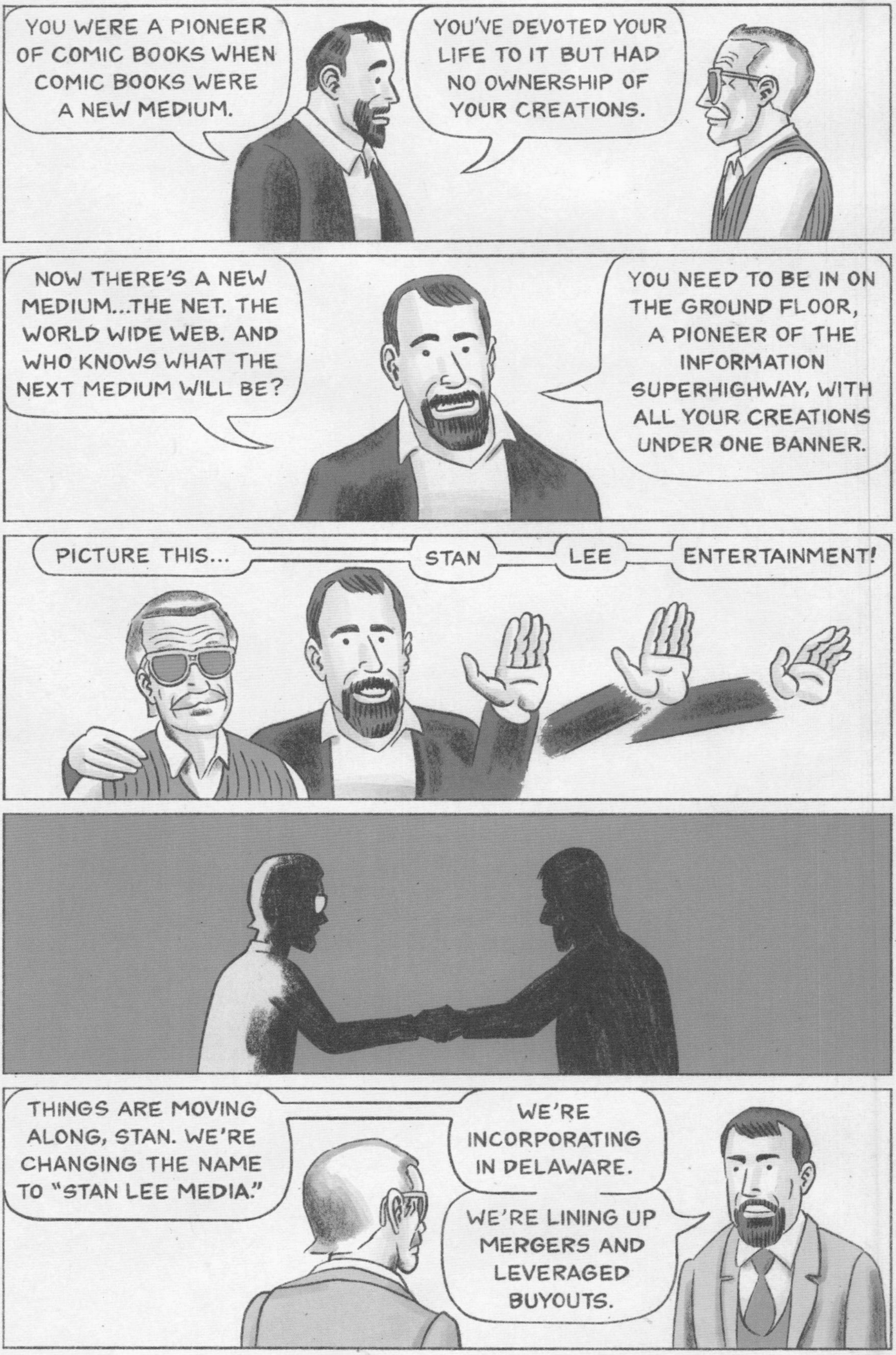
YOU WERE A PIONEER OF COMIC BOOKS WHEN COMIC BOOKS WERE A NEW MEDIUM.
YOU'VE DEVOTED YOUR LIFE TO IT BUT HAD NO OWNERSHIP OF YOUR CREATIONS.
NOW THERE'S A NEW MEDIUM...THE NET. THE WORLD WIDE WEB. AND WHO KNOWS WHAT THE NEXT MEDIUM WILL BE?
YOU NEED TO BE IN ON THE GROUND FLOOR, A PIONEER OF THE INFORMATION SUPERHIGHWAY, WITH ALL YOUR CREATIONS UNDER ONE BANNER.
PICTURE THIS...
STAN
LEE
ENTERTAINMENT!
THINGS ARE MOVING ALONG, STAN. WE'RE CHANGING THE NAME TO "STAN LEE MEDIA."
WE'RE INCORPORATING IN DELAWARE.
WE'RE LINING UP MERGERS AND LEVERAGED BUYOUTS.

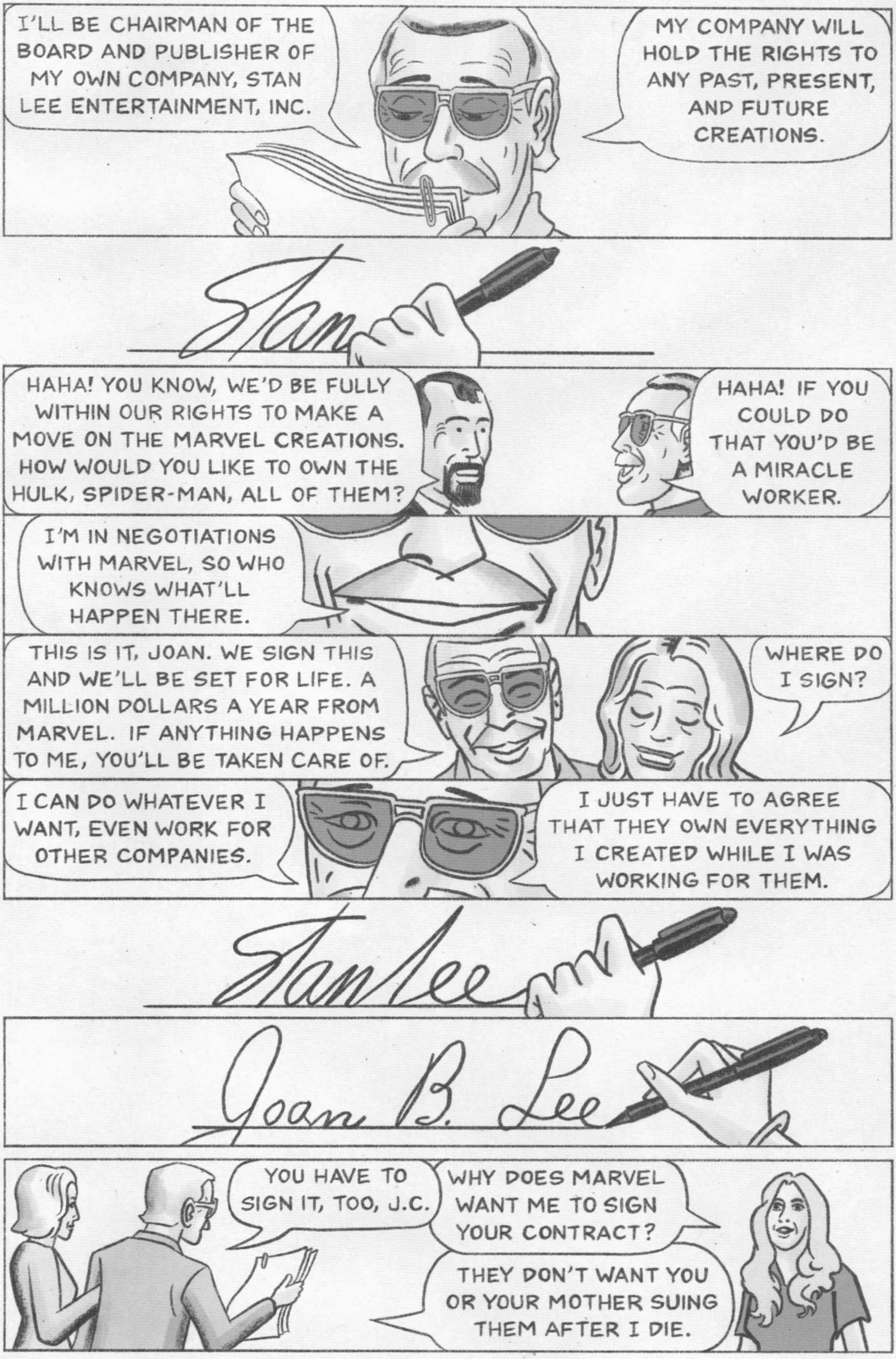

I'LL BE CHAIRMAN OF THE BOARD AND PUBLISHER OF MY OWN COMPANY, STAN LEE ENTERTAINMENT, INC.
MY COMPANY WILL HOLD THE RIGHTS TO ANY PAST, PRESENT, AND FUTURE CREATIONS.
Stan
HAHA! YOU KNOW, WE'D BE FULLY WITHIN OUR RIGHTS TO MAKE A MOVE ON THE MARVEL CREATIONS. HOW WOULD YOU LIKE TO OWN THE HULK, SPIDER-MAN, ALL OF THEM?
HAHA! IF YOU COULD DO THAT YOU'D BE A MIRACLE WORKER.
I'M IN NEGOTIATIONS WITH MARVEL, SO WHO KNOWS WHAT'LL HAPPEN THERE.
THIS IS IT, JOAN. WE SIGN THIS AND WE'LL BE SET FOR LIFE. A MILLION DOLLARS A YEAR FROM MARVEL. IF ANYTHING HAPPENS TO ME, YOU'LL BE TAKEN CARE OF.
WHERE DO I SIGN?
I CAN DO WHATEVER I WANT, EVEN WORK FOR OTHER COMPANIES.
I JUST HAVE TO AGREE THAT THEY OWN EVERYTHING I CREATED WHILE I WAS WORKING FOR THEM.
Stan Lee
Joan B. Lee
YOU HAVE TO SIGN IT, TOO, J.C.
WHY DOES MARVEL WANT ME TO SIGN YOUR CONTRACT?
THEY DON'T WANT YOU OR YOUR MOTHER SUING THEM AFTER I DIE.

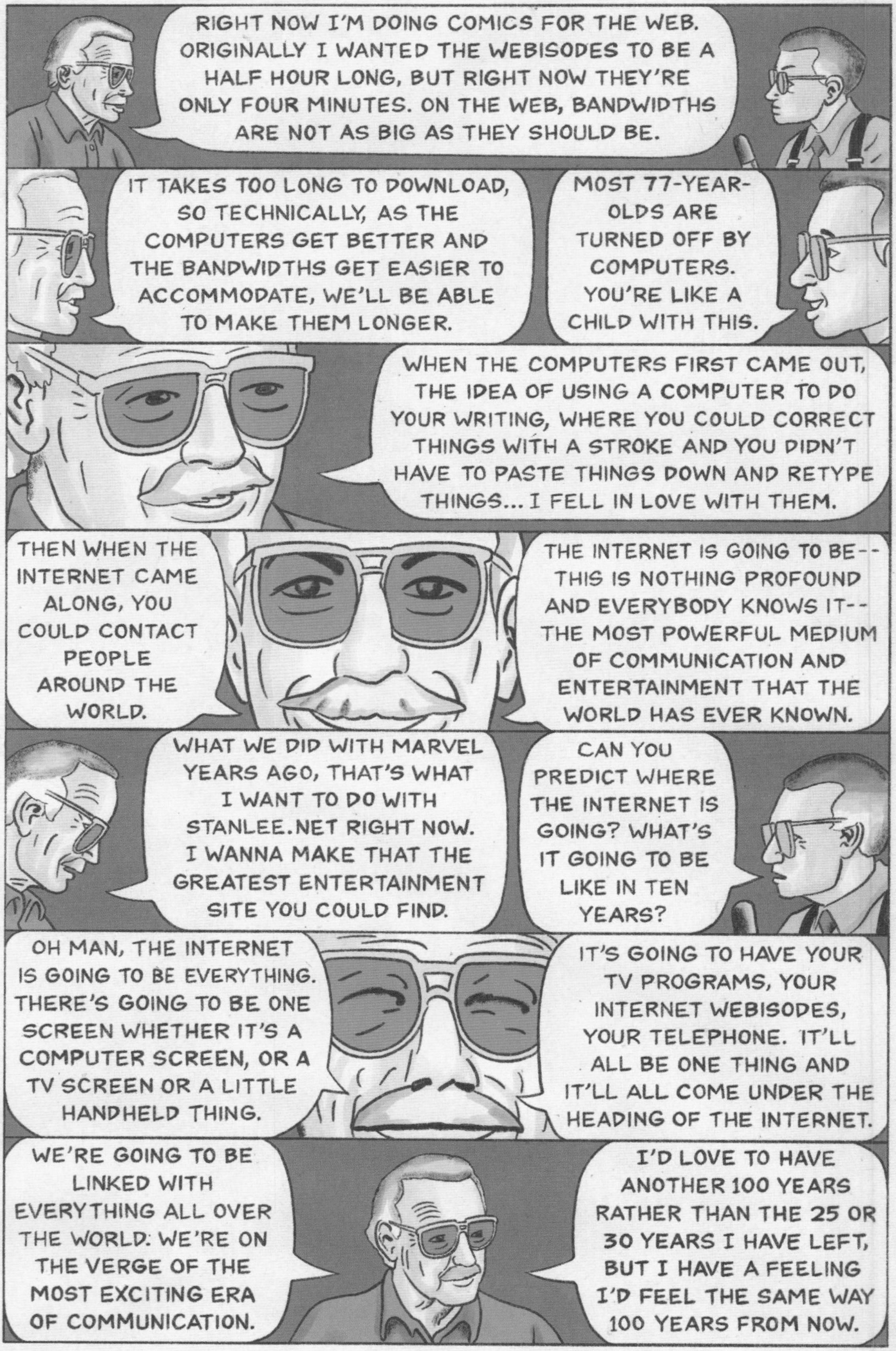
RIGHT NOW I'M DOING COMICS FOR THE WEB. ORIGINALLY I WANTED THE WEBISODES TO BE A HALF HOUR LONG, BUT RIGHT NOW THEY'RE ONLY FOUR MINUTES. ON THE WEB, BANDWIDTHS ARE NOT AS BIG AS THEY SHOULD BE.
IT TAKES TOO LONG TO DOWNLOAD, SO TECHNICALLY, AS THE COMPUTERS GET BETTER AND THE BANDWIDTHS GET EASIER TO ACCOMMODATE, WE'LL BE ABLE TO MAKE THEM LONGER.
MOST 77-YEAR-OLDS ARE TURNED OFF BY COMPUTERS. YOU'RE LIKE A CHILD WITH THIS.
WHEN THE COMPUTERS FIRST CAME OUT, THE IDEA OF USING A COMPUTER TO DO YOUR WRITING, WHERE YOU COULD CORRECT THINGS WITH A STROKE AND YOU DIDN'T HAVE TO PASTE THINGS DOWN AND RETYPE THINGS... I FELL IN LOVE WITH THEM.
THEN WHEN THE INTERNET CAME ALONG, YOU COULD CONTACT PEOPLE AROUND THE WORLD.
THE INTERNET IS GOING TO BE-- THIS IS NOTHING PROFOUND AND EVERYBODY KNOWS IT-- THE MOST POWERFUL MEDIUM OF COMMUNICATION AND ENTERTAINMENT THAT THE WORLD HAS EVER KNOWN.
WHAT WE DID WITH MARVEL YEARS AGO, THAT'S WHAT I WANT TO DO WITH STANLEE.NET RIGHT NOW. I WANNA MAKE THAT THE GREATEST ENTERTAINMENT SITE YOU COULD FIND.
CAN YOU PREDICT WHERE THE INTERNET IS GOING? WHAT'S IT GOING TO BE LIKE IN TEN YEARS?
OH MAN, THE INTERNET IS GOING TO BE EVERYTHING. THERE'S GOING TO BE ONE SCREEN WHETHER IT'S A COMPUTER SCREEN, OR A TV SCREEN OR A LITTLE HANDHELD THING.
IT'S GOING TO HAVE YOUR TV PROGRAMS, YOUR INTERNET WEBISODES, YOUR TELEPHONE. IT'LL ALL BE ONE THING AND IT'LL ALL COME UNDER THE HEADING OF THE INTERNET.
WE'RE GOING TO BE LINKED WITH EVERYTHING ALL OVER THE WORLD: WE'RE ON THE VERGE OF THE MOST EXCITING ERA OF COMMUNICATION.
I'D LOVE TO HAVE ANOTHER 100 YEARS RATHER THAN THE 25 OR 30 YEARS I HAVE LEFT, BUT I HAVE A FEELING I'D FEEL THE SAME WAY 100 YEARS FROM NOW.

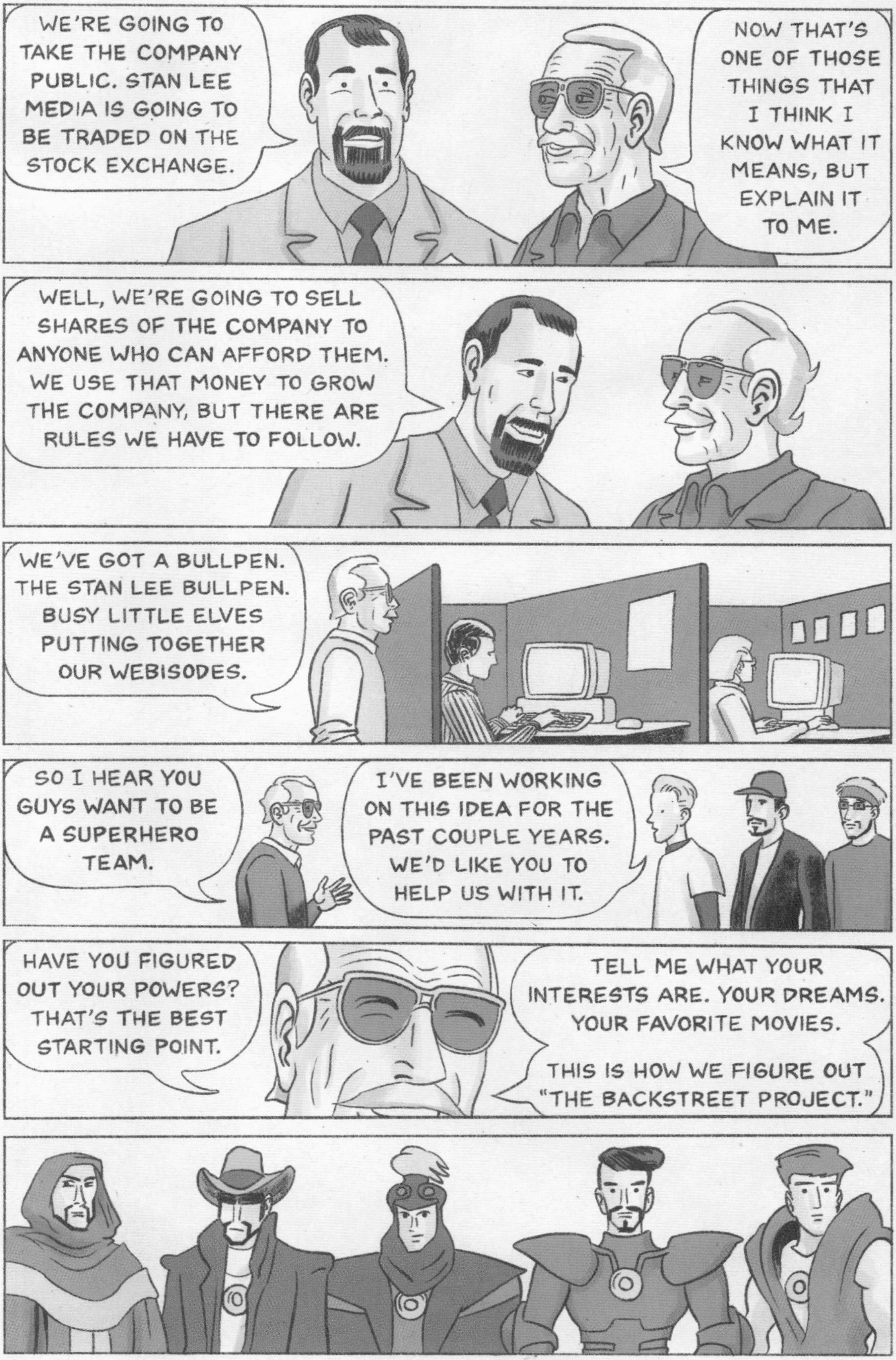
WE'RE GOING TO TAKE THE COMPANY PUBLIC. STAN LEE MEDIA IS GOING TO BE TRADED ON THE STOCK EXCHANGE.
NOW THAT'S ONE OF THOSE THINGS THAT I THINK I KNOW WHAT IT MEANS, BUT EXPLAIN IT TO ME.
WELL, WE'RE GOING TO SELL SHARES OF THE COMPANY TO ANYONE WHO CAN AFFORD THEM. WE USE THAT MONEY TO GROW THE COMPANY, BUT THERE ARE RULES WE HAVE TO FOLLOW.
WE'VE GOT A BULLPEN. THE STAN LEE BULLPEN. BUSY LITTLE ELVES PUTTING TOGETHER OUR WEBISODES.
SO I HEAR YOU GUYS WANT TO BE A SUPERHERO TEAM.
I'VE BEEN WORKING ON THIS IDEA FOR THE PAST COUPLE YEARS. WE'D LIKE YOU TO HELP US WITH IT.
HAVE YOU FIGURED OUT YOUR POWERS? THAT'S THE BEST STARTING POINT.
TELL ME WHAT YOUR INTERESTS ARE. YOUR DREAMS. YOUR FAVORITE MOVIES.
THIS IS HOW WE FIGURE OUT "THE BACKSTREET PROJECT."

WELCOME TO THE WORLD PREMIERE OF "THE SEVENTH PORTAL," A NEW ANIMATED SERIES AVAILABLE ONLY ON THE INTERNET AS A SERIES OF DOWNLOADABLE WEBISODES.

YOU ARE PRIVILEGED TO BE SEEING IT BEFORE THE REST OF THE WORLD.

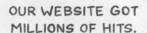

OUR WEBSITE GOT MILLIONS OF HITS.

THAT'S GOOD, RIGHT?

UNFORTUNATELY IT CRASHED THE WEBSITE, SO NOBODY GOT TO SEE THE WEBISODE.

SO IF WE DO SOMETHING REALLY POPULAR, NOBODY WILL SEE IT?

WE SIGNED A DEAL WITH DC COMICS. I'LL BE WRITING MY OWN VERSIONS REIMAGINING SUPERMAN, BATMAN, WONDER WOMAN--THE WHOLE CREW-- IN THE STAN LEE STYLE.

WE BOUGHT THE MOVIE RIGHTS TO "CONAN THE BARBARIAN."

THAT'S GREAT! I WAS THE PUBLISHER OF THE ORIGINAL "CONAN" COMICS. IT'S COME FULL CIRCLE.

WHAT IF WE BOUGHT MARVEL?

HAHA! YOU KNOW... STRANGER THINGS HAVE HAPPENED.

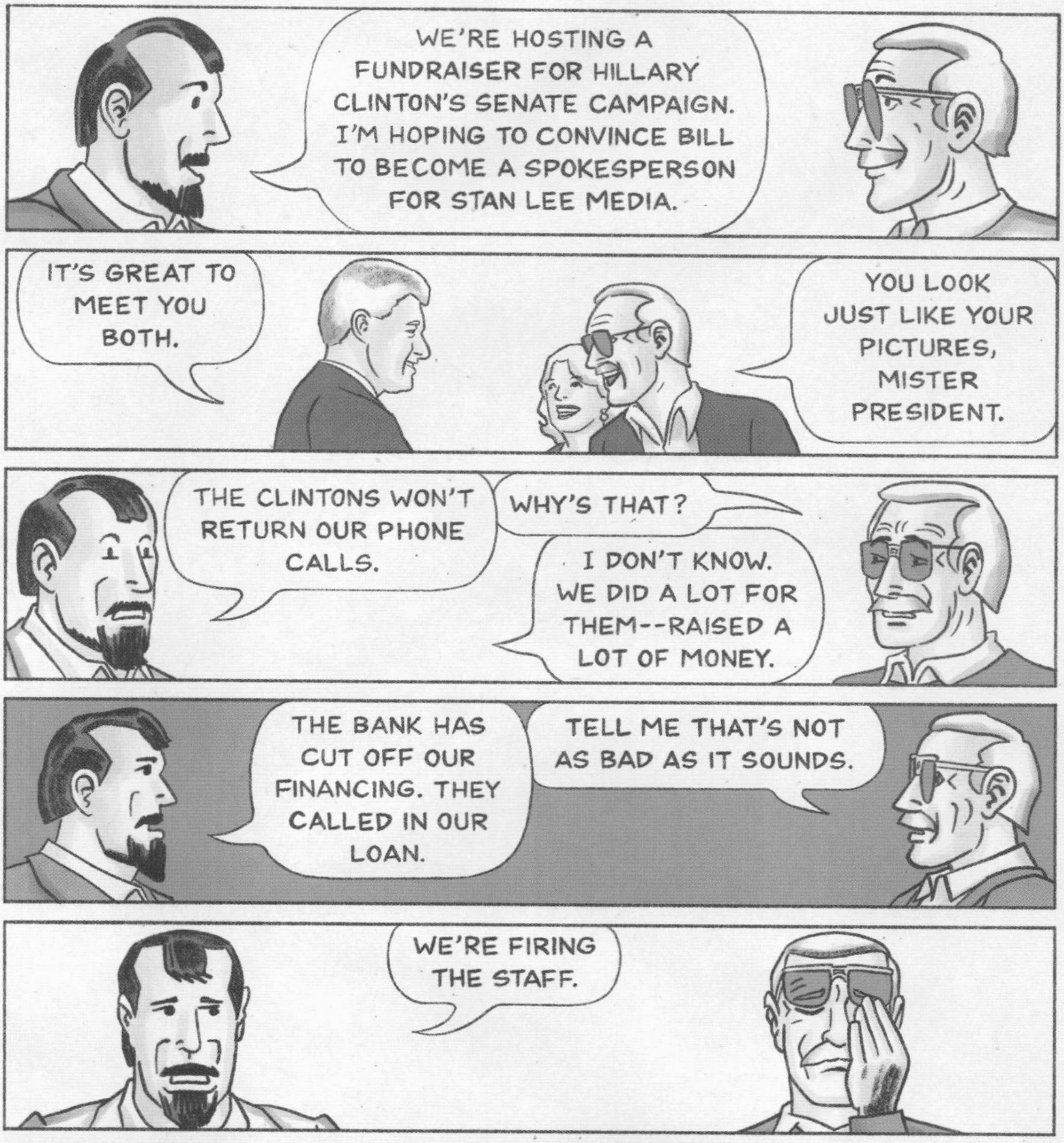
WE'RE HOSTING A FUNDRAISER FOR HILLARY CLINTON'S SENATE CAMPAIGN. I'M HOPING TO CONVINCE BILL TO BECOME A SPOKESPERSON FOR STAN LEE MEDIA.
IT'S GREAT TO MEET YOU BOTH.
YOU LOOK JUST LIKE YOUR PICTURES, MISTER PRESIDENT.
THE CLINTONS WON'T RETURN OUR PHONE CALLS.
WHY'S THAT?
I DON'T KNOW. WE DID A LOT FOR THEM--RAISED A LOT OF MONEY.
THE BANK HAS CUT OFF OUR FINANCING. THEY CALLED IN OUR LOAN.
TELL ME THAT'S NOT AS BAD AS IT SOUNDS.
WE'RE FIRING THE STAFF.
YOU'VE GOT TO BE KIDDING ME.
WHO'S GONNA SIGN FOR THIS SPIDER-MAN STATUE?
SOMEBODY'S GOTTA SIGN FOR THIS.

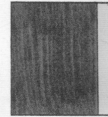

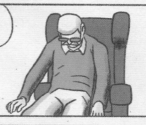

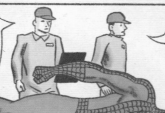

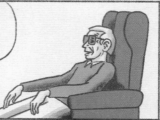

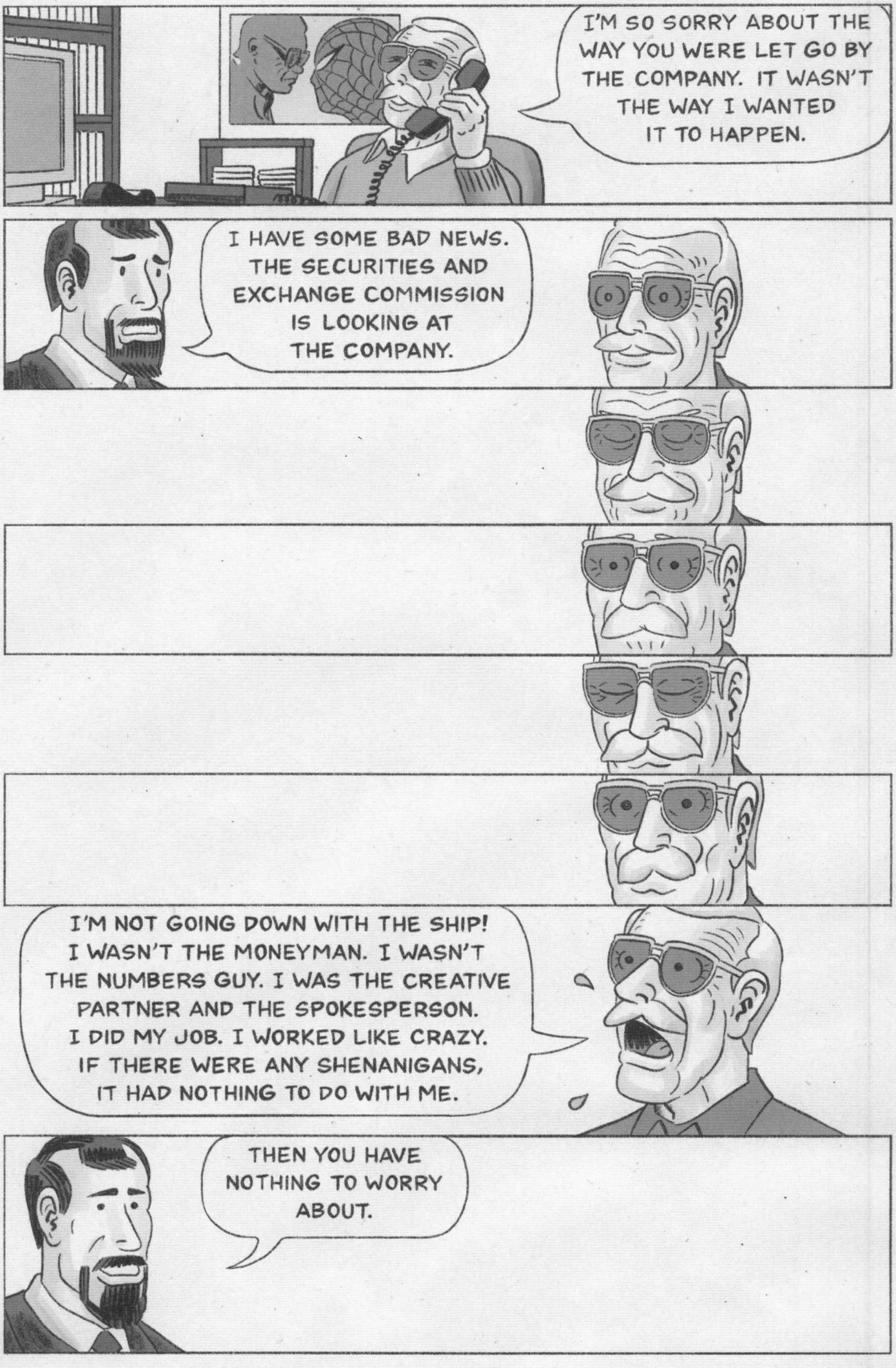
I'M SO SORRY ABOUT THE WAY YOU WERE LET GO BY THE COMPANY. IT WASN'T THE WAY I WANTED IT TO HAPPEN.
I HAVE SOME BAD NEWS. THE SECURITIES AND EXCHANGE COMMISSION IS LOOKING AT THE COMPANY.
I'M NOT GOING DOWN WITH THE SHIP! I WASN'T THE MONEYMAN. I WASN'T THE NUMBERS GUY. I WAS THE CREATIVE PARTNER AND THE SPOKESPERSON. I DID MY JOB. I WORKED LIKE CRAZY. IF THERE WERE ANY SHENANIGANS, IT HAD NOTHING TO DO WITH ME.
THEN YOU HAVE NOTHING TO WORRY ABOUT.

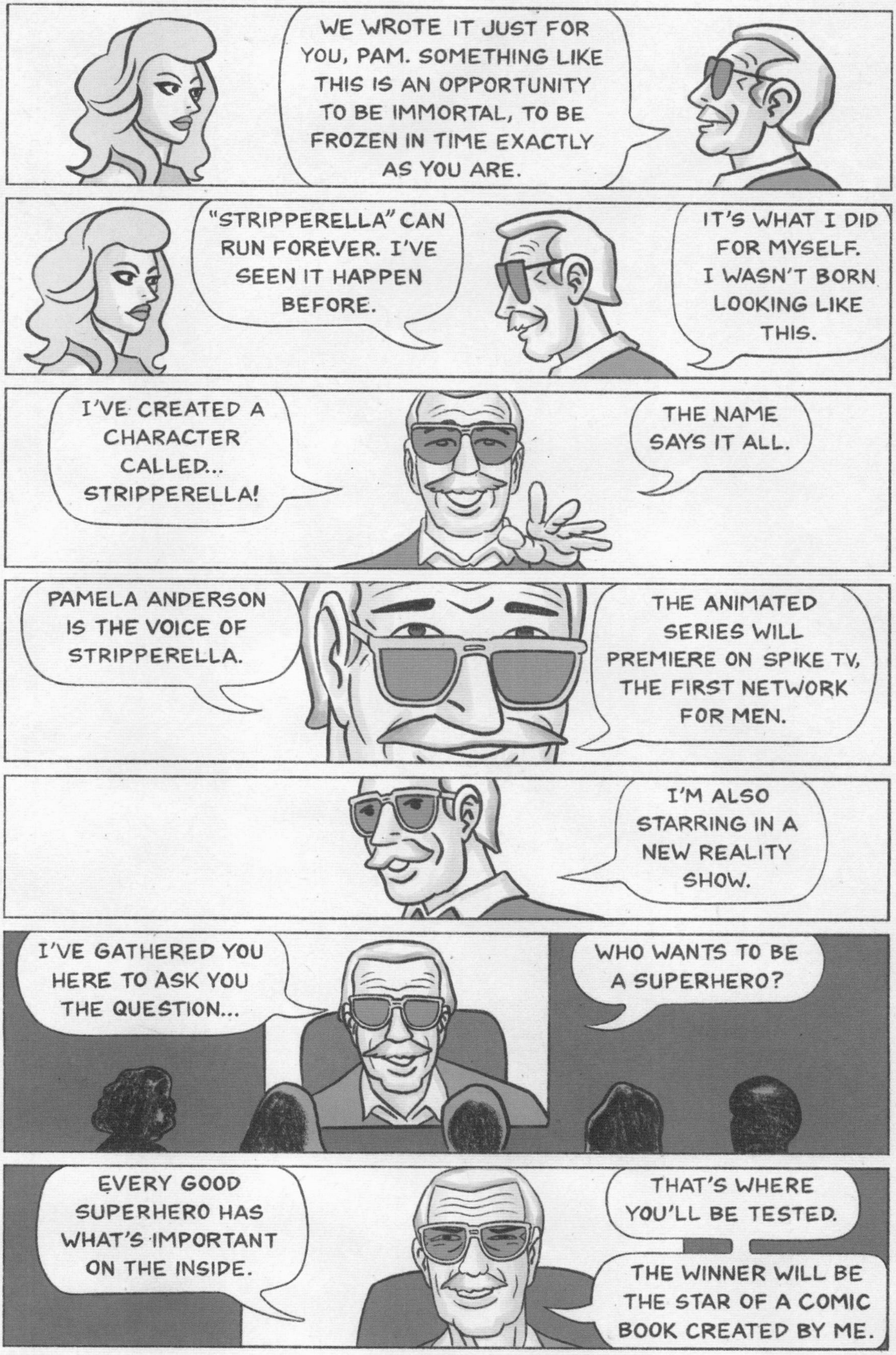
WE WROTE IT JUST FOR YOU, PAM. SOMETHING LIKE THIS IS AN OPPORTUNITY TO BE IMMORTAL, TO BE FROZEN IN TIME EXACTLY AS YOU ARE.
"STRIPPERELLA" CAN RUN FOREVER. I'VE SEEN IT HAPPEN BEFORE.
IT'S WHAT I DID FOR MYSELF. I WASN'T BORN LOOKING LIKE THIS.
I'VE CREATED A CHARACTER CALLED... STRIPPERELLA!
THE NAME SAYS IT ALL.
PAMELA ANDERSON IS THE VOICE OF STRIPPERELLA.
THE ANIMATED SERIES WILL PREMIERE ON SPIKE TV, THE FIRST NETWORK FOR MEN.
I'M ALSO STARRING IN A NEW REALITY SHOW.
I'VE GATHERED YOU HERE TO ASK YOU THE QUESTION...
WHO WANTS TO BE A SUPERHERO?
EVERY GOOD SUPERHERO HAS WHAT'S IMPORTANT ON THE INSIDE.
THAT'S WHERE YOU'LL BE TESTED.
THE WINNER WILL BE THE STAR OF A COMIC BOOK CREATED BY ME.

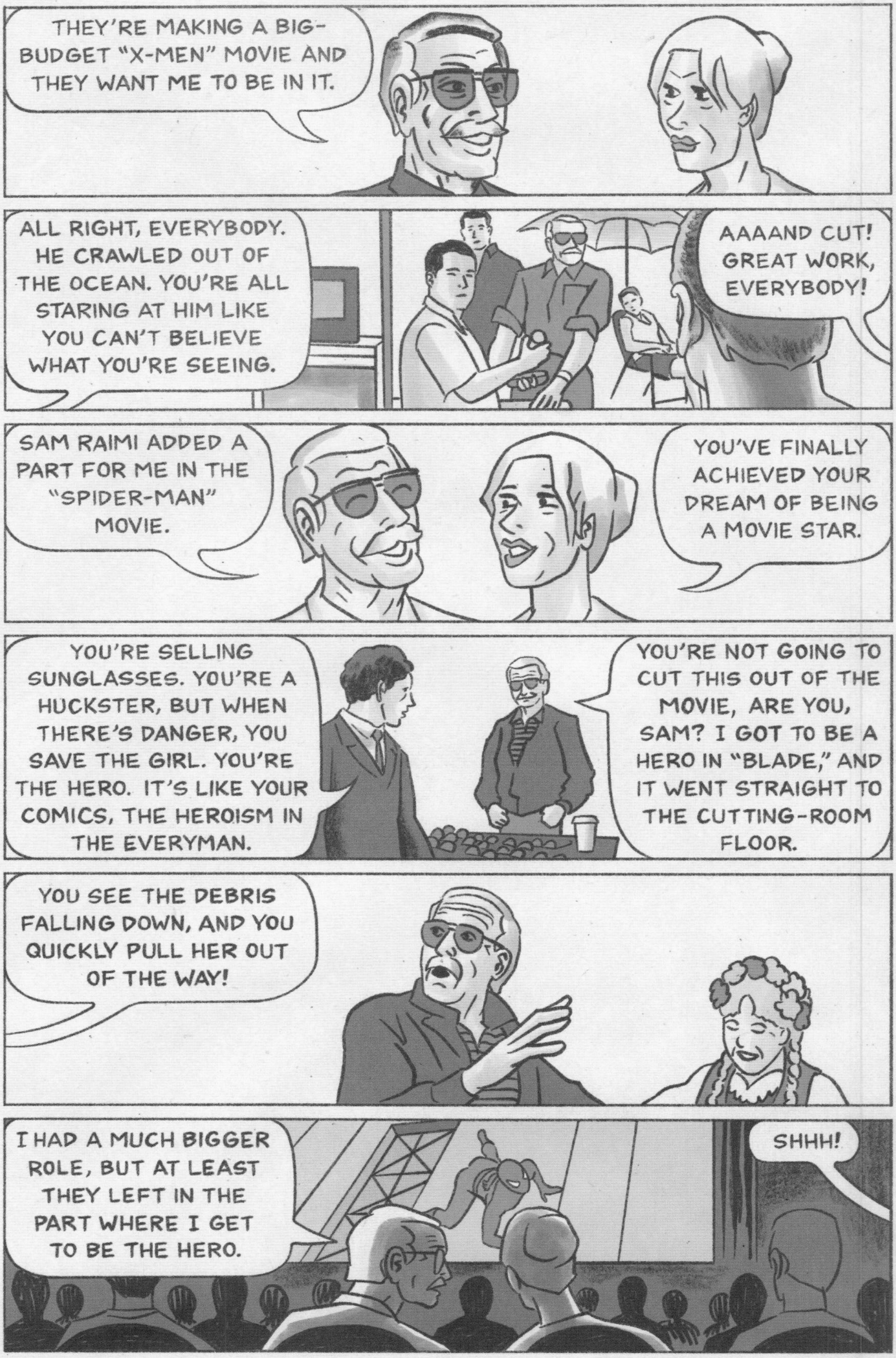
THEY'RE MAKING A BIG-BUDGET "X-MEN" MOVIE AND THEY WANT ME TO BE IN IT.
ALL RIGHT, EVERYBODY. HE CRAWLED OUT OF THE OCEAN. YOU'RE ALL STARING AT HIM LIKE YOU CAN'T BELIEVE WHAT YOU'RE SEEING.
AAAAND CUT! GREAT WORK, EVERYBODY!
SAM RAIMI ADDED A PART FOR ME IN THE "SPIDER-MAN" MOVIE.
YOU'VE FINALLY ACHIEVED YOUR DREAM OF BEING A MOVIE STAR.
YOU'RE SELLING SUNGLASSES. YOU'RE A HUCKSTER, BUT WHEN THERE'S DANGER, YOU SAVE THE GIRL. YOU'RE THE HERO. IT'S LIKE YOUR COMICS, THE HEROISM IN THE EVERYMAN.
YOU'RE NOT GOING TO CUT THIS OUT OF THE MOVIE, ARE YOU, SAM? I GOT TO BE A HERO IN "BLADE," AND IT WENT STRAIGHT TO THE CUTTING-ROOM FLOOR.
YOU SEE THE DEBRIS FALLING DOWN, AND YOU QUICKLY PULL HER OUT OF THE WAY!
I HAD A MUCH BIGGER ROLE, BUT AT LEAST THEY LEFT IN THE PART WHERE I GET TO BE THE HERO.
SHHH!

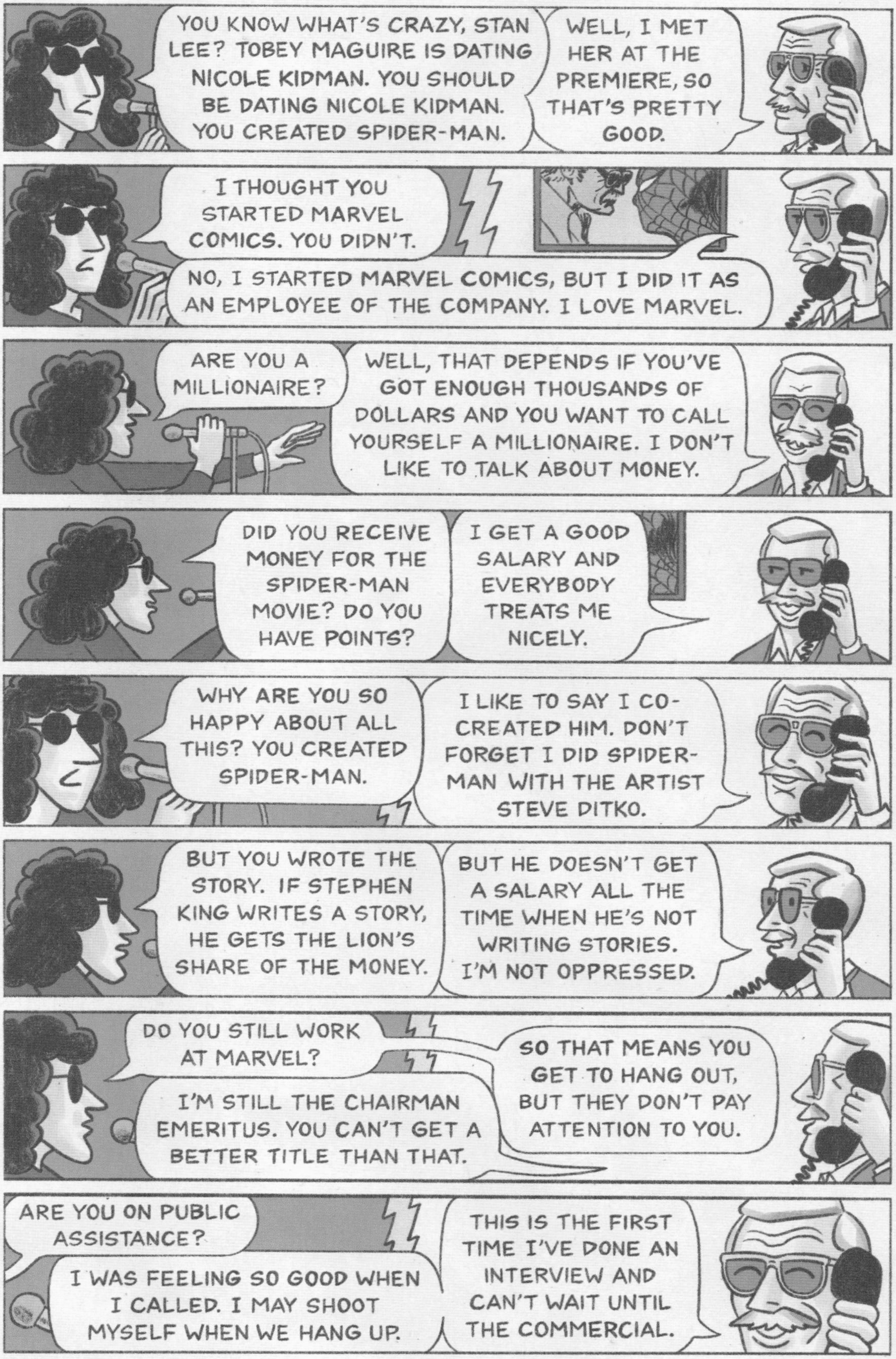
YOU KNOW WHAT'S CRAZY, STAN LEE? TOBEY MAGUIRE IS DATING NICOLE KIDMAN. YOU SHOULD BE DATING NICOLE KIDMAN. YOU CREATED SPIDER-MAN.
WELL, I MET HER AT THE PREMIERE, SO THAT'S PRETTY GOOD.
I THOUGHT YOU STARTED MARVEL COMICS. YOU DIDN'T.
NO, I STARTED MARVEL COMICS, BUT I DID IT AS AN EMPLOYEE OF THE COMPANY. I LOVE MARVEL.
ARE YOU A MILLIONAIRE?
WELL, THAT DEPENDS IF YOU'VE GOT ENOUGH THOUSANDS OF DOLLARS AND YOU WANT TO CALL YOURSELF A MILLIONAIRE. I DON'T LIKE TO TALK ABOUT MONEY.
DID YOU RECEIVE MONEY FOR THE SPIDER-MAN MOVIE? DO YOU HAVE POINTS?
I GET A GOOD SALARY AND EVERYBODY TREATS ME NICELY.
WHY ARE YOU SO HAPPY ABOUT ALL THIS? YOU CREATED SPIDER-MAN.
I LIKE TO SAY I CO-CREATED HIM. DON'T FORGET I DID SPIDER-MAN WITH THE ARTIST STEVE DITKO.
BUT YOU WROTE THE STORY. IF STEPHEN KING WRITES A STORY, HE GETS THE LION'S SHARE OF THE MONEY.
BUT HE DOESN'T GET A SALARY ALL THE TIME WHEN HE'S NOT WRITING STORIES. I'M NOT OPPRESSED.
DO YOU STILL WORK AT MARVEL?
I'M STILL THE CHAIRMAN EMERITUS. YOU CAN'T GET A BETTER TITLE THAN THAT.
SO THAT MEANS YOU GET TO HANG OUT, BUT THEY DON'T PAY ATTENTION TO YOU.
ARE YOU ON PUBLIC ASSISTANCE?
I WAS FEELING SO GOOD WHEN I CALLED. I MAY SHOOT MYSELF WHEN WE HANG UP.
THIS IS THE FIRST TIME I'VE DONE AN INTERVIEW AND CAN'T WAIT UNTIL THE COMMERCIAL.

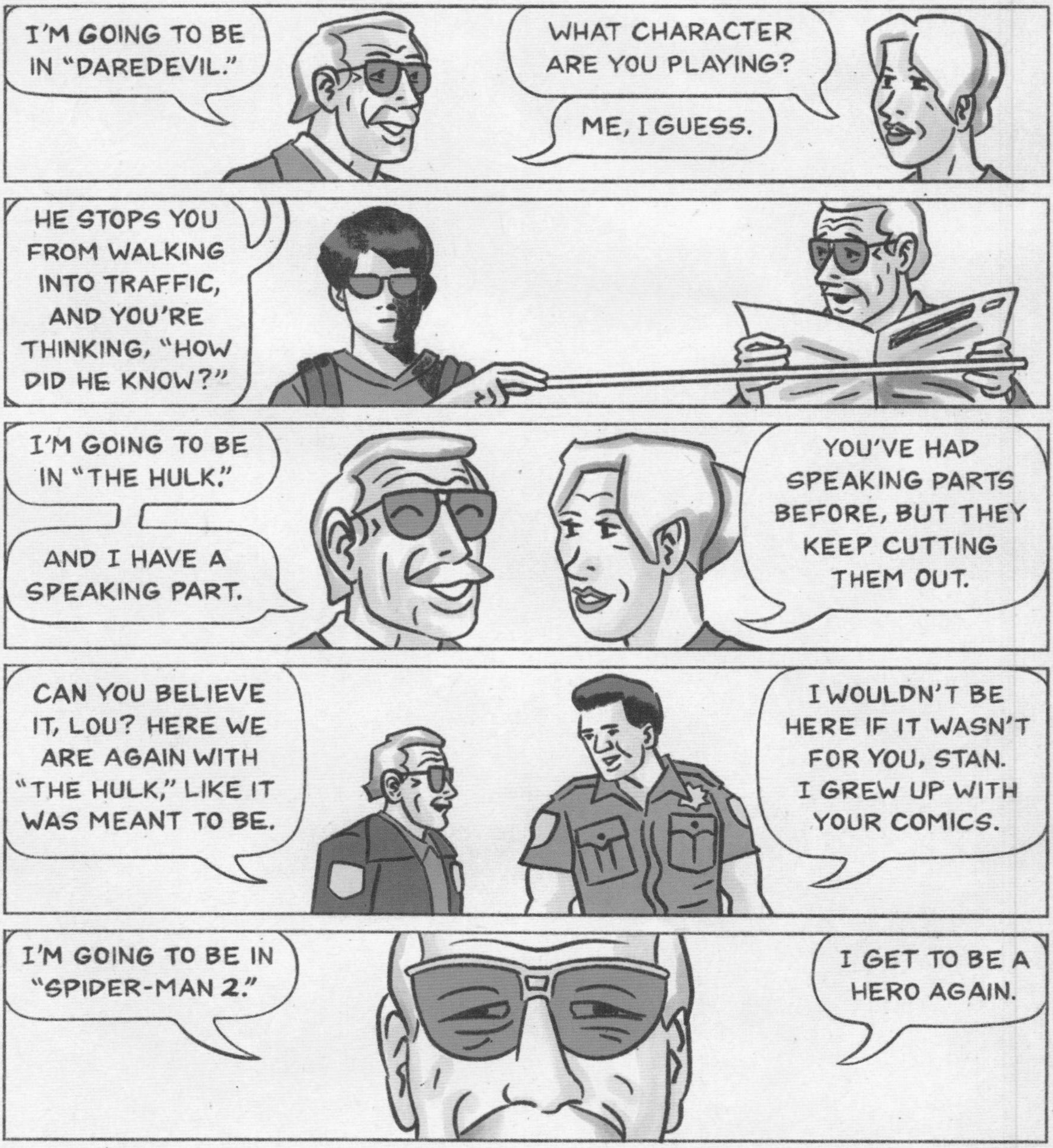
I'M GOING TO BE IN "DAREDEVIL."
WHAT CHARACTER ARE YOU PLAYING?
ME, I GUESS.
HE STOPS YOU FROM WALKING INTO TRAFFIC, AND YOU'RE THINKING, "HOW DID HE KNOW?"
I'M GOING TO BE IN "THE HULK."
AND I HAVE A SPEAKING PART.
YOU'VE HAD SPEAKING PARTS BEFORE, BUT THEY KEEP CUTTING THEM OUT.
CAN YOU BELIEVE IT, LOU? HERE WE ARE AGAIN WITH "THE HULK," LIKE IT WAS MEANT TO BE.
I WOULDN'T BE HERE IF IT WASN'T FOR YOU, STAN. I GREW UP WITH YOUR COMICS.
I'M GOING TO BE IN "SPIDER-MAN 2."
I GET TO BE A HERO AGAIN.
I'M GOING TO BE IN "FANTASTIC FOUR." YOU'RE NEVER GOING TO BELIEVE WHO I'M PLAYING.
WILLIE LUMPKIN!
WELCOME BACK TO THE BAXTER, MISTER RICHARDS.

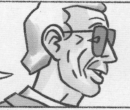

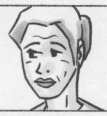

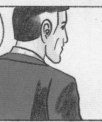

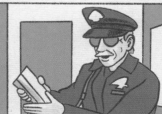

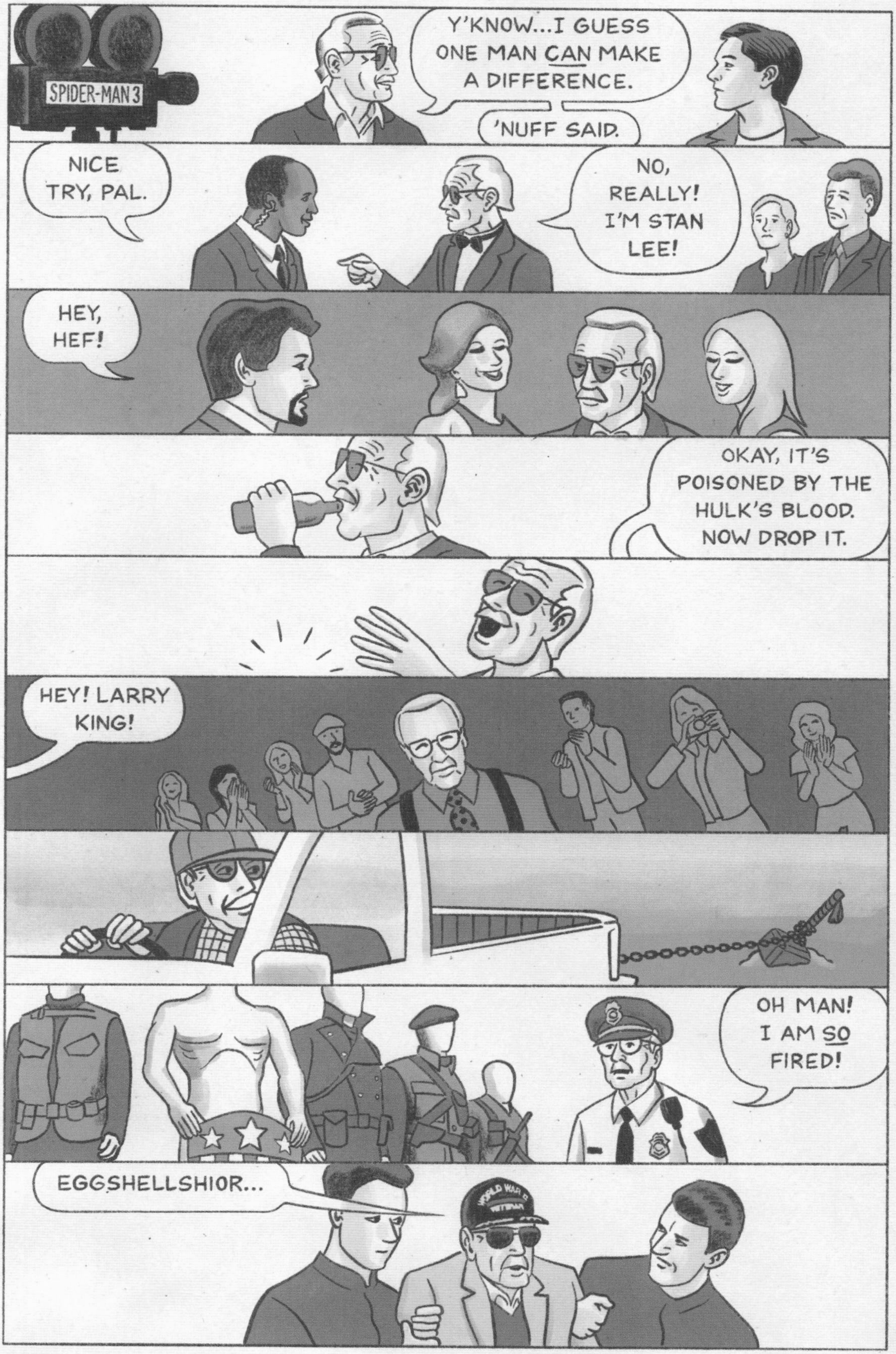
SPIDER-MAN 3
Y'KNOW...I GUESS ONE MAN CAN MAKE A DIFFERENCE.
'NUFF SAID.
NICE TRY, PAL.
NO, REALLY! I'M STAN LEE!
HEY, HEF!
OKAY, IT'S POISONED BY THE HULK'S BLOOD. NOW DROP IT.
HEY! LARRY KING!
OH MAN! I AM SO FIRED!
EGGSHELLSHIOR...

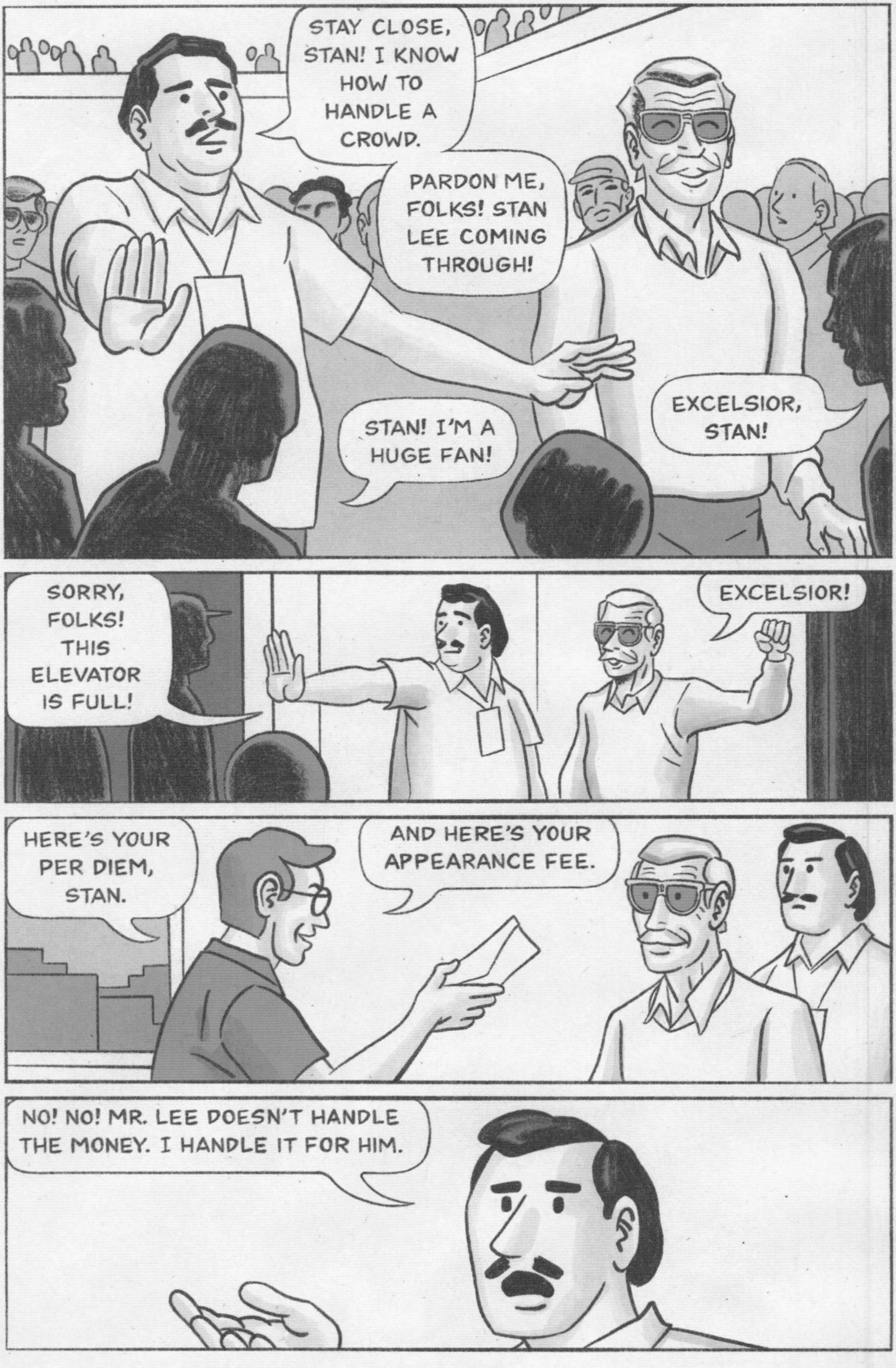
STAY CLOSE, STAN! I KNOW HOW TO HANDLE A CROWD.
PARDON ME, FOLKS! STAN LEE COMING THROUGH!
STAN! I'M A HUGE FAN!
EXCELSIOR, STAN!
SORRY, FOLKS! THIS ELEVATOR IS FULL!
EXCELSIOR!
HERE'S YOUR PER DIEM, STAN.
AND HERE'S YOUR APPEARANCE FEE.
NO! NO! MR. LEE DOESN'T HANDLE THE MONEY. I HANDLE IT FOR HIM.

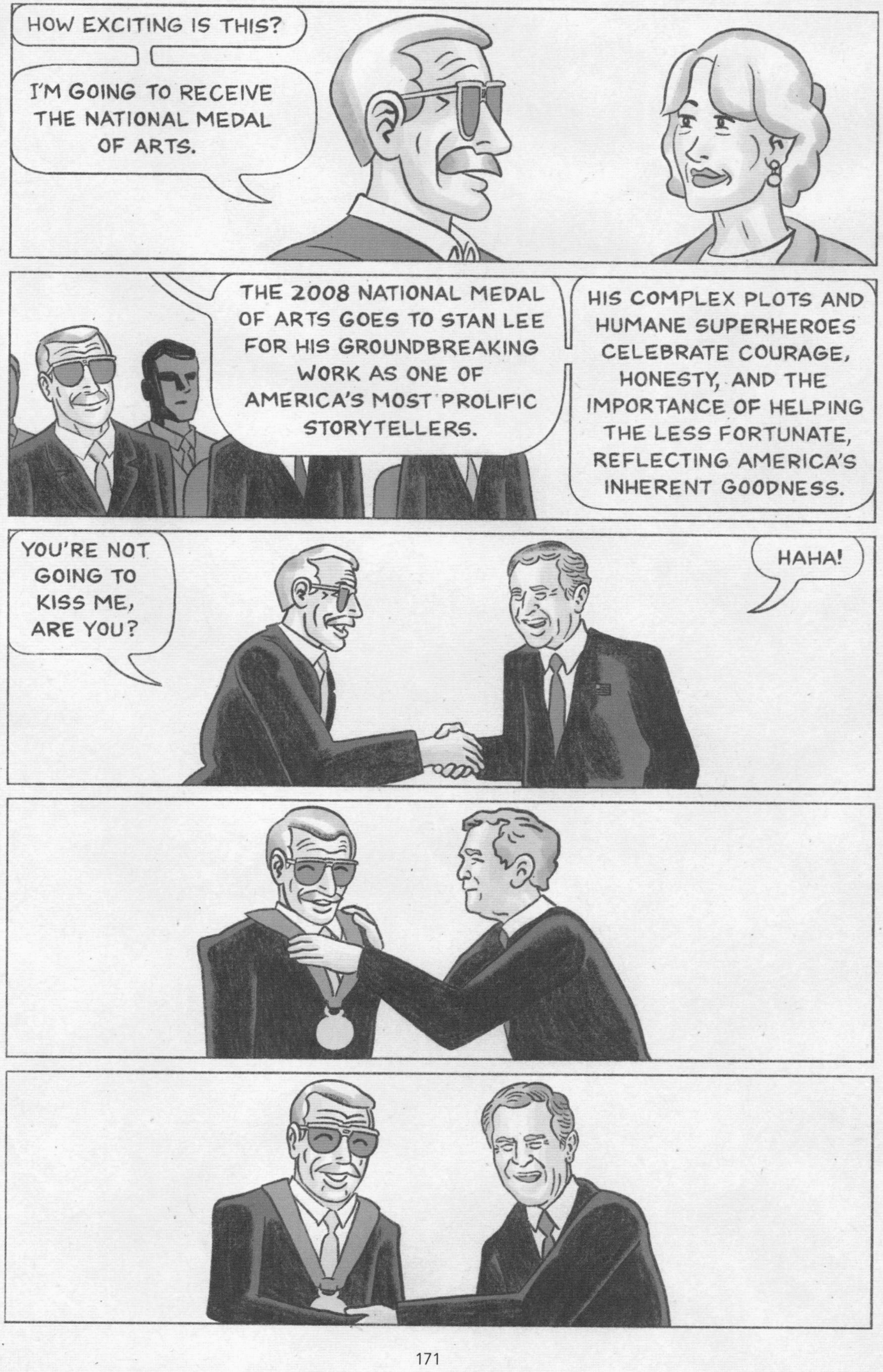
HOW EXCITING IS THIS?
I'M GOING TO RECEIVE THE NATIONAL MEDAL OF ARTS.
THE 2008 NATIONAL MEDAL OF ARTS GOES TO STAN LEE FOR HIS GROUNDBREAKING WORK AS ONE OF AMERICA'S MOST PROLIFIC STORYTELLERS.
HIS COMPLEX PLOTS AND HUMANE SUPERHEROES CELEBRATE COURAGE, HONESTY, AND THE IMPORTANCE OF HELPING THE LESS FORTUNATE, REFLECTING AMERICA'S INHERENT GOODNESS.
YOU'RE NOT GOING TO KISS ME, ARE YOU?
HAHA!

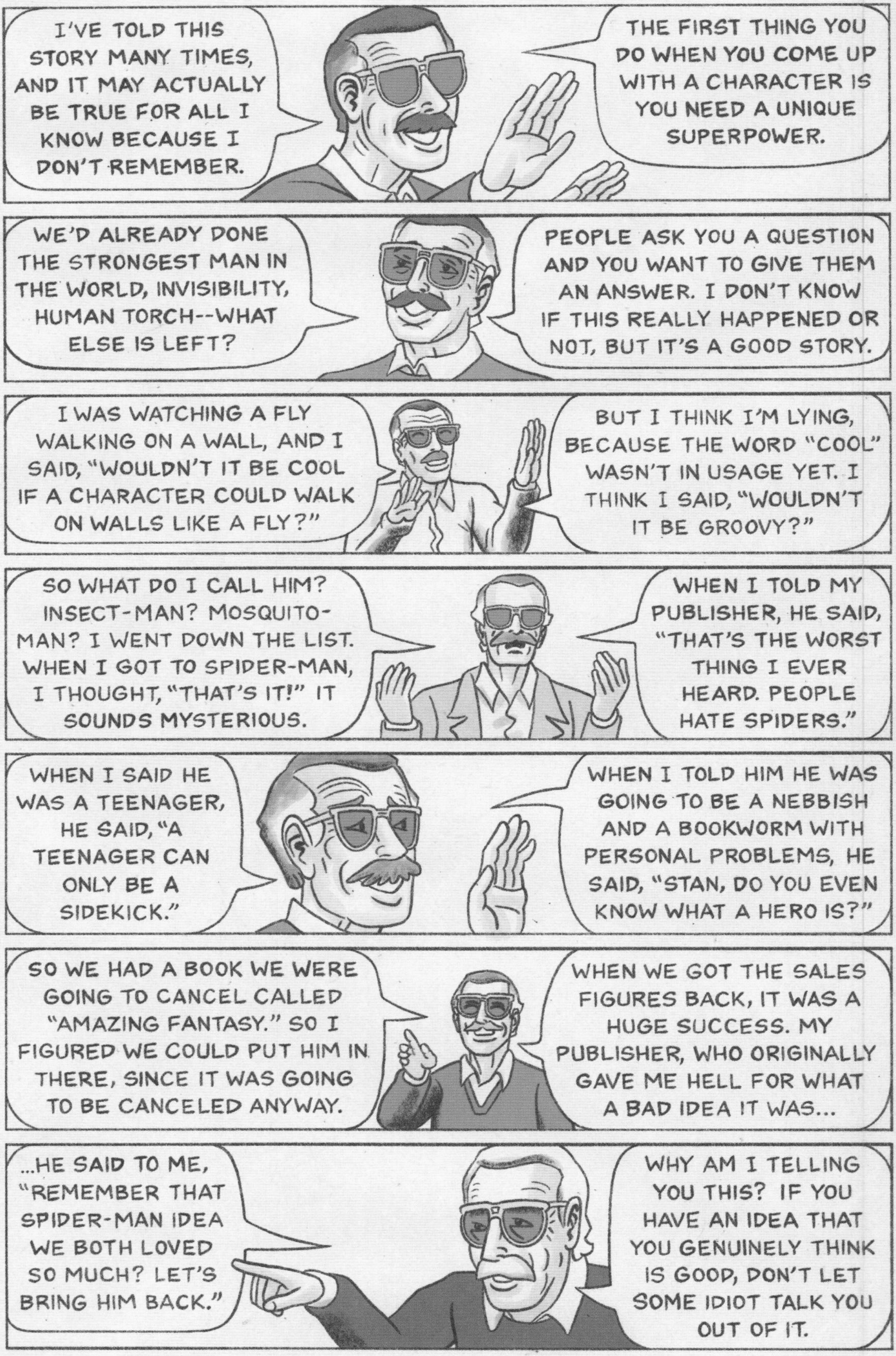
I'VE TOLD THIS STORY MANY TIMES, AND IT MAY ACTUALLY BE TRUE FOR ALL I KNOW BECAUSE I DON'T REMEMBER.
THE FIRST THING YOU DO WHEN YOU COME UP WITH A CHARACTER IS YOU NEED A UNIQUE SUPERPOWER.
WE'D ALREADY DONE THE STRONGEST MAN IN THE WORLD, INVISIBILITY, HUMAN TORCH--WHAT ELSE IS LEFT?
PEOPLE ASK YOU A QUESTION AND YOU WANT TO GIVE THEM AN ANSWER. I DON'T KNOW IF THIS REALLY HAPPENED OR NOT, BUT IT'S A GOOD STORY.
I WAS WATCHING A FLY WALKING ON A WALL, AND I SAID, "WOULDN'T IT BE COOL IF A CHARACTER COULD WALK ON WALLS LIKE A FLY?"
BUT I THINK I'M LYING, BECAUSE THE WORD "COOL" WASN'T IN USAGE YET. I THINK I SAID, "WOULDN'T IT BE GROOVY?"
SO WHAT DO I CALL HIM? INSECT-MAN? MOSQUITO-MAN? I WENT DOWN THE LIST. WHEN I GOT TO SPIDER-MAN, I THOUGHT, "THAT'S IT!" IT SOUNDS MYSTERIOUS.
WHEN I TOLD MY PUBLISHER, HE SAID, "THAT'S THE WORST THING I EVER HEARD. PEOPLE HATE SPIDERS."
WHEN I SAID HE WAS A TEENAGER, HE SAID, "A TEENAGER CAN ONLY BE A SIDEKICK."
WHEN I TOLD HIM HE WAS GOING TO BE A NEBBISH AND A BOOKWORM WITH PERSONAL PROBLEMS, HE SAID, "STAN, DO YOU EVEN KNOW WHAT A HERO IS?"
SO WE HAD A BOOK WE WERE GOING TO CANCEL CALLED "AMAZING FANTASY." SO I FIGURED WE COULD PUT HIM IN THERE, SINCE IT WAS GOING TO BE CANCELED ANYWAY.
WHEN WE GOT THE SALES FIGURES BACK, IT WAS A HUGE SUCCESS. MY PUBLISHER, WHO ORIGINALLY GAVE ME HELL FOR WHAT A BAD IDEA IT WAS...
...HE SAID TO ME, "REMEMBER THAT SPIDER-MAN IDEA WE BOTH LOVED SO MUCH? LET'S BRING HIM BACK."
WHY AM I TELLING YOU THIS? IF YOU HAVE AN IDEA THAT YOU GENUINELY THINK IS GOOD, DON'T LET SOME IDIOT TALK YOU OUT OF IT.

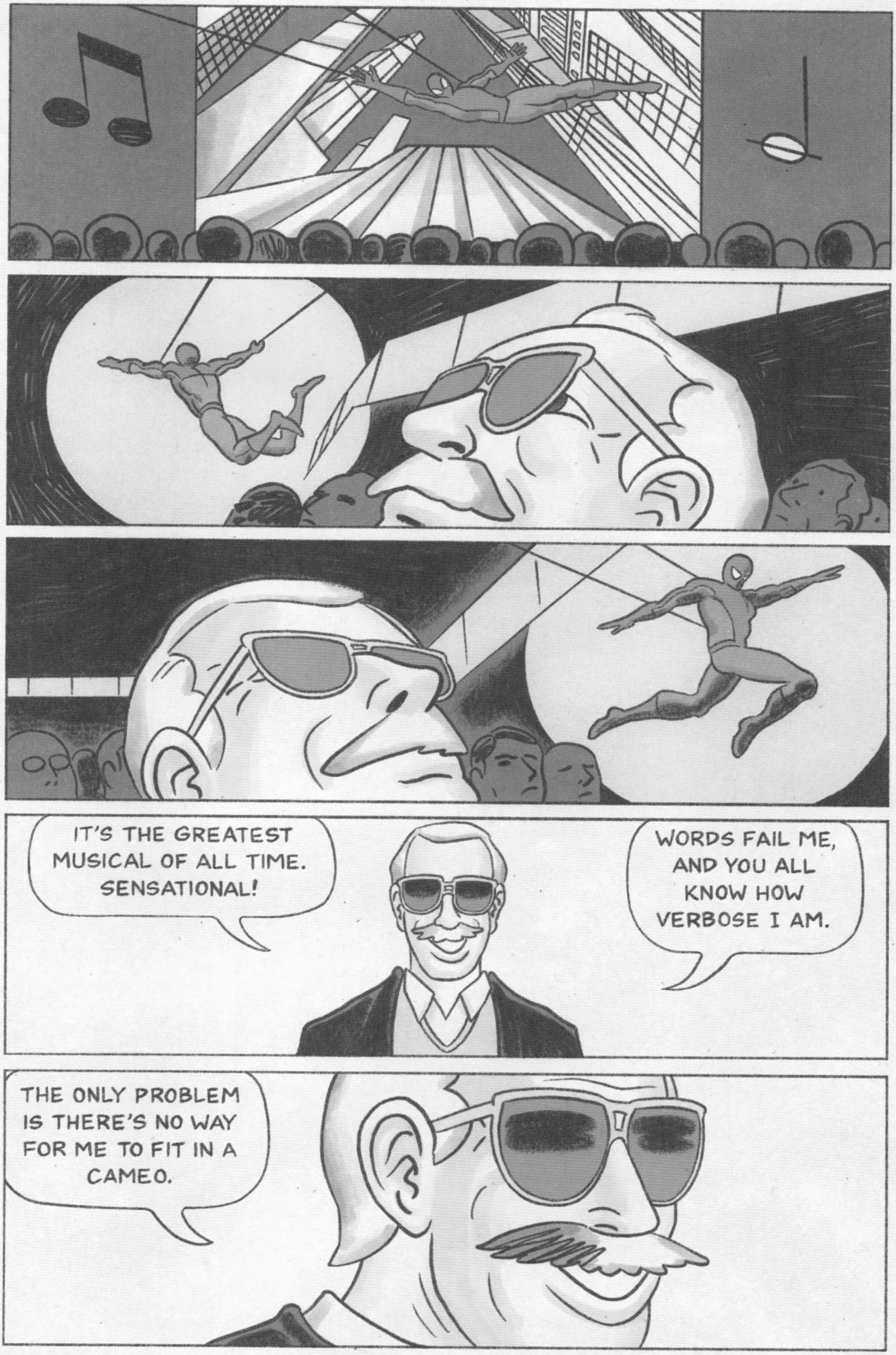
IT'S THE GREATEST MUSICAL OF ALL TIME. SENSATIONAL!
WORDS FAIL ME, AND YOU ALL KNOW HOW VERBOSE I AM.
THE ONLY PROBLEM IS THERE'S NO WAY FOR ME TO FIT IN A CAMEO.

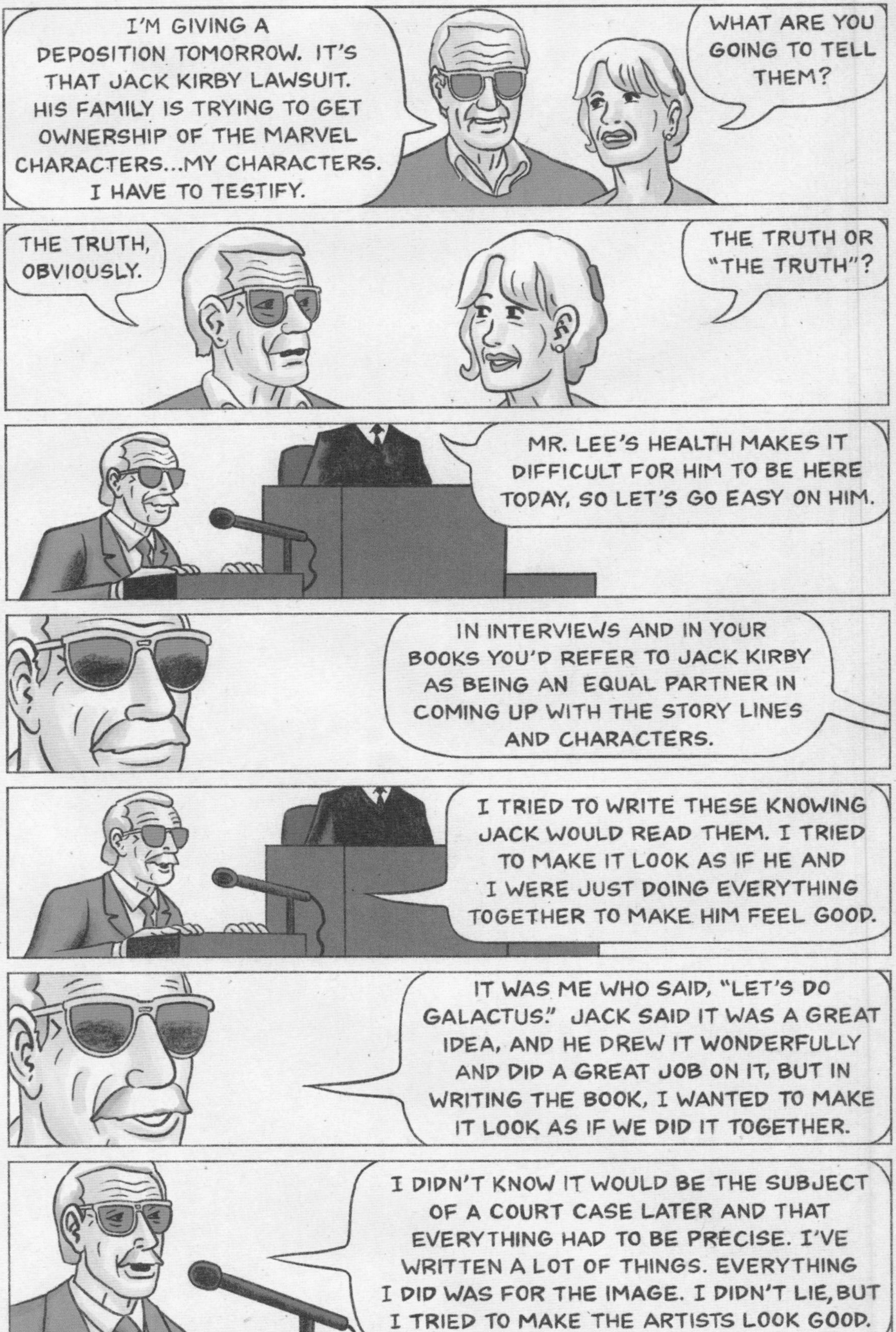
I'M GIVING A DEPOSITION TOMORROW. IT'S THAT JACK KIRBY LAWSUIT. HIS FAMILY IS TRYING TO GET OWNERSHIP OF THE MARVEL CHARACTERS...MY CHARACTERS. I HAVE TO TESTIFY.
WHAT ARE YOU GOING TO TELL THEM?
THE TRUTH, OBVIOUSLY.
THE TRUTH OR "THE TRUTH"?
MR. LEE'S HEALTH MAKES IT DIFFICULT FOR HIM TO BE HERE TODAY, SO LET'S GO EASY ON HIM.
IN INTERVIEWS AND IN YOUR BOOKS YOU'D REFER TO JACK KIRBY AS BEING AN EQUAL PARTNER IN COMING UP WITH THE STORY LINES AND CHARACTERS.
I TRIED TO WRITE THESE KNOWING JACK WOULD READ THEM. I TRIED TO MAKE IT LOOK AS IF HE AND I WERE JUST DOING EVERYTHING TOGETHER TO MAKE HIM FEEL GOOD.
IT WAS ME WHO SAID, "LET'S DO GALACTUS." JACK SAID IT WAS A GREAT IDEA, AND HE DREW IT WONDERFULLY AND DID A GREAT JOB ON IT, BUT IN WRITING THE BOOK, I WANTED TO MAKE IT LOOK AS IF WE DID IT TOGETHER.
I DIDN'T KNOW IT WOULD BE THE SUBJECT OF A COURT CASE LATER AND THAT EVERYTHING HAD TO BE PRECISE. I'VE WRITTEN A LOT OF THINGS. EVERYTHING I DID WAS FOR THE IMAGE. I DIDN'T LIE, BUT I TRIED TO MAKE THE ARTISTS LOOK GOOD.

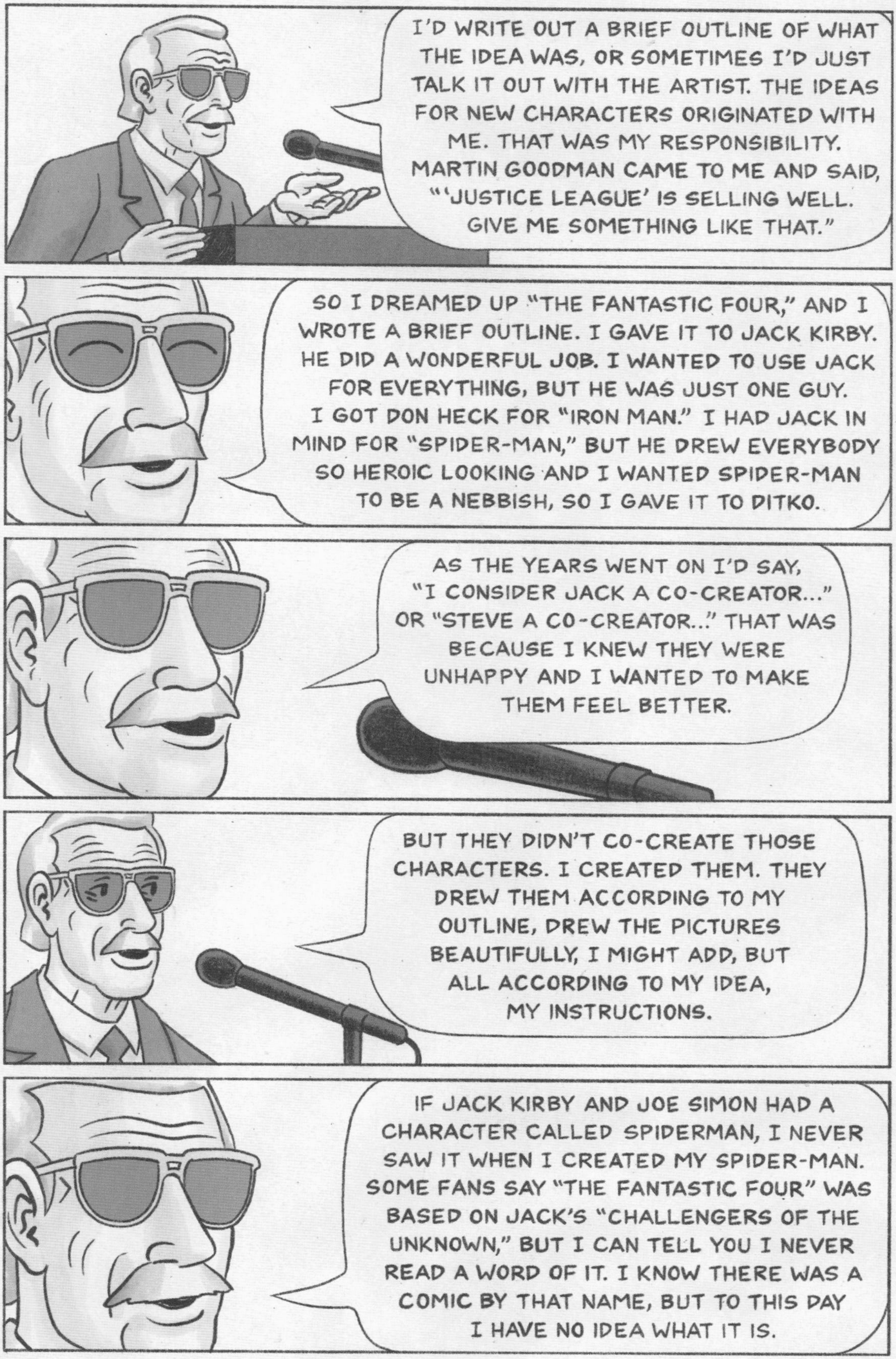
I'D WRITE OUT A BRIEF OUTLINE OF WHAT THE IDEA WAS, OR SOMETIMES I'D JUST TALK IT OUT WITH THE ARTIST. THE IDEAS FOR NEW CHARACTERS ORIGINATED WITH ME. THAT WAS MY RESPONSIBILITY. MARTIN GOODMAN CAME TO ME AND SAID, "'JUSTICE LEAGUE' IS SELLING WELL. GIVE ME SOMETHING LIKE THAT."
SO I DREAMED UP "THE FANTASTIC FOUR," AND I WROTE A BRIEF OUTLINE. I GAVE IT TO JACK KIRBY. HE DID A WONDERFUL JOB. I WANTED TO USE JACK FOR EVERYTHING, BUT HE WAS JUST ONE GUY. I GOT DON HECK FOR "IRON MAN." I HAD JACK IN MIND FOR "SPIDER-MAN," BUT HE DREW EVERYBODY SO HEROIC LOOKING AND I WANTED SPIDER-MAN TO BE A NEBBISH, SO I GAVE IT TO DITKO.
AS THE YEARS WENT ON I'D SAY, "I CONSIDER JACK A CO-CREATOR..." OR "STEVE A CO-CREATOR..." THAT WAS BECAUSE I KNEW THEY WERE UNHAPPY AND I WANTED TO MAKE THEM FEEL BETTER.
BUT THEY DIDN'T CO-CREATE THOSE CHARACTERS. I CREATED THEM. THEY DREW THEM ACCORDING TO MY OUTLINE, DREW THE PICTURES BEAUTIFULLY, I MIGHT ADD, BUT ALL ACCORDING TO MY IDEA, MY INSTRUCTIONS.
IF JACK KIRBY AND JOE SIMON HAD A CHARACTER CALLED SPIDERMAN, I NEVER SAW IT WHEN I CREATED MY SPIDER-MAN. SOME FANS SAY "THE FANTASTIC FOUR" WAS BASED ON JACK'S "CHALLENGERS OF THE UNKNOWN," BUT I CAN TELL YOU I NEVER READ A WORD OF IT. I KNOW THERE WAS A COMIC BY THAT NAME, BUT TO THIS DAY I HAVE NO IDEA WHAT IT IS.

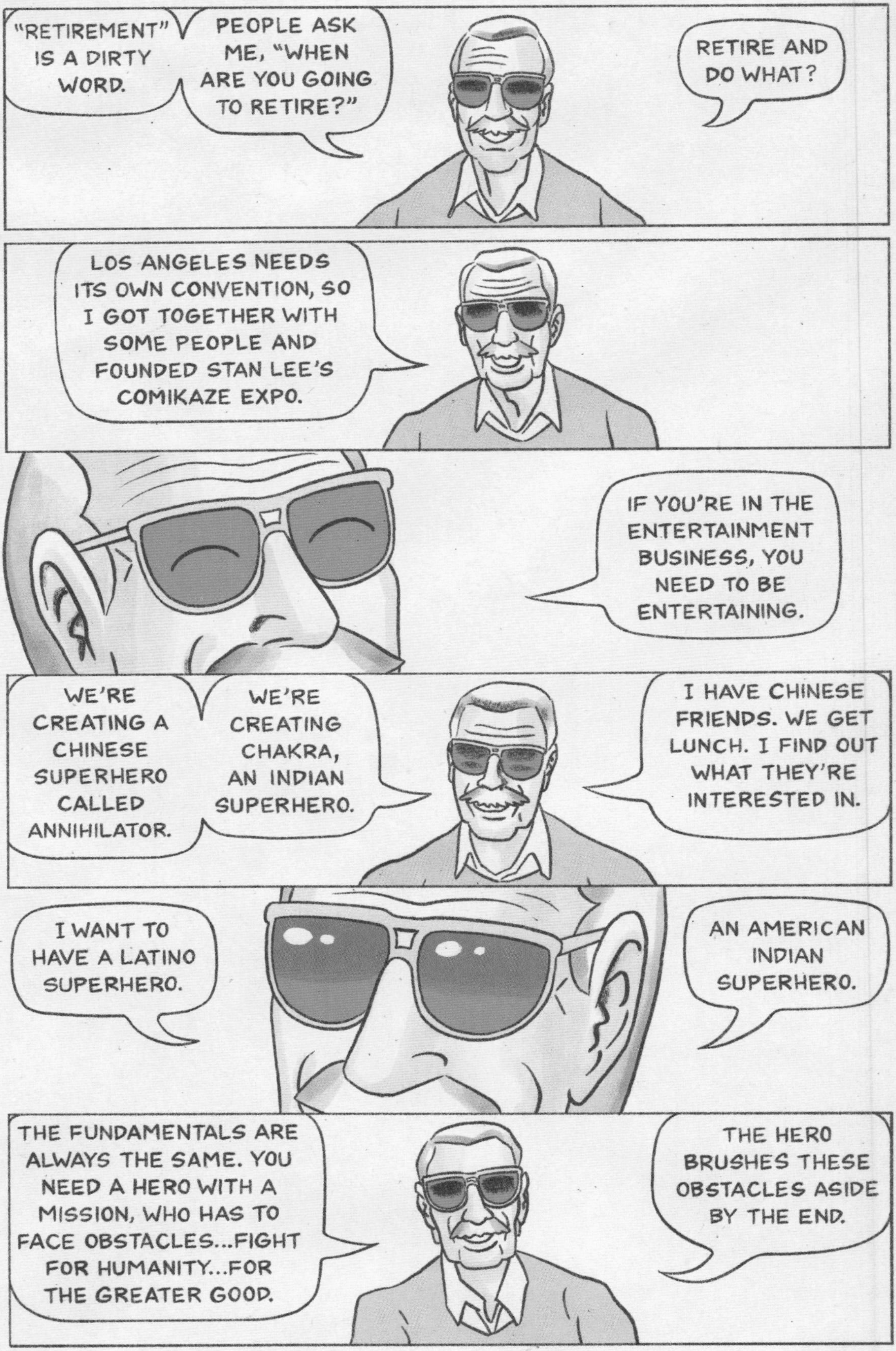
"RETIREMENT" IS A DIRTY WORD.
PEOPLE ASK ME, "WHEN ARE YOU GOING TO RETIRE?"
RETIRE AND DO WHAT?
LOS ANGELES NEEDS ITS OWN CONVENTION, SO I GOT TOGETHER WITH SOME PEOPLE AND FOUNDED STAN LEE'S COMIKAZE EXPO.
IF YOU'RE IN THE ENTERTAINMENT BUSINESS, YOU NEED TO BE ENTERTAINING.
WE'RE CREATING A CHINESE SUPERHERO CALLED ANNIHILATOR.
WE'RE CREATING CHAKRA, AN INDIAN SUPERHERO.
I HAVE CHINESE FRIENDS. WE GET LUNCH. I FIND OUT WHAT THEY'RE INTERESTED IN.
I WANT TO HAVE A LATINO SUPERHERO.
AN AMERICAN INDIAN SUPERHERO.
THE FUNDAMENTALS ARE ALWAYS THE SAME. YOU NEED A HERO WITH A MISSION, WHO HAS TO FACE OBSTACLES...FIGHT FOR HUMANITY...FOR THE GREATER GOOD.
THE HERO BRUSHES THESE OBSTACLES ASIDE BY THE END.

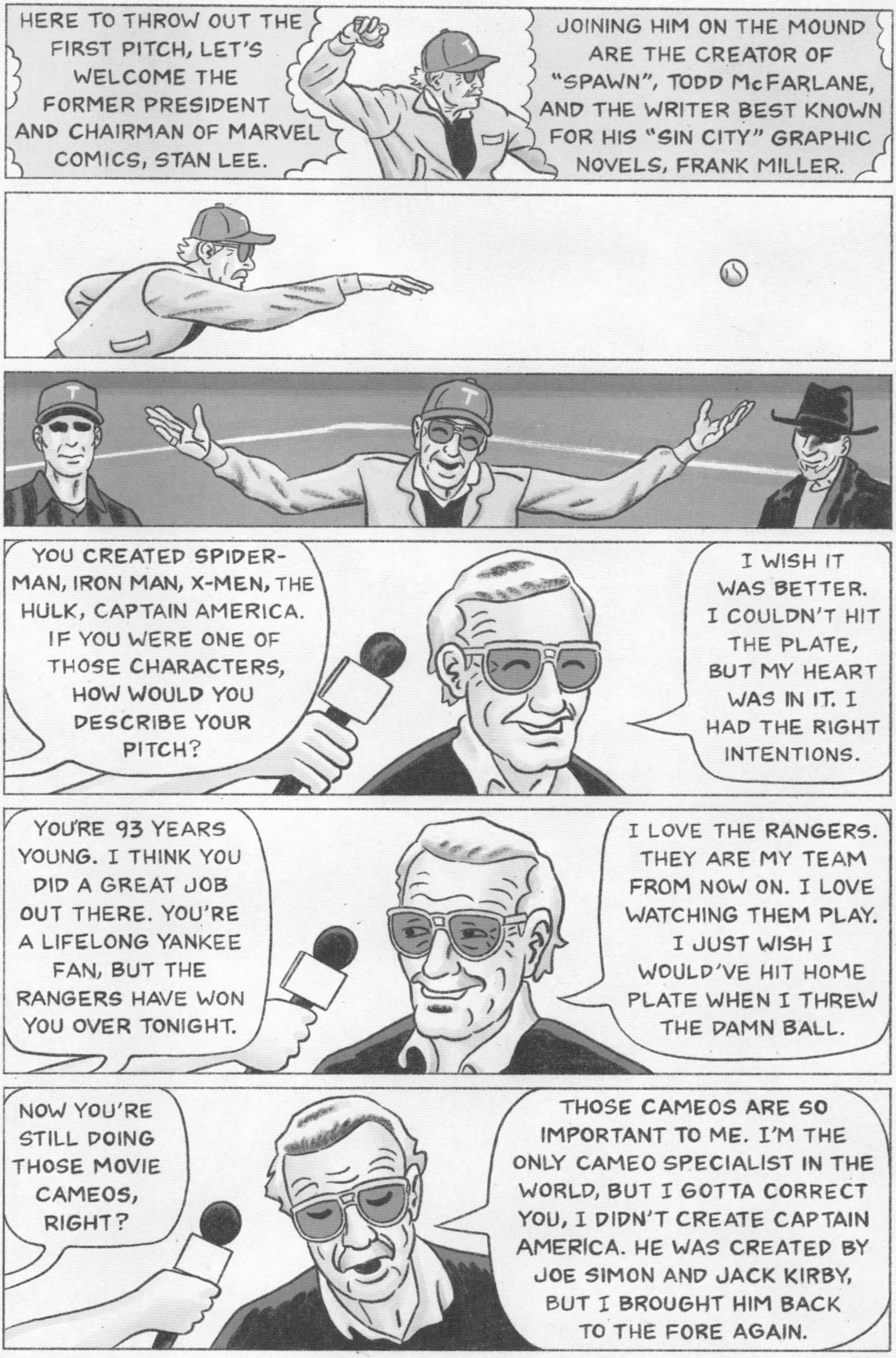
HERE TO THROW OUT THE FIRST PITCH, LET'S WELCOME THE FORMER PRESIDENT AND CHAIRMAN OF MARVEL COMICS, STAN LEE.
JOINING HIM ON THE MOUND ARE THE CREATOR OF "SPAWN", TODD McFARLANE, AND THE WRITER BEST KNOWN FOR HIS "SIN CITY" GRAPHIC NOVELS, FRANK MILLER.
YOU CREATED SPIDER-MAN, IRON MAN, X-MEN, THE HULK, CAPTAIN AMERICA. IF YOU WERE ONE OF THOSE CHARACTERS, HOW WOULD YOU DESCRIBE YOUR PITCH?
I WISH IT WAS BETTER. I COULDN'T HIT THE PLATE, BUT MY HEART WAS IN IT. I HAD THE RIGHT INTENTIONS.
YOU'RE 93 YEARS YOUNG. I THINK YOU DID A GREAT JOB OUT THERE. YOU'RE A LIFELONG YANKEE FAN, BUT THE RANGERS HAVE WON YOU OVER TONIGHT.
I LOVE THE RANGERS. THEY ARE MY TEAM FROM NOW ON. I LOVE WATCHING THEM PLAY. I JUST WISH I WOULD'VE HIT HOME PLATE WHEN I THREW THE DAMN BALL.
NOW YOU'RE STILL DOING THOSE MOVIE CAMEOS, RIGHT?
THOSE CAMEOS ARE SO IMPORTANT TO ME. I'M THE ONLY CAMEO SPECIALIST IN THE WORLD, BUT I GOTTA CORRECT YOU, I DIDN'T CREATE CAPTAIN AMERICA. HE WAS CREATED BY JOE SIMON AND JACK KIRBY, BUT I BROUGHT HIM BACK TO THE FORE AGAIN.

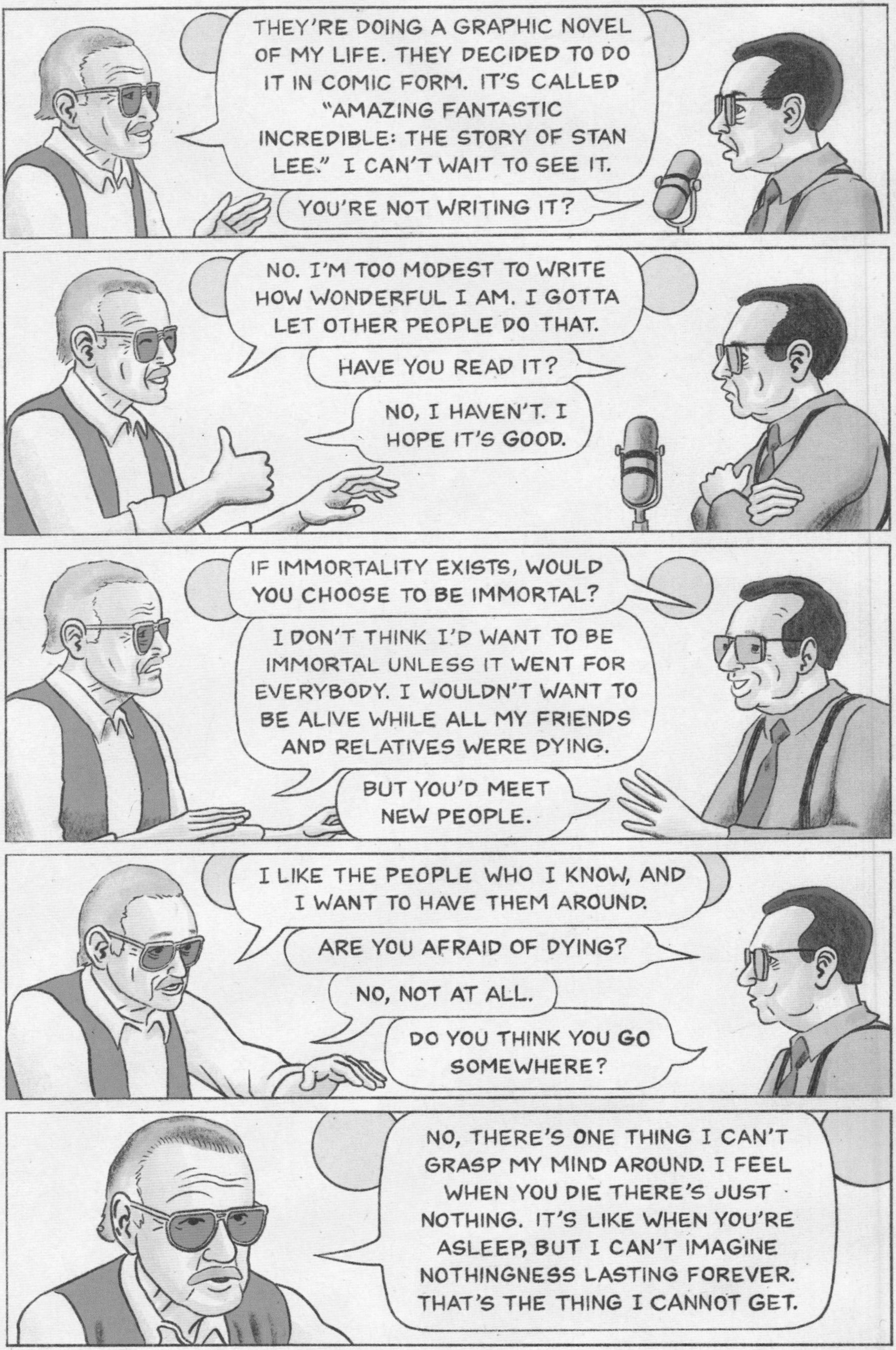
THEY'RE DOING A GRAPHIC NOVEL OF MY LIFE. THEY DECIDED TO DO IT IN COMIC FORM. IT'S CALLED "AMAZING FANTASTIC INCREDIBLE: THE STORY OF STAN LEE." I CAN'T WAIT TO SEE IT.
YOU'RE NOT WRITING IT?
NO. I'M TOO MODEST TO WRITE HOW WONDERFUL I AM. I GOTTA LET OTHER PEOPLE DO THAT.
HAVE YOU READ IT?
NO, I HAVEN'T. I HOPE IT'S GOOD.
IF IMMORTALITY EXISTS, WOULD YOU CHOOSE TO BE IMMORTAL?
I DON'T THINK I'D WANT TO BE IMMORTAL UNLESS IT WENT FOR EVERYBODY. I WOULDN'T WANT TO BE ALIVE WHILE ALL MY FRIENDS AND RELATIVES WERE DYING.
BUT YOU'D MEET NEW PEOPLE.
I LIKE THE PEOPLE WHO I KNOW, AND I WANT TO HAVE THEM AROUND.
ARE YOU AFRAID OF DYING?
NO, NOT AT ALL.
DO YOU THINK YOU GO SOMEWHERE?
NO, THERE'S ONE THING I CAN'T GRASP MY MIND AROUND. I FEEL WHEN YOU DIE THERE'S JUST NOTHING. IT'S LIKE WHEN YOU'RE ASLEEP, BUT I CAN'T IMAGINE NOTHINGNESS LASTING FOREVER. THAT'S THE THING I CANNOT GET.

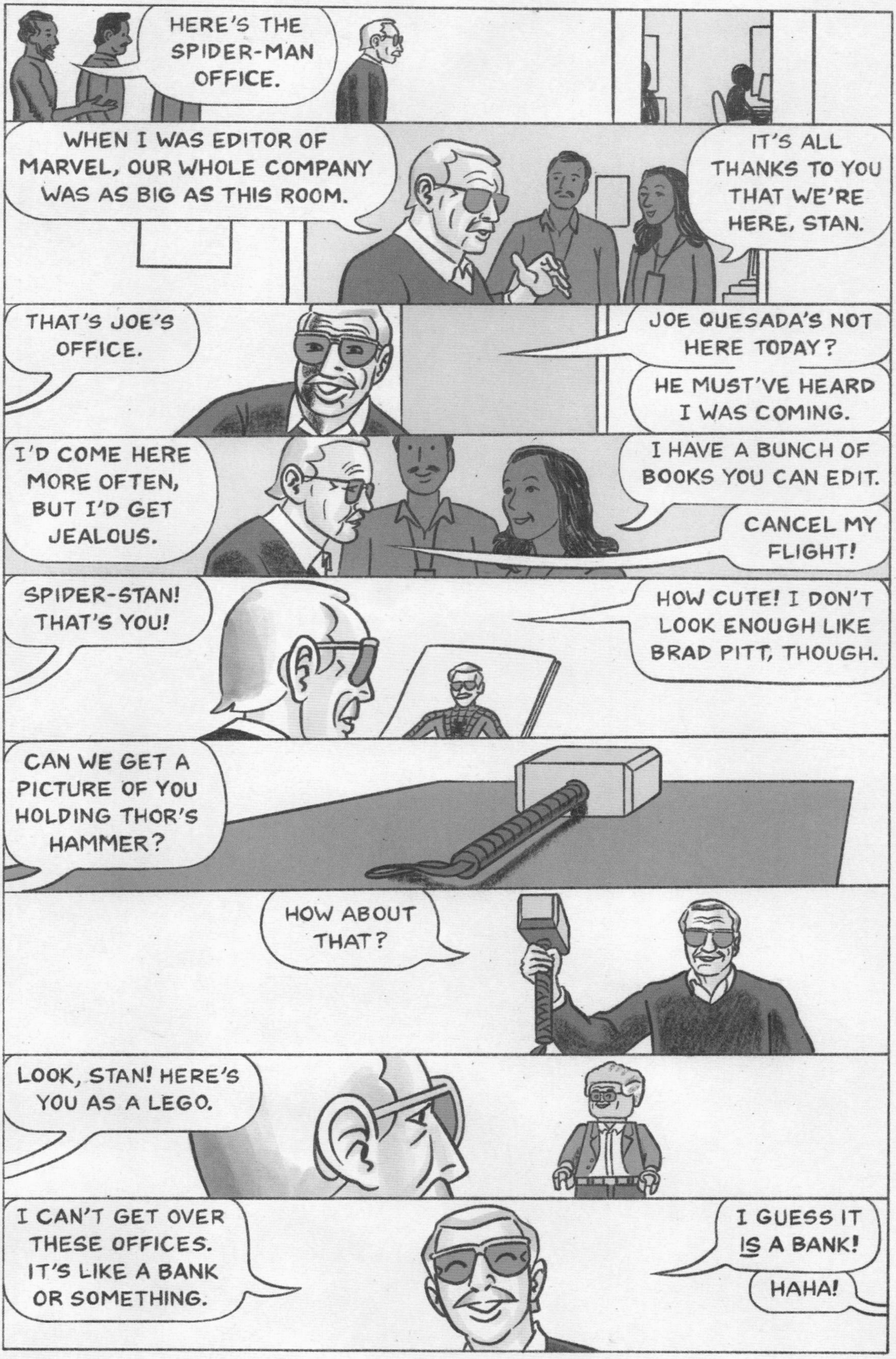
HERE'S THE SPIDER-MAN OFFICE.
WHEN I WAS EDITOR OF MARVEL, OUR WHOLE COMPANY WAS AS BIG AS THIS ROOM.
IT'S ALL THANKS TO YOU THAT WE'RE HERE, STAN.
THAT'S JOE'S OFFICE.
JOE QUESADA'S NOT HERE TODAY?
HE MUST'VE HEARD I WAS COMING.
I'D COME HERE MORE OFTEN, BUT I'D GET JEALOUS.
I HAVE A BUNCH OF BOOKS YOU CAN EDIT.
CANCEL MY FLIGHT!
SPIDER-STAN! THAT'S YOU!
HOW CUTE! I DON'T LOOK ENOUGH LIKE BRAD PITT, THOUGH.
CAN WE GET A PICTURE OF YOU HOLDING THOR'S HAMMER?
HOW ABOUT THAT?
LOOK, STAN! HERE'S YOU AS A LEGO.
I CAN'T GET OVER THESE OFFICES. IT'S LIKE A BANK OR SOMETHING.
I GUESS IT IS A BANK!
HAHA!

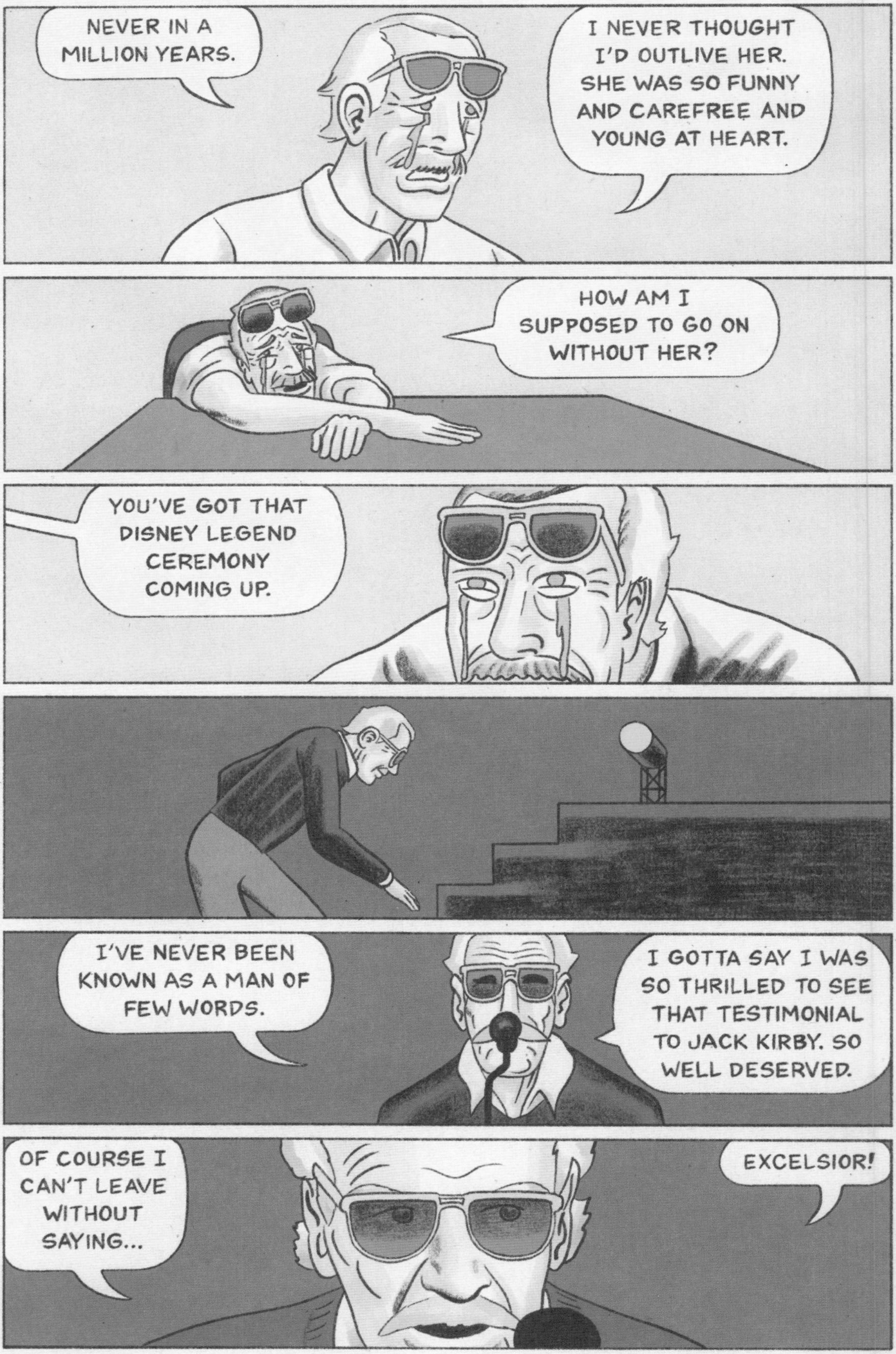
NEVER IN A MILLION YEARS.
I NEVER THOUGHT I'D OUTLIVE HER. SHE WAS SO FUNNY AND CAREFREE AND YOUNG AT HEART.
HOW AM I SUPPOSED TO GO ON WITHOUT HER?
YOU'VE GOT THAT DISNEY LEGEND CEREMONY COMING UP.
I'VE NEVER BEEN KNOWN AS A MAN OF FEW WORDS.
I GOTTA SAY I WAS SO THRILLED TO SEE THAT TESTIMONIAL TO JACK KIRBY. SO WELL DESERVED.
OF COURSE I CAN'T LEAVE WITHOUT SAYING...
EXCELSIOR!

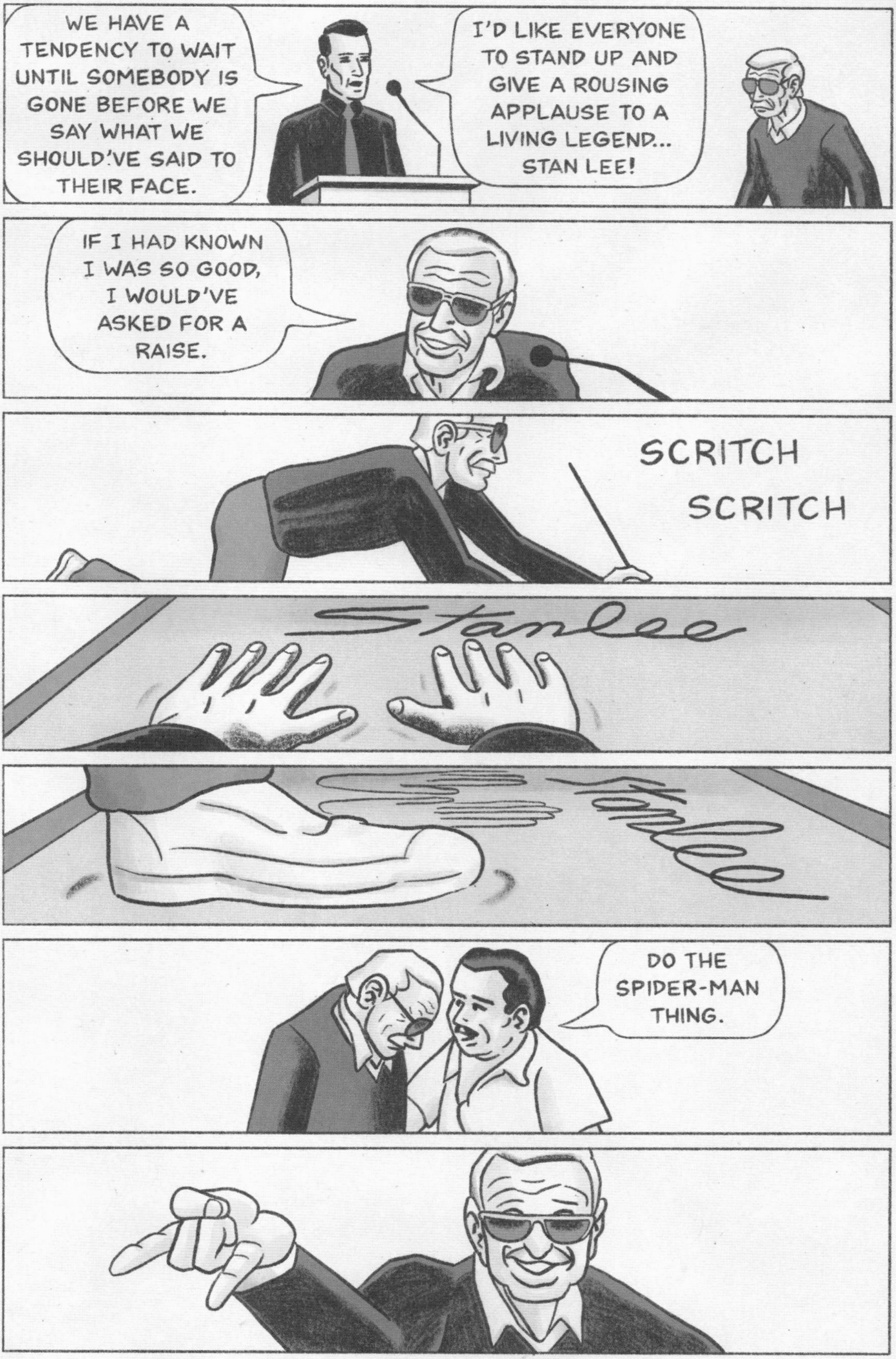
WE HAVE A TENDENCY TO WAIT UNTIL SOMEBODY IS GONE BEFORE WE SAY WHAT WE SHOULD'VE SAID TO THEIR FACE.
I'D LIKE EVERYONE TO STAND UP AND GIVE A ROUSING APPLAUSE TO A LIVING LEGEND... STAN LEE!
IF I HAD KNOWN I WAS SO GOOD, I WOULD'VE ASKED FOR A RAISE.
SCRITCH
SCRITCH
Stan Lee
DO THE SPIDER-MAN THING.

WE'VE DESIGNED THESE PINS TO WEAR AS A SYMBOL OF RESPECT AND HARMONY BETWEEN ALL RACES.

IF YOU JOIN THIS MISSION, IT CAN BECOME YOUR CAUSE. YOU CAN BE THE SPOKESPERSON.

SO WHERE DOES ALL THE MONEY GO?

TO THE CHARITY.

WHICH CHARITY?

THE WHOLE PROJECT IS A CHARITABLE ENDEAVOR. THE MISSION IS TO ENCOURAGE RACIAL HARMONY AND MUTUAL RESPECT. IF WE GET EVERYONE TO WEAR IT, WE'LL SPREAD THE MESSAGE.

I'VE DONE A LOT IN MY LIFE, BUT ONE THING BOTHERS ME: THAT I HAVEN'T SEEMED TO HAVE MADE AN IMPACT, IS THE RELATIONSHIP BETWEEN BLACKS AND WHITES IN PARTICULAR.

IF PEOPLE COULD LEARN TO HAVE RESPECT FOR EACH OTHER AND REMEMBER THAT WE WERE ALL MADE BY THE SAME...WHOEVER MADE US MADE US THIS AND THAT COLOR. WE NEED TO GET ALONG AND RESPECT EACH OTHER.

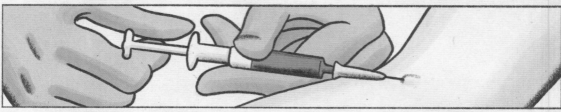

THESE COMICS ARE SPECIAL COLLECTOR'S ITEMS SIGNED WITH INK CONTAINING STAN LEE'S DNA.

WE ARE NO LONGER ASSOCIATED WITH THAT COMPANY.

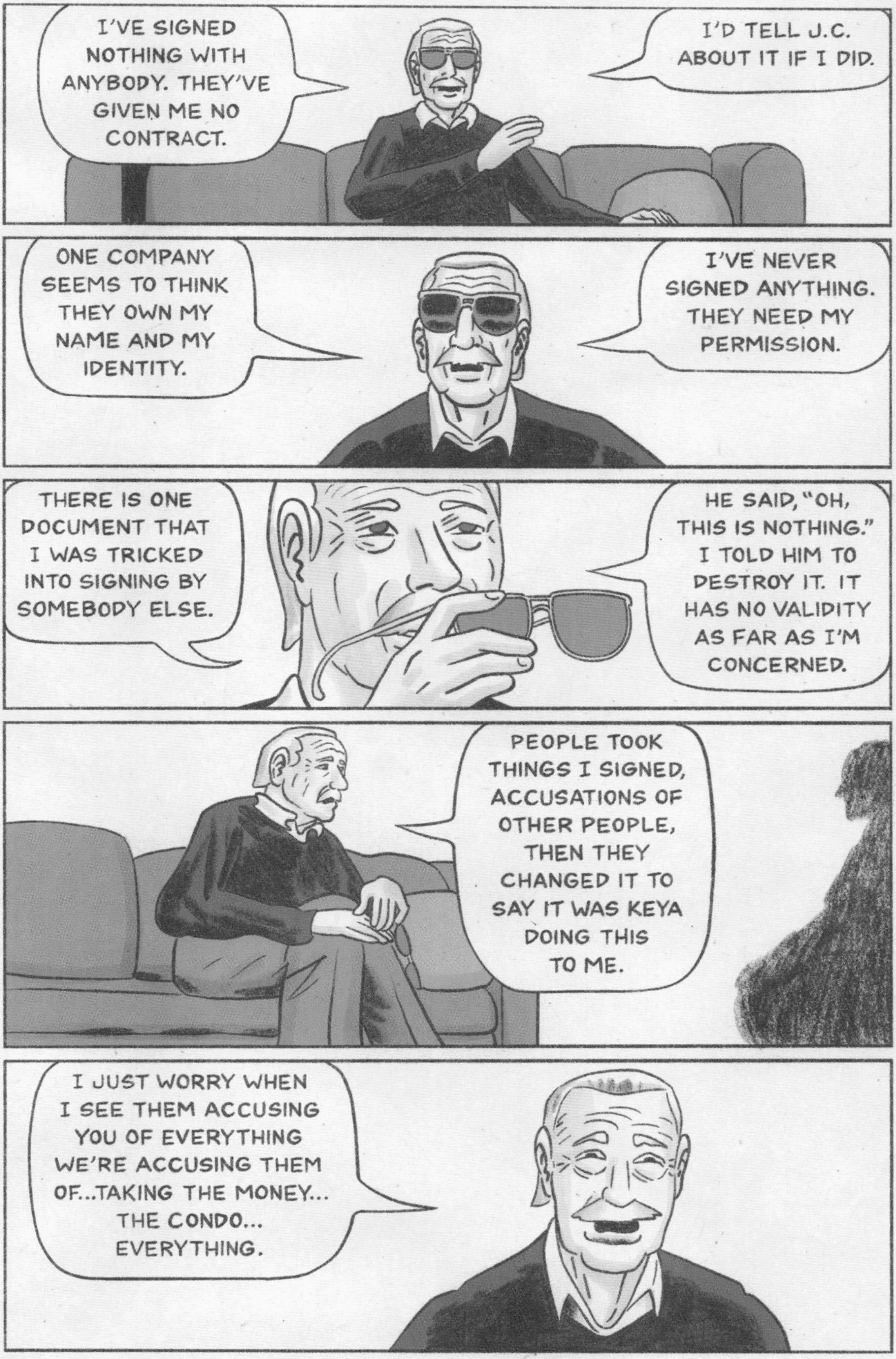
I'VE SIGNED NOTHING WITH ANYBODY. THEY'VE GIVEN ME NO CONTRACT.
I'D TELL J.C. ABOUT IT IF I DID.
ONE COMPANY SEEMS TO THINK THEY OWN MY NAME AND MY IDENTITY.
I'VE NEVER SIGNED ANYTHING. THEY NEED MY PERMISSION.
THERE IS ONE DOCUMENT THAT I WAS TRICKED INTO SIGNING BY SOMEBODY ELSE.
HE SAID, "OH, THIS IS NOTHING." I TOLD HIM TO DESTROY IT. IT HAS NO VALIDITY AS FAR AS I'M CONCERNED.
PEOPLE TOOK THINGS I SIGNED, ACCUSATIONS OF OTHER PEOPLE, THEN THEY CHANGED IT TO SAY IT WAS KEYA DOING THIS TO ME.
I JUST WORRY WHEN I SEE THEM ACCUSING YOU OF EVERYTHING WE'RE ACCUSING THEM OF...TAKING THE MONEY... THE CONDO... EVERYTHING.

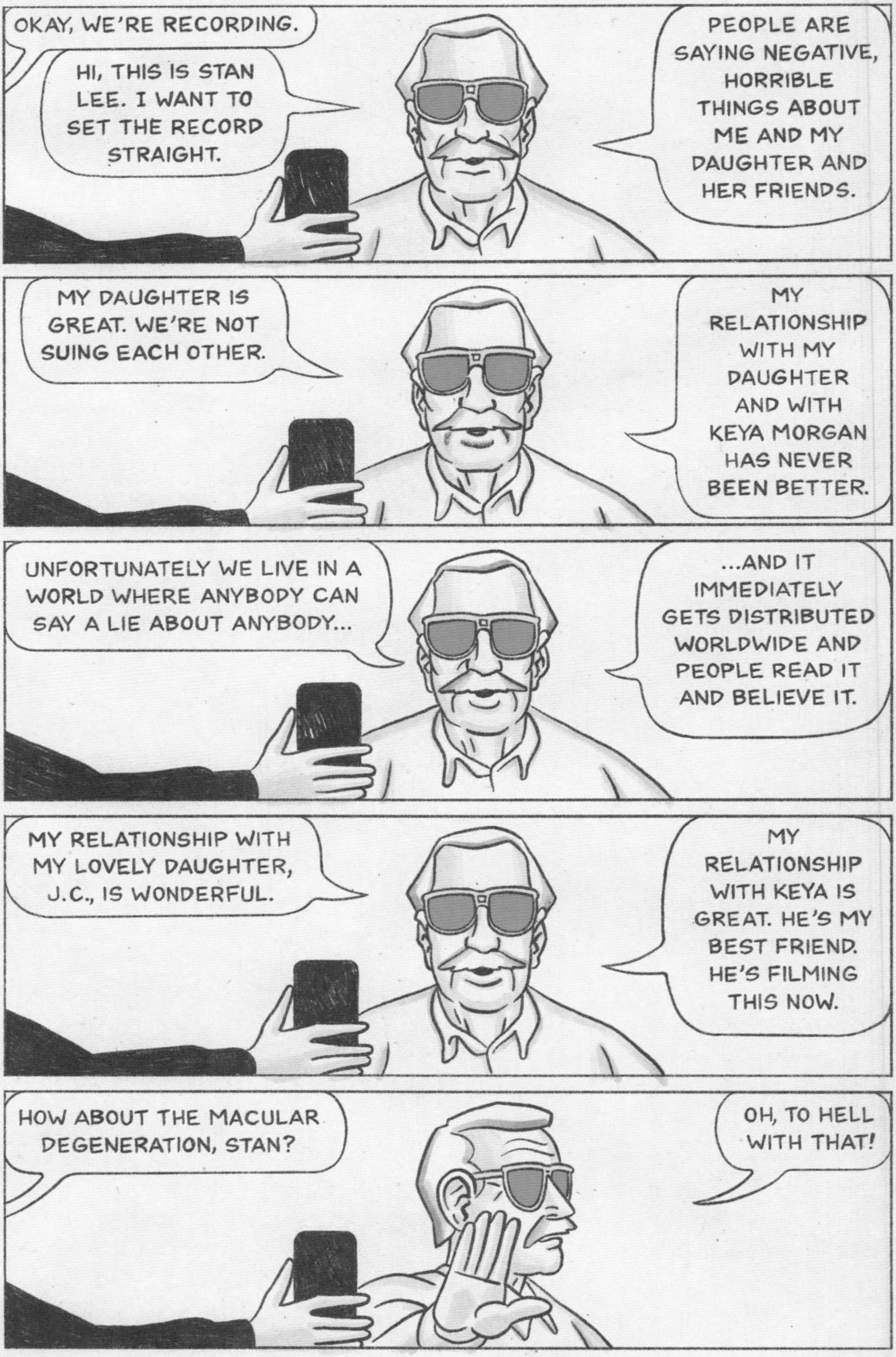
OKAY, WE'RE RECORDING.
HI, THIS IS STAN LEE. I WANT TO SET THE RECORD STRAIGHT.
PEOPLE ARE SAYING NEGATIVE, HORRIBLE THINGS ABOUT ME AND MY DAUGHTER AND HER FRIENDS.
MY DAUGHTER IS GREAT. WE'RE NOT SUING EACH OTHER.
MY RELATIONSHIP WITH MY DAUGHTER AND WITH KEYA MORGAN HAS NEVER BEEN BETTER.
UNFORTUNATELY WE LIVE IN A WORLD WHERE ANYBODY CAN SAY A LIE ABOUT ANYBODY...
...AND IT IMMEDIATELY GETS DISTRIBUTED WORLDWIDE AND PEOPLE READ IT AND BELIEVE IT.
MY RELATIONSHIP WITH MY LOVELY DAUGHTER, J.C., IS WONDERFUL.
MY RELATIONSHIP WITH KEYA IS GREAT. HE'S MY BEST FRIEND. HE'S FILMING THIS NOW.
HOW ABOUT THE MACULAR DEGENERATION, STAN?
OH, TO HELL WITH THAT!

 JUST TO LET YOU KNOW, I'VE BEEN HERE NUMEROUS TIMES, SO I UNDERSTAND A BIT OF WHAT'S GOING ON.

IS THERE ANYTHING THAT HAPPENED TODAY?

 MY DAUGHTER ACTED BETTER TODAY THAN SHE HAS IN A LONG TIME.

USUALLY WHEN WE ARGUE SHE SCREAMS AND YELLS. THIS TIME SHE WAS VERY CALM. SHE SAID, "DAD, I LOVE YOU."

SO EVERYTHING'S GOOD WITH KEYA?

 KEYA IS MY BEST FRIEND. HE'S MY PARTNER. WE'VE GOT A MILLION IDEAS WE'RE WORKING ON.

I NEED SOMEONE LIKE KEYA. KEYA IS MY FRIEND. HE'S LIKE MY PARTNER. HE'S LIKE A BODYGUARD. I WISH I HAD TWO OF HIM. HE'S A GOOD FRIEND.

 YOU SEEM HESITANT, OFFICER.

I'M LISTENING. YOU SEEM REASONABLE.

 DOES ANYTHING I SAY STRIKE YOU AS BEING NOT WHAT IT SHOULD BE?

 I THINK IT'S FINE. I JUST NEED YOU TO UNDERSTAND THAT YOU NEED TO MAKE YOUR OWN DECISIONS AND NOT LET KEYA MAKE DECISIONS FOR YOU.

 WELL, SOMETIMES HE MAKES BETTER DECISIONS THAN I WOULD.

 IF YOU WANT EVERYBODY GONE TONIGHT...

 NO, I NEED THEM FOR A MEETING.

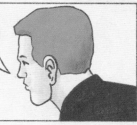

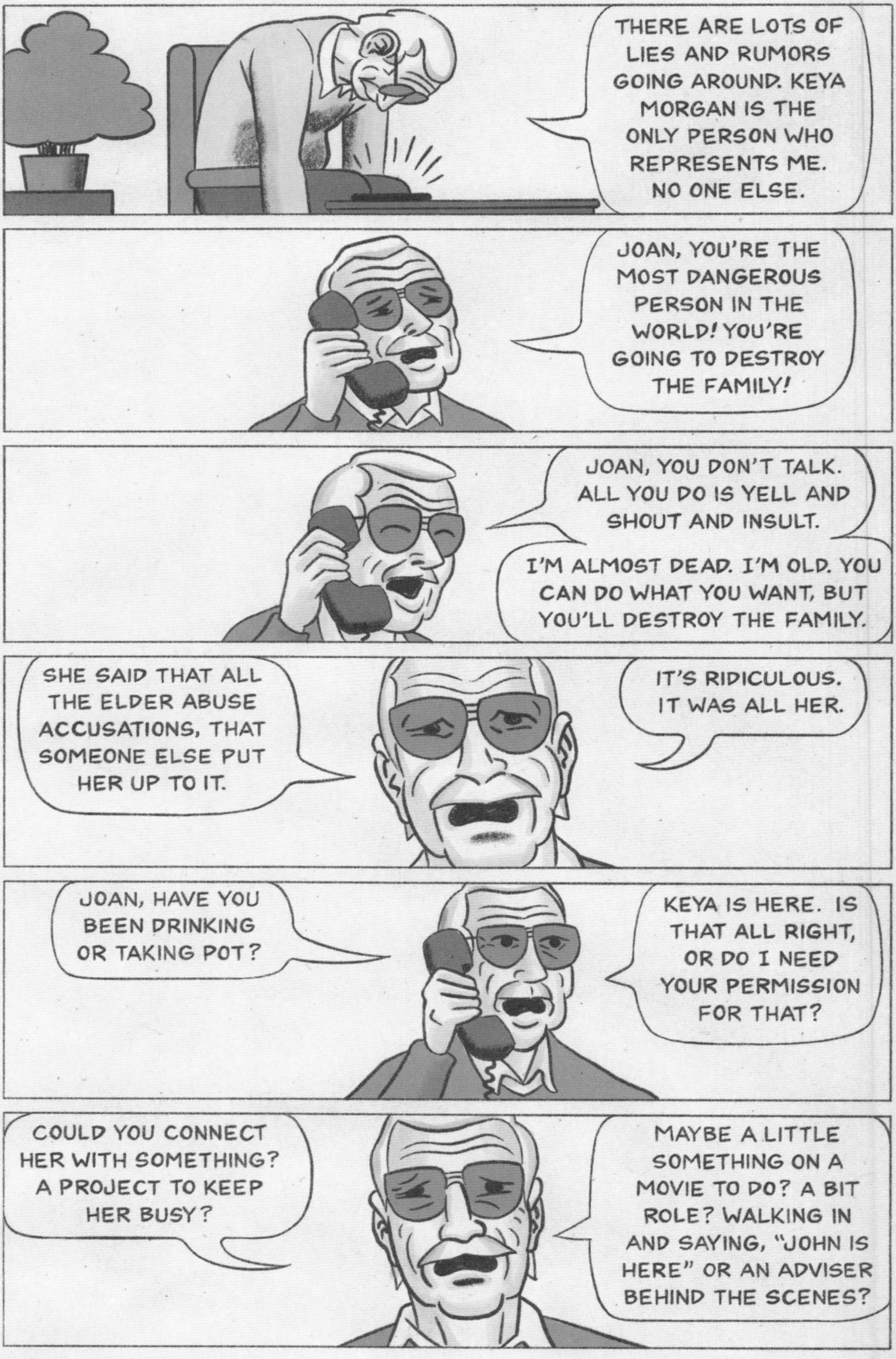
THERE ARE LOTS OF LIES AND RUMORS GOING AROUND. KEYA MORGAN IS THE ONLY PERSON WHO REPRESENTS ME. NO ONE ELSE.
JOAN, YOU'RE THE MOST DANGEROUS PERSON IN THE WORLD! YOU'RE GOING TO DESTROY THE FAMILY!
JOAN, YOU DON'T TALK. ALL YOU DO IS YELL AND SHOUT AND INSULT.
I'M ALMOST DEAD. I'M OLD. YOU CAN DO WHAT YOU WANT, BUT YOU'LL DESTROY THE FAMILY.
SHE SAID THAT ALL THE ELDER ABUSE ACCUSATIONS, THAT SOMEONE ELSE PUT HER UP TO IT.
IT'S RIDICULOUS. IT WAS ALL HER.
JOAN, HAVE YOU BEEN DRINKING OR TAKING POT?
KEYA IS HERE. IS THAT ALL RIGHT, OR DO I NEED YOUR PERMISSION FOR THAT?
COULD YOU CONNECT HER WITH SOMETHING? A PROJECT TO KEEP HER BUSY?
MAYBE A LITTLE SOMETHING ON A MOVIE TO DO? A BIT ROLE? WALKING IN AND SAYING, "JOHN IS HERE" OR AN ADVISER BEHIND THE SCENES?

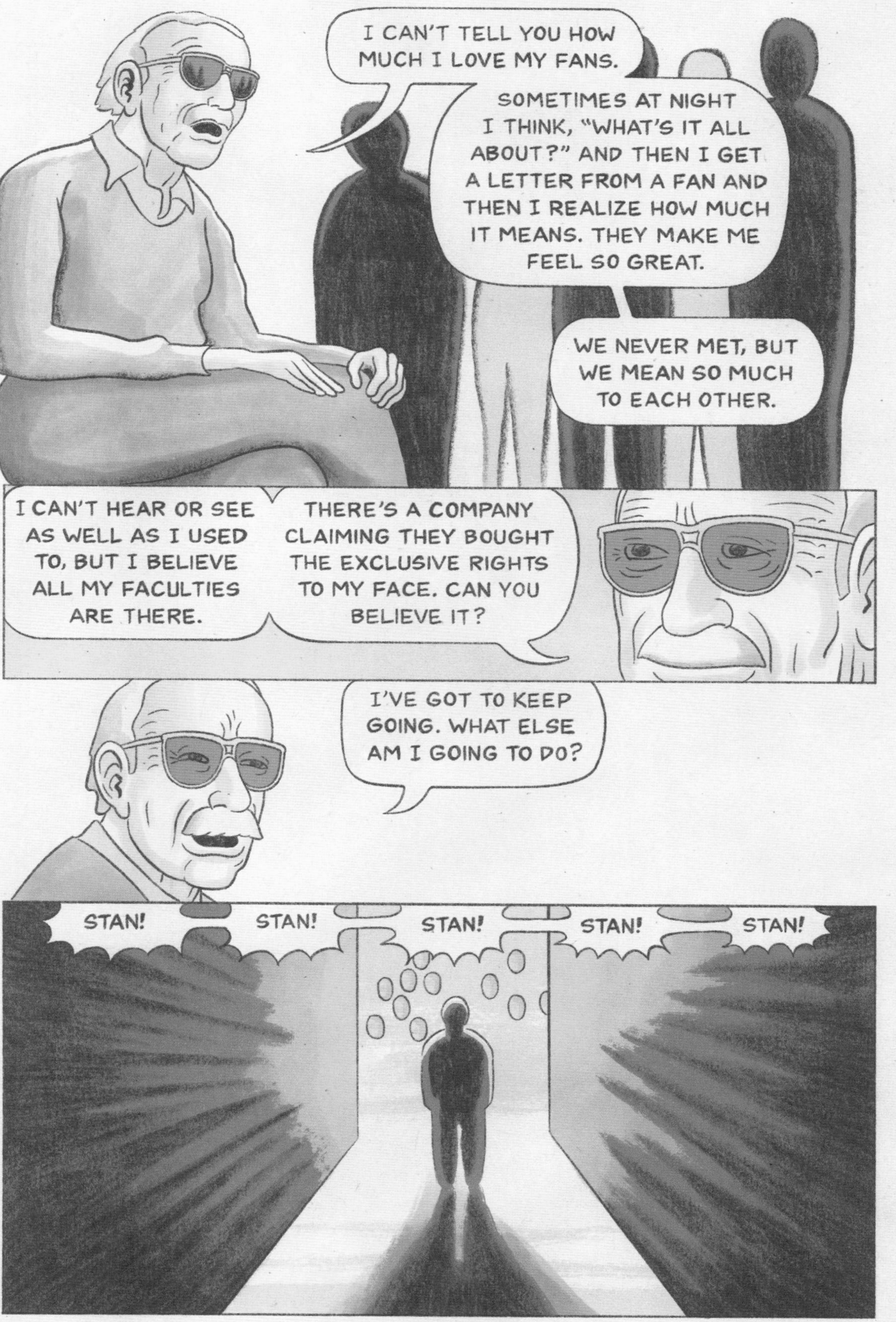
I CAN'T TELL YOU HOW MUCH I LOVE MY FANS.
SOMETIMES AT NIGHT I THINK, "WHAT'S IT ALL ABOUT?" AND THEN I GET A LETTER FROM A FAN AND THEN I REALIZE HOW MUCH IT MEANS. THEY MAKE ME FEEL SO GREAT.
WE NEVER MET, BUT WE MEAN SO MUCH TO EACH OTHER.
I CAN'T HEAR OR SEE AS WELL AS I USED TO, BUT I BELIEVE ALL MY FACULTIES ARE THERE.
THERE'S A COMPANY CLAIMING THEY BOUGHT THE EXCLUSIVE RIGHTS TO MY FACE. CAN YOU BELIEVE IT?
I'VE GOT TO KEEP GOING. WHAT ELSE AM I GOING TO DO?
STAN!
STAN!
STAN!
STAN!
STAN!

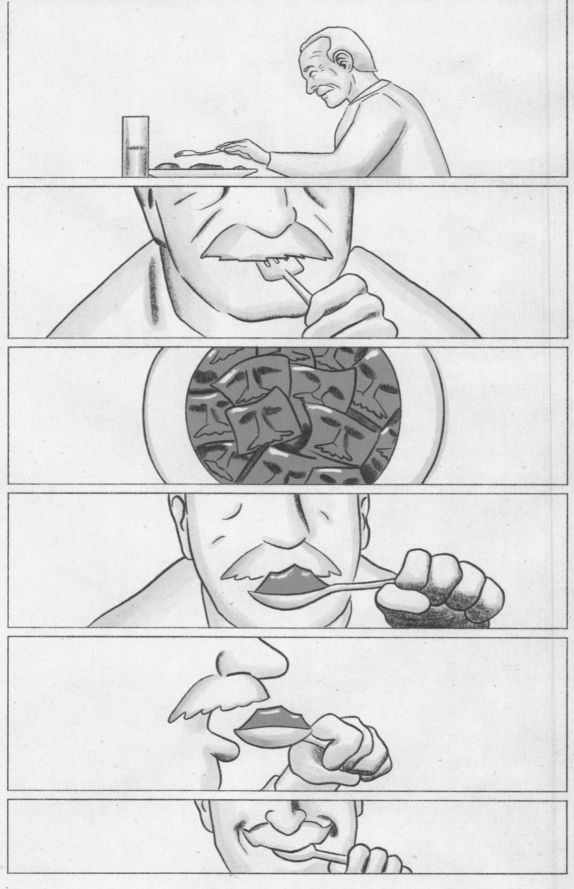

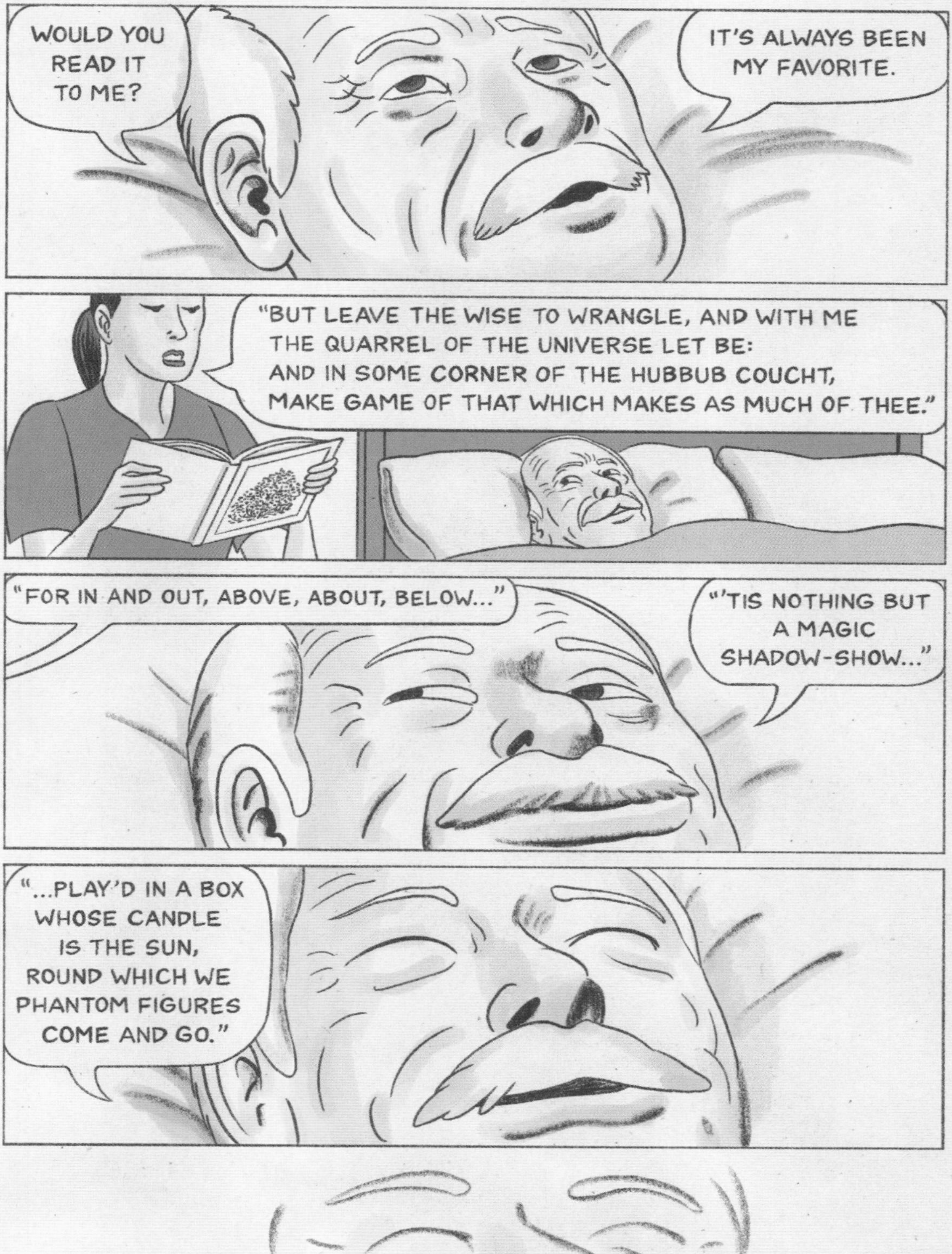
WOULD YOU READ IT TO ME?
IT'S ALWAYS BEEN MY FAVORITE.
"BUT LEAVE THE WISE TO WRANGLE, AND WITH ME THE QUARREL OF THE UNIVERSE LET BE: AND IN SOME CORNER OF THE HUBBUB COUCHT, MAKE GAME OF THAT WHICH MAKES AS MUCH OF THEE."
"FOR IN AND OUT, ABOVE, ABOUT, BELOW..."
"'TIS NOTHING BUT A MAGIC SHADOW-SHOW..."
"...PLAY'D IN A BOX WHOSE CANDLE IS THE SUN, ROUND WHICH WE PHANTOM FIGURES COME AND GO."

NOTES

PAGE 5: "They must have loved each other when they married, but my earliest recollections were of the two of them arguing, quarreling endlessly. Almost always it was over money or the lack of it . . . I used to see that poor guy, day after day, sitting at a little table in our small living room reading the want ads." *Excelsior!: The Amazing Life of Stan Lee*, by Stan Lee and George Mair. P 7–8.

PAGE 6: "One of the first presents my mother bought me was a little stand to keep on the kitchen table to rest a book against while eating." *Excelsior!: The Amazing Life of Stan Lee*, by Stan Lee and George Mair. P 9–10.

PAGE 7: *A Marvelous Life: The Amazing Story of Stan Lee*, by Danny Fingeroth. P 16.

PAGE 8: *Excelsior!: The Amazing Life of Stan Lee*, by Stan Lee and George Mair. P 17.

PAGE 10: Stan would often tell this story with "Stan Lee Is God" even though he didn't yet go by "Stan Lee."

PAGE 14: "I remember she told me once when he was a child that one of the school teachers said about him something 'he reminds me of our President Roosevelt.' Well, that's a hell of a thing." Larry Lieber interviewed in *Stan Lee: The ComiX-Man*, documentary by Nat Segaloff, 1995.

PAGE 25: *A Marvelous Life: The Amazing Story of Stan Lee*, by Danny Fingeroth. P 28.

PAGE 30: "Stan told me that he had to pick up cigarette butts on the ball field. He'd peel off the white paper and put it in something. And he'd let the excess tobacco scatter to the wind. That's the way he described it." "I Let People Do Their Jobs!" "A Conversation with Vince Fago—Artist, Writer, and Third Editor-in-Chief of Timely/Marvel Comics," Interview by Jim Amash, *Alter Ego* 3, #11 (November 2001), edited by Roy Thomas.

PAGE 31: "Reaching the barracks, I ran over to the red-hot potbellied stove and stood so close to it that my brand-new uniform, coat and all, caught on fire." *Excelsior!: The Amazing Life of Stan Lee*, by Stan Lee and George Mair, P 33–34.

PAGE 35: "So I took a screwdriver, walked to the small mailroom, unscrewed the hinge holding the padlock, opened the door, took my letter and then locked everything up again." *Excelsior!: The Amazing Life of Stan Lee*, by Stan Lee and George Mair, P 42–44.

PAGE 39: *Excelsior!: The Amazing Life of Stan Lee*, by Stan Lee and George Mair, P 48–50.

PAGE 42: "There's Money in Comics," by Stan Lee. *Writer's Digest*, November 1947.

PAGE 43: *The Secrets Behind the Comics*, by Stan Lee. 1947.

PAGE 44: *Excelsior!: The Amazing Life of Stan Lee*, by Stan Lee and George Mair. P 57.

PAGE 45: "The Two Faces of Stan Lee" by Paul Wardle, *The Comics Journal* #181, October 1995.

PAGE 46–50: *Excelsior!: The Amazing Life of Stan Lee*, by Stan Lee and George Mair. P 65–68.

PAGE 52: *Stan Lee: The ComiX-Man*, by Nat Segaloff.

PAGE 55–57: "The Two Faces of Stan Lee," by Paul Wardle, *The Comics Journal* #181, October 1995.

PAGE 62: "Student and Teacher," by Jerry Robinson in *The Art of Ditko*, edited by Craig Yoe, 2010.

PAGE 64–65: *With Great Power: The Stan Lee Story*, directed by Terry Dougas, Nikki Frakes, and Will Hess, 2010.

PAGE 75: *Stan Lee and the Rise and Fall of the American Comic Book*, by Jordan Raphael and Tom Spurgeon. P 55.

PAGE 76: *A Marvelous Life: The Amazing Story of Stan Lee*, by Danny Fingeroth. P 79–80.

PAGE 80: *Excelsior!: The Amazing Life of Stan Lee*, by Stan Lee and George Mair. P 113–114.

PAGE 81: *The Stan Lee Universe*, edited by Danny Fingeroth and Roy Thomas, 2011.

PAGE 85: *Origins of Marvel Comics*, by Stan Lee, 1974. P 182.

PAGE 86: "The Highs and Lows of Henry Pym," by Mike Gartland. *Jack Kirby Collector* #18, 1998.

PAGE 88: "Stan Lee Keynote Speech at UCLA Graduation Ceremony 2017," posted by UCLA Extension on YouTube.

PAGE 90: *Robert Kirkman's Secret History of Comics*, produced by Robert Kirkman and Dave Alpert, AMC Network.

PAGE 95: *Excelsior!: The Amazing Life of Stan Lee*, by Stan Lee and George Mair. P 109–110.

PAGE 110: "Why I Quit S-M, Marvel," essay by Steve Ditko. *Four Page Series* #9, 2015.

PAGE 114: "John Buscema Interview," by Jon B. Cooke. *Jack Kirby Collector* #18, January, 1998.

PAGE 115: *The Stan Lee Universe*, edited by Danny Fingeroth and Roy Thomas.

PAGE 116: *Marvel Mon Amour: Stan Lee and Alain Resnais's Unmade Monster Movie*, video by Daniel Raim, 2018 Criterion Collection.

PAGE 119: "Stan Lee Talkshow 1968," posted by misterx1964 on YouTube, 2015.

PAGE 121: *Marvel Mon Amour: Stan Lee and Alain Resnais's Unmade Monster Movie*, video by Daniel Raim, 2018 Criterion Collection.

PAGE 122: *With Great Power: The Stan Lee Story*, directed by Terry Dougas, Nikki Frakes, and Will Hess.

PAGE 123: *Stan Lee and the Rise and Fall of the American Comic Book*, by Jordan Raphael and Tom Spurgeon. P 154.

PAGE 124: *Kirby and Lee: Stuf' Said: The Complex Genesis of the Marvel Universe in Its Creators' Own Words*, edited by John Morrow. P 104–105, 107.

PAGE 127: "A Marvelous Evening with Stan Lee," featuring archival reviews of Stan Lee's Carnegie Hall show, tombrevoort.com.

PAGE 130: *The Stan Lee Universe*, edited by Danny Fingeroth and Roy Thomas.

PAGE 132: "Stan the Man and Roy the Boy: A Conversation Between Stan Lee and Roy Thomas." *Comic Book Artist* #2, Summer 1998.

PAGE 133: "Marc Bolan of T-Rex Interviews Marvel's Stan Lee in 1975," video posted by Matt Hawkes on YouTube, 2016.

PAGE 134: *True Believer: The Rise and Fall of Stan Lee*, by Abraham Riesman. P 189–190.

PAGE 135: " 'It's like Nazi Germany and the Allies in World War II.' Stan Lee Letter to Freelancers Regarding Competing Publishers, 1974," seanhowe.tumblr.com, December 28, 2015.

PAGE 137: "Stan Lee Talks About Disliking the American Spider-Man TV Series," video posted by Foundation Interviews on YouTube, 2011.

PAGE 138: "Japanese Spider-Man." *Marvel 616*, episode 1, Disney+, 2020.

PAGE 139: "Stan Lee Discusses the Incredible Hulk TV Series," video posted by Foundation Interviews on YouTube, 2011.

PAGE 140: "Father's Day Special." *Midday with Bill Boggs*.

PAGE 143: "Marvel Productions," by Robert Strauss, *Comics Feature*, January, 1985.

PAGE 144: "John Buscema Interview," by Jon B. Cooke, *Jack Kirby Collector* #18, January 1998.

PAGE 145: *The Toys That Made Us*, season 3, episode 2, "Mighty Morphin' Power Rangers," Netflix, 2019.

PAGE 146: *Marvel Comics: The Untold Story*, by Sean Howe.

PAGE 148: "Stan Lee—Thicke of the Night—1984," video posted by misterX1964 on YouTube, 2015.

PAGE 150: "Spider-Man's Wedding—Shea Stadium 1987," video posted by Jeff Gutman on YouTube, 2007.

PAGE 151: "1987—Jack Kirby's 70th Birthday Earthwatch with Robert Knight with Warren Reece and Mac Schmid Call in from Stan Lee," video posted by Jack Kirby Museum and Research Center on YouTube, 2011.

PAGE 152: "The Comic Book Greats: Interview with Bob Kane," video interview by Stan Lee, Stabur Home Video, 1992.

PAGE 153: "The Comic Book Greats: Overkill with Todd McFarlane and Rob Liefeld," video interview by Stan Lee, Stabur Home Video, 1991.

PAGE 154: *A Marvelous Life: The Amazing Story of Stan Lee*, by Danny Fingeroth. P 293–294.

PAGE 155: "Roy Thomas Interview," by Jim Amash, *Jack Kirby Collector* #18 June 1998.

PAGE 157: "Kevin Smith and Yara Shahidi Remember Stan Lee," video posted by IMDB on YouTube, 2019.

PAGE 160: "Stan Lee on Creating Spider-Man (Full 2000 CNN Interview)," video posted by CNN on YouTube, 2016.

PAGE 161: "AH—Backstreet Boys & Stan Lee—Superhero Comics," video posted by suzi98babe on YouTube.

PAGE 163: *True Believer: The Rise and Fall of Stan Lee*, by Abraham Riesman. P 262.

PAGE 165: "Who Wants to be a Superhero? S1E1," developed by Bruce Nash, Stan Lee, and Scott Satin, 2006.

PAGE 167: "Gone But Not Forgotten." *Howard Stern Show*, Sirius/XM, October 2020.

PAGE 170: "The Last Days of Stan Lee," by David Hochman. *AARP The Magazine*, October/November Issue 2020.

PAGE 171: "Stan Lee Receives the National Medal of Arts and National Humanities (C-SPAN)." Archival video posted by C-SPAN on YouTube, 2018.

PAGE 172: "Stan Lee Keynote Speech at UCLA Graduation Ceremony 2017," video posted by UCLA Extension on YouTube, 2018.

PAGE 175: "Marvel v Kirby: Full Deposition of Stan Lee Los Angeles, May 13, 2010." ohdannyboy.blogspot.com.

PAGE 177: "SEA@TEX: Stan Lee joins booth, throws out first pitch," video posted by MLB on YouTube, 2016.

PAGE 178: Stan talks about an upcoming book that would eventually become *Amazing Fantastic Incredible: A Marvelous Memoir*. In this interview Stan refers to it as *Amazing Fantastic Incredible: The Story of Stan Lee*. Stan says he didn't write the book. The eventual "memoir" has Stan Lee listed first as author of the graphic novel, followed by Peter David and Colleen Doran. "Stan Lee Discusses His Career, Movie Cameos & Bonding with Marvel actors," video posted by *Larry King Now* on YouTube, 2018.

PAGE 179: "Stan Lee Visits the Marvel Offices," video posted by Marvel Entertainment on YouTube, 2014.

PAGE 180: "Stan Lee Receives Disney Legends Award at D23 Expo 2012," video posted by Marvel Entertainment on YouTube, 2012.

PAGE 181: "Stan Lee Adds Handprints to Grauman's Chinese Theater . . . ," video posted by ABC News on YouTube, 2017.

PAGE 184: "Stan Lee Sets the record straight on relationship with daughter J.C. and friend Keya Morgan," video posted by the Shape Lurks on YouTube.

PAGE 185: Two different video edits of LAPD body-cam footage of Stan being interviewed by the police posted on YouTube—one posted by a channel called Stan Lee Cameos and one by a channel called True Crime DEADLINE.

PAGE 186: "Marvel Legend Stan Lee Unpublished Audio . . . ," video posted by Stan Lee Cameos on YouTube.

PAGE 188–189: "On the last evening of Lee's life, he had his usual early supper—plain fish, a roll with butter, strawberry Jell-O for dessert . . . before bed, Lee enjoyed having one of his nurses read to him from the epic Persian poem 'The Rubaiyat of Omar Khayyam,' with its ancient wisdom about living life to the fullest, including lines such as 'Ah, make the most of what we yet may spend before we too into the dust descend.' " "The Last Days of Stan Lee," by David Hochman. *AARP The Magazine*, October/November 2020 Issue.

BIBLIOGRAPHY

Currie, David, and Daniel Herman. *Ditko Shrugged: The Uncompromising Life of the Artist Behind Spider-Man*. New Castle, PA; Hermes Press, 2021.

Fingeroth, Danny. *A Marvelous Life: The Amazing Story of Stan Lee*. New York, NY; St. Martin's Press, 2019.

Fingeroth, Danny, and Roy Thomas, editors. *The Stan Lee Universe*. Raleigh, NC; TwoMorrows Publishing, 2011.

Howe, Sean. *Marvel Comics: The Untold Story*. New York, NY; Harper, 2012.

Lee, Stan, and George Mair. *Excelsior!: The Amazing Life of Stan Lee*. New York, NY; Simon & Schuster, 2002.

Lee, Stan. *Origins of Marvel Comics*. New York, NY; Simon & Schuster, 1974.

Morrow, John, editor. *Kirby and Lee: Stuf' Said: The Complex Genesis of the Marvel Universe in Its Creators' Own Words*. Raleigh, NC; TwoMorrows, 2019.

Raphael, Jordan, and Tom Spurgeon. *Stan Lee and the Rise and Fall of the American Comic Book*. Chicago, IL; Chicago Review Press, 2003.

Ridout, Cefn, editor. *Marvel Year By Year A Visual History*. New York, NY; DK Publishing, 2008.

Riesman, Abraham. *True Believer: The Rise and Fall of Stan Lee*. New York, NY; Crown, 2021.

PERIODICALS

Cooke, Jon B., editor. *Comic Book Artist*. Raleigh, NC; TwoMorrows Publishing; 1998–2005.

Groth, Gary, editor-in-chief. *The Comics Journal*. Seattle, WA; 1977–present.

Hochman, David. "The Last Days of Stan Lee." *AARP The Magazine*, October/November 2020.

Lee, Stan. "There's Money In Comics." *Writer's Digest*, November 1947.

Morrow, John, editor. *The Jack Kirby Collector*. Raleigh, NC; TwoMorrows Publishing, 1994–present.

REFERENCE

FILM/DOCUMENTARIES/TV

Boggs, Bill. *Midday with Bill Boggs*, "Father's Day Special."

Dougas, Terry, Nikki Frakes, and Will Hess. *With Great Power: The Stan Lee Story.*

Kirkman, Robert, and Dave Alpert, producers. *Robert Kirkman's Secret History of Comics.* AMC Network.

Raim, Daniel. *Marvel Mon Amour: Stan Lee and Alain Resnais's Unmade Monster Movie,* Criterion Collection, 2018.

Ross, Jonathan. *In Search of Steve Ditko.*

Segaloff, Nat. *Stan Lee: The ComiX-Man.*

Thicke, Alan. *The Thicke of the Night.*

WEBSITES

The Jack Kirby Museum & Research Center, https://kirbymuseum.org/

ohdannyboy.blogspot.com

Seanhowe.tumblr.com

Timely-Atlas-Comics by Michael J. Vassallo, Timely-Atlas-Comics.blogspot.com

Tombrevoort.com

Youtube.com

ABOUT THE AUTHOR

GREGORY NEISER

Tom Scioli is an Eisner Award–nominated writer and artist who specializes in comics and graphic novels. He's the author of the nonfiction graphic biography, *Jack Kirby: The Epic Life of the King of Comics*, as well as several science fiction and superhero originals like *American Barbarian*, *The Myth of 8-Opus*, and *Godland*. He has also reinvented established series with Fantastic Four: Grand Design, Super Powers, Transformers vs G.I. Joe, and a cyberpunk reimagining of *Go-Bots*. He is known for his singular drawing style, kinetic page layouts, and imaginative writing, and he is one of a small number of auteur cartoonists who writes, draws, colors, and hand-letters his comics. He's also the host of the pop culture–centered *Total Recall Show* and a frequent contributor to the *Cartoonist Kayfabe* podcast.

INDEX

A

Academy of Comic Book Arts, 132
Adams, Neal, 132
"Amazing Adult Fantasy," 80, 89
"Amazing Fantastic Incredible," 178, 194
"Amazing Fantasy," 89, 91, 172
Anderson, Pamela, 165
Annihilator, 176
Ant-Man, 86
Army Pictorial Center, 32
Atlas Comics, 62, 74
The Avengers, 94
Avison, Al, 25, 26
Ayers, Dick, 86, 94

B

"The Backstreet Project," 161
"Barney's Beat," 76
Batman, 115, 152, 162
Ben Grimm, 81
Black Knight, 68
Black Rider, 63, 69
"Blade," 166
The Blob, 79
Blonde Phantom, 58, 61
"Blushing Blurbs," 78
Boocock, Joan. See Lee, Joan Boocock
Brodsky, Sol, 83, 84, 95, 101, 110, 124
Bruce Banner, 84, 139, 142
"Bullpen Bulletins," 100
Burgos, Carl, 21
Buscema, John, 108, 114, 144
Bush, George W., 171

C

Caniff, Milt, 71
Cannell, Stephen, 155
Captain America, 19, 22, 24, 25, 41, 61, 177
Chakra, 176
"Challengers of the Unknown," 175

Clinton

Clinton, Bill, 163
Clinton, Hillary, 163
Comics Code Authority, 70, 120, 157
Comikaze Expo, 176
Conan the Barbarian, 162
Courageous Cat, 152

D

Daredevil, 99, 104–5, 168
DC Comics, 74, 97, 126, 162
DeCarlo, Dan, 69, 76
The Destroyer, 23
Ditko, Steve, 62, 88, 89, 91, 93, 94, 101, 106, 110, 117, 154, 155, 167, 175
Doctor Doom, 109
Doctor Droom, 93
Doctor Strange, 93, 94, 133
Donald Blake, 85
Dormammu, 133

E

Eisenhower, Dwight, 109
Everett, Bill, 21, 99

F

Fago, Vince, 29, 32, 38
Famous Enterprises, 43
The Fantastic Four, 81–83, 86, 90, 107, 109, 117, 157, 168, 175
Father Time, 22
Fellini, Federico, 116
Ferrigno, Lou, 168
The Fly, 88

G

Gaines, Bill, 67
Galactus, 107, 133, 151, 174
The Glop, 79

M

N

O

P

Q

R

S

T

V

W

X

Y

Z

Published in the United States by Ten Speed Graphic, an imprint of the
Crown Publishing Group, a division of Penguin Random House LLC, New York.
TenSpeed.com

TEN SPEED GRAPHIC and colophon are trademarks of Penguin Random House LLC.

Library of Congress Cataloging-in-Publication Data
Names: Scioli, Tom, author.
Title: I am Stan : a graphic biography of the legendary Stan Lee / Tom Scioli.
Description: First edition. | Emeryville : Ten Speed Press, 2023. |
    Includes bibliographical references and index.
Identifiers: LCCN 2022055884 (print) | LCCN 2022055885 (ebook) |
    ISBN 9781984862020 (hardcover) | ISBN 9781984862037 (trade paperback) |
    ISBN 9781984862044 (ebook)
Subjects: LCSH: Lee, Stan, 1922-2018—Comic books, strips, etc. | Cartoonists—
    United States—Biography—Comic books, strips, etc. | Authors, American—
    20th century—Biography—Comic books, strips, etc. | LCGFT: Biographical comics. |
    Graphic novels.
Classification: LCC PN6727.L39 Z93 2023 (print) | LCC PN6727.L39 (ebook) |
    DDC 741.5/973092 [B]—dc23/eng/20221216
LC record available at https://lccn.loc.gov/2022055884
LC ebook record available at https://lccn.loc.gov/2022055885

Hardcover ISBN: 978-1-9848-6202-0
Trade Paperback ISBN: 978-1-9848-6203-7
eBook ISBN: 978-1-9848-6204-4

Printed in China

Acquiring editor: Kaitlin Ketchum | Project editor: Vedika Khanna
Production editor: Natalie Blachere | Editorial assistant: Kausaur Fahimuddin
Art director: Chloe Rawlins | Designer: Meggie Ramm
Colorist: Tom Scioli
Letterer: Tom Scioli
Production manager: Dan Myers | Copyeditor: Nancy Tan
Proofreader: Mikayla Butchart | Indexer: Ken DellaPenta
Marketer: Monica Stanton

10 9 8 7 6 5 4 3 2 1

First Edition